· HIGHLANDS INSTITUTE SERIES 1 ·

God, Values, and Empiricism

• HIGHLANDS INSTITUTE SERIES 1 •

God,
Values,
and Empiricism

Issues
in Philosophical Theology

edited by
W. Creighton Peden
and
Larry E. Axel

PEETERS

MERCER

BT
40
.G58
1989

ISBN 0-86554-360-7

God, Values, and Empiricism
Issues in Philosophical Theology
Copyright ©1989
Mercer University Press, Macon, Georgia 31207
All rights reserved
Printed in the United States of America

The paper used in this publication meets
the minimum requirements of American National Standard
for Information Sciences—Permanence of Paper
for Printed Library Materials, ANSI Z39.48-1984.

Library of Congress Cataloging-in-Publication Data

God, values, and empiricism : issues in philosophical theology /
   edited by W. Creighton Peden and Larry E. Axel.
vii + 252pp. 6 × 9″ (15 × 23cm)—(Highlands Institute series : 1)
   "The essays in this volume were selected from those presented
at the First International Conference on Philosophical Theology
held at Oxford University in 1988" —Preface.
   Includes bibliographical references.
   ISBN 0-86554-360-7 (alk. paper)
   1. Philosophical theology—Congresses. 2. Naturalism—
Congresses. 3. Liberalism (Religion)—Congresses. 4. Chicago
school of theology—Congresses. I. Peden, Creighton, 1935–   .
II. Axel, Larry E., 1946–   . III. International Conference on
Philosophical Theology (1st : 1988 : Oxford University).
IV. Series.
BT40.G58   1989   89-28704
200′.1—dc20   CIP

Contents

Preface

The essays in this volume were selected from those presented at the First International Conference on Philosophical Theology sponsored by the Highlands Institute for American Religious Thought. The conference was held at Somerville College, Oxford University, in 1988. The Highlands Institute is a community of scholars who unite in a perspective which emphasizes the following: (1) the interface between theology and philosophy, especially where theological efforts have utilized the American philosophical tradition; (2) the history and development of liberal religious thought in America; (3) themes of relevance to the "Chicago School" of theology; and (4) Naturalism in American theology and philosophy. The purpose of the Highlands Institute is to enhance the dialogue in American religious thought, as it relates to philosophical theology, by sponsoring conferences, seminars, and publications. While most of the essays in this volume reflect the scholarly perspective of the Highlands Institute, other papers are included that reflect broader concerns in philosophical theology.

> —*Creighton Peden and Larry Axel*
> Highlands, 1989

Religious Creaturalism
and a New Agenda for Theology

Larry E. Axel

In this presentation I seek to reorient the doing of theology in a fairly radical manner, inviting you to call into question, or to go beyond, or perhaps actively to repudiate some of the angles of vision of the prism through which much of traditional western theology has been viewed for centuries. In the process, in noting how some of the suggestions found in Bernard Meland's work may provide material for this enterprise, I hope to lay the beginnings of a foundation for a new vision, a "religious creaturalism" that may provide an alternative to the theisms and humanisms that have dominated the west. I realize that one essay is woefully inadequate to advance the discussion beyond anything more than an exploratory, suggestive stage. But I do hope to lay the groundwork for thought experiments in the field that may assist us in moving beyond some of the dualism, egocentrism, and hierarchalism that block proper theological reflection based on the creaturalism, organicism, and contextualism of our common human experience.

As we review theologically a few events of the twentieth century and look toward a proper agenda for the twenty-first, it may be fitting to recall some words of one of our era's most profound philosophers in America: Woody Allen. Allen has said: "Today humankind stands at the crossroads: one path leads to *despair* and *utter hopelessness*; the other path leads to *total annihilation*. I pray that we have the wisdom to choose wisely." Allen saw only two options, as he looked at existence. So also, in religious philosophy, have we frequently thought there were only two options: theism and humanism, traditionally conceived. Perhaps we have not exercised sufficient vision and adventurousness, and we have become entrapped in outworn models and structures. It is one of my aims to call into question the validity and vitality of both of these two options as we close this century, to challenge an accepted notion that there are— broadly conceived—only two options, and to sketch at least the beginnings of a third possibility, labeled (tentatively, at this stage of my reflections) "religious creaturalism."

In a post-Shoah world, we can no longer do theology in the same manner anymore. When we look back at some of the events of our century, especially at those (in Poland and Japan and elsewhere) in the 1940s, we may conclude that our situation—religiously—has become radically different. We must realize that the situation of our culture has changed—theoretically, existentially, historically, theologically—that the older theisms and humanisms must grow dim, that the traditional presuppositions are now in question.

While most of the world looked on—as did, presumably, any divine beings that exist—Hitler and his Nazi forces operated killing centers that gassed children by the hundreds of thousands. The twentieth century has given us a new symbol, *Auschwitz,* for the barbarity and rampant evil that ruled the earth for a time. With perhaps unprecedented magnitude and clarity, Auschwitz brings theologians and philosophers face to face with the facts of suffering on an incredibly mass scale, with issues poignantly raised concerning the absence of divine intervention or the inadequacies of divine power or benevolence; and we are led eventually to what theologians and philosophers have called the Problem of Evil or the issue of theodicy. For theists, terrible dilemmas are raised. Much has been made—quite rightly, I believe—of the negative implications for traditional theism of these kinds of events. Irving Greenburg and others have insisted that in a post-Shoah world, no theological utterance should be affirmed today that is not credible in the presence of the burning children of Auschwitz. Anyone who wishes to take evidence and experience seriously, to be ''empirical,'' must recognize in evil (both so-called moral evil and so-called natural evil) a substantive threat to traditional forms of theism that posit a God of omnipotence, omniscience, omnibenevolence and control. Not only have many people concluded that there is an absence of substantive evidence for traditional theism, but also that there may be evidence—in the widespread presence of natural and moral evil in the world—*against* theism. There are certain things that cannot be ignored or eradicated by a theological vocabulary. We can legitimately ask: should anyone who wishes to take experience seriously and who does not seek refuge in some kind of dualistic fideism, assert a theistic position after Auschwitz?

So, as is obvious to all of us, it *has* been recognized that the Problem of Evil in the context of events like Auschwitz poses a real dilemma for the theist. To be sure, in many circles, traditional theism—advocating a personal supernatural agent, active in the world—has been repudiated in the light of suffering, natural disasters, extermination camps, and bombs of mass destruction. In large part I agree with this repudiation. But I question the main alternative—the alternative that in some quarters is advanced as the *only* alternative. While there have been various revisionist theisms that have gained currency from time to time, in most circles in the general culture where *theism* has been rejected, *humanism* flourishes. Indeed, humanism is usually seen as the logical alternative, the one remaining positive alternative, to theism. And it is a humanism that, true to its etymology, often places the human at the very center, indeed, even presenting the human being as a legitimate object of virtual worship. Many forms of humanism, including certain traditions of religious humanism with a distinguished history, highlight the human structure as the most advanced of the many structures to emerge on this planet, or even, indeed, in the universe itself. A form of anthropocentrism or even anthropos-inflation replaces the earlier monotheism. This can hardly be characterized as a very radical change. For if this kind of humanism simply moves into the vacuum created by the removal of the old theisms, if the older, hierarchically-ordered theism is simply replaced by an hierarchically-ordered humanism in which humankind is placed at the top, then—structurally considered—neither a substantive nor a radical change has occurred. The patriarchy has simply been revised—not dismantled. One potentate, as it were, has simply been replaced by another. This kind of humanism, as the second option, often becomes then a form of anthropos-inflation, celebrating the achievements and status of the human. In point of fact, the place reserved for God in the earlier religions is given now to humankind. Humankind is then proclaimed to sit at the top of creation's ladder, or at the apex of some pyramidal structure of worth and value, or at the very center of the universe itself. Humanity's rationality and achievements are celebrated, its creativity and ability are lauded, and its development toward greater future goods is confidently announced. The human structure is separated out and set apart from that of other creatures and from other natural forms.

But let us remember the events that have posed so serious a threat to theism in our century. Surely these events are even more damaging to a humanist position. Must not anyone who has encountered Auschwitz conclude that it would be blasphemous to put humankind on any kind of pedestal, let alone at the center of a religious system. An empiricist, one who takes account of the evidence of experience, cannot easily or trivially engage in an idealizing of the human structure, and, of course, should hardly engage in making a deity of that structure. The achievements of humankind can scarcely serve as adequate material for a religion; the activities of contemporary twentieth-century humanity would hardly warrant unqualified praise in contrast to those of pre-literate peoples or of other creatures. We can have no grounds for praising humanity as the best creature on this planet, or the most beneficent resident of this planet, let alone of the universe itself. The absurdity of that kind of talk must be recognized. We must call for an end to the human arrogance that would lead to these kinds of claims. And the student of theology must be especially vigilant for, and stridently critical of, any religious or non-religious option that encourages such arrogance. It is certainly nonempirical, and ignorant—if not blasphemous—to laud humanity as the crowning glory of the universe.

Heading into the twenty-first century, are there really only two religious possibilities: the worship and adulation of God and the worship and adulation of humanity? And are these two positions, usually seen as diametrically opposed, actually all that dissimilar? Can many forms of theism be criticized, in fact, on *religious* grounds? The normative strands of theism in Judaism, Christianity, and Islam have all been humanocentric forms. That is, they have confidently (arrogantly) claimed that human affairs are the center of divine concern. These religious peoples have not only assumed that the human species was the focus of the universe and its most valued entity; they have made this claim a central and explicit part of religious teaching. Rather than representing a system of faith that lets God be God, this approach encourages species-egocentrism, human provincialism, and species arrogance. A theistic ideology that persists in placing humanity at the center of the universe, assuming that we are *the focus* of divine attention and concern, is not very different from a blatant humanism that claims supremacy for the species on an hierarchical structure. For any of us who wants to take the evidence of our experience seriously, and who wishes to look beyond a humanly provincial perspective, these two religious perspectives—

humanocentric theism and humanism, as we have known them up to this point—hardly seem adequate or appropriate for tomorrow. (An illustration of my point here may be found in some of the language surrounding the discussion of a nuclear exchange and nuclear holocaust. On occasion we encounter the term *omnicide* in the literature: "the destruction of all." If planet Earth is destroyed by a massive nuclear exchange, it will be an immensely sad, very tragic, occurrence. But it will not be the destruction of all. It will be a very significant, regrettable, preventable rearrangement of the matter-energy in this little part of the universe. But the universe will not be destroyed. It will not be omnicide. It will not be the end of existence. It will be the end of the human experiment in this solar system, along with that of the other creatures with which we share this planet. It will be this—nothing more, and nothing less.)

But are theism and humanism all we have? Is there a third alternative, perhaps just now emerging, yet to be worked out in any detail or with clarity, still embedded in a web of ambiguity, but potentially offering resources for our future? Is there another alternative for those who are compelled to reject transcendental and humanocentric theism and species-arrogant forms of humanism? I think there *may* be, and I find it exciting to be involved in this search. There may be another vision, a larger and more enriching vision, grounded in our creatural sense of connectedness and texturedness in an organic context.

As part of a thought experiment in this field, I find it intriguing to look at some suggestions made by Bernard Meland, a poet of faith, author of *Modern Man's Worship, Faith and Culture, Higher Education and the Human Spirit,* and *Fallible Forms and Symbols,* among other books. Meland has spoken of theology as being "midway between art and philosophy."[1] He has pointed to a recovery of what he calls the "creatural stance," calling for an attending to experience at a more elemental level, discovering there "an efficacy [which] persists within the structure of experience."[2] According to Meland: "We need that first-hand creature-feeling to stir us with wonder, awe, and profound appreciation."[3] For him, it is essential that the theologian, that anyone attempting to render sense of religiousness and its expressions, make touch at an elemental level with this creatureness of our experience. Indeed, as Meland reported last year: "Almost everything I have done and said roots in that elemental sense of creaturehood."[4]

Accordingly, categorizing Meland's position within the purview of normal theological labels is difficult. In the mid-1930s, when Meland was first dealing with this problem explicitly, he called his stance "mystical naturalism." At that time, he explained: "Mystical Naturalism is rooted in the realization that man is a child of the

---

[1]Bernard E. Meland, *Faith and Culture* (London: George Allen and Unwin, 1955) 97.

[2]Meland, *Fallible Forms and Symbols: Discourses on Method for a Theology of Culture* (Philadelphia: Fortress Press, 1976) xiii.

[3]Meland, *Modern Man's Worship: A Search for Reality in Religion* (New York: Harper and Brothers, 1934) 26.

[4]Letter, Bernard E. Meland to Edgar A. Towne, 11 February 1987.

earth, a genuine product of the natural order, and therefore intimately akin to its life."[5] He quoted with reverence and approval one of the leading religious humanists of the day, Albert Eustace Haydon, who praised a form of non-theism that would not encourage species-arrogant self-adulation and that would not belittle contextualism. In Haydon's words,

> Man himself is one phase of the natural order, the result of aeons of cosmic development— an earth child, molded and trained in body and mind by constant interaction with environment. . . . Man's being is so attuned to the nature from which he sprang, and which has nursed his long racial infancy, that some of the finest emotional experiences he has are rooted in the unconscious past. Love of nature is not an affair of reason, but deeper, a more sensuous appreciation of unity with the whole of things. A modern understanding of our relation to all the manifold phases of the patterns of life borne by the great Earth Mother may add to the mystic feel of oneness. . . . A mystical naturalism has its roots here.[6]

Meland wishes to eschew individualism and emphasizes, instead, a note of contextualism in the cosmic matrix. As he says, anticipating Christian theologians' interest in Buddhism,

> if we are right . . . in viewing all such human categories as body, mind, personality, and the like as convenient symbols for certain intricate organizations of related behaviors, then we are confronted with the very reasonable hypothesis that the boundaries which mark off the individual or the self are merely apparent. These selves are simply intensified centers in which the widespread, intricate workings come to focus. And the boundaries which mark off the self from the not-self simply become the effect of the shading as the focus of behaviors intensifies into visible organisms.[7]

This is a view that at once wants to jar us out of our dualistic theisms and also to expand our perspective beyond the narrowness of an overly rationalistic or moralistic individuated ego-consciousness. This kind of approach contrasts sharply with a supernaturalism that bifurcates the world into a dualism of the "natural" and the "supernatural." It is critical of a humanism that truncates the range of experience and reality and that too frequently identifies "reality" within the confines of human rationality.

There is an intriguing contemporaneity to Meland's suggestions, for he has anticipated perceptively one of the cultural crises of our time here. Meland does not want to follow the normal pattern of hierarchical language in religious thought, which

[5]Bernard E. Meland, "Mystical Naturalism and Religious Humanism," *The New Humanist* 8 (1935): 72.

[6]Albert Eustace Haydon, *The Quest of the Ages* (New York: Harper and Brothers, 1929), quoted by Meland, "Mystical Naturalism and Religious Humanism," 72.

[7]Bernard E. Meland, "Mystical Naturalism," 74.

almost always trades in "what is above" statements, positing either God as divine potentate (as in theism) or humanity as creatural potentate (as in humanism) as being "at the top." Instead, if we took our cues from Meland we would seek to reformulate this project toward relational and textured talk, showing the human as a connected and connectional creature within the ambiguous web of nature and of life. So, this "creatural stance" involves getting back to an elemental openness to raw experience, to an awareness of the total datum of the lived body, to an appreciation of our creature-connectedness with other beings of this earth and with nature as a whole, freed from the restrictiveness of both an hierarchical viewpoint and a focused rational structure. When we take account of the human structure at the deeper level of its creaturehood, says Meland, with an appreciative awareness of the mystery of existing, we shall be prepared "to take seriously this fresh awareness of the depth and complexity of the sheer act of living and dying, the tragedy, pathos, and hope of mere existence."[8] At this level of experience, Meland claims, the realities of relationships as immediately experienced, the fund of sensitivities associated with past events and valuations, the ultimacies attendant to the immediacies of experience as lived provide a depth of awareness and creatural meaning elicitory of awe and depth and wonder that are, indeed, truly relevant to religious inquiry.

It is here, I maintain, that we may be able to forge a "religious creaturalism," a position that is neither "theistic" nor "humanistic," traditionally conceived. If we move toward a richer awareness of the nourishing aspects of the trans-cerebral matrix in which we live and move and have our being, we may gain a renewed sense of ourselves as contextualized creatures of the earth in the web of life. We can finally come to regard ourselves as part of the web, rather than as set off from it, as a creature among creatures, a natural part of the cosmic matrix, integrally nourished and patterned by the rhythmed whole of which we are a part. We can come to regard the natural world not with the eyes of a separated, observant *naturalist*, but rather with the heart of a participating *native*.

Feminists, both women and men, teach us to move beyond various patriarchal dualisms—mind over body, will over passion, intellect over feeling, competition over communion, domination over mutual nurture, unilateral power over enabling activity, humans over other creatures. If we could develop a sense of religious creaturalism in which we were not cut off from collaborative being, but rather were living in a relational way with nature, with one another, and with other creatures, our theological agenda would look very different, indeed. It would be different in at least four important ways.

Number one: we could repudiate the activity of what has been called "systematic theology," in fact realizing that the term itself is oxymoronic. "Religious creaturalism" seeks the intensification rather than merely the explanation of experience-as-lived: the depths and ultimacies that attend our experience and its matrix of living and dying, of joy and pathos, of triumph and tragedy, of renewal and deterioration. This means that we must fully recognize, incorporate, and employ our whole experience as creatures in doing our theology, so that the resources of the passionate, the

[8]Meland, *Fallible Forms and Symbols,* 142.

emotive, and the ambiguous, relational, and contextual are authenticated. Because these resources are concretely actual in our experience, not transcendent to it, theology ought to assist in this immersion in life, in the intensification of experience. As earth-creatures we do not live in straight lines; we truly do exist in a web, a network, a maze. For it must be seen that concrete experience, actuality, is always clothed in ambiguity. We must deconstruct any of our theologies that claim to name ultimacies exactly, that seek a "systematic" rendering of God, that honor abstraction at the price of intensity and creatural fullness.

Number two, I believe, follows directly: it is time for theologians and philosophers to stop constructing theodicies ("justifications of the ways of God to humankind"). We should put behind us—on religious grounds—the so-called "Problem of Evil" or at least the manner in which we have framed it. It should be seen as the height of religious arrogance, indeed, for humans to presume that instances of human suffering and disaster (while unfortunate, even in some cases *devastating,* for *us*) call into question the existence of *God.* There *are* events that cause horrible human suffering and lead to ruinous regression for us. But it is presumptuous—it is religiously presumptuous—to assume that our welfare, the welfare of *homo sapiens* on this little planet, is at the center of divine activity and concern, or that human welfare and advancement are always more important than that of other creatures or other structures or other activities of the natural order. That leads us to turn legitimate—but parochial— concerns into the theological "Problem of Evil." The jump is not warranted. If we adopt a stance of religious creaturalism, less self-centered and selfish, in which we realize that we are part of a web of life, where our particular activity is not the center of the cosmos and where nothing is guaranteed, then we need not "explain away" or attempt to find some cosmic explanation for what we have called "evil." This gives us a place and a role in the universe to which we are perhaps not entitled. And this approach has also seduced us at times to truncate our experience, marginalizing or denying those elements that bring genuine intensification. Too often, older theodicies have suggested that fullness of life has meant absence of tragedy and sorrow. It is time for us to put that aside.

Number three: I would like also to see our eschatological reflection (that is, reflection concerning doctrines of the last things and immortality) become less parochial, less individualistic, and less selfish. It is very patriarchal and phallic of us to be primarily concerned with the fate of our individuated selves penetrating into the future. It is time for us to bring less linearity and more relationality to our eschatological thinking. We can embody more awareness of our status as evolved earth-creatures, of our affinities and interconnectednesses with the rest of nature, with the matter-energy matrix that has given us birth and of which, in some form, we shall always be a part. To the extent that we can move beyond egoism toward an emphasis on relationality in community and in the universe, we can attend to the "great matrix of being," "the cosmic matrix of matter/energy," the "fabric of being" that is "everlasting."[9] A stance of religious creaturalism, aware of our nature connectedness,

----

[9]Rosemary Radford Ruether, *Sexism and God-Talk: Toward a Feminist Theology* (Boston: Beacon Press, 1983) 257.

might lead us to more empathy with the matrix itself. We could realize that the death of our individuated self constitutes in a way our permission—which is not optimal—for other combinations within the matrix to go on. In some sense, each of us might see that what we may call "eternality" (or "life") is expressed briefly through this society of matter-energy that is called the "self," and then it moves on.

And, to close, number four: I hope our agenda includes—drawing on a true understanding of "religious creaturalism"—a move beyond hierarchical thinking in our religious life. This revolution will be difficult, for this ideology has been in place institutionally and theologically for centuries. We have sought to climb Jacob's ladder rather than dance in Sarah's circle. Socially, we have established various apartheid systems, rank-ordering people so that we have human hierarchies rather than human communities, placing—in some ultimate sense of worth—men over women, whites over people of color, presidents over professors. A detachable god is posited above nature, and a certain species is praised to the exclusion of the other creatures. Perhaps we can move to a point at which we shall praise something by saying of it that it is "supremely natural" rather than missing this and always looking for the "supernatural" or that which is "above the natural."

Such a theology, a religious creaturalism, will progress beyond stasis to process, beyond individualism to contextualism, beyond hierarchy to community, beyond linearity to relationality, finally renouncing the truly damaging elements of patriarchy in our religion. This is our question now: can we build and sustain a religious ideology adequate to our experience without recourse to the hierarchical distinctions that have governed religious options in the past? Can we sustain a religious creaturalism that is both meaningful and non-hierarchically, relationally modelled?

This possibility and this agenda can set an exciting project for some of us in the years ahead. Along this path we are not particularly confident of our way; we are not yet totally clear as to what kind of "religious" position we might be led. But we must regain a sense of ourselves as one creatural structure among many of the earth, as limited, as participating ambiguously in the pathos, majesty and creaturehood of the universe as a whole. To be sure, this is only a beginning, but a beginning which hastens the day toward an end to human arrogance and creatural separation. This is no small step, indeed.

Universal Ethical Monotheism and National Usurpation

J. Edward Barrett

The purpose of this essay is (1) to examine theologically what nations have done and are doing—my answer being that they are continually deifying themselves, or, with boorish regularity, attempting to clothe the rumor of a universal God with propaganda about one who favors a particular state; (2) to examine what the God of Universal Ethical Monotheism is doing—my conclusion being that God is seeking to unite the world in spite of the pretensions of nations; and (3) to examine what we should do—my suggestion being that we should seek to promote the advancement of international law and world government.

I approach the issue from the perspective of American "pragmatism." This means that (1) *I try to stay close to evidence,* even while recognizing that metaphysics *is* (literally) going "beyond" the physical. I want to limit speculation considerably, and limit dogma totally. I make no appeal to supernatural revelation, but seek only to appeal to evidence available to everyone (in the methodological tradition of deism, though with somewhat different conclusions); and (2) that *I am satisfied with tentative answers,* which are "practical" (pragmatic) descriptions of experience (or "working" ideas), and which surely fall short of being comprehensive, logically necessary, or final descriptions of ultimate reality.

I

The cultures of the ancient Middle East—the Nile Valley and the Fertile Crescent—were all *theocracies.* Believing themselves to be "ruled by god" (or by a god), they were nevertheless different in theoretical structure.

In Egypt, the pharaoh was said to *be* a god. While the environment was polytheistic, the issue of civil disobedience allowed for no diversity. Religion and politics were blended, and the people encouraged to believe that the state (its structure, laws, and ruler) was divine. As a god the pharaoh owned all Egyptian property, and ruled with absolute authority. To challenge the state was to challenge a god, which no healthy-minded Egyptian mortal was tempted to do. This, along with the insulation from invasion provided by desert and sea, led to a relative political stability, which led to a security not enjoyed by potential competitors.

In Mesopotamia the theocratic claim was somewhat more modest. The kings claimed to rule by the sanction of a god, and even at the direction of a god, but not to be a god. Perhaps the relative military stability granted Egypt by the protection of sea and desert made the divinity of the state more tenable there than in Mesopotamia where invasions from the north constantly challenged the wisdom and power of ruling authorities. Nevertheless, states claimed divine authority, and were able to demand something close to absolute obedience—though the appearance of a law "code" (whether Hammurabi's or other) is evidence of an attempt to deal with some discontent and problems.

In Israel the theocratic idea and practice often shared much in common with the Mesopotamian model—especially centering around the claim that God made a special covenant with David and his descendants (2 Samuel 7), thereby creating a "chosen" people (Deuteronomy 7:6). From this perspective it is only a small step to the divinization of the state, including its military establishment—which is indeed what happened, for example, in Psalm 48:12-14, which reads: "Walk about Zion, go about her, number her towers, consider her ramparts, go through her citadels; that you may tell the next generation that this is God, our God for ever and ever. He will be our guide for ever." Now, *that* is what I mean by "national usurpation"—politics capturing religion.

But that is by no means the only approach to theocracy in ancient Israel. There is a quite different idea, often on conflict with the "establishment" model, demanding that Israel be ruled directly by God without the intervention of any government (Judges 8:23; 1 Samuel 8:7; 12:19; Hosea 8:4). From this perspective, governments are viewed with suspicion—as competing with God for human loyalty, and as presuming to a sacred status which is idolatrous, the point being that governments are not God. Governments are not endorsed by God. Governments are *judged, exposed,* and *challenged* by God.

This second and more "prophetic" Israelite idea is instructive. This perspective could be described as "Universal Ethical Monotheism," since it functions to reject the divinity of the state and to assert a value that both transcends the state and exposes the pretensions of the state.

It would be easy to write the rest of this essay (and perhaps a book) speaking only about the ancient world. But I would like to use this perspective to examine the modern world, where belief in one God is still twisted and tarnished by the attempt of nations to draft God into their own service.

History makes clear that the trick of domesticating God (into the service of the state) is not forgotten, whereas the implications of Universal Ethical Monotheism are hardly ever learned.

For an example from the modern world, Iran "knows" that God is on its side and is not embarrassed calling opponents the Great Satan— just as some Americans *know* they are the "second Israel," a "righteous empire," and were not embarrassed when their president called the Soviet Union an "evil empire." In America we still think in terms of "manifest destiny," and our currency is marked "In God We Trust." (What "God" are we talking about, and what do we trust this God to do? Or, does this mean it is in money we place our trust?) In Word War I every German soldier wore on his belt buckle the words "Gott mit uns" ("God with us"). Moving around the world, in 1971 a tourist guide who was a university graduate told me in Benares, when we visited a temple where a map of India was the focus of attention, "India is a god." I did not call for a definition.

Illustrations are endless, but they must end in order to answer the question, *How do nations get away with these pretensions?*

I submit the following suggestions as to why, throughout history, the pretentious claims of nations have nevertheless been found believable. (1) The power of the state, while clearly less than omnipotent, is conspicuously more than the power of the individual. And, the state's power is tangible in a way that an abstraction such as omnipotence is not. This ability to overwhelm the individual with tangible power is an important factor in the issue of believability. The state is less than ideal, but oh! so real. (2) Divinizing the state may have sometimes (rarely, but sometimes) contributed to the survival of its people by encouraging obedience, thereby consolidating power and creating unity, in situations where unity was important—though probably just as often it has gotten nations into military adventurism, leading to their defeat. Original sources (historians living at the time) survive to celebrate military successes, and often do not live to publicly mourn its failures.

What then is meant by Universal Ethical Monotheism?

Universal means that God is not deposited in the national treasury of any particular government or culture. The function of placing God "in heaven" is precisely this: to affirm that God has a perspective that we do not. "The earth is the Lord's" (Psalm 24:1), and not just part of the earth. Before this God "the nations are like a drop from a bucket, and are accounted as the dust on the scales" (Isaiah 40:15). The point should be devastating for religious nationalists—including Israel—but, alas.

Ethical means that God judges all peoples by the same standard, and is concerned not with national boundaries but with communities of responsibility. Allow me to repeat that: *communities of responsibility*. "Learn to do good. Seek justice, correct oppression; defend the fatherless, plead for the widow" (Isaiah 1:17) is the command and counsel of this God. An "ethical" God is one "who executes justice for the oppressed; who gives food to the hungry" (Psalm 146:7), and whose "delight is not in the strength of the horse" (Psalm 147:10), chariots, or warriors (Hosea 10:13). It is a God who reflects, "Too long have I had my dwelling among those who hate peace; I am for peace; but when I speak, they are for war!" (Psalm 120:6, 7). When a nation becomes self-righteous and pretentious, an ethical God asks, "Are you not like the Ethiopians to me, O people of Israel?" (Amos 9:7) And again, "Are you better than Thebes that sat by the Nile?" (Nahum 3:8) This God refuses to be enlisted in the military service of arrogant nations (whether Israel or some other).

Monotheism is not a rejection of relative values (gods), but a demand to recognize a perspective that transcends our own relative values (gods), thereby exposing them as relative. As Tillich notes, "Polytheism, whether in its religious form or in its secular form (that is, nationalism) . . . is surely not the acceptance of many gods in contrast to one God—it is the absolutizing of one space among other spaces" (*Political Expectation*, 148). "Patriotism is the last refuge of a scoundrel" (Samuel Johnson) because it is misdirected religious devotion—literally, "idolatry"—which "transmutes individual unselfishness into national egoism" (Reinhold Niebuhr, *Moral*

Man in Immoral Society, 91). Like every soldier asked to give "the last full measure of devotion" for his country, the nation-state is an idol, requiring a devotion and pretending to a worth which is unjustified by serious study of *any* nation's history.

II

I want now to explore the question as to what the God of Universal Ethical Monotheism is doing in the world. I am as aware as anyone of two great presumptions involved in proposing to answer this question.

(1) How do we know that the God of Universal Ethical Monotheism is actual or real? For those concerned with this question (and who is not?) I ask you to concentrate upon the logical *function* of the idea rather than upon its ontological status. What follows is not an argument for belief in the reality of the God of Universal Ethical Monotheism but instead an argument about how the logical extension of that idea should be expected to "work" in human thought. I ask you to grant me what could be called "a temporary epistemological suspension of ontology." What Tillich called "the God above the God of theism" may be judged empty of content (though I do not believe that judgment is correct) but surely it is not empty of perspective. It is that perspective I am concerned with.

(2) How can we mortals be expected to know what the God of Universal Ethical Monotheism (should such a divine entity be so accommodating as to exist) is doing with our planet? Given the pathetic and tragic history of answers to this question, can anyone hope to do better? Here is where I get bold and (I hope) interesting. I think I know—and therefore require your indulgence, humor, and sympathy. I intend the following to be not dogmatic or arrogant, but rather observant and suggestive.

Scenario One. Imagine you are an observer from outer space, watching our planet from your spaceship. One hundred years on earth is but a day in your life. What have you "observed" happening on earth during your last five "days"? What will your report back to mission control say about us?

Trusting in imagination, I think I know the answer. During the last five hundred years on earth (only five days for you) you have seen one dominant and obvious pattern: the drawing together of human communities that were formerly separated—often against their will and in spite of their actions to the contrary. There are actions to the contrary (nationalism), but they are actually reactions to what is happening rather than what is happening itself.

When you arrived (five hundred years ago on earth), you saw loosely connected and occasional caravan routes, developed then supplemented by shipping lanes, developed then supplemented by railroads, developed then supplemented by automobiles and highways, developed then supplemented by airplanes—tying the world together.

Transportation has connected us in ways that were beyond imagination on earth when you arrived. This development was fueled by commerce and made possible by advancing technology.

But accompanying this economic and scientific development has been increased communication—awareness of one another. Rumors and reports from travelers have been replaced by postal services, the telegraph, the telephone, the radio (linking ground, air, and sea), and television (made truly worldwide by satellites).

Unlike centuries ago, we are both aware of and influenced by one another in ways and to an extent that no one on earth then could have imagined.

Scenario Two. Evidence of this influence can better be examined by moving beyond the spaceship scenario and approaching the situation differently.

During the last week I personally drank coffee from Latin America, in a cup bought in Scotland, ate a banana grown in Guatemala, shaved with a razor made in the Netherlands, dressed in a shirt tailored in South Korea, used a watch manufactured in Singapore, wore a tie from Spain, drove in a car made in Germany fueled with gasoline from Saudi Arabia, used a calculator made in Taiwan, and loaded a camera made in Japan with film made in the United States. The world already has functioning a broadly international (though not yet universal) economic system.

Scenario Three. The Soviet Union imports more than twenty-five percent of its grain, and more than half of that is from the United States. Two 20,000-ton freighters loaded with grain leave the United States for Russia every day. If Russia were to attack the United States it would destroy more than ten percent of its own grain supply. Surprisingly related, the Siberian pipeline makes Western Europe dependent upon Russia for ten percent of its natural gas. But it also makes Russia dependent upon Western Europe for the hard currency it needs to purchase grain from the United States. Despite aims toward self-sufficiency, we have become interdependent.

I submit these three scenarios as evidence. We are being bound together in a network of interdependence, a web of relationships no one fully understands. We have moved from family to clan to tribe to nation to the global village. *Fact*: this is the emerging situation on our planet. *Theological interpretation*: this is what the God of Universal Ethical Monotheism has been and is doing with our planet. For theology this involves a "leap of faith," but that is different from a leap of credulity.

God is creating what Marshall McLuhan called the "global village"— which simple *is* this network of nations, this web of relationships that binds the world together, making us increasingly aware of, influenced by, dependent upon, and responsible to one another. Could it also be what Jesus intuitively meant by the "Kingdom of God"? Perhaps! Pierre Teilhard de Chardin thought so, and I find his suggestions both persuasive and visionary. Surely, for theology, the issue is not (with Charles Darwin) talking about the evolution of the past. But, rather, the issue is (with Teilhard) talking about the past scientifically in order to talk about the future imaginatively.

What Teilhard in the first half of this century imaginatively called "planetization," "point omega," and the "noosphere" has striking similarities both to the "global village" described by Marshall McLuhan and to what we all know and experience today.

III

I want now to turn to the question, What should we be doing? My answer, of course, is that we should be responding constructively to what God is doing, cooperating with God, contributing our resources to the goal of the source of all resources. Specifically, I believe this means encouraging global responsibility by advocating

obedience to international law and advancement toward world government of some
yet unknown (but not unimaginable) type.

In 1910 British journalist Norman Angell wrote a book, *The Great Illusion*. The
theme was that war is obsolete and improbable. In support of this conclusion Angell
argued that (1) modern technology is too deadly and devastating, and (2) the interdependence of nations is too restraining. We simply will not do it.

Four years later we did it (World War I), and a generation later we did it again
(World War II). Norman Angell was wrong! Or was he? Certainly his timing was off.
But today technology is more deadly, and interdependence (what God is doing) is
more restraining. Perhaps God is winning in spite of us. But only perhaps.

Some readers with exceptional memories will recall the idea of the "social con-
tract" (Hobbes and Locke). According to this theory, in primordial times, in order
to escape endless murder and anarchy, individuals submitted to the rule of governments (kings or chiefs), which imposed order.

Reasoning from this venerable tradition, a group of people known as "world
federalists" suggests that in order to escape endless warfare nations must submit to
the rule of world government. They usually then propose amending the charter of the
United Nations to achieve this.

Throughout most of my adult life I have heard World Federalists described as
unrealistic, idealistic dreamers. For more objective descriptions of international affairs I was referred to such theorists of realpolitik as Niccolò Machiavelli and Kle-
mens Metternich. Reinhold Niebuhr—whom I consider superior to both—seemed
charmed by their hard-nosed realism. International affairs, Niebuhr taught, is a matter of power struggles between competing and conflicting communities of national
interest. The law of love is the law of life, but history is the boringly repetitious record
of humanity's revolt against its own most fundamental law. Within a sinful world, it
cannot be expected that the powerful will submit their interests to the wishes of the
weak—unless under severe pressure such as strikes, boycotts, and so forth.

Now (as indicated in the second paragraph of this essay), I tend to think of myself as relatively hard-nosed when it comes to insisting upon evidence, and for years
I was intimidated by the argument that suggests that power plays are all that count in
international affairs. But more recently I have become persuaded that international
affairs are far more complex than realpolitik allows, and that there is an abundance
of evidence that World Federalists are on their way to getting their way—or something like it. So, what is the evidence?

Consider the degree to which *already functioning* international law under United
Nations supervision is operative in today's world.

The *Universal Postal Union,* under the United Nations, supervises international
mail and monitors whether letters sent from one country are delivered to the country
where they are sent.

International travelers a quarter of a century ago were required to carry a certi-
fication of smallpox vaccination on a separate "medical passport." But today this is
no longer necessary, because the *World Health Organization,* under the United Nations, has practically eliminated smallpox.

The United Nations' *International Civil Aviation Organization* creates the reg-
ulations governing all international flights and procedures for landing at international

airports. The pilot knows about weather patterns because of the U.N.'s *World Meteorological Organization,* and is able to communicate with ground control and with other planes because of the U.N.'s *International Telecommunications Union,* which assigns and protects the frequencies used.

Similar services apply to commerce and travel by sea.

Furthermore, the peacemaking and peacekeeping function of the United Nations during the decade of the 1980s has been monumental—with both "superpowers" (in spite of occasional lapses) increasingly relying upon the U.N.'s good offices. That organization has played an important peacemaking role in the Iran-Iraq war, in Afghanistan, Cyprus, Angola, and in the continuing conflict between Israel and the Palestinians. It has also served important relief-agency functions, especially in Africa.

Now these accomplishments are important and very relevant for us all. But, of course, they pale when compared with the importance of what has yet to be achieved: (1) the binding settlement of conflict between nations by the International Court of Justice and (2) the enforcement of international law (and therefore peace) by an empowered executive.

The concept of "nations" has always been fluid—both with reference to space and to time. Boundaries change, and during the Middle Ages there were no nations in the modern sense. There is no reason to believe that what we think of as the all-sovereign nation-state is the ultimate or "natural" way of existing. Alternatives are available. The issue is not an idealistic utopia (which can easily be dismissed) but a working system of relative law and order, which will limit though not eliminate the ambitions and frailties of finite and sinful human communities.

History holds at least one precedent (actually, more than one) suggesting it is possible. In 1948 Carl Van Doren, a Columbia University professor and Pulitzer-prize-winning historian, wrote a book titled *The Great Rehearsal.* The book tells the story of the making and ratifying of the Constitution of the United States, and was reissued last year in honor of the two-hundredth anniversary of the Constitution. Van Doren writes,

> In 1787 the problem was how the people could learn to think nationally, not locally, about the United States. [Today] the problem is how the people can learn to think internationally, not nationally, about the United Nations. . . .
> It is impossible to read the story of the making of the Constitution of the United States without finding there all the arguments in favor of a general government for the United Nations, as well as all the arguments now raised in opposition to it. . . . It is obvious that no difficulty in the way of a world government can match the danger of a world without it. . . . Their undertaking might be [considered] . . . a rehearsal for the federal governments of the future.

Van Doren's book demonstrates that political communities *can* and on occasion *do* forfeit self-centered interest for the more general welfare. It has happened before—in the "great rehearsal."

It has happened before—in part and in anticipation. It is happening today in the emergence of a united Europe.

But is the world really ready for global community under international law? Perhaps the answer is that it had better be.

Beyond that, history makes clear that there comes a time when the time has come, when what we human beings could not previously do we now can do, should do, must do. Paul Tillich called such historical moments a *kairos,* from the Greek meaning "when the time is ripe." Such a *kairos* came during the nineteenth century with the abolition of slavery. Since then the world has not looked back. Perhaps today the time is ripe for world government and international law. As Teilhard de Chardin has written, "The Age of Nations is past. The task before us now, if we would not perish, is to shake off our ancient prejudices, and to build the earth."

Bibliography

Angell, Norman. *The Great Illusion—Now.* Harmondsworth: Penguin, 1939.

McLuhan, H. Marshall, and Quentin Fiore, coordinated by Jerome Agel. *The Medium Is the Message.* New York: Bantam Books, 1967.

──────────. *War and Peace in the Global Village.* New York: Bantam Books, 1968.

Niebuhr, Reinhold. *Moral Man and Immoral Society. A Study in Ethics and Politics.* New York: Charles Scribner's Sons, 1934.

Teilhard de Chardin, Pierre. *Building the Earth.* Trans. Noel Lindsay. West Nyack NY: Cross Currents, 1959.

──────────. *The Phenomenon of Man.* Trans. Bernard Wall; introduction by Sir Julian Huxley. London: Collins; New York: Harper & Row, 1959.

Tillich, Paul. *Political Expectation.* Ed. James Luther Adams. New York: Harper & Row, 1971; ROSE (Reprints of Scholarly Excellence) 1—Macon GA: Mercer University Press, 1981.

Van Doren, Carl. *The Great Rehearsal. The Story of the Making and Ratifying of the Constitution of the United States.* New York: Penguin, 1948.

William H. Bernhardt's Value Hypothesis
A Systemic Approach

Francis W. Brush

Over the period of more than a third of a century William H. Bernhardt established himself as a philosopher of religion. In his preface to Bernhardt's *The Cognitive Quest for God and Operational Theism,* Harvey H. Potthoff says, "The years 1929 to 1964 witnessed the rise and flourishing of movements which minimized or denied the significance of philosophical theology. Influential voices encouraged a 'religious revolt against reason.' Throughout this period Bernhardt steered a steady course, insisting that careful attention to presuppositions, to clear thinking and to such knowledge as is available from various fields of inquiry is essential in serious theological work"[1] This is particularly evident in his two articles which appeared in 1958 in *The Iliff Review.* In them he not only discussed his own general theory of value but emphasized its metaphysical and epistemological base.

It may be interesting to note that some twenty years ago at the 1937 International Congress of Philosophy held in Paris there were fifty papers presented on the topic of values. Of these papers twelve related values to knowledge and seventeen related values to metaphysics. Wilbur M. Urban of that era, points out that "the problem of knowledge cannot be divorced from the problem of value."[2] He goes on to say, "One may insist upon the independence of ethics and axiology of metaphysics, but its separation can never be more than temporary and methodological in character."[3]

Bernhardt agrees and comes to his own conclusion that Value Theory cannot be considered apart from metaphysics and in turn from its epistemological base. He observes that there are three aspects in the knowledge-situation: the Object or World-as-Such, the Object or World-as-Known, and the Person or Subject-as-Knowing. He does not deal with the Object-as-such since in his theory of meaning it cannot be cog-

---

[1]William H. Bernhardt, *The Cognitive Quest for God and Operational Theism* (Denver CO: The Criterion Press, 1971) iii.

[2]Wilbur M. Urban, *Twentieth Century Philosophy,* ed. Dagobert D. Runes (New York: Philosophical Library, 1947) 64.

[3]Ibid., 66.

nitively known. He presupposes no esoteric source of knowledge. His focus, therefore, is on the Subject-as-Knowing and the Object-as-Known. He says, very simply,
"We may assume the existence of man as a thinker who is curious about his own
nature and the conditions under which he exists."[4]

The Subject-as-Knowing

Human knowledge about the world around us is for him acquired by patient and
persistent observation, formulated by moving from data to hypothesis, and justified
by facts and theories based on facts. Bernardt's cognitive quest was a search for
knowledge that is intellectually warrantable. He defines epistemology as the "critical analysis of the cognitive instruments employed by cognizers in understanding
themselves and their Existential Medium."[5]

Bernhardt had trouble finding a name for his approach, but finally picked as "the
least inadeqate" one, that used by many scientists and some philosophers, namely,
Operationalism which consists of two steps: "The first is clarification, the name applied to several steps preliminary to the actual testing of the hypothesis. It includes
the determination of (i) the nature of the problem under consideration; (ii) the meaning or meanings of the terms presumably relevant to its analysis and solution; (iii) the
development of hypotheses which may be proposed as possible solutions; and (iv)
the conditions which must be obtained if the hypothesis is to be verified."[6]

Concerning the two levels of the verification process Bernhardt wrote, "The first
we have called 'behavioral' verification for the reason that some human action is required by it . . . the second level of verification is called 'implicative verification.'
This may be defined as that form of verification which consists of support drawn from
other theories verified in terms of observed verification. This could be called 'cor-
rorobative' verification if one wished to do so."[7]

When Bernhardt accepted "operationalism" as a method he acknowledged that
through its use knowledge had increased—that the increase improved the reasoning
ability of the Subject-as-Knowing, as well as providing wider access to reliable information about the Object-as-Known. He believed this method to be demonstrably
more efficient than other ways of knowing. In his words it contributed to "Increasing
Cognitional Efficiency." He states, "The presupposition of Increasing Cognitional
Efficiency is . . . oriented toward the verifiability and the verification of the ɔngru-
ence of concepts with the realities they symbolize, designate or denote. As such it is
located at the level of the efficiency of human thinking rather that that of immediate
practicality. It is a type of 'practicality' but it is that form of practicality which characterized pure science (and) critical philosophy . . . it presupposes that efficiency in
living depends, in the long run, upon reliable, that is, accurate information concerning the realities upon which life depends and upon the nature of life itself."[8] This,

---

[4]Bernhardt, *The Cognitive Quest,* 149.
[5]Ibid., 95
[6]Ibid., 85
[7]Ibid., 152-53.
[8]Ibid., 116.

then, is the method Bernhardt uses in the process of valuing or evaluating. It is the same as is used in any other efficient type of thinking.

The Object-as-Known

In his second article, entitled "A Metaphysical Base for Value Theory and Religion," Bernhardt says that man does not live in a vacuum. He lives in some context, environment or medium. In his words, "The more inclusive medium within which he exists I normally speak of as the Existential Medium. As I am using the word metaphysics it constitutes that study which focuses upon the Existential Medium as broadly defined."[9] In another context he defines the term as, "a dynamic process in which novelty, creativity and differentiation are constant and continuous factors."[10] He says, "Metaphysics may now be defined as the organization of knowledge of the all-pervasive characteristics, qualities, trends, or tendencies of the Existential Medium in order to provide a framework for the understanding of man and that in which he exists."[11] In other words, Bernhardt suggests that the World-as-Known may be organized around certain all-pervasive characteristics of the cosmos, envisioned or conceived as a whole in order to better understand the parts—nature and man.

In order to understand Bernhardt's terminology it is important to recall that he uses Greek drama as an analogue for his metaphysical concepts. Like Shakespeare he says, "All the world's a stage." A key concept for Bernhardt is that of "episode," which in Greek tragedy occurs between two songs, on a stage and introduces variety into the story being told. While the episode has it's own separateness, it also has its togetherness. In a succcessful play all the parts constitute a unity. Bernhardt chooses "episode" because it has the characteristics of emerging within a context, being temporal in character, subject to change, and as it does so throwing light or new light on old situations. There is a time in which an episode persists or lasts., hence "duration" is also an all-pervasive characteristic. Nothing or "no thing" can be discussed without this characteristic. Bernhardt combines these two characteristics to form his world-hypothesis of Episodic Durationality.

For Bernhardt the Existential Medium, characterized by durationality furnishes the stage. On it the world drama takes place. It is a world in the process of change which includes both continuity and creativity. It is the matrix from which emerges the drama which is made up of episodes. While each existent is seen specifically, it is at the same time a part of, rather than apart from, the environment. It is "episodic."

In the development of the analogue as it relates to his world-hypothesis he proposes a set of categories applied to "that which is." In this he follows a suggestion made by Bertrand Russsell that one may begin with undefined terms that take on meaning by inference. Bernhardt's three undefined terms are "existence," "relation," and "modality." Briefly sketched he says that meaning is given to "exis-

[9]Ibid., 149.
[10]Ibid., 125
[11]Ibid., 152

tence'' by focusing on the characteristics of each particular episode. In defining any "thing" or existent there is an identifiable organization, developing in a definable way, capable of change, yet somewhat permanent, and having the ability to produce modifications in other episodes.

Meaning is given to "relation" by focusing on the characteristics due to the plurality of episodes. In defining "things" or existents there is the fact of otherness, novelty or newness, plurality, involvement, and the effect upon other episodes as a result of interaction.

Meaning is given to "modality" by focusing on the characteristic way episodes function because of their own characteristics and their relationship to other episodes. In defining the function of episodes one must consider that there are the characteristics of being limited in extent and endurance, being partially restricted, and yet partially "guided," leading to consummation and replacement. (A more formal table of categories may be found on p. 157 of his article on "A Metaphysical Basis for Value Theory and Religion.")

Commenting on the importance of this "cosmological" hypothesis, Charles Milligan, a colleage of Bernhardt's and a participant in this Conference, wrote, "in my judgment this metaphysical scheme is one of Bernhardt's most ingenious and useful contributions."[12]

However, until the world-hypothesis or reinterpretation is tested it is, in Whitehead's terms "an imaginative experiment." As he puts it, "The true method of discovery is like the flight of an airplane. It starts from the ground of particular observations, it makes its flight in the thin air of imaginative generalization, and it again lands for renewed observation rendered acute by rational interpretation. . . . The success of the imaginative experiment is always to be tested by the applicability of its results beyond the restricted locus from which it originated."[13]

In summary one can say that Bernhardt believed that man's values are to be found in the World-as-Known—the Existential Medium— and are to be cognized by the Subject-as-Knowing by the same methods as are used in other areas, that is, Operationalism. The objective is Increasing Cognitional Efficiency.

This, then, is the metaphysical and epistemological base on which rests Bernhardt's general theory of the person valuing and of the object considered valuable.

Bernhardt's Value Hypothesis

Moving to his general theory of value per se we find that Bernhardt's first concern is with definition of the term "value," second with the characteristics of any general theory of value, third with his own value-hypothesis.

Concerning definition he wrote: "The first problem in value theory is that of identifying the objects, entities or events which are to be called 'valuable'."[14] In this process he analyses "as presumably typical of tradition and contemporary usage"

---

[12]Ibid., xii.

[13]Alfred North Whitehead, *Process and Reality: An Essay in Cosmology* (New York: The Macmillan Co. 1929) 7, 8.

[14]Bernhardt, *The Cognitive Quest*, 131.

the positions of four quite different philosophers: the Realists Aristotle and Nicoli Hartmann, the Idealist Bernard Bosanquet, and the Instrumentalist, John Dewey.

His analysis of these four systems indicates "that value 'facts' consist in experienced events, occurrences or activities characterized by culminations, consummations or realizations accompanied by satisfactions, appreciations and enjoyments."[15] That is, there are two basic categories that can be said to describe a value experience: the culminative—an objective process, and the appreciative—a subjective satisfaction.

The culminative category, also referred to by Bernhardt as the consummative or ends-realization category, includes "all culminative change, process or activity in which there occurs more or less temporary 'forms,' 'ends,' or 'realizations' which are recognized as intended, desired or satisfying."[16]

The second value category—the appreciative—includes "all recognitions and prizings of some phase or phases of the world which are considered worthy of honor, respect, love or reverence."[17]

He goes on: "In order to search out the invariants among the four systems it will be necessary to look more deeply into each of them to define more precisely the culminative and appreciative categories."[18] The result of this further analysis revealed five factors or characteristic elements he considered basic to a general theory of value. They are:

(i) the continuous emergence of novelty,
(ii) some tension, momentum, or directionality,
(iii) some culminative results or consummative experiences,
(iv) varying degrees of satisfaction, and
(v) some change in the quality potential of the situation.[19]

Bernhardt explains these characteristics in the following manner.

(i) *Emergence of Novelty*. "Value experiences apparently presuppose some change in a situation before they become possible. . . . The emergence of novelty is not confined to things or productions. Geniuses appear in various fields who invent the new in response to new possibilities which they discern. And they appear in all fields, from mathmatics to music. It is the creative person who plays a significant role in the origin of all value-experiences. . . . The emergence of novelty is not confined to the human level. Changes in the surface of the sun have their effects upon weather and climate. Cosmic rays play a role in human productivity and inventiveness, even though we do not yet know what their effects are. Yet changes here produce responses on the part of man and reactions on the part of nature. And these changes are factors in value situations. There is then some emergence of the new in the experi-

---

[15]Ibid., 143.
[16]Ibid., 140.
[17]Ibid., 141.
[18]Ibid., 138
[19]Ibid., 143-44

ence of value."[20]

(ii) *Tension, momentum, or directionality.* After discussing various views concerning tension as a basic characteristic of a general theory of value, Bernhardt says, "Granted that tension may be a factor, . . . my own studies lead me to accept the view that there is a factor of directional momentum operative at all levels of existence. . . . Directionality combined with momentum may be traced through all the levels superimposed upon the atomic. The universe is dynamic, and it is directional. And what is true of the whole appears to be true of the lesser wholes. With the emergence of some novelty, the new contains its own directional momentum with its own tendency toward some culminative activity."[21]

(iii) *Culminative or consummatory results.* Bernhardt says, "Value experiences appear to be episodic in character. . . . That is with the emergence of some novelty there occurs a development climaxed by some culmination. . . . Yet culminative results are never wholly lost. They appear to be cumulative in character . . a cumulative factor at work which carries something of each earlier value experiences into those which emerge later."[22]

(iv) *Satisfactoriness.* "Culminative and appreciative experiences are accompanied by feelings of satisfaction or dissatisfaction." What satisfies the mind is accepted, what does not is rejected. "It judges and this capacity to judge is the basis of valuation. But satisfaction is also a feeling tone that is deepened and enriched."[23]

(v) *Changes in quality potential.* Bernhardt defines "quality" as "that in objects, events and ideals capable of evoking modification in other objects, events and ideals."[24] For example, at the human level, "Every experience, *something lived through,* leaves it's imprint upon us physically and psychically. . . . The culminative events or experiences defined as valuable have this capacity also. Each aesthetic experience may deepen and enrich our capacities for such enjoyment."[25]

Conclusion

In the concluding paragraph of his first article on Value Theory Bernhardt summarizes: "The term value refers to, denotes or designates those culminative episodes which satisfy some need, interest or directional momentum of living beings."[26]

To put this in the context of his metaphysical base he says, "Values . . . are related positively to the Existential Medium. They are not accidents or incidents. Rather they are expressions of the Existential Medium at one level of existence. [Again] Values belong in the larger context of the Existential Medium . . . they are 'at home' in and are of the nature of Existence."[27]

---

[20]Ibid., 145.
[21]Ibid., 145
[22]Ibid., 145-46
[23]Ibid., 147.
[24]Ibid., 146.
[25]Ibid., 146
[26]Ibid., 147
[27]Ibid., 173

From an epistemological point of view he says, "Values, in the long run, depend upon increasing man's knowledge of himself and his Existential Medium. . . . It is the intelligent quest for human values viewed in the perspective of the centuries, and conditioned by more adequate and reliable knowledge of realities."[28]

To put it simply, for Bernhardt the *location* of values is in the Existential Medium; the *selection* of values is by the method of Operationalism; and the *realization* of values occurs in such experiences as may be described as ethical, intellectual, aesthetic, or religious which are discussed by other participants in this conference. What is important to understand is that Bernhardt's value-hypothesis is systemic.

---

[28]Ibid., 115-16.

The Importance
of the Notion of Being
for Philosophical Theology

J. Harley Chapman

I

In this essay I argue for the theoretical importance of the notion of being, which means that being is to be taken as the central and determining category of the theory put forth to explain what most needs explaining in philosophical theology: (1) the nature of the experienced referent and (2) ontological shock. I am arguing that the theory of ontological creativity best does the job needing to be done and thus ought to be accepted by others. But as with any theory, it is vulnerable and invites collegial challenge and correction.

The structure of the essay is as follows: (1) an introduction in which both the claim and the assumptions of the argument are laid out; (2) a phenomenological section in which experience is probed, and that in two modes: experiential and existential; (3) a theoretical section in which the theory of ontological creativity is sketched out; and (4) a concluding section with some suggested applications and vulnerabilities.

The claim of the theoretical importance of being is of course not new as Western theological history testifies, with the Greek Fathers, Augustine, Aquinas, Neo-Thomists, transcendental Thomists, Tillich, Macquarrie, and Neville all finding an important place for the notion of being in their systems.[1] But affirmation has always been followed by protest: being, it has been said, is too abstract, too static, too banal, too lifeless, too removed from the welter of history with its myriad of natural, social, and personal becomings to serve as the organizing category of theological theory. However, the "ontologists" have never been fully convinced, converted, or silenced. Consider Paul Tillich's response to the proposal that becoming be made co-

---

[1]Among many possible treatments of this theme see O. C. Thomas, "Being and Some Theologians," *Harvard Theological Review* 70 (January-April 1977): 137-60.

ordinate with, if not superior to, the notion of being in theology:

> [Being] is meant neither as the object in contrast to a subject nor as the last-
> ing in contrast to the changing; it is meant as the negation of non-being, as
> not-not-being, or as the underivable fact that there is something and not
> nothing. Subjectivity as well as objectivity, dynamics as well as form, the
> changing as well as the lasting are implied in "being" in this sense. I sus-
> pect that much theological criticism of the first (not last) statement about
> God, that he is "being-itself," results from the confusion of being in the
> absolute sense of not-not-being with a particular element of being, the static
> or objective.[2]

And further he writes:

> one who has experienced the shock of non-being cannot make any conces-
> sions to the ultimacy of being.[3]

It is important to note here what has often been overlooked by the critics of ontological theories: the proponents of such have usually been deeply concerned to give
a faithful accounting for *experience*. The only good reasons for holding such a theory
are that lacking such a theoretical category certain crucial areas of experience cannot
be given adequate voice nor can the proper ordering of interpretants to account for
what is central in experience be made.

In the following argument I make three assumptions about the discipline of
philosophical theology, the referent and the experience of it, and the relation between
theory and experience. First, philosophical theology is a *theological* discipline, with
the referent of the discourse being understood in some sense as real and positive. With
apologies to Gertrude Stein, "There is a there there." The force of the claim that the
referent is real is to distance such claim from all constructivist and fictionalist interpretations; this does not entail a naive-realist interpretation, however. At this point
we can be satisfied with a certain vagueness about what the referent is. Yet *that* it is,
that it is encounterable, that multidimensional interaction therewith is possible is an
assumption (a) most natural to make considering the pervasive experience of the
world's various spiritual paths, including the testimony of transformed lives and
communities; and (b) dialectically justifiable, assuming of course the reality of the
norms governing the dialectic and the dialectical nature of reality itself.

Second, philosophical theology is *philosophical* and thus takes as primary not
the adhesion to a unique revelation nor its elaboration in abstract categories but the
pervasive, seemingly universal responses of wonder and fascination, of awe and fear
in the face of the primordial mystery, and the desire to give oneself unreservedly to
it. It proceeds by reflecting on the experiences of the various adherents of the world's
religions and quasi-religions in a non-reductive way: the terror and bliss of the Shaiv-

---

[2]Paul Tillich, "Rejoinder," *The Journal of Religion* 46/1/2 (January 1966): 185.

[3]Ibid., 186. Owing to an unfortunate misprint in the original article, I have interpreted
this passage *ad sensum*.

ite, the ecstasy of the hasid, the limpidity of nirvanic consciousness of the bhikku, the committed resolve of the Muslim warrior, the Marxist revolutionary, or the Calvinist doing the will of God. It ponders the healing and transformation of lives in depth psychotherapy, mutual support groups, and intentional communities. It considers the mystery felt in nature, sexuality, human friendship and love, and art. It meditates on the secular testimonies of those who no longer believe in a God or explicitly follow an approved spiritual path but who find "a holy space within the heart" (Ingmar Bergman). The referent, alluded to above, is thus variously and pervasively apprehended.

Third, importance in experience ought to determine the shape of the theory; that is, the organizing category or categories ought to be as close a theoretical rendering as possible of the primordial experience. What is central in experience ought to be centrally determinative in theory. Theory, however, is not the recreation of experience nor a substitute for it but an explaining of what is important in experience. Unfortunately, not all philosophical-theological systems adequately express the experience of the referent previously alluded to. Some theories better express the experience of novel cosmic advance; others, aesthetic richness of undetermined extent; yet others, moral regeneration or the increase of virtue; yet others again, creative interaction with oneself, others, and nature; and so on. Of course, it is very much to the point just what the central experience is and whether in fact a given theory—or any theory, for that matter—adequately explains it. Yet the ideal of theoretical conformation to what is experientially important remains.

II

In this section I proceed to focus on that referent of ultimate responsiveness which appears as the unity or integration of mystery, meaning, and power. Though theoretical language is unavoidable, my intent here is to engage in phenomenological probings into the dimensions of whatever it is that philosophical theology takes as the referent of the primordial and ultimate responsiveness. So approached, the most important thing that we can say about the referent is that it is *mysterious*. Surdly situated among things and concepts, persons and institutions, the referent is inexpungeably present yet rationally impenetrable, by which is meant that whatever this-something-which-is-there-is, it defies rational analysis; it cannot be broken down into more nearly fundamental parts. Language of whatever sort gimps here, and necessarily so; "person," "event," "essence," "form," "substance," "actual entity," and the like go almost nowhere in revealing what this-something-which-is-there fundamentally is.

However, for all the forbidding difficulties, the mysterious is hauntingly attractive. It cannot be rationally penetrated or broken down in constituent parts, yet it entices, beckons, lures, draws. If it did not lure, there would be no reason, no impetus for considering it; it could and would be safely ignored. Yet if human history is any guide, people seemingly need to discourse and debate about it, make decisions about it, and organize their individual and communal lives in light of it.

This fact suggests another aspect of the mysterious: the experiencer cannot distance himself/herself from it. It is not a hurdle or roadblock or some other obstacle which is troubling if but only if one chooses to take up a particular inquiry but which inquiry can be laid aside or abandoned at will. No, the mystery grabs one by the vitals and makes one unable to distance oneself from it. Distantiation implies a power to manage, to make a problematic situation of what one does not comprehend, to objectify it over against oneself as subject. Mystery transcends the distinction between subject and object. The mystery experienced in the object is already present in the subject.[4]

Because of the preceding features, mystery is insoluble (one "cannot get a wrench on it") and must simply be lived with. At crucial junctures, at the times of decision in a life, the techniques for adjustment to prevailing conditions are greatly reduced in both scope and effectiveness, if they do not in fact utterly fail. Further, one moves from a more agentive role to a more receptive or participative one. There is nothing much one can do except to be open to the impenetrable and insoluble mystery.

Mystery bears down upon the world as its limit: "Hitherto shalt thou come, and no further." Mystery is that which finitizes all processes, including processes of understanding, and dethrones every claim of any contingent reality to be ultimate. And yet the limit is paradoxically the transcendence of the world. Mystery is that which lures the mind beyond the facts, forms, and values of this world. It is in contrast with mystery that the world is seen to be the world and in contrast with the world that mystery is seen to be mystery.

All things and events, categories and values are seen to have their meaning, ultimately, in their relation *to* mystery. Thus, while mystery is rationally impenetrable, it relates to, constitutes itself in relation to, things which are more or less rationally penetrable. Some "margin of intelligibility" (Meland) is thereby assured.

As far as I can tell, there is one mystery, not many. The mystery of existence, of life, of death, of creativity, of love, of personhood, of the intelligibility of the universe (Einstein's perpetual wonder), of suffering, of evil is not two (or more). There is no non-mysterious principle by which we could parcel out the alleged mysteries.

The second dimension of the referent to be explored is its power. Mystery acts; it impacts, thwarts, enhances, envelopes, forbids. Whatever, mystery is effective; it makes a difference. It strikes in such a way that one has to respond—"not in curse or jest" (William James) but in serious and sober account-taking of one's life; one has to make a vow, sell the business, proclaim the good news, go on a pilgrimage, feed the hungry, seek enlightenment, do theology.

As active, the mystery cannot be kept at arm's length. It is self-involving. You cannot explore the mystery without having to explore yourself. Furthermore, the mystery wounds and makes us thereby vulnerable (*vulnus,* "wound"): Hound of Heaven; Abraham and Gautama Siddhartha having to leave their families; Jacob wrestling to the point of permanent injury with the angel; Muhammad running away from the angel on Mt. Hira into the comforting arms of Khadijah; Yahweh seeking

---

[4]I am influenced in these reflections by Gabriel Marcel's seminal essay, "On the Onto-logical Mystery," in his *The Philosophy of Existentialism,* trans. Manya Harari (New York: The Citadel Press, 1962) 9-46. I do not, however, restrict my reflections to the sphere of the personal, as Marcel seems to do.

to kill Moses. The impenetrable mystery now penetrates us.

The third dimension of the referent to be explored is meaning. The mystery which acts upon us confronts us with meaning, with structure and value content. It is not a matter of a highly charged blank or blur. There is always some element of meaning, something *meant* in the experience. The meaning can be largely structural—grids, patterns, logical forms, configurations—or valuational—harmonies, tonal clusters, focal points, thrusts. It can be cognitive or emotional, logical or paradoxical. But in any case there is something which engages the imagination if not directly the rational intellect; meaning grabs one by the vitals, providing a matrix and lure for feeling and acting. For this reason, the arts are very important for our understanding. Meaning emerges from opposition, contrast, juxtaposition, location, and arrangement, to name a few. Furthermore, because of this I prefer "meaning" over "logos"; the latter term almost inevitably suggests to Western minds logic, rationality, and science.

The meanings may be coalescent, fluid, complex. But they are there in a rich and powerful way in the primordial experience. They present the "heart-mind" (Wang Yang-ming) with values to be embodied in experience; they are possibilities for incarnation. They are the "whats" which can make up our identities and the constitutive elements for the face we put on the world.

Sometimes one of the three aspects or dimensions of the referent (mystery, power, meaning) is more to the fore than the others in a given experience so that we should not think that there are so many unrelated or only loosely related experiences: sometimes of mystery; here and there of meaning; now and then of power. (One thinks of the charming art of children of a very young age when they can separate the color of a cat from the shape of the cat and then place a set of more or less parallel lines over in the corner of the page for the cat's whiskers.) No, the power, meaning, and mystery are integrated. The power is not mere energy or brutishness; rather, it is power shot through with mystery and meaning. The meaning may be paradoxical, certainly it is not manageable; yet somehow it coheres. The mystery does not cancel the meaning or depotentiate it. Because there is an integration of these dimensions, there can be healing; otherwise, we would be stuck with necessary fragmentation, schizophrenia, uncoordinated power, sheer chaos. The testimony is that there are important instances of healing, integration, and overcoming in the various dimensions of personal and social existence. Only the integration, the unity, the harmony of these three dimensions can or should evoke an ultimate response, a total self-giving. Mystery without meaning is mystification and is not worthy of an intelligent response. Meaning without power is not effective enough to make a difference (it cannot be "mighty to save"). Power without meaning is raw, undirected, and destructive energy.

Let us cast a quick glance ahead to possible theoretical implications. The unity of mystery, meaning, and power can be interpreted as *being*. Though at this point we should not demand theoretical closure, there are still good reasons for interpreting this referent as *being*: (1) we must say of the experienced referent that somehow it *is*; it is not nothing; we must acknowledge its effectiveness; and (2) because of the mystery of the referent we cannot subsume it under categories of lesser scope, each of which suggesting a complementary category (temporal/eternal, subject/object, enduring/changing, etc.), which also must be said to *be*.

Let us now take a second step in our phenomenological exploration. If the first with its treatment of the referent is the experiential, then let the second be termed the existential. Consider the following situation.

> "I might not be here next year," I suddenly blurt out to my dinner companions at the conference banquet in Oxford.
> "Likely not," says one," the conference is going to be in Chicago."
> "No," I reiterate with increased emphasis, "I might not *be* here next year."
> "Of course you will *be* next year," another interjects, "although you may *be* a corpse. And if you have a good mortician, you may *be* a rather nice-looking one at that!
> I am not comforted.

In both of my companions' comments the radicality of my not being was missed or denied. For both, to not-be was simply to be *other* than I am now. This is understandable since we often think of the negation of a certain state x to be y; that is, *non-x* is y. To not-be *this* is to be *that*. Most Western philosophers since Plato have held that non-being is otherness. However, it seems that in addition to being this or that (righthanded or left-handed, insightful or dull, etc.), there is the possibility of just simply being as opposed to the possibility of not being at all. I am, when and if I am, rather than simply not being at all. And it is this permanent possibility actualized moment by moment in and by my existence that concerns me. At moments I am surprised that I am. I marvel that I am since there was a time when I was not and there will yet be a time when I am no more and since there is the permanent possibility at each present moment of my not being at all. Against the perpetual and pervasive backdrop of not being at all, I am.

Now this seems to be true no matter how we decide on *what* I am (my identity). If we hold with Buddhist and process philosophies that my identity is genetic rather than strict and that to some degree where we draw the boundaries of my identity, between what is me and what is not-me, is arbitrary, we have only addressed the question of what my identity is to include (how wide should the net be cast to catch all of me?). We are still left with the question whether or not Chapman-wide-or-narrow belongs to reality, whether or not Chapman *is*. That I am, if I am—that is the mystery! And a perpetual concern. This, of course, creates some thorny conceptual problems—the problem of the status of nothingness being one—but existentially the matter is real, poignant, and inescapable.

III

What theory when fleshed out would best account for the experiences I discussed in the preceding section? I claim that a theory making being central best accounts for this and allows best for application to further experience. As with any explanation, the transition from description to theory requires a shift in the context of presuppositions and is signaled usually by the semantic redescription of the data of experience. In the previous section we considered the experience of ultimate response to something encountered as mysterious, powerful, and meaningful; in addition, we adverted to our linguistic expressions of "being here" versus "not being here." Relative to our purpose these are all pre-theoretical expressions however much they may function theoretically in other explanatory contexts.

Earlier I indicated that ontological language naturally suggested an ontological theory. This is not necessarily the case since verbs in ordinary language implying existence usually do not have ontological-theoretical import. "Where *is* the damn thing?" usually means which drawer, closet, or file folder did I absent-mindedly put it in. Ordinary language, and even naming the Cartesian coordinates of a point, does not get us very far into ontology. Nevertheless when I say, "Oh my God, I might not *be* here next year" as a way of voicing my sense of radical limitedness, of the fragility and contingency of my being (whatever that may be), I am expressing an important datum for theoretical redescription into ontological terms. Moreover, when I say that I experience something there as mysterious power to give life meaning or to destroy it, thus robbing it of meaning, I am expressing an important datum for theoretical redescription into ontological terms.

Let us, therefore, redescribe ourselves and by extension all other things of our experience as *beings*. As such, they necessarily have some identity; otherwise they would not be at all. I have not defined beings as agents or parts of agents since this needlessly prejudices the case for reality as actual (to be is to be actual), which of course it is in part, but only in part. The identity of a being is complex; it is composed of relations with other beings and its ownmost features. This is true whether the being is a person, a historical fact, a scientific law, a metaphysical principle, or a fantasy. Each being has enough power to resist collapse into the other and enough vulnerability to relate to the other.

But any being might not be, and this in at least three ways: it might never have been; it might not at this moment be; and it might not continue to be. Any being is therefore bounded by nothingness, and to be in the face of the possibility of not being at all is to be contingent. In part, a being is contingent with respect to other beings since *what* a being is, is partly constituted by its relations with other beings. If the other beings were to change or to cease, then the being in question would change necessarily. This is horizontal or cosmological contingency. It is contingency in the face of the other. Even a radical empiricism, which rightly makes much of the relationality of existence, has no doctrine of *radical* contingency, ontologically considered, but only contingency in the face of the other.

Granted that I would be a different being if my friends were fools from what I would be if my friends were philosophical theologians (or perhaps foolish philosophical theologians), still we can ask what it means to *be*, whatever my relations to others as well as myself are. What if constitutive identity should cease to exist in toto (or fail to come into being) so that it should not be encounterable in its mode, should not be a positive anything? We have here a more radical contingency related to the horizontal or cosmological contingency necessarily, but not collapsible thereinto. This is vertical or ontological contingency. It is contingency in the face of nothingness. This is truly a radical empiricism.

Let us focus on this vertical or ontological contingency. Since a thing might not be at all (not just qualified differently) yet somehow *is*, its existence judged simply for itself and in itself is *absurd*. If it does not exist at all, its non-being is not necessary and its non-existence judged simply for itself and in itself is *absurd*. Thus each being is poised between two absurd possibilities, each possessing in itself no necessity. If a thing exists, it exists against the contrasting nothingness, out of which it came and into which it will go. If a thing does not-exist, it does not-exist against the contrasting existence, from which it came (if it did) and to which it might go (if it does).

Generally, we are unaware of this situation of radical contrast. However, on some occasions, relatively infrequent it must be admitted, we become suddenly aware of, and appreciate the distance between, the absurd fact that something exists—it may be our own being— and the absurd fact that it might not. This is ontological shock and is the redescription into the theoretical language of ontology of the ''I-might-not-be-here'' experience as I earlier described it. On other occasions, more to the fore is the sense that something positively is, though it might not be, because some grounding source causes it to be. The experience of the contrast between contingent being and the non-contingent grounding source is also ontological shock. The oscillation in emphasis between these two aspects (nothing and being) in the experience of ontological shock I find puzzling, even paradoxical, but nonetheless undeniable.

So far two primary terms of the theory have emerged: finite or determinate being and nothing.[5] To this a third must be added: Creative Being or Being Itself. Beings, one and all, are contingent, finite, absurdly existing when and if they do. Their existing when they might not cannot be explained by another finite being, which is in the same ontological fix; namely, it exists contingently and cannot make either itself or some other thing be. If anything exists at all, it is because it has been made to be by whatever grounds its being (whatever that should turn out to be). If the grounding source did not cause a thing to be by giving being to it, it would not be at all. If the grounding source did not cause each component of a thing to be by giving being to each component, the component would not exist at all. The existence of each thing, in whole or part, is totally dependent upon an ontologically causative source. This I have termed Creative Being or Being Itself.

Of this source we know nothing other than it makes each being to be. What it is in and for itself we do not, will not, or cannot know; it is sheer mystery. In itself it is indeterminate, though making itself determinate, hence to that degree knowable, when and as it makes beings to be. If Being Itself were not essentially indeterminate, then it could not be the creative source of determinate being. It too would be essentially determinate and thus also in need of explanation. But Being Itself creates; and as Creative Being it makes itself the source, the norm, and the act by which beings come to be. These technical terms are the theoretical redescription of mystery, power, and meaning discussed in an earlier part of the paper.

---

[5]It is extremely difficult to talk about the concept of nothing—and in short compass—but we can say the following: (1) nothing should not be treated as if it were some thing or some kind of thing—a chaos, a blankspace, an undifferentiated continuum, etc.; (2) it is doubtful if we ever directly experience nothing, but that is not a crucial difficulty since (3) nothing is a theoretical term and takes its meaning not from direct experience but from its relationship to other concepts in the theory and from the model(s) which suggest the theory, and we know how nothing functions theoretically; (4) we know the rule for negating something.

IV

This theory has been very sketchily laid out, but a few words need to be said about application. We cannot just remain with Aristotle's God thinking on thinking. One has to specify the necessarily vague theory with interpretations closer to lived experience. If we start on home turf, which for philosophical theology are the specific claims of religion, we find that this theory can be specified variously, and with varying degrees of adequacy, by the Tao, the God of Western religions, Brahman, Suchness, Nirvana, etc. The theory should help us, first of all, understand the meaning of the claims, then grasp the hitherto unsuspected meanings and all implications of these claims, show possible links from one set of claims to another, reveal the insufficiencies of certain formulations, and finally to suggest possible testings of the truth-values of given claims. Frankly, that is no small service to religion and to culture, which is now global. And fragile.

As to the vulnerabilities, the critics will be better able than I to spot them. However, I might mention a few. One, has the theory assumed accurately what is central in experience for philosophical theology? Does ontological shock adequately describe this, or does it only capture what at best is a rather limited type, the type that sages, philosophers, and other reflective sorts tend to pick out for understanding? Can it make sense of the experience of the bhakti yogi, the householder, the evangelist, the born-again convert, the one *doing* the truth? Another, does it interpret secular experience sensitively enough to be of service to a world shaped by science and technology? Some mediating interpretations would in any case be needed. Yet again, is the theory weighted too much toward the theistic systems of the West so that other important intuitions are not seen to warrant serious and sustained reflection? Does it prize unity more than the facts warrant? And again, is the theory so abstract (in itself no necessary defect) that little guidance is offered for doing anything other than banging the drum for the theory? Does it stimulate other theoretical and experimental efforts? And so on. It seems to me, however, that the theory is worth living with long enough and with enough diligent and caring concern to try to answer these questions.

Whitehead's God
and the Dilemma of Pure Possibility

Donald A. Crosby

> *If there be a God, he is no absolute all-experiencer, but simply the experiencer of widest actual possible span.*   —William James[1]

Three basic roles assigned to God in the metaphysics of Alfred North Whitehead are: God as (1) the foundation of metaphysical order; (2) the ground of emergent value (and, consequently, also the ultimate basis of contingent or cosmological order); and (3) the everlasting preserver of all attained value. In this essay I deal with the first of these roles, noting its implied requirement of omniscience in God and showing this requirement to be one factor leading to Whitehead's insistence on the nontemporal character of God. I also critically analyze the first role, concluding that a fundamental dilemma it poses can only be resolved by entirely eliminating this function of God in Whitehead's system. And I discuss implications of this resolution for conceiving the metaphysical character and status of possibility.

1. God as Ground of Metaphysical Order

According to Whitehead, the conceptual or primordial aspect of God's nature "at once exemplifies and establishes the categoreal conditions" for any possible universe (1929:522). The whole gamut of eternal objects or forms of definiteness is here fused into a tightly integrated, hierarchical realm of *pure* possibility that must be expressed in all subordinate orders of *real* possibility and in every concrete actualization, or process of actualization, of this or any other cosmic epoch. God is thus the ground of metaphysical, as contrasted with mere cosmological, order or stability (Whitehead 1929:64).

---

[1] "The Essence of Humanism," in James 1977:304-10, p. 306.

God must be omniscient in this first role, because his/her[2] conceptual envisagement must encompass every possible type or grade of realization, and every possible
pattern of relatedness. For example, every realizable shade of color; variation of heat;
discrimination of taste; pitch or intensity of sound; degree of hardness; change of place;
geometrical configuration; tonality of emotion; passing phase or stable outcome of
cosmic, organic, or cultural evolution and all their entwined conditions and ramifications are already anticipated in the primordial nature of God. There can be no surprises for God when it comes to pure possibilities; all such possibilities are fully and
completely envisioned.

Someone might object that since Whitehead contends that God is not conscious
in his/her primordial nature (1929:522-23), it makes no sense to speak of the absence
of *surprises* or of an omniscience or completeness of *knowledge* in that nature. Three
responses can be made to this objection. First, the primordial nature is simply an abstract way of speaking of God (Whitehead 1929:521-22); in his/her concrete reality,
there is complete conscious awareness. Second, even if we were to concur momentarily with Lewis Ford's suggestion (see his "Whitehead's Differences from Hartshorne," in Ford 1973:58-83, pp. 59, 61) that God becomes conscious of details of
his/her primordial nature only with the emergence of facts in the world, as these are
taken into account in his/her consequent nature, the point is that those primordial details are already there to be drawn upon. We can find an analogy in the familiar claim
of rationalist philosophers that experience merely *occasions* the awareness of innate
ideas. These are not derived from experience but are already present in the mind,
even if not always consciously entertained. By this reading, God is omniscient in his/
her primordial nature, in the sense of already having in mind, innately even if not
consciously, the exhaustive set of pure possibilities, ordered into their hierarchical
patterns.

But third, we should note that Ford's interpretation is plausible only if we assume that there can be *times* when God is not yet aware of certain emerging occasions
and therefore not yet conscious of parts of his/her primordial nature. This cannot be
the case, however, since Whitehead conceives of God's consequent nature, whereby
he/she prehends facts of the world, as an everlasting "now," with neither past nor
future, memory nor anticipation. From the standpoint of this everlasting now, no finite entities await their actualizations; the whole span of time is consciously entertained by God. Therefore, there is no time when the full panoply of eternal objects
that ever have been, or ever will be, ingressed, has not yet entered into God's conscious awareness. Because the fullness of Whitehead's God, in the words of Bowman Clarke, "is one everlasting present which includes every other present, his glance
is carried everlastingly over all things as they are in their presentiality." Thus, "it
would not make sense, or it would be false, to say 'God has known such and such'
or 'God shall know such and such'" ("God as Process in Whitehead," in Clarke and
Long 1984:169-87, pp. 182-84).

The envisagement of all possibility requires timelessness, as well as omniscience, in the primordial nature of God, because as pure, complete, and final, it can-

[2]I use this conjunction of pronouns throughout to avoid sexism in talk about God; Whitehead employs only the male pronoun.

not be altered, augmented, or in any way affected by what happens in the temporal world (Whitehead 1929:46, 70, 522).[3] For Whitehead, this means that, in direct contrast with temporal occasions, God's mental pole cannot be derived from, or dependent upon, his/her experiences of the world. It also means that no novel pure possibilities can emerge in the creative advance of nature or the course of temporal events; all are eternally present in God. Every new actualization is the actualization of some logically anterior, timeless pattern of possibility. This is Whitehead's celebrated Platonism, but he seeks to harmonize it with an Aristotelian insistence on the absolute priority of concrete actuality (which Whitehead labels the "ontological principle") by conceiving of the unchanging, eternally ordered realm of possibilities as having its locus and source in a particular actual entity, namely, God (see 1929:63-64). Hence, this realm is no mere free-floating "heaven of ideas" but is anchored in the "static majesty" and primordial, once-for-all "decision" of the divine mind (Whitehead 1929:75, 248, 378, 530).

2. The Dilemma Lurking in This Role of God

This move, although it seems to solve the problem of the "where" of pure, ordered possibilities, and to explain the "how" of their ordering, does so at the price of posing a dilemma that, in my judgment, admits of only one solution. Consideration of this dilemma shows the folly of claiming the need for divine omniscience and nontemporality with regard to this first function of Whitehead's God and provides a compelling case for eliminating the function altogether. The dilemma is implicit in the previously quoted allegation of Whitehead that God's primordial nature both "exemplifies and establishes the categoreal conditions" of any possible universe.

The dilemma's first horn is as follows. If we acquiesce in Whitehead's claim that the eternal objects would be a mere multiplicity of unrelated disjuncts did not God create their relational essences and thus establish them as an ordered realm (see Whitehead 1929:64, 392; Ford, in Ford 1973:69; Suchocki 1975:240), then two disastrous consequences immediately follow. (1) Such an act of establishment or ordering would have to be itself contingent, even while defining metaphysical necessity, a situation that produces an absurd infinite regress. (2) If God can create the categoreal conditions by a contingent act, however timeless that act may be conceived to be, then he/she becomes an exception to Whitehead's metaphysical system, thus introducing radical incoherence into the system. Let us analyze these two consequences in more detail.

That Whitehead considers the divine ordering of possibility to be contingent, rather than necessary, is suggested by his description of the primordial nature of God as "the limitation for which no reason can be given: for all reason flows from it." He continues in this vein, observing that "God is the ultimate limitation, and His existence is the ultimate irrationality" (1967:178). Citing this passage, Jorge Nobo states that "aside from God's own primordial autonomy, no reason can be given for

---

[3]Marjorie Suchocki makes the point, in this connection, that a "physical origination cannot ground all possibility, since it necessarily requires elimination of possibility" by exclusion (1975:240).

the ideal creative order being what it is. God's primordial nature *could have been different.*'' Had it been different, ''the course of universal history would have ex-hibited a different, but no less peculiar, no less arbitrary, flux of realized forms'' (1986:121). But if this divine ordering is contingent and arbitrary, then it must be a selection from a wider realm of ordered possibility that can explain its existence as one realizable system of order among others. That wider realm, then, by the onto-logical principle, would have to have its own ground, and so on ad infinitum!

The second unfortunate consequence flowing from the first horn of the dilemma is that God has to be seen as an exception to Whitehead's metaphysical scheme. God's primordial decision must be anterior to the interlocking system of eternal objects that defines all metaphysical possibility, because it is this decision which is said to confer a structure of relational essences upon those objects. So here is something taking place, however timelessly, with no account of how it could be *possible* for it to take place. The incoherence thus introduced into Whitehead's metaphysics is no less serious than the ''arbitrary disconnection of first principles'' in the metaphysics of Descartes of which he rightly complains (1929:9-10).

The dilemma's second horn is this: if, as Whitehead believes, the generic cate-gories enshrined in the realm of pure possibility define what is metaphysically pos-sible, then they must also define what is possible for God as one type of real entity. The structure of possibility is accordingly presupposed in anything God may be or do. Because it is presupposed, it makes no sense to claim a need for the structure to be ''established'' by a primordial decision of God. Since everything that God is or does or can only ''exemplify'' the system of metaphysical possibility, God cannot be the ground of that system or of the metaphysical order it provides.

This means that the order of eternal objects must be seen as necessary, rather than contingent—necessary in the sense of defining all metaphysical possibility, in-cluding the possibility of God. If necessary in this sense, then this order requires no ground, because the claim for such a requirement would be viciously circular. More-over, what is metaphysically necessary requires no divine decision to constitute it, since by definition it cannot be *contingent* upon such a decision. Instead of seeing the eternal objects only in their disjunctive individual essences as given, as Whitehead does, we must now see them in their ordering relational essences as also given, in which case there is no need to posit God as the explanation for their patterns of in-terrelatedness. We can say of eternal objects what William James says of experience: here relations are as primitive or underived as things related (1967:1:42-44).

To sum up the dilemma: either we go along with Whitehead's requirement of God as the ground of ordered possibility, thus generating an infinite regress, as well as making God an exception to the metaphysical system, or we abandon altogether the idea that God is needed to ground metaphysical possibility. Seizing the second horn of this dilemma seems to be our only intelligent recourse, given the extremely high cost of opting for the first horn. As Whitehead himself notes, ''there must . . . be limits to the claim that all the elements in the universe are explicable by 'theory.' For 'theory' itself requires that there be 'given' elements so as to form the material for theorizing'' (1929:67). Since *something* has to be accepted as given in any meta-physical system, the only alternative being an unending regress of explanatory ent-ities or principles, why not simply say that possibility is what experience and reflection show it to be, and leave it at that? Why posit God as its ground, since that move only generates the need for further grounds, as already demonstrated?

3. The Problem of the Ontological Principle

It might be objected that seizing the second horn of the dilemma exacts its own steep price, namely, that of having to jettison the ontological principle and of thereby being forced to conceive of an ordered realm of possibility that simply "floats into the world from nowhere" (Whitehead 1929:373). One response to this objection is to argue, as Justus Buchler does, that Whitehead's ontological principle is not necessarily a good thing, that a certain arbitrariness, one-sidedness, and internal inconsistency results from his assertion of the absolute priority of actual entities to everything else in his metaphysical scheme.[4] Another type of response is to outline a way of preserving at least a modified form of the ontological principle, and of giving status in actuality to the realm of possibility, even while continuing to cling to a version of the second horn of the dilemma now under discussion. Let me explain what I have in mind.

Whitehead at one place in *Process and Reality* defines the ontological principle in this way: "apart from things that are actual, there is nothing—nothing either in fact or in efficacy" (1929:64). This definition has at least two distinct advantages. The first one is that it speaks only of "things that are actual," rather than of actual entities proper, thus avoiding Whitehead's contention, to which Buchler properly objects, that actual entities must be seen as "more real" than other actualities such as societies and nexūs (Ford and Kline 1983:283-84). The second advantage of this particular formulation of the ontological principle is that it makes no explicit claim to the priority of actuality over possibility.

The statement as written, and as isolated from Whitehead's other definitions of the ontological principle, is compatible with Buchler's insight that it is equally valid to say that apart from *possibility* there can be "nothing either in fact or in efficacy" (Ford and Kline 1983:288). Thus, while actuality is still of bedrock importance, possibility has bedrock importance as well. This is in keeping with Whitehead's statement early in *Process and Reality* that among the "eight categories of existence, actual entities and eternal objects stand out with a certain extreme finality" (1929:33). This statement can be brought fully into line with the position being endorsed here by stipulating that the term *eternal objects* be interpreted as encompassing both the relational and individual essences of those objects.

Neither possibility nor actuality is prior to the other, in this view. Instead, they are correlative concepts, the one implying the other and neither having meaning in independence of the other. Not only can a given actuality be regarded as the concrete manifestation of a particular possibility or set of possibilities, but it can also be seen as suggesting a much wider range of possibilities or conceivable alternatives from which it is a determinate selection. Conversely, not only can a given possibility be

---

[4]For the details of Buchler's criticism of the ontological principle, see his "On a Strain of Arbitrariness in Whitehead's System," in Ford and Kline 1983:280-94. Ross 1983 is also critical throughout of this principle.

viewed as a potential ingression in some world (the very meaning of metaphysical possibility); it is also important to understand that the concept of any specific possibility, to say nothing of the idea of an ordered realm of all possibilities, would be devoid of meaning were there no actualities of our experience with which such envisioned possibilities could be contrasted and compared. As Stephen David Ross observes, "If we can entertain a concept, it is because that concept is conditioned by our lived experience, therefore, neither pure nor eternal in relevant respects." He illustrates the point by noting that the "look of a person never seen must be related to persons seen (or experienced in some other way) . . . " (1983:229).

Accordingly, the distinction between actuality and possibility should not be viewed as a hard-and-fast opposition of two "worlds," the one temporal and the other timeless. Instead, the distinction must be seen as relative and perspectival, dependent on variations of focus and context. "From such a perspectival point of view," writes Ross, "what is prior in one sense is secondary or derivative in another" (1983:235). Understood in this way, we have no warrant for thinking of possibilities as floating into the world from nowhere. They have their status and significance in relation to actuality, i.e., as one kind of perspective or reflection upon actuality, just as actuality can be brought into the perspective of possibility. The objection, based on the ontological principle, to our grasping the second horn of the dilemma has therefore been answered with a modified, more tenable version of that principle. With this answer, we have removed any need for an omniscient, nontemporal God to ground or establish a realm of possibility or structure of metaphysical necessity.

4. Some Further Consequences

In this concluding section I want briefly to indicate three other implications of this analysis of possibility. One is that the distinction, so basic in Whitehead's metaphysics, between *pure* and *real* possibility (1929:34) can now be abandoned.[5] All the conceivable possibilities of a given time are to be seen as real possibilities,[6] in the sense of their being made manifest in past experience: either in its actualizations or in the alternatives those actualizations open up to view. Hume's missing shade of blue, discussed in one of the better known passages of Whitehead's principal work, is a vivid case in point (1929:132-33). Having experienced, as Hume says, colors of all kinds with the exception of one shade of blue, and having all those colors laid out before one in their degrees of variation from the deepest to the lightest, one would then be able to conceive or imagine the missing color as a possibility not previously

---

[5]A real possibility is a proposition or "impure" potentiality, with its subject some past actuality or nexus of actualities, and its predicate, some simple or complex eternal object. Its meaning is therefore conditioned by the past (see Whitehead 1929:33-34).

[6]In addition to the distinction between possibilities that are now real in the sense of having been made *conceivable* by past fact and those that are not (but may be later), we need also to distinguish between real possibilities that are presently *realizable* and those that are not. Part of what Whitehead means by real possibility I propose to call *realizable* possibility. For example, once I have passed 50th Street on the subway, the possibility of getting off there is not presently realizable, although it is perfectly conceivable.

evidenced in one's experience (Hume 1978:5-6). The possibility of that shade is thus neither timeless nor unconditioned; it becomes apparent in the course of time and is conditioned by previous experience.

How does it become apparent? Where does it come from? Questions such as these led Whitehead to posit a primordial being with no causal past, i.e., a finished, complete ordering of pure potentials timelessly constituted by God's conceptual feelings (1929:134). But I contend that we need only two things to provide a reasonable answer to such questions, one that does not embroil us in the difficulties previously discussed. The first thing needed is past ingressions of possibility, and the second is the power of reversion in present actualities. What Whitehead calls *reversion* (1929:40) is a capacity in things to actualize in fact (or, in the case of conscious beings, also in thought) possibilities suggested by, but not ingredient in, the past of those things. It is an expression of the principle of creativity, the dialectic of continuity and novelty operative everywhere in the experienced world.

The example cited from Hume's *Treatise* might mislead us into thinking that such reversion can only introduce proximal or immediately relevant novelties, e.g., a shade of blue adjacent to a another hue only slightly different from it. But though this may usually be the case, there is no reason to think that it must always be true, particularly if we consider the creative workings of the human imagination. Flashes of insight sometimes introduce bold innovations that are, in at least in some particulars, quite remote from the experienced facts that may have occasioned them. Or recognition of a proximal novelty may quickly bring awareness of more remote possibilities in its train. An example of this second kind of creative process is the person who first thought to alter a single postulate of Euclid's system and then, by following out the implications of that slight change (a proximal novelty), began to dream of non-Euclidian space and of whole new systems of geometry (more remote novelties).

A second consequence of our analysis of the nature and status of possibility is implicit in the first consequence. The latter can be summarized in this way: since there is no longer any need for a static, unconditioned, complete and thus, pure realm of possibilities, all possibilities are now to be regarded as real, i.e., as dynamic, open-ended, and emergent. Past actualities provide the raw materials for innovation via present reversions, the resulting ingressions of these novel possibilities occasion further reversions, and so on. This being so, it also follows (and here is the second consequence) that no justification can be found for the distinction Whitehead draws between metaphysical categories and so-called derivative notions, i.e., cosmological categories that elucidate only the more restricted possibilities of the present cosmic epoch (see 1929: pt. 1, ch. 3).

Because all possibilities are emergent and correlated with actualities in the manner described, there can be no unalterable boundaries of metaphysical possibility, no unchanging limits constraining all future epochs or universes. Not only could such not be known by us; they are in principle unknowable by any being and cannot be said to exist. As has been argued, both that which is conceivable and that which is realizable are now to be seen as functions of what Whitehead terms the "creative advance of nature" (1929:443). Therefore, ineliminable elements of contingency and unpredictability must pertain to both. To assume the present knowability of all future possibility is inconsistent with Whitehead's own "category of the ultimate," the principle of creativity, because it purports to take the precise measure of incalculable, inexhaustible novelties lying in the womb of this principle. As Whitehead himself observes, a nature that exhibits the tireless operations of the principle of creativity "is always passing beyond itself" and "never complete" (1929:443).

Moreover, by introducing the distinction between eternally fixed metaphysical categories and emergent derivative notions, presenting sets of both, and claiming the former to be enshrined in God's primordial nature, thus serving as the basis of metaphysical stability, Whitehead shows a streak of rationalistic apriorism that violates his own announced method of "descriptive" or "imaginative" generalization, with its accompanying criterion of adequacy to experience (1929:5,7-8,15-16,24-26). The categories derived by the method of descriptive generalization can only be tested by experiences of the past, present, and forseeable future. No empirical tests could be devised of their adequacy for all subsequent worlds. Categories alleged to apply to such worlds are bogus and ill-advised, having no place in an empirically grounded metaphysics.

The third consequence of our critical revision of possibility in Whitehead's system is that a major reason for his reversal of the poles of physicality and mentality in God is removed. As we saw earlier, Whitehead maintains that God is the exception to all other entities because in God the mental pole is prior to the physical pole, thus insuring that the former be wholly unaffected and unaffectable by events in the world. Only in this way, Whitehead reasons, can the realm of possibility be kept pure. But by eliminating the need for a realm of pure possibility, we have also eliminated a basic reason for the reversal of God's poles.[7]

---

[7]Is not the reversal of poles still needed, however, for God to function as the ground of absolute, timeless *value* (the second role of Whitehead's God mentioned at the beginning of this essay)? I think not. I shall argue in a subsequent essay (a) that the very notion of absolute, timeless value is inconsistent with certain overriding themes of Whitehead's metaphysics (as well as with any genuinely *process* metaphysics); and (b) that there is no need for God to be either timeless or omniscient to function with full effectiveness in the way Whitehead intended, namely, as the principal goad to novelty and lure to value in the universe.

Works Cited

Clarke, Bowman L., and Eugene T. Long, eds.
  1984   *God and Temporality*. New York: Paragon House Publishers.
Ford, Lewis S., ed.
  1973   *Two Process Philosophers: Hartshorne's Encounter with Whitehead*. AAR Studies
         in Religion 5. Tallahassee FL: American Academy of Religion.
Ford, Lewis S., and George L. Kline, eds.
  1983   *Explorations in Whitehead's Philosophy*. New York: Fordham University Press.
Hume, David
  1978   *Treatise of Human Nature*, L. A. Selby-Bigge, ed. 2nd ed. Oxford: Oxford Uni-
         versity Press.
James, William
  1967   *Essays in Radical Empiricism and a Pluralistic Universe*. 2 vols. in 1. Gloucester
         MA: Peter Smith.
  1977   *The Writings of William James*, John J. McDermott, ed. Chicago: University of Chi-
         cago Press.
Nobo, Jorge Luis
  1986   *Whitehead's Metaphysics of Extension and Solidarity*. Albany: State University of
         New York Press.
Ross, Stephen David
  1983   *Perspective in Whitehead's Metaphysics*. Albany: State University of New York
         Press.
Suchocki, Marjorie
  1975   ''The Metaphysical Ground of the Whiteheadian God.'' *Process Studies* 5/4 (Winter
         1975): 237-46.
Whitehead., Alfred North
  1929   *Process and Reality: An Essay in Cosmology*. New York: The Macmillan Company.
  1967   *Science and the Modern World*. New York: The Free Press.

Pluralism and the Problem of God:
A Sketch of an American Predicament

William Dean

When they saw themselves as an exceptional people, the Puritans thought of themselves as God's elect, as a New Israel with a prophecy to fulfill in a promised land. God was involved in their history as God was not involved in the history of other peoples. As Calvinists, the Puritans knew what it was to speak about a transcendent and unknowable God, and they often did speak of such a God.[1] But when they spoke in their more distinctively American voice, they spoke of God as directly operative in their history—so definitely present that America would become God's holy people. In their seventeenth- and eighteenth-century eyes, the sacred entered the secular in the history of America.

American Enlightenment thinkers, such as Jefferson and Franklin, followed the same exceptionalist style, thinking that to America belonged in a special way the high promise of historically embodied natural reason. American romantic thinkers and artists, such as Emerson, Thoreau, Hawthorne, and Melville, continued that style when they focused on the intuition of the common person, and treated that as the channel through which the divine blessing would enter the American national life.

It was partly through this exceptionalist emphasis that Americans became historical monists.[2] That is, through telling their exceptionalist story they found a way

---

[1]For all their extra-Calvinist and pro-scientific attempts to rationalize and naturalize Christian truth, the Puritans in England and Holland and their followers in America retained an orthodox allegiance to God's transcendence and inscrutability. See Perry Miller, "The Marrow of Puritan Divinity," *Errand into the Wilderness* (Cambridge MA: The Belknap Press, 1981) 48-98.

[2]I have used here the old conventional picture of American intellectual development (from the Puritans, to the Enlightenment liberals, to the Transcendentalists and their cohorts, to William James) rather than the new conventional picture of American intellectual development (from the Puritans, Edwards particularly, to the several generations of Calvinist scholarship, up to and including the Andover Liberals, to John Dewey), Bruce Kuklick's 1985 *Churchmen and Philosophers* being its most prominent expression. While I continue to find the old conventional picture more useful, my argument here is only slightly affected by this choice, for the Calvinists (while they did not confine their God to history) were exceptionalists and monists, just as much as their more secular counterparts that I have described.

to reduce—at least for purposes of national self-understanding—the multiplicity of historical events to a single narrative guided by a single and ideal reality; they unified their national meaning under one comprehensive theory.

However, at the same time and through this same exceptionalism and monism that had made them exceptionally blessed, Americans created the conditions that would make them exceptionally condemned. This change of affairs resulted from a deeper change: the monistically unified history teetered and for professional historians collapsed under the weight of evidence and was replaced by a plurality of historical events.

The movement from monism to pluralism now appears virtually fated. When the historical evidence began to say that actual international and domestic history not only gave the Americans no grounds for seeing themselves as God's New Israel but in fact militated against that view, they were a people with a shattered self-understanding and a shattered interpretation of their sense of meaning. This must be understood in its full magnitude. First, when the Americans concluded that the sacred that could be known and used was located within their secular history, they denied themselves the comforts of a sacred beyond history—at least the comforts of a sacred that they could know or that they could understand as active. The Americans' European cousins were capable of seeing their own secular history as merely one history among other histories or as fraught with ambiguity and in ineradicable declension from the ideal world; but, then, such realism was not particularly costly because, when secular history seemed most inhospitable, the Europeans always could repair to the ideal world. But when Americans presumed to surmount declension, to affirm that their history contained in a special way the only knowable and active God there was, they blocked any significant escape to a sacred refuge beyond history. Consequently, when in mid-twentieth-century American historical monism collapsed, this led to the collapse of the active sacred as well—and, in turn, to the collapse of the myth of America and, in David W. Noble's phrase, to "the end of American history."[3] What remained was a chaos of pluralities; and skepticism, relativism, and varieties of nihilism seemed to be the only respectable positions left standing.

When the Americans found the sacred in their history, this history appeared monistic rather than pluralistic. Divine providence unified, made one and whole, their history. But, as America's unique lack of an indigenous culture, its unique history of immigration, and its twentieth-century international and domestic problems suggested, for America historical monism had never been quite right. All along there was a pluralism tugging at the sleeve of American religious chauvinism. When monism collapsed, the most obvious indicator was a new pessimism—not merely the implicit pessimism of the American renaissance thinkers like Emerson, Thoreau, Hawthorne, and Melville, but an explicit pessimism born of dashed hopes.

My question is, How do these historical developments limit or otherwise determine American thought about God? Without justifying it here, I assume that this is

[3]David W. Noble, *The End of American History: Democracy, Capitalism, and the Metaphor of two Worlds in Anglo-American Historical Writing, 1880–1980* (Minneapolis: University of Minnesota Press, 1985).

a historical question, and that it is properly answered—not through the introduction of a priori reasons—but through ideas based on history.

(In what follows I speak in speculative and generic ways, talking about the "Americans," the "Europeans," and "the meaning" of America, as though these terms had distinct, clear, and verifiable meanings. But obviously, these are abstractions, problematic in a statement largely devoted to defending empirical thought. I recognize, however, that this is nothing more than a preliminary sketch, sustainable only with elaboration.)

1. Pluralism and God: the Problem

America's pluralism has two aspects, one quantitative and the other qualitative. First, there is too much that the notion of America's "errand into the wilderness" does not explain to permit the unification of America under the rubric of a single mission. The diversity of America's peoples, cultures, and purposes makes a mockery of any such actual unification of America, whether through the power of God or not. If this quantitative plurality undermines monism one way, then a qualitative plurality undermines it another way. America, whatever her quantitative complexity, does not give sufficient moral signs of being God's chosen nation. Here it is that the startling events of the twentieth century—from the Great Depression, through Vietnam, to the moral corruption of Watergate and Irangate—recently have been so convincing. This nation does not act like a nation unified by any quality of goodness, whether divine or human.

It appeared that Americans had either to abandon all talk about God or to accept that God is impotent and/or morally ambiguous. And the answer to this can seem virtually automatic, for a God either impotent or only ambiguously good appears not to conform to any reasonable definition of God at all, so that talk about God simply should be abandoned. When, for example, most process theologians have felt that God could be deprived of omnipotence and the omniscience that attends omnipotence and remain God, they have tended to identify God all the more with unambiguous goodness. But the evidence in American history for God's goodness is too scarce. However, if God is separated from unambiguous goodness as well as from omnipotence, is not God as understood by process as well as classical theologians put seriously into question?[4]

This atheistic implication can be illustrated by reference even to the empirical theologians of this century, from Henry Nelson Wieman through Bernard Meland. They have argued that God possessed some kind of universal creativity—not an omnipotent and irresistable creative influence, but a persuasiveness nevertheless. And this persuasiveness was always for the good; it would urge the world toward higher forms of life, where communities would be more inclusive, imaginative, harmonious. Then in his late-1970s essay, "The Size of God," Bernard Loomer looked at "the basic characteristics of individuals and societies," and concluded that in moral

---

[4]See Nancy Frankenberry's development of this indictment of process theology's God in "Some Problems in Process Theology," *Religious Studies* 17 (1971): 179-97.

terms they were inevitably ambiguous.[5] He argued that if all historical creatures are morally ambiguous, then a strict adherance to theological empiricism requires that God, as a dimension of historical activity, also must be seen as morally ambiguous. He suggested that the process and empirical theologians had associated God not so much with the empirical world, as with their cherished moral abstractions, and that that was not a very empirical thing to do. The only consistent empirical consequence of the moral ambiguity of finitude, Loomer argued, was that God's influence must itself be morally ambiguous. Loomer was hard pressed, however, to justify that the word God was appropriate for a reality that was neither omnipotent nor unambiguously beneficent.

Loomer's effort to save the notion of God may simply have extended the problems he had identified so adroitly in other process and empirical theologians. Loomer suggested that God, however morally ambiguous, nevertheless exerted an unambiguous aesthetic influence. God was the name for that "restlessness of the whole body of creation"—a restlessness that always sought higher forms of stature, where stature is the mark of how much diversity of experience an individual could internalize without losing its unity of experience. This divine tendency Loomer saw as the telos of the universe. In other words, while God might be morally ambiguous, God was aesthetically unambiguous.[6] In this respect, then, Loomer himself spoke metaphysically, universally, eternally, and unambiguously: God was a kind of aesthetic *perfection* within the world consistently urging the world towards ever greater aesthetic realization. I am suggesting that Loomer did not carry through his recognition of ambiguity—which should include the aesthetic as well as the moral. As Hannah Arendt suggested when she stressed the "banality of evil," evil is evil for aesthetic reasons as well as for conventionally moral reasons. Loomer, despite his high empiricist intentions to prevent the religious elevation of abstractions, appears to have reified beauty just as surely as his colleagues (Wieman, Hartshorne, Whitehead) reified goodness.

But if this is accepted, how does one avoid the conclusion that, if God operates in history or not at all, there is nothing left of God? Does not quantitative pluralism lead to polytheism? And to a Westerner, who sees God as transcultural, transubjective, and metaphysical, is not polytheism virtually the denial of God? Further, does not qualitative pluralism make God a qualitative nullity? In a context where God is

---

[5]Bernard M. Loomer, "The Size of God," in *The Size of God: The Theology of Bernard Loomer in Context*, ed. William Dean and Larry E. Axel (Macon GA: Mercer University Press, 1987) 45ff.

[6]This is an argument requiring more elaboration than I can offer here. Such elaboration would hinge on reading sentences like the following with appropriate interpolations: "God is expressed as the organic restlessness of the whole body of creation, as this drive is unequally exemplified in the several parts of this societal web. This discontent, which is an expression of the essential 'spirit' of any creature, may exemplify itself as an expansive urge toward greater good. It may also become a passion for greater evil that, however disguised or rationalized as a greater good, also has its attractiveness." (Ibid., 41) Loomer's point, I believe, is that God's involvement in "greater evil" is necessary for God because it contributes, as God must *always* contribute, to the growth of aesthetic value.

typically treated as unambiguously valuable, is not the qualitative ambiguity of God a virtual denial of God? Is this not then the time to avoid all talk about God and to acknowledge that the American empiricist tendency issues naturally in atheism?

2. Historicism and God: An Imaginative Hypothesis

Agreeing with William James that atheism tends to diminish the quality of life, I would prefer to avoid atheism. Again like James, I would seek a religious theory subject to pragmatic corroboration; and, wanting to avoid merely guessing at a theory, I would consult experience as a source for a theory that is more likely, subsequently, to square with experience. (I say this, but at the same time admit that no matter how deliberately a theory is based on experience and pragmatically correlated to experience, the theory and its confirmation are loaded with constructions based on nothing more than private imagination.)

My candidate for a theory springs from analogies. Just as external physical laws are not given in nature, but built in time through interpretations of the world, and just as the Earth's atmosphere is not simply the given context for living things, but is built in time by those living things themselves, so God is not given, but is built in time by all the finite entities in the world. To say that God is built in time by all finite entities in the world is, I will argue, a mere extension of the neonaturalism of the American classical philosophers and theologians.

John Wheeler, a theoretical physicist, has advanced the first analogue. Wheeler has argued that this is a "participatory universe." Following the Copenhagen interpretation of quantum physics, he claims that the indeterminacy of nature is not merely an epistemological problem (that the observer's errors or limitations make her uncertain), but an ontological reality. Further, he claims that one source of the indeterminacy is the observer; that is, the observer's indeterminate reaction, as it issues in action, makes of the so-called purely objective world something that it would not be apart from that reaction. Wheeler contends that over time the effects of all interpreters, from the nuclear atom to the human Adam, not only alter local histories, but create natural history itself, so that the so-called "laws of nature" or "laws of science" are simply the universal, but temporary, consensuses of the general history of observer-observed interactions.[7]

James Lovelock, an independent English scientist, is the source of the second analogue. His Gaia hypothesis tells in biological terms a story formally identical to Wheeler's. Lovelock argues that it is backwards to exclaim, How wonderfully strange that the Earth's temperatures, gases, minerals, and oceans just happen to fall within that highly improbable range of possibilities that subsequently permits life. Lovelock

---

[7]John Archibald Wheeler, "Beyond the Black Hole," in *Some Strangeness in Proportion: A Centennial Symposium to Celebrate the Achievements of Albert Einstein,* ed. Harry Woolf (Reading MA: Addison-Wesley Publishing Co., 1980) 341-75, and Freeman Dyson, "Comment on the Topic 'Beyond the Black Hole'," in ibid.; J. A. Wheeler, "Genesis and Observership," in *Foundational Problems in the Special Sciences,* ed. R. E. Butts and J. Hintikka (Dordrecht and Boston: D. Reidel Publishing Co., 1977) 3-33.

and a growing body of colleagues (including Freeman Dyson and Lynn Margulis)[8] argue that it makes better sense to say that, from microbes through humans, living things themselves have created, through countless separate decisions, just those environmental conditions suitable for their own survival. They have accomplished this through taking a planet much like Mars was three and a half billion years ago (a planet we now say was then incapable of supporting life), and found ways of gradually altering the environment to make it capable of supporting life. Further, they have accomplished this in part through keeping the Earth climate stable during a period when the Sun's output has increased steadily, from a time when it was thirty per cent less than it is now, until now—an enormous change, in view of the fact that we say that a two per cent drop from present output would cause an ice age.[9]

I introduce Wheeler and Lovelock not with the pretense of inductively arguing for a notion of God. The analogy is rhetorical rather than argumentative. That is, Wheeler, Lovelock, and others suggest a model for theology that should be tested by theologians, historians of relgion, and philosophers of religion, using data and criteria appropriate to religious inquiry. This critical discussion should ask if and how Earth-creatures have created laws and environments of value that operate just as surely and "objectively" as the laws of science or the Earth's environment operate, but that are no more given than they are. Does not this axiological environment have its own momentum, inertia, and otherness that must be respected—just as laws of nature and the physical environment have their own momentum, inertia, and otherness? Is not what humans have called the law or word of God equivalent to an axiological environment? Is not the term "God" a way of speaking of the authority and yet availability of this value-creating process? For example, traditionally Westerners have said that the Hebrews were the passive recipients of God's action and laws, and in one sense that is true. But during the last 150 years of scholarship it has become increasingly evident that the Hebrew biblical writers and the rabbis imaginatively constructed their religious world.[10] Through a chain of interpretations, shaping and reshaping their heritage creatively to speak to new needs and address new problems, the Hebrews not only deconstructed earlier religious and moral laws, but constructed new laws. In the process, they shaped the God who was also and at the same time reflected by those laws. Equally, we say that the Christian community passively re-

---

[8]Freeman J. Dyson, *Infinite in all Directions* (New York: Harper & Row, 1988) ch. 5; Lynn Marguils "Early Life. The Microbes Have Priority," in *Gaia: A Way of Knowing* (Great Barrington MA: Lindisfarne Press, 1987) 98-109.

[9]J. E. Lovelock, *GAIA: A New Look at Life on Earth* (New York: Oxford University Press, 1982) 23-24. See also James Lovelock, "Gaia: A Model," in *Gaia: A Way of Knowing,* 83-97.

[10]This is implicit in tradition history criticism (see, e.g., Gerhard von Rad, *The Problem of the Hexateuch and Other Essays* [New York: McGraw-Hill Book Co., 1955] and *Tradition and Theology in the Old Testament,* ed. Douglas A. Knight [Philadelphia: Fortress Press, 1977]) and in recent deconstructionist analysis (see, e.g., Susan A. Handelman, *The Slayers of Moses: The Emergence of Rabbinic Interpretation in Modern Literary Theory* [Albany: State University of New York Press, 1982] and José Faur, *Golden Doves with Silver Dots: Semiotic and Textuality in Rabbinic Tradition* [Bloomington: Indiana University Press, 1986]).

ceived a new revelation, and in one sense that is true. But, again, many scholars argue with increasing effectiveness that the Christian theories, including the theory of God, were imaginative reconstructions of a variety of ancient Near Eastern influences. This religious and sociohistorical creativity continues today; it can be traced and has been traced—perhaps most sensitively, but in ways now generally forgotten, by the sociohistorical analysis of the old "Chicago School."

The rhetorical analogues for this suggestion are not limited to Wheeler's participatory universe or to Lovelock's Gaia hypothesis. While these are best seen as preliminary and challengeable hypotheses, they extend, nevertheless, current and growing movements in the natural sciences and American philosophy. Wheeler is extending Werner Heisenberg's uncertainty principle of quantum physics and Neils Bohr's principle of complementarity. Heisenberg argues that what the observer does is to select from all the potentialities of the world those that will be made actual; and, of course, those that will be made actual then determine to a limited extent the future. Bohr's principle of complementarity recognizes, in Heisenberg's words, that "the term 'happens' is restricted to the observation."[11] Equally, Lovelock's claim that living things can change the environment extends Darwin's notion that over the long run it is the spontaneous variations that compose the guidelines of natural selection. In Darwin's words, "changed habits produce an inherited effect,"[12] and the sum of these inherited effects constitutes the general set of conditions that, in turn, rewards and penalizes future variations. In the middle of these developments, American classical philosophers, James, Dewey, and Whitehead in particular, summarized this evolutionary world in philosophical language, arguing, in James's words, that truth, like health and wealth, "is made."[13] If Whitehead's primordial nature of God, his fixed metaphysical principles, are dropped (and he usually dropped them after his 1929 *Process and Reality*), then these three great American thinkers are insistent in spelling out the general picture that offers a philosophical context for both Darwin and for quantum physics. This has been called neonaturalism, pragmatism, radical empiricism, or organicism; in every instance what was real was not given, but evolved through interaction of past and present entities.

Over against these terms, I prefer the term "historicism" because it seems more explicitly comprehensive than the other terms, involving human as well as natural history; because it seems more explicitly to involve a worldview as well as an epistemology; and because the term fits with the phrase "new historicism," which several contemporary philosophers of religion use to distinguish their postmodern historicism from deterministic and idealistic sorts of historicisms.

Within such a new historicism, God can be defined in ways that avoid the problems noted earlier. This redefinition would stop making religion the enterprise devoted to convincing a people that religious truth originates from beyond history. Further, a historicist approach to theism can take with new seriousness Jewish and

[11]Werner Heisenberg, *Physics and Philosophy: The Revolution in Modern Science* (New York: Harper & Row, 1958) 52.

[12]Charles Darwin, *The Origin of Species* (New York: Collier Books, 1962) 33.

[13]William James, *Pragmatism* (Cambridge MA: Harvard University Press, 1975) 110.

Christian claims that faith should be historical, and that God is known in history.

Today's new historicist philosophers of religion see a local, temporary, communal history as the final religious authority, and define religious truth as some version of the historical truth. As historical needs change, so religious thought changes; as religious thought changes, so does the known and used God change—for, to be sure, such a God is the only God available. Among religious new historicists I would emphasize Gordon Kaufman, Mark C. Taylor, Jeffrey Stout, and Cornel West— acknowledging that their historicisms vary greatly.[14] However, while these religious thinkers emphasize history, they neglect the natural history discussed by people such as Wheeler and Lovelock—and, more importantly and far earlier, by James, Dewey, Whitehead, the Chicago School theologians, and by process theologians.

Based as it is, on a specifically American, naturalistic, and nondualistic form of new historicism, this hypothesis about God should not be seen as mere projection. Admittedly, it has this appearance if one works from a dualistic position typical of mid-nineteenth-century Continental thinkers and if one assumes, therefore, that something nonobjective is merely subjective—a creation of the isolated self, a mere delusion. However, the historicist God, derived from the American context to which I have pointed, works beyond such dualisms. There it is inaccurate to treat God as either objective and real or subjective and illusional. God, like any entity, is the creature of current interpretation; equally, God is historically creative just as any historical force is creative. God is both a signified, created by the signifiers; and God is a signifier, a contextual influence capable of altering the present. More specifically, God is the word people use to indicate the otherness of those values that appear to originate from beyond themselves and to influence them most profoundly. Add to this the neonaturalist proviso: the observers, the signifiers, the interpreters who create God, include nonhuman beings just as surely as human beings, bacteria just as surely as homo sapiens.

3. Pluralism and God: Toward a Specifically American Notion of God

Any consistent historicism requires a closer look at history than the more or less methodological talk that has preceded. While covering some of the same ground, I want to focus more specifically on what in the late twentieth century in the United States God might be. Again, my comments are imaginative gestures seeking pragmatic corroboration; and they are sketchy and exploratory rather than finished.

---

[14]See esp., Kaufman, *The Theological Imagination: Constructing the Concept of God* (Philadelphia: The Westminster Press, 1981) and *Theology for a Nuclear Age* (Philadelphia: The Westminster Press, 1985); Taylor, *Erring: A Postmodern A/theology* (Chicago: University of Chicago Press, 1984) and *Altarity* (Chicago: University of Chicago Press, 1987); Stout, *The Flight from Authority: Religion, Morality, and the Quest for Autonomy* (Notre Dame IN: University of Notre Dame Press, 1981) and *Ethics after Babel: The Languages of Morals and Their Discontents* (Boston: Beacon Press, 1988); Cornel West, *Prophesy Deliverance: An Afro-American Revolutionary Christianity* (Philadelphia: The Westminster Press, 1985) and *Prophetic Fragments* (Grand Rapids MI: Eerdmans Publishing Co.; Trenton NJ: Africa World Press, Inc., 1988).

Any American historicist approach should begin with a picture of the American religious context. I would describe that context in terms of a recent disillusionment coming at the end of a sequence of American ideas about God. America has had its counterparts to sixteenth- and seventeenth-century European Protestant orthodoxies and neoorthodoxies, where faith was warranted by the sure guidance of a God standing outside history. And it has had its Transcendentalist counterparts to nineteenth-century Continental idealism, where faith was warranted not only by a God standing outside history, but by God's sure guidance of history itself. I am contending, however, that what specifically set America up for pessimism was its movement from a distinctively American exceptionalism, where everything depended on history and faith was warranted by a historical God's fulfilment of history, to a distinctively American post-exceptionalism. Under that post-exceptionalism there was neither a God beyond history nor a good God controlling history. There seemed to be no warrant for faith at all. Post-exceptionalism meant that ideal realities no longer controlled things, that this source of optimism was eliminated, and that either pessimism or some new and definite reason to avoid pessimism was required.

The key to this last and distinctively American step is the movement from a monistic paradigm to a pluralistic paradigm. Previous to this step a unifying historical narrative was posited. From the post-exceptionalist standpoint this narrative appeared to be based on hopes reified and made the objects of faith. What remained after the elimination of the monistic narrative were concrete, plural, and disparate experiences. Then there was nothing binding the world together, giving it general coherence or absolute purpose. How, under those conditions, is religion even possible?

To put it differently but no less accurately, a post-exceptionalist theology may allow, as we indicated earlier, a God active in history, but this God is ambiguous. Pragmatically, however, what is the point of a God who does not act unambiguously for the good and who does not provide even an unambiguous incentive for the good? To affirm such a God may be to affirm that there is a value-created and value-creating process, but if those values are quite ambiguous, what is accomplished by focusing on that process? Hence, the pessimism that underlies American religious thought for those who have abandoned American exceptionalism.

But here I want to challenge the negative thrust of this line of reasoning, and ask whether these skeptical questions are the last questions. Is not the pessimistic tone too much a function of dashed hopes? Does pessimism necessarily follow because the axiological process is no longer omnipotent and unambiguous?

If pessimism would necessarily follow here, then so would it necessarily follow in the natural sciences. Thus, when the teleological understanding of nature was disconfirmed in the nineteenth century, natural science should have been abandoned. Scientists should have stormed out of their studies and labs saying, If the natural world is not driven by a benign purpose, the hell with it! Of course, this is a temptation. Offering security does seem sometimes to be the purpose of science as well as religion. Einstein can appear to say to Niels Bohr, If the physical universe is not driven by a universal, eternal, determined order, well then, the hell with it. But, increasingly, it seems that the Niels Bohrs have had the last word, that he and his disciples have found, even, some new way of discussing meaning. Of course, there are the

Anthony Flews of the 1950s, who suggest that the only God is the traditional God, and that this God has suffered "the death by a thousand qualifications."[15] And there are the neoorthodox and fundamentalist religious thinkers of twentieth-century America, who say that the gods of modernism and postmodernism are false Gods. As Einstein did, they treat earlier interpretations as authoritative, and conclude that to abandon the earlier interpretation is simply to abandon meaning.

On the other hand, if Wheeler and Lovelock did not conclude that a participatory universe is meaningless, why should a new historicist theologian conclude that a world with an ambiguous God is meaningless? If for Wheeler and Lovelock finite creatural gestures yield meaning, why should not finite creatural gestures constructing a series of finite valuational interpretations yield meaning for the new historicists? Religious pessimism, in short, is not simply required by the fact that there may be no omnipotent, unambiguous, extrahistorical, and evil-eradicating historical process—anymore than that the end of given laws and environments required pessimism for Wheeler and Lovelock.

In fact, Lovelock argues that his hypothesis gives new meaning, mandating new responsibilities to humans to create a better environment. Equally, a new historicist notion of God might carry a new pragmatic value and truth—that of inciting people to accept as their own the responsibility for enhancing ultimate values. To shift the analogy, the loss of absolute and benevolent monarchies caused only the old order to be pessimistic; for others it made governance pluralistic, evolutionary, and usually better.

Admittedly, the pragmatic approach I have emphasized is, by itself, shallow, equating the growth of God with the addition of pragmatically successful reinterpretations of past value. To be religiously significant, the empiricist part of the American tradition must be added—that is, its development of Lockean sensationalism, from Jonathan Edwards's sense of the heart, through the radical empiricism of James, the immediate empiricism of Dewey, and the causal efficacy of Whitehead, to the appreciative awareness of Bernard Meland.[16] Without this empiricist element, hitting on new interpretations of the past is sheer guesswork, accomplished as well by the ignorant and indifferent as by the informed and the experienced. With this element there is a reason to conclude that a religious interpretation is more likely to be pragmatically confirmed if it is informed by tradition and is offered by those who have experienced deeply the religious value of the past. Here, theology can speak meaningfully of how those deeper dimensions of past value are intuited. It is just these intuitions that will be reconstructed, made into new interpretations, and pragmatically tested. But that is another story—one which most new historicists, with their neoKantian distaste of any vestige of empiricism, are unequipped to tell.

---

[15]Anthony Flew, "Theology and Falsification," in *New Essays in Philosophical Theology,* ed. Anthony Flew and Alasdair Macintyre (New York: The Macmillan Co., 1964) 97.

[16]For sketches of this development see my *American Religious Empiricism* (Albany NY: State University of New York Press, 1986) 20-39; and *History Making History: The New Historicism in American Religious Thought* (Albany NY: State University of New York Press, 1988) chs. 4 and 5.

Here then is an American way of talking about God, at odds in some ways with the traditional God, who not only is an other, but an other that is in some sense truly absolute. From the traditional standpoint, anything less, especially the conclusion that over time God is entirely created by finite beings, may appear simply absurd. But a historicist dedication to the implications of social and natural pluralism seems to suggest otherwise. For pluralism the absoluteness of God is not somehow wicked; it simply has no longer any function, for there are no longer those social or natural universals and eternals that must be explained by reference to an Absolute. And apparently good meanings for God can be put in place of the traditional God.

But, once more, if dropping the absoluteness of God appears on a rational or emotional level to some people to be unsustainable, they—like Einstein, Flew, the neoorthodox, and the fundamentalists—should dedicate themselves to a traditional notion of God, and avoid as much as possible the current American new historicist concern with pluralism.

Bernard Loomer's Concept of "Interconnectedness" A Pious Naturalism

Douglas A. Fox

Even among people who reject Bernard Loomer's conclusions, he has earned a reputation for intellectual honesty and rigor. Moreover, he strikes a responsive chord in many because of his conviction that the United States can and should develop a theological tradition less dependent than formerly on Europe and more competent to express its own experience of the creative tension between the ideals of freedom and community.

The purpose of this paper is to pay tribute to a rare spirit, and to do so in a way he would have approved: by a critical appreciation of his thought. To this end I shall outline a selection of Loomer's ideas and suggest that there are certain questions to be asked of them; then I shall argue that the attempt to unite his form of naturalism and piety was an enterprise destined to fail, but one from which much may be learned as we press toward his goal: an authentically American theology.

Central to Bernard Loomer's theology is his notion of "interconnectedness," and this shall be the pivot of the following discussion. But first it may be expedient to indicate a few of the assumptions that pervade Loomer's systematic work.

Assumptions

The world (by which he usually means the observable universe) is all the reality we can know. This means that if a term such as "God" is to have reference to reality, rather than to mere abstraction, it must be identified with the whole or part of the empirical.[1]

Further, to identify God with only a part of the whole is to relapse into abstraction. To insist, for example, that God is associated or identified with only what is

---

[1]Bernard Loomer, "The Size of God," in William Dean and Larry E. Axel, eds., *The Size of God: The Theology of Bernard Loomer in Context* (Macon GA: Mercer University Press, 1987) 20.

good, true, beautiful and benign is to tell the world more about ourselves than about God, for it expresses a value judgement and describes a "God" who is merely the idealization of that judgement. Even Whitehead's view of God as a Final Cause or Wieman's restriction of deity to *creative* process are ruled out of order here.[2] As Loomer says, "In terms of this analysis, God as a wholeness is to be identified with the concrete, interconnected totality of the struggling, imperfect, unfinished, and evolving societal web."[3]

There is no room here for a deity who transcends the universe. Loomer's God is concrete and finite.[4] "God is to be found within the natural order. . . . Process philosophy holds that the God it is talking about is observable, and observable in a fundamentally physical or bodily manner."[5]

Curiously, Loomer admits that God may be *religiously* transcendent, but we can know nothing of a transcendent source of explanation: "the reasons why things are the way they are and behave as they do are to be found within the things themselves and their relationships."[6]

Before proceeding to a second assumption, let us briefly consider some questions that may be asked of this first one.

At the outset we must acknowledge that not everyone will find Loomer's empiricism a necessary and sufficient basis for reflection. Robertson Davies somewhere gently lampoons "the simple faith of scientists in materialism" and there will be those who find human experience punctuated by what they take to be visitations of an extraordinary sort. He has dismissed, rather than refuted, the more orthodox Christian belief that in Christ we find the confirmation that the empirical is envalued by a "Reality" that transcends it, "in which we live and move and exist," and whose enfleshment is precisely the Christhood of Jesus. To say that we might touch Jesus but not what his orthodox followers would call deity is not to prove that the former is more real than the latter. Perhaps it is only to limit needlessly our apparatus of apprehension. It may also reduce theology to philosophy, and philosophy to a species of scientism—a charge that Loomer acknowledges Charles Hartshorne to have levelled with some justice.[7]

Still, it seems reasonable to concede that even if the poet's eye sees what the empiricist's microscope does not, the poet (or prophet) may lead us into dangerous or foolish realms of fantasy if he or she is allowed unlimited freedom, and a good dose of earth-bound realism is a healthy antidote. What Loomer calls "abstraction" is, indeed, often a value-laden editing of belief or knowledge, with its puissant values derived from whatever may cheer us. Loomer did not despise visionary imagination, but he would warn us that we should *know* when we are imagining something, even

[2]Ibid., 38-40.

[3]Ibid., 23.

[4]Ibid., 23.

[5]Loomer, "Neo-Naturalism and Neo-Orthodoxy," *The Journal of Religion* 28/2 (April 1948): 83.

[6]"The Size of God," 25.

[7]Ibid. 30.

if we hope it may turn out to be real. To know this is to keep our imagination relatively safe as an empirical datum. Fallacy arises when we imagine we are knowing something outside this datum itself.

Again, Loomer assumes that "God" must be a comprehensive term for a comprehensive reality. Obviously all forms of polytheism disagree, as do some theories of a limited God (such as Brightman's). Loomer has not shown such rival theories to be false, but he shares the popular hypothesis that ours is a universe rather than a multiverse, and pays the price of believing (as not all monotheism must) that God is ambivalent because the universe is. However, even if associating God with only the beneficent is abstraction, many will find the disjunction of good and evil to be sometimes so radical that it reduces Loomer's God to irrelevance or incoherence.

Loomer's argument for identifying God and the world is that God must be concrete, since the concrete is greater than the abstract. As John B. Cobb points out, Loomer seems to borrow from Whitehead here, but for Whitehead only the individual actual entity is fully concrete, and Loomer has not shown why each such entity should not be regarded as a separate God, or, as Cobb says, why it is not true that "every occasion has a different God."[8]

Delwin Brown has argued that if Loomer wishes to proclaim an ambiguous or ambivalent God, he must show what kind of ambiguity he means. Is it ambiguity of condition (God, like all of us, must work with the facts of human distortion and brokenness)? Is it ambiguity of character (God, like us, is a mixture of good and evil)? Or is it ambiguity of intention (God's decisions, like ours, are rarely single-minded)? Loomer explicitly accepts the first and second of these, but the first does not take him beyond a quite orthodox opinion, and there are questions to be raised with regard to the others. For instance, he has not shown why it may not be believed that the divine character is capable of permitting evil (for an end that justified this) rather than committing it, and he has not shown why, even if we are less than singleminded, it may not be held that God enjoys unity of intention.[9]

Finally, it may be asked how God can be religiously transcendent while not ontologically so. Loomer's reply to this is quite clear. Even though God is perfectly identified with the world, humans do not always recognize the divine. Sin blinds us to our dependence on the whole; we are insensitive to the full measure of creative power in the world; and our human consciousness "does not easily perceive those elements of our experience which are always present. We more easily observe those factors which are sometimes absent."[10]

This only means that God (the totality of things) transcends our awareness. God is, thus, not beyond the world, but is beyond our sensitivity. There is the further point that "God" is the symbol of what we value (we shall return to this later) and may therefore serve as a stimulus to our effort to realize value. There is surely a difficulty here, however. Can an ambivalent God serve such a purpose? If he does, is not the stimulus bound to be as ambivalent as our own ambitions? "God" may be a religious

[8]John B. Cobb, "Response to Loomer," in *The Size of God*, 53.
[9]Delwin Brown, "The Ambiguity of Ambiguity," in *The Size of God*, 56-58.
[10]"Neo-Naturalism and Neo-Orthodoxy," 83.

ideal that intensifies the self-serving pursuit of advantage and gives it the spurious sanctity of a "holy war."

Let us proceed to a second assumption. We acquire whatever knowledge we can have by physical experience. He writes,

> We experience our world primarily by means of our bodies. All our ideas are primarily either reflections of or derivations from bodily behavior. It is true that ideas can be derived from other ideas, but in each process mentality originates by a conceptual reproduction of a bodily feeling.[11]

"Bodily feeling" is not always a limpid phrase in Loomer's writings, but it stands for the essential contact through which things impinge on each other and whatever knowledge there may be is created. Within bodily feeling are sense perceptions, and derived from such feeling in appropriately equipped animals, come conceptions. I think we can infer from various of Loomer's suggestions a rough schedule of evolution in knowing: at the inorganic level we find only a contact, or physical prehension, out of which may come the emergence of form. Higher than this is consciousness which may at last contain sensory perception. Higher still is reasoning, which is associated with the capacity to abstract. He says, "the power to abstract forms from concrete processes is so great that mentality emerges into reason."[12]

There is little to object to in this outline, but might not the evolution of a capacity for abstraction be itself a revelatory datum? Might it not invite us at least to respect the mystic's power of intuition (even if we find reason to dissent from particular rationalizations of its meaning, or if we fail to see that it is a "higher" rather than simply a different state of consciousness)? Might not the very ability to construct imaginatively new configurations out of objects perceived be considered a kind of transcendence that points to a yet more ultimate kind? Perhaps there is missing in Loomer's account an adequate sense of wonder at the extraordinary development he describes.

A third assumption is that all knowing is a result of relationship, of encounter with whatever and whoever we meet. "What we are not related to," he writes, "we cannot experience, and what is unrelated to us is unknowable, and the unknowable is unknown."[13]

I suspect that, underlying some of Loomer's thought, looms Wieman's distinction between belief and knowledge, but one may question the implied confidence in knowledge. Every freshman philosophy student knows that we can seriously doubt whether we possess anything except belief. What Loomer is concerned to do, however, is to ground our affirmations in something tangible, and "bodily experience" seems more nearly secure than imaginations. One wonders whether a mathematician would be entirely comfortable with this. As Physics (which began as the search for

[11]Loomer, "Christian Faith and Process Philosophy," *The Journal of Religion* 29/3 (July 1949): 188. Cf. also *The Size of God*, 24.

[12]Ibid. 189.

[13]"Neo-Naturalism and Neo-Orthodoxy," 82. Cf. also *The Size of God*, 25.

a quite tangible *phusis*) becomes more mathematically abstract, it is not only the Taoist but a conventional theologian who may find her or himself comforted by release from the confinement of bodily or sensory encounter.

The fourth assumption is that if we examine our experience carefully we must find a small set of inescapable ontological principles. The first of these is that process or becoming, rather than *stasis* or being, is the essence of reality.[14] All things change. But Loomer's understanding of process is conditioned by the second of his ontological principles, which deals with the nature of entities. An entity at any given moment is a "concrete occasion" or an "occasion of experience" and it is not strictly true to say that such an occasion changes. "They cannot move or change," he writes, "they can only be superseded. They inherit from the past, and having etched their individual stamp on their inheritance, for richer or poorer, they project their decision into the future."[15] Occasions of experience, thus, are episodic.

The procession of a particular sequence of such events or occasions is what we recognize as an enduring individual or an extended event.[16] At any moment I am a concrete occasion or an event, and the story of my life is the history of an extended event (or a sequence of occasions) which draws its shape in each moment from its assimilation of data from its past encounters with other events. There is creativity and choice in this assimilation, but the data for it is always relational.[17]

I am not sure that this is entirely coherent. It reminds one of Theravada Buddhism's theory of *dhammas*, "point-instants" which arise mysteriously by an inherent power to do so, take form, and then vanish with a new set arising to assume the form conditioned by what went before. Some Mahayanists complained that such a disconnection between moments in the sequence made it impossible to account for real process. Loomer tries to overcome this by including choice and creativity in his "occasions" but in doing so he seems to come perilously close to inventing these factors as a *deus ex machina* (much as *karma* serves the Theravadin). Loomer might reply that he includes these because they are empirical data, but even if they are, their existence may demand a different description of the concrete occasion, one that owes more to Aristotle's analysis of potency or something of the sort.

The problem is not solved by Loomer's final ontological principle: order. This appears in the unfolding of the process, but is not something imposed from outside, say by a transcendent God. Rather, it is the "necessary condition in the creation of actualities."[18] Loomer explains that some possibilities are contradictory, and there must therefore be some principle of selection and harmony if process is to continue. "Order is intrinsic in events."[19] It is important to place this principle within the events because "to think otherwise would seem to deny the principle that the reasons for things are to be found within the things themselves and their relationships to each

---

[14]*The Size of God,* 26.

[15]Ibid. 26-27.

[16]Ibid. 28.

[17]"Christian Faith and Process Philosophy," 187.

[18]*The Size of God,* 33.

[19]"Christian Faith and Process Philosophy," 192.

other."[20]

More discussion is needed here to analyze more exactly the relation of order, disorder, and imperfect order. Both function and dysfunction are, presumably, elements in the whole (that is, in God) but, as we shall see, Loomer casts his vote for function and order. We shall have to ask whether he legitimizes this selectivity.

As a final assumption, Loomer says that there is a restlessness at the heart of things to move toward increase in value, to make the good better and the less more. He recognizes that this may, in the end, prove incompatible with the entropy promised in the Second Law of Thermodynamics, but in the meantime there is a discernible drive in the process of the world toward more complexity in individuals and in society.[21] To recognize this and to devote ourselves to it is the supreme objective of the wisely lived life.

Surely the assumption that there is a drive toward higher value is a considerable leap of faith. Teilhard de Chardin, who saw us caught in a vortex of centripetal and centrifugal forces may seem to have recognized more clearly the real presence of the power of diminishment and destruction. If both are equally the character of that totality we call God, why is increase better than decrease? Why is structured complexity so sure a goal—unless, like Teilhard, we impute a kind of intentionality to God that demands some measure of divine transcendence and control. Loomer's answer lies in his concept of "stature" and "size" to which we shall shortly turn.

Obviously we could dig deeper into Bernard Loomer's assumptional system, but in limited space we shall confine ourselves to what has been said. We turn now to his concept of "interconnectedness" or what he liked to call "the web of life."

Interconnectedness

Interconnectedness— relationship—is what gives content to the process of becoming. So important is it that Loomer is prepared to say that relatedness is the purpose of process.[22] In this we discover that he is not only a naturalist but evidently a teleologist as well, giving to natural process a kind of power of determination that resembles that given to historical process by Marx.

We are, as we have seen, shaped by our past relations and our responses to them. As Loomer puts it, "We live in society, but our society also literally lives in us."[23] Again, "We create each other. . . . We live within interlaced fields of energy or relational webs of interconnectedness. Individuals are created within these fields."[24] So vital is this that "we should commit ourselves to relationships and not to each other."[25]

This does not mean that we are solely dependent on others. "We are both self-creative and creative of each other, for good or ill, or for good and ill. We are de-

[20]*The Size of God,* 33.
[21]Ibid. 31.
[22]Ibid. 31.
[23]Ibid.
[24]Ibid. 31-32.
[25]Ibid. 32.

pendent and yet autonomous.''[26] Thus, although we bear a creative responsibility, to a great extent the evil as well as the good in us, mutual destruction as well as mutual support, hatred as much as love, arise through the influence of interconnectedness.

The web of interconnectedness, thus, is ambiguous as to value, and Loomer believes this is irremovable and that we would not achieve a true advance even if we could remove it. Life simply is ambiguous, and only death escapes this condition:

> The dominant tradition of western thought has proceeded on the value premise that the resolution of the ambiguous in terms of the perfect and unambiguous is a development from the less to the more. The thesis of this section is that the converse is the case, namely that this movement is a transition from the more to the less. . . . It is a movement from the concrete to the abstract.[27]

It may be hard to see why a reality with reduced ambiguity need be less than perfectly concrete, but the suggestion seems to be that unless we are torn between the poles that Tillich called "dynamics" and "form" we would be either dead or chaotic. As much can be said for other forms of tension. In one respect, however, Loomer goes further than Tillich. To root out the evil in a person would also destroy his or her capacity for goodness since both spring from the same source.[28] After all, ambivalence is not merely my personal quirk, but is the character of God since God is the totality of things. How, then, can we have an ethic? Is any action, any attitude, more admirable than any other? If we identify all behaviors with God, have we not lost any vantage point from which to exercise critical judgement? The pure humanist may make some value discriminations after establishing at least a provisional description of optimal humanity, but he or she does not deify all existents. Why is love, which Loomer eloquently advocates, better as a lifestyle than hate?

To answer this, Loomer introduces a new concept embraced by the terms "stature" or "size." Our size—and, for that matter, God's—is determined by the "range and intensity of internal relationships one can help create and sustain. The largest size is exemplified in those relationships whose range exhibits the greatest compatible contrasts, contrasts which border on chaos.''[29]

In other words, the person, society, or deity which eliminated polarities altogether would be very small: one might even say that in the loss of the tension for process they would be dead.

It must be noted that it is *contrasts*, not contradictions, that Loomer wants to see us contain, and we may concede that contrasts may, indeed, be constructive. But are there not forms of good and evil that are nothing less than contradictory, and can it be imagined that there is no progress if the latter are expunged? If we introduce a program that eliminates hunger from the world, have we not abolished one of our

---

[26]"Two Conceptions of Power," *Criterion* (Winter 1976): 22.

[27]*The Size of God*, 44-45.

[28]Ibid. 47-48.

[29]"Two Conceptions of Power," 28.

current polarities, and is the world (God) not then of lesser size? Again the construction of ethics seems to become dubious.

Loomer does, however, advocate an ethic as a way of taming the incompatible contrasts without destroying them, and in so doing he arrived at the concept of two kinds of power.

Human life has largely been governed by what he calls "unilateral power," the capacity to produce an effect, to manipulate other persons or things for our own or our group's advantage. It is unilateral because the wielder of power acts and the object is passive. When, in this spirit, we use Bacon's dictum that "knowledge is power" we mean that the more we know the better we can control others for our own ends.[30] "The practise of this kind of power is the primary condition whereby the ineradicable inequalities of life are transformed into life-denying injustices."[31]

In contrast, Loomer speaks of "relational power." "This is the ability both to produce and to undergo an effect. It is the capacity both to influence others and to be influenced by others."[32] If we operate with unilateral power, we hate being influenced because this smacks of weakness, but while openness to the influence of others may, in truth, reflect weakness, it may also reflect great strength: we may be displaying great "size" in our will to risk such openness. As he remarks, "the world of the individual who can be influenced by another without losing his or her identity or freedom is larger than the world of the individual who fears being influenced."[33]

One feels that this is true and important, although the introduction of the word "freedom" raises a question, tangential to our present task, that I do not think has been satisfactorily answered. The open person becomes free *for* things that are denied the other, but less free *from* some. But the existence of freedom is a problem in this system, and Loomer admits that "the self in its freedom cannot be explained or fathomed or rationalized. Freedom 'explains' itself. And this is no explanation."[34]

In a moving passage, Loomer acknowledges that inequality is inescapable, and because of it there is unfairness in life. He adds,

> Our only choice is to choose between two forms of unfairness. In the life of unilateral power the unfairness means that the stronger are able to control and dominate the weaker. . . . In the life of relational power, the unfairness means that those of larger size must undergo greater suffering and bear a greater burden in sustaining those relationships which hopefully may heal the brokenness of the seamless web of interdependence in which we all live.[35]

---

[30]Ibid. 19.

[31]Ibid. 13.

[32]Ibid. 21.

[33]Ibid.

[34]"The Free and Relational Self," *Belief and Ethics*, ed. W. Widick Schroeder and Gibson Winter (Chicago: University of Chicago Press, 1978) 75.

[35]Ibid. 28.

It would seem that for Loomer the superiority of great size and, therefore, the superiority of relational power (which he sometimes calls "love") is self-evident. It springs from a recognition of our mutual creativity, that we are constituted by others as much as they are by us. "We are not interdependent because there is a principle or law of love," he says. "This, again, would be to explain the concrete in terms of the abstract. We love because we are interdependent, because we enter into each other's lives."[36] He adds, "love does not create the world. It re-creates and redeems it."[37]

Again we pause for a question. I respond warmly to what Loomer says about love, but if the law of love is an abstraction which is matched by another, the law of self-interest, where does it derive its authority? Is it drawn only from the fact that Bernard Loomer, a gentle man, preferred to live in a world governed by love? Others may not! Others do not! Unless love comes to us with stronger credentials than this, the interconnectedness of our lives may be only a battle field for "selfish genes."

Loomer says, "we love because a failure to love is a denial of the other, ourselves, and our relatedness."[38] But is this denial always self-evidently bad? There are religious systems whose goal is the denial of self and other in the realization of the indivisible Nirvana or Brahman and which use passionless compassion as a means to this end. Nor, I suspect, would the disciples of Ayn Rand find Loomer's point persuasive.

In the end, I think, love's importance for Loomer rests on the wish to increase what he perceives as value, and this wish, he tells us, "carries its own warrant."[39] One wishes it were a warrant universally convincing.

We shall draw our exposition to a close with one more question. Since it seems possible to discuss all these ideas without recourse to the term "God," one may ask why Loomer persists in using it. Loomer's reply is instructive.

The term "God" is embedded in our culture as a symbol of ultimate value and meaning. It implies a claim upon our loyalty; it indicates what we consider most worthy of worship. But it is the process of becoming through interconnectedness that deserves such veneration and deserves, therefore, to be called by our highest value term.[40] Bernard Loomer's view of things is, thus, not only a naturalism, but truly a "pious" naturalism.

A few final questions are in order. Loomer attacks abstraction, but seems unable entirely to avoid it. For example, he says we are sinners because "we will not allow ourselves to be fulfilled through yielding ourselves to that process which works for the mutual good of all."[41] The concept of fulfilment may seem to be a bit of an abstraction, but even more so is "the mutual good of all." To give meaning to these may involve speculative value judgments as great as that which enthrones a tran-

---

[36]*The Size of God*, 33.

[37]Ibid.

[38]Ibid.

[39]Ibid. 42.

[40]Ibid.

[41]"Christian Faith and Process Philosophy," 194.

scendent God. We might say the same about Loomer's frequent references to the totality of things tending toward greater size.

Again, while no transcendence is to be allowed to God, Loomer often appeals to a purposiveness in the world that seems difficult to reconcile with a totality which lacks self-consciousness. For instance, he writes,

> God . . . cannot realize himself apart from the fulfillment of his creatures. God and the world are mutually dependent. Therefore, if the finite creatures are to be fulfilled, and if God is to achieve his purpose through his self-realization and the realization of his creatures, God must forgive us our sins.[42]

This certainly sounds like a God with a will of his own and some measure of transcendence, whose forgiveness is a conditional imperative.

Loomer speaks of the solitariness of the individual, then says,

> Yet the longing to be known and understood fully by another is one of the deepest bases for the life of prayer and the outreach of religious trust. No human community or relationship can provide an adequate response to such a longing.[43]

This either avows a God who is more than the world process, or it makes our religious outreach a projection as pitiable as Freud ever dreamed.

There seems to me also to be some inconsistency in the way in which Loomer identified God with the totality of things, and yet is constantly selective in his evaluations. As Cobb remarks, "What I am trying to understand is why, if Loomer's commitments are shaped in terms of specific features of the totality, the polemic against relating God particularly to these features is so sustained."[44]

"God" does not stand, for many people, for the simple totality of things. There are elements in the interconnectedness I experience that I do not worship. Here, I think, lies the reason for what I believe to be the inevitable failure of Loomer's system of thought, brave and instructive as it is. Throughout the questions and criticisms that have been threaded through this paper, one motif runs: is it possible to make coherent a system in which one espouses a selective valuation of universal processes, on the one hand, yet imputes the value implied by the term "God" to the totality? He speaks of the world as the "preserver of meaning,"[45] but it just as surely is the preserver of meaninglessness. To dismiss God altogether and make a selective choice of things and processes is one thing; to retain God but associate this term with what is constructive is another. But to be selective, yet call the whole "God" seems the most implausible of all paths.

---

[42]Ibid. 195.
[43]Ibid. 76.
[44]"Response to Loomer," 52.
[45]*The Size of God*, 42.

The goal of an American theology, based on the experience in this land of the polarity of freedom and interconnectedness, remains an important task that should enlist our sympathies. but it may entail a fresh start. Learning all we can from Loomer's effort, we may need to begin at another place, with other assumptions. But we will need Loomer's perseverance and courage to succeed.

Consequences of William James's Pragmatism in Religion

Nancy Frankenberry

Pragmatism currently appears to be enjoying the height of philosophical and literary fashion in North American intellectual circles. In the area of literary criticism, where there is much talk of a "new pragmatism," Frank Lentricchia can manage a reading of William James in the same company as Michel Foucault and Wallace Stevens.[1] The newest of the "new pragmatism" in literary studies announces itself as "against theory."[2] In philosophical studies, where "theory" is customary, pragmatism is treated chiefly as a deflationary device which offers to lift us over the old worn out metaphysical battles that few philosophers care about anymore. Richard Rorty, whose influential *Consequences of Pragmatism* depicts pragmatist philosophy as giving expression to a "post-Philosophical culture," now defines his brand of neo-pragmatism as a way of reducing objectivity to solidarity, in contrast to realism which wants to ground solidarity in objectivity.[3] Denying that neo-pragmatism is just another radical relativism, Rorty terms it "ethnocentrism" and breezily joins with positivism in dismissing what he calls "the Dewey of *Experience and Nature* and the James of *Radical Empiricism*," labelling these "the bad ('metaphysical') parts of Dewey and James."[4]

My purpose in this paper is to counter these recent readings of Jamesian pragmatism, first, by arguing that pragmatism is intimately related to James's other major doctrine of radical empiricism and implies neither relativism nor ethnocentrism, and second, by suggesting several consequences of recuperating a Jamesian pragmatism in contemporary philosophy of religion. It was, after all, from religion that James

---

[1] Frank Lentricchia, *Ariel and the Police* (Madison: University of Wisconsin Press, 1988).

[2] W. J. T. Mitchell, ed., *Against Theory: Literary Studies and the New Pragmatism* (Chicago: University of Chicago Press, 1985).

[3] Richard Rorty, "Solidarity or Objectivity?" in *Post-Analytic Philosophy*, ed. John Rajchman and Cornel West (New York: Columbia University Press, 1985).

[4] Richard Rorty, *Consequences of Pragmatism* (Minneapolis: University of Minnesota Press, 1982) 214.

drew virtually all the examples in the essays on *Pragmatism,* and pragmatism was for him a method closely tied to a defense of religion.

Richard Rorty may be only the most recent in a long line of critics who have misunderstood the consequences of pragmatism because they have misinterpreted its relation to radical empiricism. For example, James was always far from equating truth simply with "what is useful to believe," as G. E. Moore complained.[5] Neither did his pragmatism resemble Bertrand Russell's summary of it as "The truth is anything which it pays to believe,"[6] a summary that prompted James to write in the margin of his copy of Russell's review, "The question being in every case whether it really *does* pay."[7] And, finally, it would be difficult to cite a more myopic case than A. J. Ayer's dogged reading of pragmatism as a kind of phenomenalism, just on the verge of anticipating Ayer's own logical positivism.[8]

All these readings by empiricists on both sides of the Atlantic share a common failure to connect pragmatism to James' other doctrine of radical empiricism. The alternative project of restoring radical empiricism to pragmatism offers several distinct advantages. Perhaps its principal advantage, for those who are not yet thoroughly paralyzed by the strictures of post-Kantian religious thought, is to afford a way out of the throes of a Third Copernican revolution, the assumption, that is, that experience revolves around language, not language around experience. This Third Copernican revolution has been ushered in by the combined projects of Wittgenstein, Heidegger, Saussure, Ricoeur, Foucault, Derrida—by all the developments ranging from structural linguistics to hermeneutical phenomenology to grammatology—which have had the effect not just of problematizing but of displacing and sometimes erasing the very notion of "experience," except as always-already linguistically constituted through and through. In many ways recent American neo-pragmatism is only a blunter version of the continental philosophical emphasis on the utter linguisticality of experience and on language as the "House of Being." Rorty, for example, simply says it's language all the way down, you can't peek behind the public, linguistic grid to see how well or how poorly language reports actual lived experience, so you can just skip the experiences, thus eliminating possibly dishonest middlemen.

But to take pragmatism without the radical empiricism is to have method without the madness of the blooming, buzzing confusion of lived experience. Both as a method and as a theory of truth, pragmatism best "fits" with the Jamesian conception of a processive-relational matrix of experience with its open-ended "fringe" of relations, out of which are emergent both knower and known. As I have tried to show elsewhere,[9] the radically empirical world is not layered hierarchically but structured lat-

---

[5]G. E. Moore, "William James' 'Pragmatism'," *Philosophical Studies* (London: Routledge & Kegan Paul, 1922).

[6]Bertrand Russell, "Transatlantic 'Truth'," *Albany Review* 2 (1908): 393.

[7]Cited in Gerald E. Myers, *William James* (New Haven: Yale University Press, 1986) 564n.60.

[8]A. J. Ayer, *The Origins of Pragmatism* (San Francisco: Freeman, Cooper & Co., 1968).

[9]In Nancy Frankenberry, *Religion and Radical Empiricism* (Albany: State University of New York Press, 1987).

erally in "fields of force," more like a web than a pyramid. The radical empiricist does not dig for rock bottom foundations of knowledge, but instead discerns in the dynamics of concrete experience a textured pattern of relations that provide a context for conduct and belief. This makes the process of pragmatic justification of beliefs, for example, something more than a way of adjudicating claims by a social process in which linguistic propositions are understood to refer only to other linguistic propositions. More profoundly it is a process of finding, or of failing to find, in experience a felt difference that *makes* a difference contextually. This is the framework within which pragmatism "works" as a theory of truth. This is also, I believe, the epistemology and metaphysical theory that best "fits" the project of articulating the "new historicism" in American religious thought.[10]

In the lectures published as *Pragmatism,* James was at pains to dissociate pragmatism and radical empiricism, saying they were logically independent and that one could entirely reject radical empiricism and still be a pragmatist, just as Rorty in fact has done.[11] But two years later, in the preface to *The Meaning of Truth,* James changed his mind and said that if pragmatism were to be accepted, "one great point in the victory of radical empiricism would also be scored." These passages can be reconciled by close consideration of the summary James gives of radical empiricism in this same preface to *The Meaning of Truth.* Of the three central aspects outlined, the first draws pragmatism and radical empiricism into the same methodological orbit by asserting the postulate "that the only things that shall be debatable among philosophers shall be things definable in terms drawn from experience." If there is anything of an "inexperienceable nature" James says it forms no part of the material for philosophical debate. The second central aspect of radical empiricism concerns a statement of fact which asserts that "the relations between things, conjunctive as well as disjunctive, are just as much matters of direct particular experience . . . as . . . the things themselves." Viewed also as an expression of Jamesian pragmatism, this statement of fact contains a concise outline of the way in which ideas lead beliefs or inquiries in certain directions via intervening relations towards a 'terminus,' as James called it, which may verify them or fail to do so. Finally, the generalized conclusion, which is the central feature of radical empiricism, introduces its metaphysical import: "The parts of experience hold together next by next by relations that are themselves parts of experience. The directly apprehended universe needs, in short, no extraneous, trans-empirical, support, but possesses in its own right a concatenated or continuous structure."[12]

What might be the import of these strictly philosophical considerations if applied to the field of the philosophy of religion? No doubt the applications are multiple and need to be stated in connection with very particular analyses, but several general remarks can be noted here. In the first place, the point of James's postulate rules out

[10]See William Dean, *History Making History: The New Historicism in American Religious Thought* (Albany: State University of New York Press, 1988).

[11]William James, *Pragmatism* (Cambridge MA: Harvard University Press, 1978) 6

[12]William James, *The Meaning of Truth* (Cambridge MA: Harvard University Press, 1978) 6-7.

theological analysis that is only language about language, or second-order discourse about first-order doctrinal discourse, or conceptual-textual manipulation of symbolic projections, as long as these are not shown to tie in to the stream of experience at some point. This would not mean that such theological writing does not have its uses, only that it does not form part of the pragmatic method of radical empiricism in the philosophy of religions. Second, James's statement of fact, which calls attention to the role of both internal and external relations, becomes useful in querying contemporary process theologians about the extent to which their conception of the panentheistic all-inclusive whole may neglect the discontinuities that are introduced by *external* relations, while it is also useful in reminding contemporary empiricists of various stripes that they entirely overlook the reality of *internal* relations. And third, the generalized conclusion is clearly a metaphysical hypothesis to the effect that parts of experience do indeed hold together by relations within the flux, thus obviating the need for transcendental principles of explanation, or supernatural entities, or any idealistic forms of cosmic glue.

At the same time, it needs to be emphasized that a metaphysics geared to a world of process, of time and particularity and pluralism, is no less theoretical than one that features eternity and universality; it is only less pretentious and essentialist. Jamesian pragmatism dovetails with, and depends for its cogency upon, his metaphysical theory of the universe as pluralistically and loosely knit, and of experience as a flux in which we carve out derivative concepts. However, the concepts, with which pragmatism is primarily concerned, are never as rich as are the percepts, with which radical empiricism is primarily concerned. The gap between percept and concept is always being filled by relations, which are themselves neither one nor many, subjective nor objective. On this view, concepts can not really be said to "correspond" to reality, and much of our perceptual as well as intellectual life consists of a construction superimposed upon reality rather than a transcript delivered up by it, as Buddhists have long known. Furthermore, the distinction between percepts and concepts can be looked upon, as James does in the *Principles of Psychology,* as precisely the great strength of concepts, that we can think of things that do not exist for perception, that are not even derived from or found in experience itself, things, James says, like round squares, black-white things, perpetual motion machines. This shows, according to James, how independent our concepts are from our percepts. Concepts are only pragmatic tools; some work and some do not and the things we think about do not thereby force their way into existence.

As a further implication of this understanding of the link between Jamesian pragmatism and radical empiricism, I would argue in favor of three more specific consequences of pragmatism in religion. The first concerns the question of epistemological and metaphysical grounds, the second applies to issues about justification, and the third raises the problem of the religious object. In the first connection, I would argue that pragmatism in religion can safely bypass all the interminable disputes about how to ground various basic human values. Here at least is one instance in which we can agree with Rorty that foundational efforts accomplish very little simply by taking the finished first-level product, jacking it up a few levels of abstraction, inventing a metaphysical or epistemological or semantical vocabulary into which to translate it, and then announcing that it has been *grounded*.[13] As James described it, "These are but names for the facts, taken from the facts, and then treated as previous and explanatory."[14]

If this is an appropriate criticism of epistemological attempts to ground values and philosophical first principles, may it also apply to theological questions about metaphysical foundations of the universe? Or does the universe itself need to be conceived as though it stands in need of a further ground? I suggest that one consequence of pragmatism in religion is to answer this ancient question in the negative. Whereas the fundamental theologian asks, What *grounds* the universe and serves to satisfy the principle of sufficent reason in answer to the question "Why is there something and not nothing?", the religious pragmatist has no need for an answer to this question. Undaunted by the awesome requirements for cosmic intelligibility that fundamental theologians impose upon themselves, the religious pragmatist may even deplore the way in which theology exploits the pathos of contingency, its wonder and surprise, for the sake of deriving from it, and for it, a necessary being. Indeed, the religious pragmatist may worry that once necessary being is affirmed, and the rational problem solved, ontological wonder is thereby dissolved, and the explanation ends by explaining away the original sense of mystery and wonder. Religious pragmatists thus sometimes seem to lack full speculative rigor, failing as they do to push back to an unconditioned ultimate *Grenze*. They need not be suspected of an incapacity of piety, however. For it is here that the pragmatic method joins up with the radically empirical worldview for the sake of preserving appreciative awareness of the insistent particularities of the aesthetic content of experience. Rather than making these seem merely the contingent *occasion* for a religious affirmation of something else which is really real or fully concrete or a necessary contrast, religious pragmatism will resist the transcendental temptations of speculative reason. Much like literary naturalism which delights in the study of nature and the faithful description of its ways, pragmatism as a phase of religious naturalism will strive for a faithful portrayal of things as they are but offer no final explanation of *why* things are. One might judge this a laudable, if limited, employment in philosophy of religion, but, as Emile Zola and other naturalist writers discovered, faithful description can be seen by some as reprehensible. More often than not things as they are turn out too nasty to be swallowed neat, too disturbing to the mind unless given some poetic coloring, and much too offensive until clothed in a decent figleaf from the abundant tree of the theological imagination. If religious pragmatism maintains a natural piety, it is not one that partakes of the theological imagination's craving for consolations and guarantees; it is instead one that is willing to say, with William James, that the last word is not sweet, that all is not "yes, yes" in the universe, and that the very meaning of contingency is that ineluctable noes and losses form a part of it, with something permanently drastic and bitter always at the bottom of the cup.[15]

[13]Cf. Rorty, *Consequences of Pragmatism, 168.*
[14]James, *Pragmatism,* 126.
[15]Ibid., 141.

A second consequence of pragmatism concerns the central question that preoccupies many contemporary philosophers of religion, that is, the question of the justifiability of religious belief. If the pragmatic tendency is to forego foundationalist concerns with respect to questions of epistemological and metaphysical grounds, the pragmatic tendency with respect to the justifiability of religious belief is to look for radically empirical reasons and warrants for belief and to assume for these a tentative and hypothetical character. Pragmatic justifications thus appeal to radically empirical relations as given in experience, on the premise that everything in the truth-relation is experienceable. The pragmatic emphasis falls not on antecedent religious truths that stand ready-made and complete, but on the process whereby new truths are being made, engendered out of old truths, to be sure, but as genuine creations that are added by incremental human acts. As a result of this emphasis, an increasingly important consequence of pragmatism in philosophy of religion consists in exchanging an older justificationist method for a newer criticizability criterion, much as Karl Popper proposed in philosophy of science.

Conceived in this way, the pragmatic alternative to the quest for justification would have the consequence of treating particular religious beliefs as proposals or hypotheses which could, in principle, be falsified, and regarding whole religious belief systems as constructed by random mutations and selective retention of those mutations which fit the environment.

A third consequence of pragmatism is to raise with even greater acuteness the problem of the religious object and the question of what practical effects it may have. When James said that the pragmatic meaning is the difference made "in concrete fact and in conduct consequent upon that fact," [16] he was not saying, as even the eminent scholar Arthur Lovejoy took him to be saying, that the difference is solely a product of the act of believing. Whatever the deficiencies of his popular lectures on pragmatism, James was not guilty of confusing the consequences of *believing* that an idea is true with the consequences of its actually being true.

Are there specifically and uniquely religious data or "facts"? Or are there, as contemporary Wittgensteinian philosophers of religion tend to assert, only the same facts, interpreted differently in religious and non-religious perspectives as optional picture-preferences? James himself waivered on the question. Very often he wrote as though the problem of God is not a problem of the existence or the non-existence of a being, even a Supreme Being, but rather a question about the character of the universe, taken as a whole and in its parts. Religion has more to do with "total reactions" and "cosmic impressions" than with an intentional object. So in his pragmatic treatment of "God," "freedom," and "design," he could trace the meaning of each of these concepts to something like "the presence of 'promise' in the world."[17] Invariably, the pragmatic difference between theism and materialism came down to a case of "hope versus no hope."

But other times James wrote as though religion should stand for definite facts of the matter else it reduces only to a pair of rosier glasses for viewing the same facts

---

[16]Ibid., 50.
[17]James, *The Meaning of Truth*, 6.

that are seen non-religiously. He could insist, for example, that religion is not a "mere illumination of facts already elsewhere given, not a mere passion, like love, which views things in a rosier light," but something more, a "postulator of new *facts* as well." He could describe the theistic hypothesis as standing for something more than just the "materialistic world over again, with an altered expression"; rather, "it must have, over and above the altered expression, a natural constitution different at some point from that which a materialistic world would have," that is, "different events can be expected in it, different conduct must be required." He could also say "I believe the pragmatic way of taking religion to be the deeper way. It gives it body as well as soul, it makes it claim, as everything must claim, some characteristic realm of fact of its own."[18] What are the more characteristically divine facts? James did not know what they could be, he said, apart from the actual inflow of energy.

But if this is the pragmatic way of taking religion, as standing for something superabundant, some characteristic realm of fact, does it not raise a special difficulty for religious naturalism? Something of the problem can be brought out by contrasting James' approach with the very different alternative represented by those philosophical theologians, inspired largely by Wittgenstein, who have moved into a "form of life" descriptivism that views religion as a way of looking-on or seeing-as, according to a particular religious "conceptual scheme." Certain definite advantages accrue to the "form-of-lifers" (also known as "seers-as" and "conceptual schemers") in religion. Since in their use the term "God," like the present King of France, no longer refers, there is no danger here of idolatry, of identifying "God" with some limited being or aspect of existence. Neither is there any risk of science putting religion out of business with a few more quick cuts of Occam's razor, for this is a position which signs an easy non-aggression pact with science, easy because it has no cognitive claims to offer, so none that could possibly conflict with scientific claims. Form-of-lifers also consider it an advantage of their position that it allows them to avoid abstract metaphysical disputes, in favor of romping, relativistically it appears, through a startling variety of metaphors, models, myths, and paradigms.

By contrast, the pragmatic method of looking for a discernible difference, a felt difference that *makes* a difference in religion, where the difference made is not only in the individual but a difference in fact in the world, seems to offer none of these advantages and even to risk the alternative disadvantages. That is, some of the claims made on behalf of the religious hypothesis might be such as to make Occam reach for his razor, particular cognitive claims might conflict with or fail to be supported by current scientific theory, and abstract metaphysical disputes will once again become centerstage, occasioning continuing argument over the question of what in fact the theistic hypothesis adds as distinct from a non-theistic one, or a religious as distinct from a non-religious perspective. For on the pragmatic maxim, something must be different in the world, some state of affairs incompatible with atheism must be said to obtain or else the distinction between theism and atheism is finally vacuous and god-talk is empty. And yet the current dilemma of religious naturalism is that the

---

[18]William James, *The Varieties of Religious Experience* (Cambridge MA: Harvard University Press, 1985) 407-408.

pragmatic difference is so difficult to discern. Or if discernible, then it seems that much the same meaning could be expressed without religious language at all. Even within the comparatively austere religious naturalism of Henry Nelson Wieman, Bernard Meland, and Bernard Loomer, the question "why call it 'God'?" receives no fully satisfactory answer. And this is currently a question which comes, increasingly, no longer from neo-orthodox theologians or from conservative fundamentalists, but from secular critics who simply regard a naturalistic version of "God" as a superfluous half-way house on the way to its natural successor, atheism. To this, the pragmatic tendency in religious naturalism has but one reply: "If the word offends thee, pluck it out—but don't skip the experiences."

Religious pragmatism can also be understood as supplying a melioristic option between classical theism, on the one hand, and neo-classical process theism, on the other hand. For example, in Charles Hartshorne's neo-classical theism, the principal difference that God makes is to garner all the value, everlastingly preserving it within the ongoing divine life. Religious pragmatists, however, do not think that every value has to last everlastingly in order for anything to have any meaning. They suspect that Hartshornian theism is just another version of idealism, intent on seeing its own human urgencies mirrored and matched by nature. They look to lived experience, with all its finite, particular, contingent, and temporal values, in order to find there all that they need religiously. Like James, they are willing that there be "real losses and real losers, and no total preservation of all that is."[19] Hartshornians, on the other hand, hold that "without belief in a cosmic and permanent receiver of value-experiences, we cannot make sense of the idea, which we all presuppose at some level, that our experiences and decisions have an ultimate meaning."[20] The differences between the two methods are crucial. In the end, neo-classical theism stands for the idea that only a God of dual transcendence and of the conservation of value is a proper object of worship. Religious pragmatists reply that a proper object of worship cannot be one to which we pay unlimited metaphysical compliments in an age in which fewer and fewer of us are disposed to make those metaphysical moves in the first place. Finally, confronted with the Hartshornian notion of a totality that at each moment is totalizing itself into a new unity, religious pragmatists find themselves, with James, "willing to believe that there may ultimately never be an all-form at all, that the substance of reality may never get totally collected, that some of it may remain outside of the largest combination of it ever made."[21] They agree with James that "ever not quite has to be said of the best attempts anywhere in the universe at attaining all-inclusiveness."[22]

So far I have been suggesting some of the consequences of pragmatism as a method. Considered in its second aspect as a theory of truth, the consequences of

---

[19]James, *Pragmatism,* 142.

[20]David Griffin, "Charles Hartshorne's Postmodern Philosophy" (unpublished paper), citing Hartshorne, *Beyond Humanism,* 13-16; *Omnipotence and Other Theological Mistakes,* 15; *Logic of Perfection,* 286.

[21]William James, *A Pluralistic Universe* (Gloucester MA: Peter Smith, 1967) 34.

[22]Ibid., 321.

pragmatism with respect to religious arguments are strictly limited in at least the following five ways. First, pragmatic justifications, like radically empirical reasons, are partially dependent on rational and theoretical considerations; that is, pragmatism can supplement but never totally supplant theoretical argument and evidence, upon which it is largely parasitic.

Second, the understanding of what constitutes "experience" in pragmatic discernments seeks expression in categories as widely applicable as possible in order to avoid the highly idiosyncratic and the merely anecdotal. Otherwise, the altar of experience becomes so cluttered with everyone's icons that generality is hard to see and particularity may mask wishful thinking and self-deception. In religion pragmatism leads to the consequence that we live with much uncertainty and a very low degree of probability in connection with the full particularity of the various world religious systems. Therefore, tolerance and pluralism are further inescapable consequences.

In the third place, the effectiveness of pragmatic arguments is a contextually dependent and historically situated matter. The acceptance of any religious argument depends upon individual acceptance of various other beliefs and assumptions which are not beyond question, and which stand in need of their own epistemological defense. This is a simple consequence of the fact that any analysis of experience such as offered by radical empiricism, while hypothetically projected as generally applicable and adequate, is not universally accepted as valid. Therefore, it is entirely appropriate, at this stage, that pragmatists be reminded by historicists, feminists, marxists, and other critics that its categories may not be trans-culturally and trans-temporally valid.

Fourth, good arguments can be provided for showing that the contextual and perspectival character of a pragmatic theory of truth does not entail radical relativism. Therefore, pragmatism need not be construed as representing in religion the kind of relativism that Rorty implicitly presents as its consequence in philosophy.[23]

Fifth, partly as a consequence of the first and the third points, pragmatic defenses of religion do not authorize any final resolution of the most basic disputes in the philosophy of religion. Even if one can effectively argue that experiential considerations do justify some form of religious belief, the question as to the exact form of that belief remains open. This is to raise the question, once again, not of the *ideally adequate* but of the *actually available* religious object.

Severe as these qualifications are, I conclude that it should still be possible to defend the sorts of considerations advanced by the pragmatic defense of religious belief as having relevance to the on-going, agonizing, always unfinished work of deciding questions of religious truth.

---

[23]Space does not permit me to provide those arguments here, but I hope to develop them elsewhere.

Naturalism and Existentialist Interpretation
Methodological Parameters
for a Naturalistic Christian Theology

Charley D. Hardwick

This paper contributes to an argument that Christian theology can be construed naturalistically by combining Henry Nelson Wieman's naturalistic philosophy of religion with the existentialist interpretation of Rudolf Bultmann and Fritz Buri. The claim is that the content of Christian affirmation, interpreted existentially, is compatible with philosophical naturalism. The present essay consists of an analysis of three troublesome points in Bultmann's program. These must be clarified in order to show that existentialist interpretation can be construed naturalistically. I shall have space in the conclusion only to suggest the naturalistic application, but some of these implications will be obvious from the analysis itself, especially for those familiar with Wieman's position.

I

The first issue concerns how we are to understand Bultmann's claim that the real content of myth is existential. Bultmann's demythologizing proposal is radical because it entails a twofold methodological claim: (1) that the underlying meaning of *all* religiousness is existential, and (2) that its theological interpretation derives its entire content from this existential character. The locus for these claims is Bultmann's analysis of mythology in his programmatic essay. There he says that "the real purpose of myth is not to present an objective picture of the world as it is, but to express man's understanding of himself in the world in which he lives," and he goes on to say that "myth should be interpreted not cosmologically, but anthropologically, or better still, existentially."[1] These statements require careful attention. Note

---

[1] Rudolf Bultmann, "New Testament and Mythology" in Hans Werner Bartsch, ed., *Kerygma and Myth: A Theological Debate*, trans. Reginald H. Fuller (London: S.P.C.K.; New York: Harper and Row, Publishers, 1953) 10. Hereinafter this essay is abbreviated as KM.

that myth requires an existentialist interpretation[2] because it expresses our understanding of ourselves *in* the world, or in Heidegger's language, which Bultmann assumes throughout, because it expresses *Dasein*'s understanding of her existence given in and with her "being-in-the-world" (*In-der-Welt-sein*).[3]

Bultmann's language requires attention because, I shall argue, it demands an interpretation different from a common one, and this alternative is crucial for a naturalistic program. Such thinkers as Ogden, Oden, and MacQuarrie construe Bultmann as saying that myth expresses our understanding of ourselves *and* the world. They then develop a theological interpretation that simply replaces myth with some version of *metaphysical* theism suitably informed by existentialist insights about human existence. Ogden is clearest because he sees that if a metaphysical theism is to be defended under the form of existentialist interpretation, then it must be developed directly out of Heidegger's argument that the question of being requires a fundamental ontology. The latter is an analysis of the being of *Dasein* as the being who can ask the question of being because an understanding of her being is given with her being. *Dasein* has ontological priority because *Dasein*'s being is determined by *Dasein*'s concernful questioning of her own being in her existing. The question is not at first philosophically explicit or even conscious but appears in her *Sorge* or "care," so that being first appears, is first "uncovered," in this "care-laden" questioning. Ogden turns Heidegger to account by construing the analysis of *Dasein* as *Existenz* in terms of Whitehead's reformed subjectivist principle and thereby proceeds to a full blown metaphysical theism along process lines.

It is admittedly not easy, especially with "God terms," to clarify precisely how Bultmann understands existentialist interpretation. But note again that he does not say that an existentialist interpretation will interpret a myth's understanding of our existence *and* the world but of our existence in the world. It is implausible to think that his intent in criticizing myth in favor of existentialist interpretation is an equivalent of criticizing it for its inadequate metaphysics in favor of a more adequate metaphysics—especially given the strictures he otherwise places on "objectification." This would trivialize his proposal, for, as I have emphasized, its radicality lies in its proposal to interpret both religion and theology in terms of an *existentiell* self-understanding. Such an understanding does include an understanding of ourselves *In-der-Welt* as *In-der-Welt-sein,* and thus includes an understanding of "world," but, given existentially in terms of the way we are "in the world," it carries no implication that an existentialist interpretation of "faith" should be developed metaphysically. It makes no claim to replace an incoherent mythological metaphysics with a better one. Rather, it is a formal claim about the nature of religion and theology themselves. It does raise the crucial question of how "God referents" are to be construed, and this issue is one of the most powerful points at which Wieman's naturalism can clarify Bultmann and Buri on this difficult issue, but Bultmann's proposal for an existentialist interpretation cannot immediately be taken in a metaphysical direction. So, what might be a different reading?

---

[2]Cf. KM, 16.
[3]Cf. Martin Heidegger, *Sein und Zeit* (Tübingen: Max Niemeyer, 1927, ⁹1960) 63-88.

Bultmann specifies the self-understanding implicit in mythological thinking by three further features. First, myth involves a kind of transcendence by expressing our existential awareness that the familiar world of our daily lives is limited and defined by powers that lie beyond it and are its source and limit. Second, myth expresses our awareness that we cannot simply be masters of ourselves or our lives because we find ourselves dependent both on powers within our familiar world and also on those mysterious and unknown powers that circumscribe us. Finally, myth expresses the confidence that we can become free from these powers. In sum, Bultmann seems to say that what distinguishes a mythological self-understanding is that it expresses our understanding of ourselves as limited by transcendent powers and our confidence that through some of these powers we can find liberation.[4]

The question is how this notion of transcendence qualifies an existentialist interpretation. If it turns out that "man's understanding of himself in the world in which he lives"[5] already includes a reference to transcendent powers, then it is not so clear how this intent is different from the more typical conception of mythology as involving simply a conception of "God, man, *and* the world" requiring more adequate metaphysical translation. But then it becomes difficult to see that there is anything distinctive about an existentialist interpretation.

It seems clear that there must be another reading of what Bultmann means by transcendence that is more compatible with an existentialist understanding of myth. I propose (and I believe this is consistent with Bultmann's meaning) that we understand "transcendence" entirely in reference to our being-in-the-world. "Transcendence," then, would be entirely *functional*, with no metaphysical intent at all. Taken existentially, it serves the function, embedded directly in our being-in-the-world, of bringing to expression a *concrete, immediate* experience of life that we all have, namely, that we lack any ultimate control over our lives, which are bounded by powers beyond our ability to determine and even (existentially) to understand. By thus taking "transcendence" functionally as an expression of a pervasive type of experience actualized concretely throughout our lives, we can preserve its existential character that seems required by Bultmann's proposal.

This reading gains support from Bultmann's argument that, given the nature of myth, it calls for its own demythologizing. The argument is that the "beyondness" and dependence myth intends is expressed inappropriately in terms of the known and familiar world. Myth "speaks of the other world in terms of this world, and of the gods in terms derived from human life."[6] By so doing, myth betrays its own intent and "contains elements which demand its own criticism."[7] Such incoherence within myth is an important example of what Bultmann regards as inappropriate objectification, and he often subjects metaphysics and other theological positions to this same criticism. As he says in concluding this argument, "the importance of the New Testament mythology lies not it its imagery [by which he means its objective character]

---

[4]Cf. KM, 10-11.

[5]Ibid., 10.

[6]Ibid., 10.

[7]Ibid., 11.

but in the understanding of existence which it enshrines."[8] Again, it seems highly implausible that Bultmann intends simply to substitute one metaphysical form for another.

II

A second issue requires an analysis of how Bultmann's conception of the kerygma advances the notion of existentialist interpretation. The Greek word *kerygma* became a technical term in twentieth century theology through form criticism. The latter tried to identify the earliest layer of oral tradition in primitive Christianity which later took literary form in the New Testament. *Kerygma* has come to refer to this earliest version of Christian proclamation—which probably took form as something like: "Jesus is the Lord" or "Jesus is Christ [i.e., the Messiah] come." Appropriated theologically, the term has been broadened beyond this strictly critical or literary sense and has come to mean the normative content of the Christian message as a proclamation or a gospel rooted in the earliest New Testament tradition. As such, "kerygma" has a twofold force in theological usage. It refers *normatively* to the *content* of the earliest Christian message which may be specified as God's eschatological act in Jesus Christ. But it also has a *formal* meaning, which refers to the nature of that message as a proclamation of the event of God's action. In this formal sense, the weight of the kerygma falls on its event character.

This double meaning is relevant to Bultmann's argument about the nature of myth because he criticizes all previous efforts at demythologizing for failing to preserve the kerygma as kerygma.[9] But he fails clearly to specify how the weight of this criticism is divided between the two meanings. They are typically collapsed into one, as in the following characteristic statement of this criticism in reference to liberal theology and the History of Religions school: " . . . , they are silent about a decisive act of God in Christ proclaimed as the event of redemption."[10] This ambiguity raises the following question about which of the two possible meanings of kerygma is lost: Is it the *content* of the kerygma, the action of God in a series of specific events some two thousand years in the past that is lost? Or is it the *event* character of what is proclaimed as action of God that is lost?

This question drives straight to the center of the controversy over Bultmann's demythologizing proposal. At issue is whether demythologizing requires surrendering the idea that redemption is possible now only because God acted in some special way in specific events of past. The statement above seems to imply that preserving the kerygma means not surrendering the idea of God's special constitutive action in specific past events. But this is contradictory, for, on the one hand, Bultmann sees that demythologizing must be exhaustive, yet, on the other hand, this position seems to insist on a content for the kerygma that is patently mythological. Recognized by many critics, this problem has come, through the powerful analyses of Ogden and Buri, to be known as the "structural inconsistency" in Bultmann's position. Here I

---

[8]Ibid.
[9]Ibid., 12-15.
[10]Ibid., 15; cf. 13.

shall simply assume this critique and accept its conclusion that the Christ event itself must be demythologized.

Assuming this conclusion, it becomes possible to see how kerygma has implications for how we ought to understand the method of existentialist interpretation. We should note that despite the unclarity noted above, there are good reasons to understand the force of Bultmann's criticism in terms of the second, formal meaning of the kerygma, namely, as the proclamation of an event (which has the content of God's action of redemption). Three considerations in Bultmann's language itself support this interpretation.

First, after the statement quoted above directed at failed attempts at demythologizing, Bultmann continues:

> So we are still left with the question whether this event and the person of Jesus, *both of which are described in the New Testament in mythological terms,* are nothing more than mythology. Can the kerygma be interpreted apart from mythology? Can we recover the truth of the kerygma for men who do not think in mythological terms without forfeiting its character as kerygma?[11]

Bultmann thus implies that his own phrase for the content of the kerygma, "decisive act of God in Christ," has a mythological form. This would imply that, undemythologized, such language cannot be identified with the kerygma that was lost in other efforts at demythologizing. It further implies that the phrase here should not be taken as determining the *content* of the Christian gospel but is intended *formally* to designate the character of the gospel as kerygma, as present *event* offering the possibility, *existentiell,* of a new self-understanding. Or, perhaps better, it implies that the content of the kerygma, mythologically expressed as "decisive act of God in Christ," must itself be determined by the formal character of the kerygma as *existentiell* event. Second, in criticizing past attempts at demythologizing, Bultmann repeatedly insists that what was lost is the "*event* through which God has wrought man's redemption,"[12] and we have established that this cannot be an event of the distant past (or any past event, for that matter). What is at stake, in other words, is the event character as such of the kerygma as a present proclamation. Finally, nothing could be clearer from all of Bultmann's writings than his insistence that the decisive issue in the Christian proclamation of the kerygma (and also in the resurrection) is an event of God's action of redemption that happens again and again in the present, not in the past— regardless of his apparent attachment to an undemythologized Christ event.

What is really behind Bultmann's demythologizing proposal is this notion of God's action in the present (as it occurs in and through proclamation). It is not a metaphysical world view that is at stake but the event character of God's action. Myth makes such present action unintelligible. Other demythologizing efforts reduce the content of Christianity to ideas or ethical principles and thereby surrender the notion

---

[11]Ibid., 15; emphasis mine.
[12]Ibid., 14; Bultmann's emphasis.

of God's redemptive action in present life. What is at issue in the theological objection to philosophical attempts to describe human existence is not that they fail in their description of the structure of existence but that they fail to see that we cannot make the transition from inauthentic to authentic existence without an event by which we are liberated to choose authentic life.[13] In other words, the real force of the kerygma is its event character, which points to God's redemptive act in the present, and it is this that divides Christianity from its alternatives.

So understood, Bultmann's or any other Christian use of the mythological phrase, "the decisive act of God in Christ," must be so interpreted as to elucidate this formal character of the kerygma as event. Furthermore, its formal character as present event must determine how one gives content to "decisive act of God in Christ" because, if the formal character of the kerygma as event is decisive for thinking about *any* "act of God," then no simply past event can ground or constitute its intrinsic character as present event. The *content* of the kerygma, the content of the phrase "decisive act of God in Christ," is not the historical events of the distant past, however interpreted, but the formal character of the kerygma which, through the proclamation of the action of God in Christ, becomes an event of redemption in the present. Thus, the question of the truth of the kerygma, which Bultmann often asks,[14] is not a question about the truth of some past event but is the question whether an act of God or the encounter with an event of redemption is necessary at all in order for human existence to be authentic.

Of course, the question may still be raised whether any such reference to "the event character of God's action" is still not some sort of metaphysical claim, and I believe Wieman's naturalism provides resources for a negative response consistent with Bultmann's existentialist interpretation. The point here, however, is that when Bultmann claims that myth betrays the event character of the kerygma, it is not a false versus a more adequate metaphysics that is at issue.

III

The final issue to be discussed here is probably the most difficult in Bultmann's thought. (It is also the most difficult and pressing issue in contemporary theology generally and one where Wieman's naturalism is especially powerful.) Bultmann himself poses the issue in his reply to his critics when he asks whether the notion of an act of God is mythological as such.[15] He treats the question as almost rhetorical. He rejects outright the charge that he reduces the idea of God's action to a "symbolical description of a subjective experience," and explicitly states that any proper

---

[13]Cf. KM, 27-33. Cf. also Bultmann, "The Historicity of Man and Faith," *Existence and Faith: Shorter Writings of Rudolf Bultmann,* Schubert Ogden, trans. and intro. (New York: Meridian Books [World Publishing Co.], 1960) 107.

[14]Cf., e.g., KM, 11.

[15]Cf. Bultmann, "Bultmann Replies to His Critics," in *Kerygma and Myth,* 196. Cf. also Owen Thomas, ed., *God's Action in the World: The Contemporary Problem* (Chico CA: Scholars Press, 1983).

language about God and God's action "must denote an act in a real, objective sense."[16]
The problem, as we saw above, is that any language is mythological if it speaks of
God, the beyond, in terms drawn from this world, but on these terms, it seems difficult to see how we could speak of God at all without our language becoming mythological, since all language is necessarily this-worldly. Bultmann does admit that there
can be an appropriate *analogical* way of referring to God's action,[17] and Ogden,
making a great deal of the analogy between an existentialist, non-objectifying, conception of human being and a process conception of God's being, has used this ad-
mission to develop a *proper* way of referring to God and God's action which then
justifies incorporating a full blown process metaphysics into Bultmann's demythologizing.[18] Bultmann, however, resisted this development of his theology, and never
endorsed it in writing despite an extended discussion with Ogden over many years.
What was his reason?

Bultmann commonly describes the inappropriateness of mythological language
in terms of conceiving of God "as a worldly phenomenon."[19] How this is a problem,
however, receives two different emphases in his thought. On the one hand, mythological language sees divine activity as interference in the world which tears it asun-
der.[20] In this sense, "it objectifies the divine activity and projects it on to the plane
of worldly happenings."[21] The problem here is at least partly that such a conception
is simply incompatible with a view of the natural world based on scientific regularity.
But this is not the whole problem, for, on the other hand, when mythology speaks
this way, it also treats God and God's action as though, like worldly events, they can
be apprehended independently, objectively, or neutrally, apart from their existential
reference. What is at stake here is a notion of God's transcendence, in the twofold
sense both of *indisposability* and of *worldly nonobjectivity* (not of metaphysical and
therefore *objective* transcendence). This latter emphasis on the problem of objectivity is what justifies Bultmann's characteristic claim that there is no neutral language
about God but only a language that is simultaneously about myself as existentially
concerned:

> . . . it is clear that for my existential life, realized as it is in decision in face
> of encounter, the world is no longer a closed weft of cause and effect. In
> faith the closed weft presented or produced by objective observation is tran-
> scended, though not as in mythological thought. For mythology imagines it
> to be torn asunder, whereas faith transcends it as a whole when it speaks of

---

[16]Ibid., 196-97, 199.

[17]Cf. ibid., 197. Cf. also Bultmann, *Jesus Christ and Mythology* (New York: Charles
Scribner's Sons, 1958) 60ff.

[18]Cf., esp., Schubert M. Ogden, "The Temporality of God" and "What Sense Does It
Make to Say, 'God Acts in History'?" in Ogden, *The Reality of God* (New York: Harper and
Row, Publishers, 1966) 144-63, 164-87.

[19]Bultmann, "Bultmann Replies to His Critics," 196.

[20]Ibid., 197, 199.

[21]Ibid., 197.

the activity of God. *In the last resort it is already transcended when I speak of myself, for I myself, my real self, am no more visible or ascertainable than an act of God.* When worldly happenings are viewed as a closed series, as not only scientific understanding *but even workaday life requires,* there is certainly no room for any act of God.[22]

This emphasis accounts for Bultmann's resistance to all objective language *about* God and is made still clearer by his rejection of the criticism that his position is pantheistic (identifying God with all worldly happening). Pantheism, he responds, is a world-view consisting of a set of *anterior* convictions about God and the world. Christianity is not such an anterior world-view but, resting as it does on the experience of grace, "believes that God acts upon us and addresses us in the specific here and now."[23] This is incompatible with a world-view because the latter is a set of beliefs that can be possessed whereas faith in God's gracious action must be constantly renewed through the actual *events* by which God does indeed act.[24]

From this analysis it follows that one cannot immediately translate Bultmann's willingness to speak of analogy into his endorsement of a metaphysics based on such analogies. That would amount to an "anterior world-view." What then does he mean by analogy? The context makes clear that the analogy is between God's transcendence (in both senses of "indisposability" and "non-objectivity") and a dimension of human existence similarly transcendent. In other words, Bultmann wants to say that there is a dimension of human existence which cannot be objectified like a worldly phenomenon. This is the dimension clarified by Heidegger's existential analysis, in which the reality at stake is a reality that cannot be grasped except by one's own concernful engagement with it, since what is at stake is one's own being being at stake. This analogy permits us to relate God's action to this realm of human agency or personhood. The analogy is appropriate because the human question of God, as well as God's gracious action, deals precisely with this existential dimension of our lives.[25] The analogy warrants no metaphysical conception. What it warrants is the independence of God's action exactly analogously to the way our own existential actions are "transcendent" and independent. The latter are misunderstood if treated psychologically as intra-psychic processes. Rather, they involve our full, yet non-objective, engagement with a world independent of us:

> Christian faith . . . believes that God acts upon us and addresses us in the specific here and now. This belief springs from an awareness of being addressed by the grace of God which confronts us in Jesus Christ. . . . This kind of faith, however, is not a knowledge possessed once and for all, not a *Weltanschauung.* It can only be an event occurring on specific occasions, and it can remain alive only when the believer is constantly asking himself

[22]Ibid., 198-99; emphasis mine.
[23]Ibid., 197.
[24]Cf. ibid., 198.
[25]Cf. ibid., 202 and 205-207.

what God is saying to him here and now.[26]

When we say that faith alone, the faith which is aware of the divine encounter, can speak of God, and that therefore when the believer speaks of an act of God he is ipso facto speaking of himself as well, it by no means follows that God has no real existence apart from the believer or the act of believing. It follows only if faith and experience are interpreted in a psychologizing sense. If human being is properly understood as historic being, whose experiences consist of encounters, it is clear that faith, which speaks of its encounter with the acts of God, cannot defend itself against the charge of illusion, for the encounter with God is not objective like a worldly event.[27]

Thus, the analogy is between "act of God" and our *existentiell* acts in encounter with a world. Just as speaking of the transcendence and non-objectivity of our "historicity" does not entail subjectivizing our experience but implies a full encounter with a world, so speaking of God's action does not reduce it to human subjectivity. It has the real form of our existential encounter with a world—this is the analogy. But just for this reason, we can only speak of God when we speak of ourselves existentially.

This, I believe, is the only sense of analogy that Bultmann's position warrants. But, though it makes clear where the analogy is located, non-objective *events* within human existence, and what the analogy excludes, a metaphysical interpretation, there is no question that there still remains the problem of specifying the "God side" of the analogy. Wanting to avoid a merely subjectivistic reduction while also preserving the event character of grace in the moment of faith, yet also lacking any objective language apart from that interior event, Bultmann is forced into a kind of neo-Kantian, phenomenal/noumenal, two-aspect theory in which he wants to say that God's action is visible only to the eyes of faith through what is effectively a noumenal action. He is forced to say that faith will see events in the world as God's action, even though, of course, nothing has changed.[28] In this way, his discussions of the "invisibility" of God's action except to the eyes of faith become simply garbled. He has no effective way of specifying God's action except as personal address to the existential self, no way of specifying why the *existentiell* events of personal address, which support the analogy, are appropriately termed *God's* action, and thus finally no successful rejoinder to the charge he himself articulates that "action of God" seems no more than a manner of speaking about the occasion for a change in self-understanding.[29] This issue does create a genuine opening for construing his position metaphysically, which Ogden has exploited, but we have seen why this option is not

---

[26]Ibid., 197-98.

[27]Ibid., 199-200.

[28]Cf., e.g., ibid., 198, and *Jesus Christ and Mythology*, 62-66.

[29]*Jesus Christ and Mythology*, 73. Bultmann's analysis in response to this charge does clarify the issue of a transformation in existential self-understanding as arising from encounters, but it does not further clarify the other issue which has to do with the "non-self" side of the analogy and therefore his response remains locked in his neo-Kantianism. Cf. ibid., 74-77.

acceptable within Bultmann's program. This is where Wieman's conception of God and God's action is more clarifying. But for that, it would be necessary to understand Bultmann's position naturalistically.

IV

Bultmann's position is attractive for a naturalist theology because his argument that theological terms are to be construed exhaustively in terms of modes of human existence (i.e., an *existentiell* self-understanding) remains neutral as between a naturalist or anti-naturalist conception of the world as a whole. I have tried to suggest an interpretation of his position that adheres strictly to such an existentialist conception of theology. There is space to make only suggestions about how this interpretation might be coordinated with Wieman's naturalism.

The first and most obvious point is the solution Wieman provides for Bultmann's difficulties in referring to God's action. Wieman's naturalistic, yet entirely formal conception of God as the creative event (or the processes in nature that lead to transformations in value) provides a non-subjectivistic reference for God that is both real and actual but which avoids Bultmann's neo-Kantian mystifications. Taking Wieman naturalistic conception of God as a starting point, more interesting and powerful correlations follow.

The second of these is the fit between the anti-metaphysical force of Bultmann's existentialist conception of religion and Wieman's own non-metaphysical, "empiricist" treatment of both the human problem and human religiosity. Understanding God as the "source of human good" realized in naturalistic processes of creative transformation, Wieman was led toward an analysis of theological and confessional notions that sees their content entirely in terms of the meanings they have within the structure of devotion to God (or faith), or, alternatively stated, as deriving their entire meaning from "consummations within experience."[30] The structural similarity with Bultmann is very close. At this point the coordination can run in the opposite direction, for the rich existentialist analyses of the content of faith in Bultmann and Buri, properly applied, can fill out the hinted at, but largely undeveloped, theological resources latent in Wieman's position.

This potential is especially well grounded in the "event" character of faith and of God's action which can be drawn out of Bultmann's conception of the kerygma. If we ask how God is active, the answer is that the event of grace in Bultmann's sense would be equivalent to Wieman's conception of God's action as a transformative moment within natural processes given particular valence within human existence by the structure of human valuing. Particularly important is that this transformative moment can be, and indeed requires to be, understood as an event in all of the ways that this

---

[30]Wieman's naturalism might be thought itself to be a metaphysics. Perhaps it implies one, but in this respect it emerges only in what—if we are naturalists—we *cannot* say about God—for instance, that God is personal, or that faith requires a belief in either final causality or the conservation of value. More important, parallel with Bultmann, Wieman consistently affirmed that any metaphysics that might support his naturalism was strictly irrelevant when it comes to the issues that concern "faith" or religion.

notion figures in Bultmann's position. The reason is that the relevant transformative moment should be conceived not as a linear series of valuing events but concerns the overall orientation by which an intentional agent commits itself to value.[31] In remarkable continuity with Bultmann's Lutheran analysis, Wieman sees the human problem as the attempt to increase value by controlling it and its production. The issue, then, has to do with an orientation (an existential self-understanding), not with a series of valuing acts. Wieman argues that such an orientation is self-defeating because growth in value is not a human achievement but an action of "God." This position is formally identical to Bultmann's Pauline analysis that sin is constituted as "life after the flesh" by which we attempt to control the conditions of life in "mistrust of God," the sole source and ground of those conditions.

The change from "unfaith" to "faith" is also identical in the two thinkers, for it is a transformation of orientation from one seeking to control life (value and goodness) on one's own terms to one of openness and trust in the only true source of value. Furthermore, the change in orientation is itself a transformation, which makes it structurally and functionally identical with the event of grace that, in both thinkers, accords exactly with the traditional content of justification by faith.

These formal parallels between Bultmann and Wieman make it possible to introduce Bultmann's notion of event into Wieman's analysis, thus wedding an existentialist interpretation to the latter's conception of the religious life (including Bultmann's notion of the non-objective character of faith and the non-objective force of theological doctrines). Since faith is *constituted* by a *transformation* in existential self-understanding, it is an event in exactly Bultmann's sense. In an exactly parallel way, God for Wieman must be seen to be unavailable except in the moment of God's action which, properly understood, is always gracious.[32] In other words, God is non-objective in the only way non-objectivity can make sense in Bultmann. And God remains so for Wieman also because the transformative moment always recedes into the past. For Wieman, the orientation of commitment to God must always be a moment of openness to God's transformative action, which moment, theologically analyzed, must always be seen as itself transformative, a gift, God's grace, an event of interior action that doubles back upon itself and rests upon a moment of passive receptivity. Stated differently, the only way God can be known for Wieman is in an orientation of commitment to the source of human good, and the moment of this commitment is for him, as for Bultmann, a moment of God's gracious, transformative action. Thus, the meaningful notion of faith for both requires that the action of God is not a single transformation but a continuous one; commitment to God is itself an always new and transformative moment of openness to God's transformative action wherein the openness can never be possessed but recedes behind itself into another

---

[31]For the argument supporting this interpretation of Wieman, cf. my essay "What Is the 'Good' of Religion for Wieman?" *American Journal of Theology and Philosophy* 9/3 (September 1988).

[32]Cf. my essay "Faith in a Naturalist Theology: Henry Nelson Wieman and American Radical Empiricism," *Religion and Philosophy in the United States of America,* 2 vols., ed. Peter Freese (Essen: Verlag der Blaue Eule, 1987).

transformative action. In this sense, faith for Wieman, when the notion of justification by faith is taken with full seriousness, must be seen to be existentially nonobjective in exactly Bultmann's sense. Faith for both is an existentially and phenomenologically thick conception. In both cases, it must be formulated so as to include God's action. The consequence is that for Wieman, faith should be termed "openness to transformation" (just as in Bultmann's it can be termed "openness to the future").

A Dual Theory
of Theological Analogy

Charles Hartshorne

Always there have been some philosophers who incline to stress the difficulties of the philosophical task, or even its hopelessness. The ancient skeptics illustrate this. Their kind is common today. On the other hand there have always been the daring speculators. A. N. Whitehead, the Anglo-American, is an outstanding example, more so than any other Englishman for many centuries. In France and the U.S.A., Bergson and C. S. Peirce preceded him. How shall we relate the two types of thinker? One way is to take the skeptics as having the function of keeping the speculators sane and modest, or more so than they otherwise would be. As a speculative philosopher, I would surely be far more conceited than I now am were there not positivists, linguistic analysts, Heideggerians, deconstructionists around playing remarkably agile games that I only partly comprehend. But it seems obvious to me that we need a wisdom more positive and adequate than they, or the scientists, including psychologists, or the religionists without benefit of philosophy can offer us. Scientists too need some philosophy, and psychologists most particularly need it. When scientists philosophize, they may do it well or not so well. But this is true of philosophers.

Consider the psychologist B. F. Skinner. He deals with some philosophical questions, in my opinion partly well and partly ill. But where he is wrong, so are many in my profession. His determinism and his materialism are common doctrines in both professions. What is right in Skinner is his stress on *positive* reinforcement, compared to negative. Neither strict, classical determinism nor materialism is required to make the valid point Skinner makes here. Life is essentially enjoyment, not pain, essentially hope, not fear. However, the proper definition of reinforcement is in terms of probability, not strict determination of effects by causes. In quantum physics, and in the half-life laws of atoms and particles, science has begun a new epoch in which the very ideas of causality and of physical substances are being changed. Perhaps few philosophers, even few physicists or psychologists, are aware that two great scientists, one of them both a psychologist and a philosopher, Charles Peirce, with flashes of genius, partly anticipated the recent change in causal ideas and in ideas of substance. The statistical laws of gases, Maxwell had suggested, might be taken to mean that all natural laws are of this nature. Peirce, perhaps independently, and partly for additional reasons, came to this conclusion, and stated it emphatically and definitely. Many philosophers and scientists still do not see what these great minds saw then. Nowadays, however, many do see it, both in the sciences and in philosophy. It takes less genius to see it now than it did then.

Skinner, aware that the uncertainty principle in physics does somewhat qualify causal determinism, says that psychology can live with that much concession to indeterminacy. My response to this is, who is Skinner to settle an issue that is moot in physics about the extent to which classical causality must be qualified? Bohr, Wigner, Prigogene, Heisenberg, and others have suggested that there will probably be further changes in the same direction. As for materialism, as Whitehead has shown, what the Greeks meant by matter has dropped out of physics. The Greek *atomism*, in qualified form, remains, but not the classical concept of *matter*. More and more, Whitehead rightly argues, the traits attributed to matter as distinguishing it from mind have been disconfirmed. Peirce said of materialism that it was "that mode of philosophizing that leaves the world as unintelligible as it finds it." As a trained chemist, physicist, and astronomer, as well as outstanding mathematical logician, Peirce deserves attention in such a judgment. Quantum theory strengthens a case already strong.

I wish now to turn to the science of biology. Here too I see philosophers and psychologists as having a hard time keeping up with significant changes in basic sciences. Since Darwin and Wallace, we know how basic biology is. It is the evolutionary process, and our and our ancestors' freedom, that have made us what we are, not some single act of deity. This need not at all mean that God was not required. After all, Wallace was a natural-selection evolutionist independently of Darwin, and he was and remained a theist. The English author and clergyman Kingsley accepted Darwinism and gave it a theistic interpretation, as did Asa Gray, the great American botanist, and Peirce. Also my father, F. C. Hartshorne, about a hundred years ago. Millions of people take this line now.

Darwin himself was not an atheist, only an agnostic. And his main reasons for this were essentially philosophical. One of them was even theological. It was the contradiction between two religious ideas, human freedom and divine omnipotence. In my book *Omnipotence and Other Theological Mistakes*, I argue that Darwin was right: as omnipotence was usually conceived it does contradict human freedom. The issue was not scientific but metaphysical. And the metaphysicians were mostly confused, as Darwin saw. Even Darwin's other reason for disbelief was metaphysical, his determinism, for which also theologians were partly responsible.

I recall some biologist saying or writing that psychologists are insufficiently biological in their thinking. On this point, I have an axe to grind. I hold that my theory of sensations as a subclass of feelings—physical pleasures and pains being only the clearest instances—is better biology than the account of sensation given by many psychologists. Many, not all, for some have supported me in this matter as I show in my book, *The Philosophy and Psychology of Sensation*, the most biological chapter of which is on "Sensation and Environment." Mine is a directly adaptational theory of sensory qualities. Most other theories are only indirectly and weakly adaptational.

Consider pain. It directly tells us we are being injured. We do not first learn this by association. We *feel* the badness. Pain is a warning, an inhibitor, a discourager. Pleasure is the opposite, an encourager, a positive reinforcer. Again we do not have to *learn* this meaning. Consider the taste or smell of sweetness; it is akin to pleasure and encourages us to eat or to smell. Foul odors, sourness, bitterness, saltiness, are all more or less opposite to this. Of substances directly encountered in nature, sweet ones are wholesome and nourishing; of foul, bitter, salt, or sour ones, many, unless in small quantities, are useless or poisonous. So these tastes or smells are directly adaptive. My view is that *all* the sensory qualities tend to favor certain appropriate types of response. Redness is opposite to greenness, yellowness to blueness; it can be shown that the feeling tones of these color sensations are appropriate to the facts that in nature the biologically important red substance is blood, the important or pervasive green substance is vegetation; the important or massive blue object is the sky (or distant mountains or bodies of water), while yellow is the color predominant in sunlight. I argue that these feeling tones are appropriate to the pragmatic import of the objects mentioned. Experimental tests seem to show that the feeling tones in question are not mere associations but are intrinsic to the sensations. On this point my book has not been refuted. Quite a few psychologists have taken a position something like mine in this matter.

One advantage of the doctrine is that it gives by far the best explanation there is for the power of sensation in art, especially in music. Music expresses feeling partly because sound sensations are feelings already. By association they may express further feelings that are more than sensory, but this is association by similarity, not by mere contiguity.

There are further advantages. If our knowledge of the physical world is by sense perception, and if sensation is feeling, then our direct intuition of the physical world is of forms of feeling, not forms of mere dead, insentient matter. The basic idea of materialism is a logical construction not a datum. So far as direct perception goes there may be no such thing. Further, if all direct intuition is of feeling, then *either,* by direct intuition, we are aware only of our *own* feelings, and are thus shut up in a solipsistic isolation, *or* we directly intuit feelings not simply our own but those of other sentient subjects. If so, all experience is *social* in structure. This has enormous implications for many sorts of problems.

In feeling pains or physical pleasure, including sexual pleasures, what we are most directly aware of is matter that is not outside our bodies but inside them. We feel pain when at least *some* bodily cells are being injured, or mistreated. A cell is an integrated individual, it *acts as one.* How do we know it does not feel as one? If so, it surely does not enjoy being injured. On that view our physical suffering is participation in *cellular* suffering. It is innate sympathy. Generalize this and we have a unique clue to the mind-body, as well as the mind-other-mind, relation. If we throw away this clue, what other equally good clues will be left?

Leibniz may have said some absurd things, but he said one not absurd and very important thing. It was that while there are some insentient things in nature, yet feelings are everywhere. There is no contradiction in this. My hand does not feel, a tree probably does not feel, and a rock does not feel. But the cells of my hand, the cells of the tree, and the molecules or atoms of the rock may feel. The principle is, what acts as one feels as one; what does not act as one does not feel as one. There is good evidence that rocks do not feel, for they do not act as single agents. A tree grows, but this need not be action of the tree as a single agent. The tree-cells multiply and this *is* the growth. But a waking animal with a nervous system acts as one and thereby expresses its feeling as one. So do atoms or molecules. Leibniz thought trees did this too, but he seemed less sure on this point. His hesitation was justified and a botanist long ago argued against the idea of Fechner, the psychologist, that trees are conscious. The question remains, do their cells not at least feel?

The upshot of the foregoing is that psychology may in principle or ideally be the universal science in the following sense. Every active agent in nature at least feels and its internal stuff is feeling, but there are many layers and levels of feeling. The lower the level the less we can, even vaguely, imagine the feelings. Hence, as we go down the scale of active agents, behaviorism becomes more and more nearly the whole story, so far as our possible definite knowledge goes. Physics, then, is the almost entirely behavioristic psychology of the lowest and most universal types of agents. Some physicists believe this. With the higher animals it becomes more and more worthwhile to try to imagine their feelings. My book on bird song, *Born to Sing,* gives arguments for this.

A serious weakness of Western thought, illustrated in both philosophy and psychology, is in the failure, with a few exceptions, to realize that the inclusive values are aesthetic. Animals, including people, survive partly because they *want* and try to survive. This means, to put it simply, that living gives them pleasure, joy, satisfaction, or other aesthetic, that is intrinsive values, and the thought (if they do think) on continuing to live gives them more of this value than the thought of not continuing. This holds, whatever they may say or not say about it. Even moral values are intrinsically aesthetic to the extent that the sense of harmony with the good of others is an element in one's own aesthetic good, and that genuinely moral conduct favors aesthetic good in the future for others and, for the most part, for oneself. If living were not good in itself there would be no point in being ethical, or in anything.

What reinforces behavior is either positive or negative aesthetic values; Skinner rightly emphasizes the positive side. Either way it is aesthetic value that does the job. Moral value reinforces only if it contributes to the aesthetic value. One who has no enjoyment from being good can hardly be very good. This does not justify the reduction of altruism to enlightened self-interest. The self-enjoyment needed for action is enjoyment *in the present.* One may *now* enjoy acting for one's own or *another's* future enjoyment. The first is self-interest, the other is altruism. Both have basic roles to play. As Hume saw, it is fallacious to reduce one to the other. The genuinely universal motivation is the interest of present life in other life, including one's *own future life* as a special though often predominant case of other life. Enlightened *interest,* not self-interest, is what is needed. Interest exclusively in and for oneself is subhuman, no matter how much reasoning is involved in it. Indeed, it is subanimal. Sympathy is truly basic, it is even what unites us to our own bodies.

A delightful psychiatrist friend of mine, Adam Blatner, likes to say that a great neglect in his profession is to overlook the importance of play. So far as what we do is not partly play for us it is our cells, not we, that tend to take over. They at least are doing what they enjoy doing with whatever qualifications pain and disease require.

To be a healthy live animal is an aesthetic achievement in itself. Life is the inclusive art. Well do scientists speak of the beauty of their theories, and the greater the scientists the more likely they are to do this. They must have this enjoyment to do well in their subject. There is no *mere* altruism (not even in God, in spite of a long tradition to the contrary), and there is also no mere self-interest. There are only good (ideally good in God) or poor, *proportions* in these two factors of life.

Students of animal behavior have been naively surprised to find that solving a puzzle may be more rewarding for a subhuman animal than food. Animals are *interested* in their situations, and interesting is an aesthetic term. Animals can enjoy novelty and they dislike or ignore stimuli reiterated many times at short intervals. Beauty is no longer defined, as it traditionally was, in terms of pure order, but rather as a judicious departure from pure order, a median between the entirely, and the not at all predestined. Freedom is subtly involved, and sheer determinism was always an unaesthetic view of reality. Any artist can achieve order; what is needed is neither order nor chaos but something transcending both. Kant partly saw this in his aesthetics, but failed to generalize. Whitehead is, among other things, the first great system maker who was abreast of twentieth century aesthetics. Peirce had already said that aesthetic value is fundamental. Had Whitehead not had the aesthetically cultured wife to whom he gives the credit for his thought on this topic, he might have made little progress in it beyond Peirce. However, Whitehead did read Wordsworth and Shelley extensively and intensively.

If it were not for the war-peace problem, and some other intractable practical issues, this would be a magnificent time to be alive. In theoretical reflection about nature, God, and the past of the human species, we can now understand so much more than was possible in other centuries that we could be very proud of our collective achievements, were it not that we face a future which, so far as anyone has shown, could crush us all, quickly with nuclear war; more slowly by population-pollution-problems, or the malcontent produced by the grossly uneven distribution of benefits the world over. These are now the crucial issues.

Our (or my) conclusion so far is that reality as we know it in its concrete forms involves feelings which are never those of a single subject or feeler but are either feelings of other subjects or feelers—in the paradigm case those of the first subject's bodily cells—or of a previous subject or experience in the same personally ordered series. The latter are what we ordinarily call cases of memory. Memory in this sense is not the verbalized account one gives of it, but, for example, a present feeling of a just previous experience of joy or sorrow. With Whitehead I argue for the view that in sensory feelings, where bodily constituents are the other feelers, the feelings felt (called by Whitehead "objective forms" of the person's feelings) are not in the absolute present but are just previous in time. The significance of this is that our sensory feelings are effects whose causes, or necessary *antecedent* conditions, are cellular feelings. It is also to be understood that all feeling has what Peirce called spontaneity and Bergson, Berdyaev, and Whitehead called creativity in the sense incompatible with the classical idea of sufficient, or fully determining causal conditions. Rather, feelings partly determine *themselves* in the precise way in which they feel the feelings of their predecessors. In short there is a pervasive social duality in feeling, an aspect of sympathy or love (with antipathy as a more or less distorted, unfortunate form) and an aspect of libertarian freedom.

If this is what we find reality to be, what are the theological bearings of the doctrine? Theologians come close to agreement on two propositions: for the idea of deity to have human relevance, there must be some *analogy* between a human being and the divine being; however, the analogy must not be too close, there must be a *difference in principle* between the divine and the human. There is widespread agreement also upon what sort of concepts are to be used in stating this difference in principle. What philosophers call categories, meaning extremely general and abstract terms, including necessary vs. contingent, absolute versus relative, infinite versus finite, perfect versus imperfect, one versus many, unitary or singular versus plural or composite, eternal versus temporal, immutable versus mutable or changing, cause versus effect—it is such polarities or "ultimate contrasts," as I call them, that we must employ in conceptualizing the divine *Difference*. But, most amazingly, one has only to look at the list to see certain illogicalities. Many terms applied to God are *negative,* but not all of them. Eternal is negative, meaning either non temporal or temporally beginningless and endless, and so is absolute, meaning not relative or dependent, also infinite, not finite. But is *cause* negative? Is *knowledge* negative? Is *love* negative. The so-called *negative theology* was never consistently or merely negative! Moreover, if we try to make it consistently so we end with the collapse of relevant religious meaning. That we are images of God ceases to make sense.

That God *differs* categorially from all else is correct, what needs to be added is that God is also, in another aspect of the divine reality, categorially *similar* to all else, but in such a way that there remains a difference in principle in both aspects. I call this double likeness-difference *dual transcendence*. If God contrasts with all else in being in a uniquely excellent sense cause, God, to be worshipful, must equally contrast with all else in being in a uniquely excellent sense effect, responsive to influence by others; similarly with the other contraries, absolute-relative, infinite-finite, simple-complex, object-subject. If this is contradictory, then so is theism.

I believe the contrasting predicates can be taken to apply to different aspects of deity, and that this removes the apparent contradiction. A grammatical subject S can have predicates p and not-p if the negative application is to a different aspect of S than the positive. The negative applications are to an abstract aspect of deity and the positive ones are to God as concrete. Moreover, the old contention that deity entails absolute "simplicity" and can admit of no distinction between abstract and concrete clearly begs the question. The divine simplicity is the abstract and the divine complexity the concrete side of the divine nature. It is scarcely a paradox that the concrete is richer than the abstract. Moreover there is no least contradiction in saying that the complex can have a simple constituent, although the simple can have no complex constituent. Neoclassical theism is the logical and classical theism the illogical version.

Long ago another analogy was proposed additional to the usual likeness-difference between a human being as one and the divine being as one. Plato's World Soul was this other analogy. It takes a human being or person as a one-many, the one is the person's flow of experiences, the many (to modernize) are the person's bodily cells, especially the neurons, each with its vastly lower levels of experience or feeling. In the thought of Plato, God is cosmic Soul of which all else forms the inclusive body. I hold that this proposal was a stroke of genius, one of the greatest and most underestimated of philosophical discoveries. Whereas kings have never had a truly divine right to rule, you or I can and should achieve something like a divine preeminence over our bodily cells. Each of these cells is almost nothing in comparison to you or me as an individual. How we think or feel is immensely important for our cells' welfare; only collectively do they count a great deal for us. Whitehead, who calls his view a "cell theory of reality," yet harshly refuses to employ the platonic analogy theologically. Luckily for me, who can almost claim to have invented it in its modernized form! However, there have been and are others.

Of course one can argue against the World Soul analogy, but so can one against the more usual analogy, which in Plato is called the Demiurgos or creator. But note two things: where one analogy is strong the other is weak; in addition, modern science immensely strengthens Plato's second analogy because what we know about the cellular, molecular, atomic, particle-wave structure of a vertebrate animal supplies what Plato most lacked in spelling out his sublime idea of soul. I stand on this: show me a conception of the psycho-physiological structure of the vertebrate animal that in your view prevents it from symbolizing the divine-creaturely relation and I will show you that you misrepresent either or both the religious requirements and the actual psycho-physiological natures of ourselves.

If classical physics were the absolute truth then, I admit, the analogy would break down hopelessly. Also, if human thoughts or feelings had no bodily effects, then too the analogy would not work. But there is no expert unanimity for this "epiphenomenalism." More and more I have come to the belief that for every theological error there is a corresponding error about human nature. Ugly ideas of God, and there have been many, go with ugly ideas of ourselves, and vice versa. Only so can we understand the possibility of intelligent and trained minds dividing so stubbornly, for thousands of years, between theists and atheists.

Is the God of dual transcendence personal? Our secular knowledge of personhood is derived from our experience of ourselves as social animals and of other higher animals, all of whom are in some way and degree social. To be a person is to have relations to other persons, to be a member of one or more societies, including families as societies and to interact with other members. If God in no sense interacts with us, it is nonsense to use the analogy of personhood theologically. Nor will the Trinity solve the problem, for God is said to love us and all creatures, not just the divine Son and Holy Spirit. On the other hand, no relation between human persons will do to express the difference in principle between God and all else. No king and no parent (whether father or mother, and preferably the mother) helps much to symbolize the radical supremacy and yet intimate relatedness of God to every creature. The mind-body analogy does help to symbolize it.

Theistic metaphysics in this century has oppportunities not effectively open to it in any previous century.

Omnipotence
Must God Be Infinite?

Yeager Hudson

Although a handful of thinkers in the history of Western philosophy have examined and advanced the idea of a finite deity—Plato, John Stuart Mill, and Edgar S. Brightman are examples—for the most part, the notion that God is and must be infinite has been a fixed and nearly universal belief. And omnipotence has nearly always[1] been regarded as an essential characteristic of the infinite deity. In most cases, the motivation for putting forward the concept of a finite God has been to provide a way of dealing with the problem of evil. A being Whose power is in some small measure limited might be excused for creating a world containing evil on grounds that She did not have the power to eliminate all evil. My concern here is not primarily with the problem of evil. I have addressed that issue elsewhere.[2] Here I want to examine the concept of omnipotence itself, for its own sake and the sake of its implications.

On the face of it, the claim that God is omnipotent appears to be the claim that "God can do anything at all." Despite Peter Geach's contention that "no graspable sense has ever been given to this sentence that did not lead to self-contradiction . . . ,"[3] philosophers have certainly assumed that the sentence has a graspable and noncontradictory sense, and in fact that it expresses a truth. And yet the sense conveyed by the sentence has not been thought to be transparent on the face of it; thus many attempts have been made to explicate the claim, already by such medieval thinkers as Anselm and Thomas, but especially in recent literature. However, when philos-

---

[1] A conspicuous exception is Peter Geach who argues that the biblical and Christian theological teaching is that God is almighty, not omnipotent. See his "Omnipotence and Almightiness," *Philosophy* 48 (1973), in Louis Pojman, *Philosophy of Religion: An Anthology* (Belmont CA: Wadsworth, 1987).

[2] See my articles: "Is There Too Much Evil in the World?" *International Philosophical Quarterly* 25/4 (December 1985) and "Response to Chrzan's 'Hudson on Too Much Evil'," *International Philosophical Quarterly* 27/2 (June 1987).

[3] Geach, "Omnipotence and Almightiness."

ophers who maintain that God is omnipotent attempt such explication, they often do what amounts to conceding limits to the divine power in the interest of consistency and of not implying that God can do things which are incompatible with other aspects of the divine nature. As early as the time of Thomas Aquinas, philosophers and theologians began to list the kinds of things an omnipotent deity cannot do—while still maintaining that a being who could not do these things was nonetheless omnipotent. I shall briefly analyze a typical list of things an omnipotent being cannot do and then examine the implications of accepting these disabilities for the concept of omnipotence. I shall contend that when all of these concessions are summed up, it becomes plausible to ask whether the resulting conception of God is not of a less-than-infinite deity; whether, in other words, even the orthodox theologians and philosophers have not unwittingly put forward a theology of a finite deity while still supposing they believe in omnipotence.

When the problems with the claim that an omnipotent being "can do anything at all" begin to be noticed, more modest or less sweeping definitions are often attempted. A typical one is: Omnipotence is the ability to do whatever is possible, or to actualize any possible, and every compossible, state of affairs. I am not interested here in examining the adequacy of the definition. Rather I want to note that already in the definition there is the concession that there may be things which even an omnipotent being cannot do, or that not every state of affairs is possible for God to actualize. It is at this point that lists of what kinds of things cannot be done or what kinds of states of affairs are not possible emerge. I shall briefly discuss five kinds of things or states of affairs which are sometimes said to be impossible even to an omnipotent being, namely: (1) doing anything that is logically contradictory; (2) altering the past; (3) causing the free acts of other agents; (4) doing evil or other things incompatible with impeccability; (5) creating rather than merely exemplifying universals.

Although a few philosophers, Descartes, for example, have insisted that God must be the creator of the laws of logic and mathematics and thus could have decreed laws quite different from the actual ones, most philosophers have conceded that an omnipotent being cannot do what is logically contradictory. God, if She is omnipotent, can do many great things such as creating the universe and redeeming all mankind, but She cannot create a square circle, nor can she make $2+2=7$. God cannot create a square circle because there is no such thing; the words do not name anything which can consistently be thought, much less which could exist. And although God might have brought it about that the symbol "7" stood for this many: " | | | | ," rather than this many: " | | | | | | | ," and if She had done so then $2 + 2$ would indeed have equaled 7, this is only a playing with definitions. It does not require a God to perform such a feat. We humans could adopt the convention of using the symbol "7" to stand for this many: " | | | | " and then we too would have made $2+2=7$. What is clear is that the relations of quantity remain what they are regardless of the symbols we use to designate them, and it is these relations and not the symbols which constitute the laws of mathematics. And it is not a question of how much power a being has as to whether that being can change these laws. The laws of logic and mathematics are not like civil statutes which can be altered if the requisite authority and power are there. It does not matter who makes a contradictory claim, whether man or God; the result is the same: either unintelligible non-sense or falsehood. If God were to attempt to promulgate laws contrary to the principle of identity and the principle of contradiction, She would perforce be faced with the necessity of exemplifying those principles in Her speech, for if She attempted to do otherwise, nothing intelligible would be communicated. It is for reasons such as these that most philosophers and theologians have conceded that not even an omnipotent God can change or act contrary to the fundamental laws of logic and mathematics. Some would say that there is a sense in which these are antecedent to God Herself; others such as Brightman would say that they are simply an unalterable part of the divine nature—what Brightman calls God's "rational given."[4] In either case, these laws bind God. To violate or change them is something that is not possible even for an omnipotent being.

As with logic, so also with the past: a few philosophers have argued that God can alter the past—Peter Damian is an example—but the clear majority have said that altering the past was something that is impossible even for an omnipotent being. The specific example often discussed in the Middle Ages is whether God can restore the virginity of a woman who had lost it. The issue is complicated by the claim put forward by many thinkers to the effect that God is timeless, that God transcends time, or that what happens in a temporal sequence from our point of view is actually present to God in an eternal, unchanging now. But Anselm, Jerome, Aquinas, and most others concluded that although God might have prevented the loss of virginity, once it was lost it could not be restored even by God. Time seems clearly to be unidirectional; it appears definitely to have the characteristic of being irreversible; and once a part of it has passed, it is fixed for all future times. Even an omnipotent being cannot change the past.

It has been the so-called predestinarians earlier on and the so-called "compatibilists" today who have maintained that God can cause the free acts of human agents, but once again this has been the minority view, although by perhaps not quite so large a margin. One issue here is the freedom of the wills of created beings and the claim that freedom is a necessary condition of moral responsibility. If human wills are free in the sense that God cannot control them, this would appear to be a severe limitation on God's power. Thus, it has been argued, if God is omnipotent, then She must be able to control my actions. But if God causes my actions, the counter-argument goes, then it is not I but God who is responsible. Unless human wills are free, humans are only puppets with God pulling the strings; thus human actions have no moral standing. Furthermore, it would be unfair for God to reward our virtues or punish our sins, since they are not really ours but Hers. Both the predestinarians and the compatibilists have attempted to have it both ways; i.e. to insist that God controls our wills and actions *and* that nonetheless we are responsible and therefore justly punishable for our sins. Persons of other persuasions have vigorously argued that this having one's cake and eating it is actually fancy theological footwork or, to speak more plainly, duplicity. The claim that free will and moral responsibility are compatible with God's having control of our will and actions, which is essentially what the compatibilists

---

[4]Edgar S. Brightman, *Person and Reality* (New York: Ronald Press, 1958).

claim, amounts to asserting both p and not-p, or at least asserting p and a series of propositions which implies not-p. To examine the arguments in detail would require several papers longer than this one. It must suffice here to say that even more fundamental than the important moral issues involved is the inconsistency of claiming that one being controls the free acts of another. For the very meaning of calling them free is that no one else controls them. If someone else does, they are not free; and if they are free, no one else controls them. Thus, either we must give up the belief that human actions are ever free, or else we must concede that God cannot determine the free actions of other agents. The moral issues are considerations in favor of refusing to give up the belief that human actions are free, but there are other significant considerations having to do with the very vivid sense of sometimes being able to deliberate and decide uncoerced what we shall do. To be sure, such a vivid impression might be mistaken—just as vivid sense impressions sometimes turn out to be mistaken—but in the absence of strong contrary evidence the presumption is in its favor. Thus, for both moral and what we might call epistemological reasons, the belief in human free will has been widely supported, and I would argue ought to be supported, and it has therefore been conceded that there are actions of other free agents which it is impossible for God to control.

The major concern with regard to the compatibility of omnipotence with impeccability is the question whether God can sin or do evil. Clearly sinning or doing evil is something which is possible. Humans can do it. But can God? If She can, then She would appear not to be morally perfect. If She cannot, She would seem not to be omnipotent. One way to answer the dilemma is to say that sinning or doing evil simply means doing what is contrary to God's will. But surely God could not do what is contrary to Her own will. This, it has been asserted, is no limitation of God's omnipotence since it is compatible with God's being able to do whatever She wills. But the solution has problems of its own. It implies the so-called divine command theory of morality: that what is right and what is good is merely a product of the divine will. This implies that God might have made lying, torture, or murder morally right merely by saying so. But surely morality is not so slight a matter as whim—even divine whim. And surely the unprovoked murder of innocent persons would still be wrong even if God commanded it.[5] Furthermore, if what is good is just what God wills, it makes no sense to say that God is good or does good since that would amount merely to saying that God is what She wills to be or that She does what She wills.

Another attempt to solve the tangle involves saying that although God can sin, i.e., is able to sin, it is only minimally likely that She ever would because of Her moral nature. This amounts to recognizing, as I am prepared to argue that we must recognize, that morality is independent of God's will, thus suggesting that it is antecedent to God and something to which God Herself must conform—like the laws of logic and mathematics. But it does enable us to say that God's omnipotence is not compromised, since it is possible for Her to sin, and also to say that Her impecca-

---

[5]The case of Abraham's proposed sacrifice of his son Isaac and its interpretations by S. Kierkegaard under the concept of the "teleological suspension of the ethical" is interesting and important. Unfortunately, it is not possible to pause to examine it here.

bility is intact so long as She does not exercise the option of committing sin.

There is another issue which has certain similarities to the one we have just been discussing which might be mentioned at this point. It is a problem which Mackie calls the "Paradox of Omnipotence."[6] The question is whether an omnipotent being can perform an action which places limits on what that being can subsequently do. If the answer is affirmative, the implication is that although the being was initially omnipotent, after performing the action it is no longer omnipotent. On the other hand, if the answer is negative, there is already the concession that there are things an omnipotent being cannot do. As Mackie points out, there is a parallel paradox with regard to the sovereignty of a king or parliament, which suggests that supreme sovereignty over time is impossible. If the king or the parliament is initially supremely sovereign, it has the power to make laws which subsequently limit its sovereignty; or if it does not have that initial power, then its sovereignty is limited from the start. In the Hebrew Bible there are instances of kings or judges making vows and then being bound by them despite the shocking consequences of having to keep their word—e.g. Jepthah vowed to sacrifice the first thing which came out of his house when he returned from battle and thus had to make of his daughter and only child a burnt offering to fulfill the vow.[7]

An instance which seems to exemplify this paradox of omnipotence is God's promises. If God makes a promise—to lead Israel out of Egypt, or to send a Messiah—then She must keep that promise. Thus She no longer has the power to do otherwise than She promised. If God creates eternal laws She subsequently will be unable to alter those laws or to act contrary to them.[8] Thus Mackie argues that God either is not initially omnipotent or is not subsequently omnipotent and so that there cannot be a being which is omnipotent for all time. But the same sort of answer might be offered here as was given concerning whether or not God could sin. It might be said that God could perform actions which would limit Her own subsequent power, but that because of Her other perfections She would never do anything which would compromise in disabling ways Her power to perform Her proper divine functions. Nevertheless, if God makes promises, as most religious traditions suggest that She does, and if She gives free will to Her created human beings, then She does perform acts which limit Her subsequent power.

Finally, some philosophers such as Plato would argue that God is limited by antecedent possibilities such that She can only create possible things; i.e. that there are eternal forms or universals which are antecedent to creation and that God can only create exemplifications of them. Plato's own view of creation was that the creator [he called him "demiurge," from a Greek work which meant something like "tink-

---

[6]J. L. Mackie, "Evil and Omnipotence," *Mind* 64/254 (1955), reprinted in Nelson Pike, ed., *God and Evil* (Englewood Cliffs NJ: Prentice-Hall, 1964) 57ff.

[7]Judges 11:30-35.

[8]This relates to the problem of miracles. If the laws of nature are universal and eternal, then even God ought not (indeed, ought not to be able) to violate them. If they are such that they bind only finite beings, in what sense is it a miracle when God makes exceptions to them, since such actions on the part of God would not be violations.

erer''] found preexisting blueprints, patterns, or universals, and preexisting matter, and that he created by imposing the preexisting forms or patterns on matter. Some contemporary modal logicians seem to construe the concept of possibility so widely that anything that can be named, apparently even what is logically contradictory, is "possible" and claim that there are "possible worlds" in which each of such things might be, or might have been, exemplified. Geach[9] has some harsh things to say about modal logicians who attempt to overstep the bounds of the laws of logic in their talk about possible worlds. But the issue is whether or not there are any limits upon what God might create or whether literally all things [even contradictory ones] are possible. Just as the laws of logic, mathematics, and morality are not the product of God's will but rather laws to which God Herself must conform, Plato insists that God creates within the constraints of a set—a very large one, no doubt, but a finite set—of possibilities, that God did not create and cannot change. Thus construed, this last item expands into a comprehensive one, including in a general way all the others, and connecting with the proposed definition of omnipotence as the ability to do whatever is possible. But it makes even more clear than the definition itself did that not all things are possible.

Unfortunately there has been time here to give these five alleged exceptions to God's omnipotence only skimpy treatment. But our immediate concern is not with the details but with the more general issue of whether or not, given the concessions exacted from the conception of omnipotence, we have not departed from the infinite deity and in effect embraced a finite one. The only one of the five which seems not necessarily to attenuate God's omnipotence is the one concerning impeccability and the concomitant "paradox of omnipotence." If we grant that God is able to sin but never does, Her power as well as her moral virtue remain intact. However, if God makes certain kinds of promises, the paradox of omnipotence returns to bedevil us with limits to future power. So even this most innocent appearing of the objections turns out not to be without fangs. The other four never even had the appearance of harmlessness. We must conclude, then, that there are at least four and perhaps five kinds of things which God cannot do: She cannot do anything which violates the laws of logic, mathematics, or innocently do anything that violates the laws of morality; She cannot alter the past; She cannot control the free acts of other agents; and She cannot make promises without attenuating Her power. These incapacities are summed up in the notion of limited possibilities: God cannot do just anything, but only some or all of the finite number of possible things; and God cannot create just anything but again only such things as are possible. And it is not up to God as to what is possible.

Does this amount to a doctrine of a finite God? The answer hinges on how far we are willing to stretch the concept of omnipotence. It is clear that it has been stretched quite considerably from the naive definition of "able to do anything at all." Has it been stretched to the breaking point? I believe that we have arrived at the point where we need to ask what is any longer gained by clinging to the term. To be told again and again that God cannot do some certain kinds of things but that that does not damage God's omnipotence, and that God cannot do some other certain kinds of things

---

[9]Peter Geach, "Omnipotence and Almightiness."

but that that also does not threaten God's omnipotence, and on down the list—causes growing anxiety about the intactness and viability of the concept of omnipotence. Perhaps it is time to point out that God's greatness is everything it ever was whether we cling to the label of omnipotence and keep trying to patch it up, or let it go in order to think and speak more candidly about our experience of the divine nature. Geach abandons omnipotence quite light-heartedly, claiming that it is not consistent either with most Christian theology or with biblical teachings. He affirms instead the notion of God as almighty.[10] If one's overriding consideration is Christian orthodoxy, that word with its pious overtones has a real advantage. But I suspect that a philosophical analysis would result in a stretching and taxing of that word until it came just as close to the breaking point. Hartshorne, typical of the process theologians, characterizes omnipotence as a theological mistake.[11] Perhaps the lesson is that a God who is able to create the heavens and the earth, to instill the order and the beauty they clearly have, and to inspire the moral, aesthetic, and religious qualities which the best of humans have, is amply great to deserve the esteem of philosophers and the worship and devotion of religious persons even if that God cannot plausibly be said to be infinite in power.

---

[10]Ibid.

[11]Charles Hartshorne, *Omnipotence and Other Theological Mistakes* (Albany: State University of New York Press: 1984).

Meland's Post-Liberal Empirical Method in Theology

Tyron Inbody

It is commonplace to speak of contemporary theology as post-Christian, post-Enlightenment, post-Newtonian, post-modern, post-liberal, and even post-theological. The modern quest for clarity and certainty has dissipated in the face of growing skepticism about our capacity to establish knowledge in secure foundations, whether those be the foundations of authority, rationality, or experience.

Two important contributions to the quest for a post-liberal methodology have been made by Gordon Kaufman in *An Essay on Theological Method,* and by George Lindbeck in *The Nature of Doctrine: Religion and Theology in a Postliberal Age.*

In Kaufman's view the predominant characteristic of liberal methodology is that it begins theological reflection by an appeal to religious experience. Liberal theology claims a pre-conceptual base in experience, regardless of whether such experience is thought of as an experience of a special object (such as the holy or God) or as a special quality of experience (such as absolute dependence or oneness with the universe). Instead, he argues, tradition and language provide the actual basis of theology, for "the raw pre-conceptual and pre-linguistic ground of religious experience is simply not available to us for direct exploration, description, or interpretation, and therefore it cannot provide us with a starting-point for theological work" (7).

The proper business of theology, then, is to take control of our construction of a world through which we can create more humane meaning and significance. The idea of God is an imaginative construct which helps to unify the totality of experience. The issue for theological method is not truth as the correspondence of our concepts with percepts, whether given in classical theology through objective descriptions of doctrine or in liberalism through our direct perceptual receptivity, but is rather coherence and the pragmatic usefulness of the concepts of world and God (71-72).

George Lindbeck is even more pointed in his criticism of liberal methodology. All such methodologies, he contends, are characterized as "experiential-expressive," by which he means they understand theology as noninformative and nondiscursive symbols of inner feelings, attitudes, or existential orientations. His cultural-linguistic alternative locates the basis of religion in a cultural system. The function of theological doctrines is their usage as communally authoritative rules of discourse, attitude, and action. Lindbeck does not deny there is a relation between experience and language, but the order of inner and the outer in liberal religious theory is reversed. Language, the means of communication and expression, is a precondition, a culturally formed a priori for the possibility of experience, including religious experience. "We cannot identify, describe, or recognize experience qua experience without the use of signs and symbols. These are necessary even for what the depth psychologist speaks of as 'unconscious' or 'subconscious' experiences, or for what the phenomenologist describes as prereflective ones. In short, it is necessary to have the means for expressing an experience in order to have it" (36-37). The effect of Lindbeck's proposal is to abandon the notion that the source of religious thought in any sense rests in experience prior to language and culture.

Neither of these post-liberal proposals takes account of the alternative of radical empiricism, or what Bernard Meland sometimes calls "empirical realism," as a basis on which to explore the relation of experience, language, and culture. While Kaufman and Lindbeck are deeply aware of the relativity of all human constructs, they seem not to give serious consideration to the empirical account of experience rooted in pragmatism and American naturalism. "At issue, finally, is not simply the question of the relativity of worlds to words, a harmless assumption, generally granted, but the question of how far are we to take this assumption? Assuming a dialectical relation between experience and interpretation, the problem becomes one of critically incorporating both as a paired phenomenon in a theory that does not displace either by the other" (Frankenberry, 67).

Bernard Meland's radical empirical method in theology and his empirical realism constitute an alternative to the impasse between liberal foundationalism, the search for a basis of beliefs in some item of knowledge that is self-evident or beyond doubt, and the implicit relativism of recent anti-foundationalism. His account of the richness of experience leads him to a subtle and complex account of the relation between experience, language, and culture. What results is an "objective relativism," a view which stands between a naive foundationalism, on the one hand, and a subjectivism which portrays experience as merely the product of language and culture, on the other. My thesis is that Meland's radical empirical realism constitutes a genuine post-liberal theology through the way he conceives the relations between pure experience, history, language, and culture to be internal and of a piece.

1. Experience in the Radical Mode

Meland's empirical method in theology provides an alternative either to the abstract concept of experience in classical empiricism or to language and culture cut off from primal experience in some post-liberal theologies. The reason Meland's empirical realism is a successful alternative both to the older liberalism of the enclosed subject and a post-liberal theology of autonomous interpretation is that his radical empiricism represents a deeper understanding of experience.

Meland's liberalism is not an appeal to religious experience or even to a dimension of experience he calls religious but to experience as such in its depth. The problem for the empirical theologian is that experience as conceived by modern empiricists is thought to consist only of sense experience. Hume, for example, taught that all of our ideas follow from and copy sense impressions. He enunciated three rules of empiricism (Frankenberry, 38-45). First, all our simple ideas in their first appearance are derived from simple impressions. Second, experience consists of atomistic, solitary impressions, so different impressions are not only distinguishable but separable. Third, these separable impressions of sensations exhibit no necessary connection; their relations to entities in the external world become attached only by practice, custom, or habit. The result is that "all relations and dynamic continuities were supposed to be foreign to experience, mere by-products of dubious validity" (Frankenberry, 44).

Meland claims that Humean empiricism is not empirical enough. Drawing on James' radically empirical notion of "the perceptual flux" and organismic thought based on the new physics and emergent evolution, he claims that the most immediate empirical datum is not sense experience but the sheer act of existing. Experience as a lived bodily event is richer than either sense experience, linguistic expression, or the conceptualization of experience.

In contrast to modes of thought which begin with a categorial scheme employed as a literal description of reality, empirical realism begins with "the primacy of perception." Perception is deeper than consciousness and richer than conception. The perceptual field is the ongoing stream of occurrences in which we participate bodily. The idea of pure experience or the perceptual flux "conveys the fullness of concrete ingredients, and it renders the internal access to meaning as knowledge by acquaintance infinitely richer than the knowledge about acquired through conceptualization" (FET, 296).

The range of meaning in empirical realism, however, is not "a penumbra of mystery that simply supervenes experience; it is a mystery and depth of the immediacies themselves" (RF, 223). Experience as lived conveys a contextual ground of relations which is part of every concrete experience and constitutes a holistic event which is more ultimate than our conceptions. Relations are not imposed by the mind on reality. Relations are experienceable and experienced in a radically empirical view of the world (FFS, 55). They are felt as immediately as anything else and are "as real as the terms they relate" (Frankenberry, 86). When perception instead of sensation or conception is given priority, experience is seen to include transitions, activity, as well as the sense of beauty, a "more," aversion and attraction, and quality (Dean, 36). This contextual or relational ground of any event is seen to be a datum in its own right prior to and independent of language and thought.

In radical empiricism this contextuality of experience appears at "the fringe of consciousness." Deeper than all forms of conscious experience are the happenings and configurations of events in which the relationships and complexity of meaning provide a depth of context which defies ready observation or analysis (FC, 39; RF, 93). Perceptual experience is "a richer event than conception can possibly be, providing every occurrence of awareness with a 'fringe,' implying a 'More,' much of which persistently evades conceptualization" (FFS, 43). The primary and initial cognitive response to this contextual depth at the fringe of consciousness is appreciative awareness, an openness to the range of data beyond our comprehension, which includes maximum receptivity, identification, and discrimination (HEHS. ch. 5).

Existence in the context of radical empiricism, then, embraces simultaneously dimensions of ultimacy and immediacy. Ultimacy is not a supervening reality which casts its shadow on experience or invades experience from outside. It is a dimension of experience within the Creative Passage which "transpires to give depth of meaning to the human situation as immediately discerned within our structured experience" (FFS, 174). Ultimacy and immediacy traffic together.

2. Experience and Culture

Although experience as a concrete event of the mutual inherence of body and relational context is the primary level of the meaning of experience for a radical empiricist, Meland does not restrict his understanding of experience to the subjective life of the individual. One of the most distinctive contributions of Meland to post-liberal methodology is his insistence that pure experience and its contextual depth are available as more than a preconscious flux awaiting conceptualization. Experience in its fuller meaning is a perception of the depth of relations within a larger world. "Subjectivity, while still of prime importance as a dimension of experience, is never viewed just as a closed track of internal reflection or reverie, but as immediate access to what opens out into the world as lived experience" (FET, 288). Individuals are integrated into a fuller orbit of meaning and valuation as they emerge from their individual tracks of perception and participate in the depth of experience within their culture.

The immediacies of experience are conveyed simultaneously within individual and culture. A persisting inheritance of contextual relations within the stream of experience is transmitted culturally as bodily feeling from age to age (FFS, 183-85). Given the relational character of experience, lived experience is to be thought of as a patterned occurrence as well as a channeling of feeling within individual tracks of perception. "Lived experience is simultaneously a patterned occurrence exemplifying and bodying forth the stream of ever recurring concretions as a communal event and an intensified channeling of that stream into individuated life-spans, each with its own legacy of inherited possibilities as given in the stream of experience and with its unique fund of possibilities as an emerging event" (FC, 56).

Another way to state this is to say that experience has both a personal and a social character. "Experience is always an internal ordering of responses within individual lives, but it assumes a corporate character. This is so because individuals exist in relationship with one another within certain geographical bounds, and partake of common occurrences which in turn give rise to specific instances of conscious experience" (RF, 210). There is an inner channeling of events in individual memories, sensibilities, and bodily characteristics which make up the psyche, but there is also an outer channeling of experience in the form of social custom and public practices.

Culture neither simply produces experience nor simply expresses experience but exists as a mode of reciprocal interaction between pure experience and structured meaning through the medium of language. Language is the primary means of culture in conveying the depth of experience and shaping our encounter with the deeper realities of lived experience. The forms of culture, which embody the contextual character of lived experience beyond the individual tracks of subjective experience, is internalized by the individual by way of symbolization (FC, 57).

When experience is defined as a relational concept, the term culture becomes intrinsic to the idea of experience. Culture is one ''particularized fruition within the realm of experience'' (RF, 214). As a component of experience, culture is ''the human flowering of existing structures and facilities, becoming manifest as an ordered way life in the imaginative activities and creations of a people, their arts and crafts, their architecture, their furniture and furnishings, their costumes and designs, their literature, their public and private ceremonies, both religious and political. It is in their formative ideas, giving direction to their educational efforts and customs, as well as to their religious notions and practices, their social graces and manners; in their habits of eating and body care; in their modes of livelihood and the social organization that follows from them'' (RF, 212).

The key to Meland's idea of culture as it relates to radical empiricism is his notion of the structure of experience. Lived experience, ''the primal flux of immediacy,'' is something more than ''an ambiguous preconscious flux, awaiting conceptualization'' (FFS, 297). Experience is always an internal ordering of responses within individual lives, an inner channeling of the events of individual sensibilities which make up the psyche of the person. But experience also assumes a corporate character, an outer channeling of accumulated meanings. ''These inner and outer dimensions of accumulated valuations and meanings, together with the physical qualities that give them actuality and limited form, comprise the structure of experience that is operative in any period of time or generation within a given society'' (RF, 210). The realities of the depth of relations are present not only in the primal context but also in the patterns of experience within any culture.

Lived experience, then, is never simply a sensory act or response; it is also a structured occurrence. It is not simply the individual response to events but is also the accumulation of effects within a structure of experience. This structure of experience forms the living nexus in which all individual experience participates. What is noteworthy in this larger concept of experience is that structure, valuation, and meaning are already present in each individual event and person; they are not added to experience. ''What we perceive in this vital immediacy is not a chaos of unformed impressions awaiting form through conceptualization. We live out of a world that is given, out of structures of meaning, already bodied forth, yet susceptible of reconception and reformulation, even re-creation. But the freedom to partake of a new historical situation is in a way defined and given by the historical fabric of occurrences which now define one's intentionality in this historical moment of time'' (FET, 298). In short, experience includes a social and cultural world. This is another dimension of the meaning of the phrases ''new realism,'' or ''empirical realism,'' namely, the ''realities outside of and other than self-experience, existing independently of it, though engaging it both continuously and in intermittent encounters'' (RF, 193). The imagery of self-experience that dominated earlier liberal thought has given way to a strong sense of otherness that is conveyed in lived experience in its primal and cultural forms.

The structure of experience is the most elemental level of meaning in any culture (FC, 96). The concept is rooted in James's version of radical empiricism and Whitehead's notion of causal efficacy, which imply that experience is continuous and that the meanings that have emerged persist in some form to give character to every successive event. The structure of experience is shaped by the ethos of a culture, the complex of sensibilities, the sentiments and the dispositions of a community (RF, 44), and by the mythos of a culture, the persistent reservoir of psychical energy and sensitivity and persisting pattern of meaning and valuation imaginatively projected through metaphor and drama (FFS, 109, 177). Mythos is not to be equated with myth ("an elemental ingredient in mythos") or mythology ("a secondary level of imaginative reflection within the mythical mode"), but is the pattern of sensibilities projected through metaphor (RF, 44). The elemental myth of a culture gives shape to this cultural mythos. It conveys to conscious experience something of the depth of awareness which would otherwise remain at the level of bodily feeling. While mythologies are expendable, myth, as a persisting expression of the primal response of sensitivity and wonder in a culture, is not (SMC, 125).

The structure of experience integrates the individual life of the person with the "fund of valuations" related to the ethos and mythos of a culture through the shaping of perception. Perception is simultaneously a bodily event in which the data are freshly encountered through participation, and a valuating event coterminous with the act of individuation by which what is encountered is felt, grasped, apprehended, valued, and finally interpreted within a frame of meaning that is organic to the life of the person (RF, 173). The cycle of responses of a culture give rise to a complex of symbols and signs which contribute to a sense of orientation and familiarity. "Like the genetic code, operating at the level of physical inheritance, this funded social inheritance becomes a given, expressing itself concretely in each individual existence as a past selectively merging with immediacies to emerge as a present moment of living in intentional acts" (FET, 288).

Perceptual experience is apprehended and interpreted through these frames of meaning. An individual internalizes the structure of experience, this nurturing context of meanings, feelings, and valuations, through symbolization. "Now the personality of the individual, existing in this structure of experience, is formed by a subtle and almost imperceptible process of taking into its consciousness and feelings, the cultural meanings and values thus transmitted. The process is called symbolization" (FC, 57). Language is not merely a tool used by the autonomous subject of experience to express the experience of the subject but is involved in a reciprocal task of conveying the fullness and shaping the meaning of primal experience. In addition to the organic structure, then, the resources of culture internalized through symbolization determine the nature of the experience of the individual. The bifurcation of experience, language, and culture is overcome in radical empiricism.

3. Meland's Post-Liberal Thelogy

In two significant ways Meland's empirical theology continues the liberal project in theology. First, he does not abandon the critical, post-authoritative or authoritarian stance in theological method which liberalism initiated. Authority rests in reality itself in its depth and richness, not in an authority who can prescribe or proscribe beliefs about reality. His appeal to experience in its depth, language, community, and culture as sources in his empirical method is quite different than the post-liberal appeal to the authority of the religious community or the authority of its language system as the basis for theology.

Second, Meland attempts to ground theology in experience. Our theological beliefs about reality depend on an empirical description of the depth and richness of reality as it is experienced in individual, cult, and culture. Although his concept of experience is more social, in both the ontological and cultural senses, than the older liberals' notion of experience as an isolatable ground of certainty within the consciousness of the individual subject, his theological method cannot be understood apart from the liberal appeal to experience as the source and authority in theology.

Nevertheless, Meland's liberal method is also post-liberal in significant ways. He speaks of his method as one which has moved through not back of liberalism (FFS, 142-43). Long before the current phrase "post-liberal" became fashionable as a way of describing the pragmatic, cultural, linguistic, and textual approaches to theology, Meland's empirical realism was critical of some of the basic characteristics and themes of liberal theology. Although he says in his last book, "I find myself moving into a post-liberal methodology" (165), that statement could have been made as readily of his first book written in 1934, which was a challenge to the restriction to the subject and mental enclosures of liberalism.

Throughout his writings, Meland's empirical method is post-liberal in at least three senses. First, his stress on realism or otherness throughout the entire corpus of writing makes him a thorough, persistent critic of all forms of liberalism which reduce experience and reality to the subjectivity of the individual, regardless of whether that subjectivity be rooted in the feelings or ideas of the person. From *Modern Man's Worship* through *Seeds of Redemption* and *Faith and Culture* to *Fallible Forms and Symbols,* the theme of objectivity or otherness (later referred to as realism) dominates his thinking.

Earlier, historic liberalism, which was basically Kantian in its philosophical method, can be characterized as an enclosure within self-experience, the result of which was to circumscribe every meaning to the human, mental sphere (RF, 196-97). Empirical realism, which "lifts up the simultaneous presence of an ultimate dimension of reality and the humanly available immediacies within the stream of experience" (FFS, 123), claims, like all forms of neoorthodox theology which had also reacted against the limitation of reality to the human equation, that otherness is real. But unlike most other post-liberal theologies which were dominant throughout Meland's career which tried to replace the subjectivity and mentalism of liberal idealism with an otherness that cast its shadow upon experience, cult, and culture from beyond this world, otherness in Meland's thought is incorporated in the notion of withness, so that ultimacy and immediacy traffic together as the depth of concrete experience.

Second, it must be granted that there is a sense in which Meland continues a kind of foundationalism characteristic of liberal methodology. His effort to ground theological method in experience, and particularly his appeal to the primal context or primal ground of experience, not only sounds like the language of one who is searching for the foundations of faith and theology behind concept and formulation but is an argument that faith and theology are indeed grounded in a reality which is deeper and richer in context than feelings, language, ideas, text, cult, and culture. If any attempt to ground theology in something more than the human equation is foundationalism, then Meland is a foundationalist and grounds his appeal in "an experienceable base" (GDN, 121) as conceived, both metaphysically and culturally, in radical empiricism.

However, if foundationalism is defined, as it is in most anti-foundationalism today, such as neopragmatism, linguistic theory, historicism, and deconstruction, as "the thesis that our beliefs can be warranted or justified by appealing to some item of knowledge that is self-evident or beyond doubt," (Frankenberry, 4), then Meland's work is anti-foundational at its core. Certainty is not only denied as an impossible achievement because of the limitations of the human structure; the lure of certainty is eschewed as a search for the kind of ultimacy that is not available in radical empiricism. "The Absolute was a creation of this modern, liberal period, supplanting the authority of the church and Scriptures. For the Absolute implies a rational certainty established by logical argument out of concern to find points of fixity and ultimate reference in a world of finitude and change" (FFS, 72; ATA).

Meland's relativism is nearly as thoroughgoing as most other post-liberal theologies. He discovers no certainty in any human equation. However, his relativism rests not only on the fact of cultural pluralism, but in the relativity of reality itself as it is given in experience. His solution to the problem of relativism is to appeal to ultimacy within the immediacy of experience itself in its various dimensions, individual, cult, and culture (SMC, 151-3, 161-2). The answer is not absolutism or even foundationalism in the strict sense, but relativity itself. "For relativity implies interrelatedness. . . . There is no immediacy in history or experience that is without its ultimate depth, its ultimate reference. The appeal from any religious witness, while it exudes the conditioning of its cultural environment, speaks also out of the depths of its own encounter with what sustains and judges its witness. Limitation and ambiguity imply an intermingling of our immediacies with ultimacy, not insulation from it. The fact that our human formulations in thought and effort are not to be taken as direct accounts or descriptions of what is ultimate and real in experience is not to be understood to mean that we stand dissociated from these depths of reality in experience" (RF, 164, 168).

Third, Meland is close to some of the post-liberal methodologies in his emphasis on the relation of language and culture to experience. As we have seen above in analyzing his concept of experience, he does not conceive of experience as isolated within the conscious subject. It has both metaphysical depth and cultural breadth. This concept of experience places him closer to the post-liberal theologies than to historic liberalism in the sense that the post-liberals stress the reciprocity between language and culture.

Experience, for Meland, however, is not reducible to language and culture, a reduction which Kaufman and Lindbeck come close to making. Even when experience is not explicitly reduced to an epiphenomenon of linguistic systems, the failure to develop a theory of the relation of experience and culture leaves the most fundamental issue between liberal and post-liberal theologies not only unresolved but even unexplored.

The genius of Meland's empirical method is that it has explored precisely this problem in great detail. He maintains the liberal project to the degree that language and culture are involved in metaphysical and empirical descriptions of experience. On the other hand, Meland does not have a concept of "pure experience" as an aspect of the human equation which could serve as foundation for clear and certain knowledge independent of the ambiguities and relativity of all linguistic and cultural systems. Experience, for Meland, is not an "autonomous" or "pure" or "abstract" concept but is a dimension of reality which partakes simultaneously of the depth of relations that constitute reality itself and the human forms of subjectivity, language, and culture.

Empirical realists deny foundationalism to the extend that the term designates the search for a transcendental starting point, but empiricists claim that to deny foundationalism is not to deny every form of realism. Empirical realism is a form of realism without an appeal to monistic foundations. Experience makes contact with reality, and an empirical account of experience points to a context and depth of relations beyond us on which we can count to support, correct, and redeem us. Unlike Kaufman and Lindbeck, who imply the kind of relativism which reduces experience entirely to the subjective or linguistic worlds, the empirical realist defends a kind of realism which simultaneously encompasses nature, individual, experience, language, and culture. The empirical realist is a relativist without subjectivism and a realist without foundationalism.

The significance of Meland's appeal to experience within a radical empirical framework for the various post-modern formulations of theological method, then, is that he provides a concept of experience which does not force one into an either/or choice, either the liberal appeal to pure experience or the post-liberal claim that experience, both of immediacy and ultimacy, is simply a product of the language or texts or other forms and symbols of culture. These cannot be either/or choices for an empirical realist because experience is a richer and more social concept than most liberal theologies conceived, including both a depth of relations and linguistic and cultural embodiments of that depth, and is more realistic than most relativists conceived, including contextual relations that exist beyond language. Experience and culture have an inherent connection with the depth of reality and a structure of experience that grounds all our fallible forms. When post-liberal theologies begin to take radical empiricism seriously as a mode of empirical grounding for theology, it may discover that empirical, linguistic, and cultural modes of theology are not discreet methods, perspectives, or options, but indeed are aspects or elements of a realism that provide a thoroughly empirical context for theology.

References

Dean, William
  1986   *American Religious Empiricism*. New York: SUNY Press.
Frankenberry, Nancy
  1987   *Religion and Radical Empiricism*. New York: SUNY Press.
Kaufman, Gordon
  1975   *An Essay on Theological Method*. Missoula MT: Scholars Press.
Lindbeck, George
  1984   *The Nature of Doctrine: Religion and Theology in a Postliberal Age*. Philadelphia:
          Westminster Press.
Meland, Bernard
  1934   MMW *Modern Man's Worship*. New York: Harper and Brothers.
  1947   SR *Seeds of Redemption*. New York: Macmillan.
  1953   HEHS *Higher Education and the Human Spirit*. Chicago: University of Chicago
          Press.
  1955   FC *Faith and Culture*. London: George Allen and Unwin.
  1962   RF *Realities of Faith*. New York: Oxford University Press.
  1965   ATA "Alternative to Absolutes." *Religion in Life* 34/3 (Summer).
  1966   SMC *Secularization of Modern Cultures*. New York: Oxford University Press.
  1969   FET *Future of Empirical Theology*. Chicago: University of Chicago Press.
  1974   GDN "Grace as a Dimension of Nature." *Journal of Religion* 54.
  1976   FFS *Fallible Forms and Symbols*. Philadelphia: Fortress Press.

Religion Generates Moral Energy
Reinhold Niebuhr's Use of William James

J. Dell Johnson

Abstract. In this paper I examine Reinhold Niebuhr's view of the social relevance of religion, a view Niebuhr borrowed from William James. That religion generated "moral" or "spiritual energy" was a key element in James's religious philosophy. Niebuhr used this idea in his analysis of the efforts of the social worker and the political activist to build a just society.

In part I, I give a summary of what James meant by his view that religion generates moral energy. In part II, I trace Niebuhr's specific use of this idea. I conclude with a criticism of Niebuhr's inconsistent application of his view to the problems facing industrial workers and Afro-Americans.

By showing that Niebuhr's use of James made it possible for him to arrive at a political understanding of religion's social relevance, I provide an explanation of the limited value Niebuhr's mature religious thought has for contemporary political theology inasmuch as he abandoned the Jamesian view in his later writings.

There have been several recent attempts to show that Reinhold Niebuhr's thought has continuing relevance for contemporary political theology.[1] Such attempts are of limited success inasmuch as Niebuhr abandoned one key element of any political theology which one would deem to be relevant today, namely, a theology which recognizes the need of oppressed groups to use their faith in their efforts to secure an end to their oppression. Niebuhr's early thought contained such a view. His mature thought did not. It is in his early writings that one finds a truly relevant view of faith's role in the quest for justice.

---

[1]Roger L. Shinn, "Reinhold Niebuhr: A Reverberating Voice," *Christian Century* 103 (1-8 January 1986): 15-17; Robert McAfee Brown, "Reinhold Niebuhr: His Theology in the 1980s," *Christian Century* 103 (22 January 1986): 66-68; Michael Novak, "Reinhold Niebuhr: Model for Neo-Conservatives," ibid., 69-71.

In his early years Niebuhr was concerned with the extent to which religion could serve as a resource in the quest for social and economic justice. The depth of his religious liberalism was evident in his view that religion did contribute in some way to the resolution of social problems. Like many heirs of the Social Gospel, Niebuhr viewed modern society as in need of redemption from its many injustices. He thought that religion had a role to play in the struggle to improve the social situation.

In 1932 Niebuhr began to abandon much of this liberal faith. He denied that a just society was realizable on earth, but held that it could be approximated by a social struggle that had as its goal the balancing of power between the privileged class and oppressed groups.[2]

In his concern for justice Niebuhr tried to determine what were the rational and religious resources available to those who were involved in the social struggle. He also wanted to find out what limitations in human imagination and self-interest inhibit the drive for social change. Much later he would define justice as the approximation of love under the conditions of sin, but in 1932 he viewed justice as the equal distribution of political and economic power.

With this overview of what Niebuhr meant by justice one can more easily see why Niebuhr borrowed from James an idea about religion's social function. James provided Niebuhr with a view of religion as an tool for change when it gave individuals the strength to persevere in their quest for justice.

Let me turn first to an examination of what James meant by his view that religion provided motive power for social change.

I

William James wrote often about his view that religion functions both to unify and to generate "spiritual" or "moral energy."[3] James thought that one way an individual reached any moral goal was to believe in the ultimate triumph of that goal. To fight against war or to struggle against the entrenched power of the rich required that the individual have the energy to stay in the battle. To firmly believe in the ultimate vindication of one's cause, James thought, validated the truth or rightness of that cause insofar as energetic effort was eventually matched by some measure of its realization.

Although James recognized that it would take more that one individual and longer than one lifetime to finally validate the rightness of any particular social goal, he was convinced that humans did not strive for high spiritual or moral objectives without

---

[2]*Moral Man and Immoral Society: A Study in Ethics and Politics* (New York: Charles Scribner's Sons, 1932) 200-30.

[3]"The Sentiment of Rationality," and "The Will to Believe," in *The Moral Philosophy of William James*, ed. John K. Roth (New York: Thomas Y. Crowell Company; Apollo Books, 1969) 132-66, 192-213; "Reason and Faith," and "The Energies of Men," in *The Works of William James*, 11 vols., Frederick H. Burkhardt, gen. ed. (Cambridge MA: Harvard University Press, 1975) vol. 11: *Essays in Religion and Morality* (1982) 124-28, 129-46; *Varieties of Religious Experience* (New York: New American Library; Mentor Books, 1958) 162 and 317.

such a faith in the final attainment of their goals. This faith in the ultimate triumph of one's ethical and spiritual values was a central principle in the religious philosophy of William James. It was his eschatological principle.[4]

II

It is this eschatological principle that the young Reinhold Niebuhr used. He first used it in his 1930 Forbes Lectures which he delivered at the New School of Social Work in New York. These lectures he published in 1932 as *The Contribution of Religion to Social Work.*[5] In this book Niebuhr described the many ways in which religion supported and sometimes hindered the efforts of the social worker. He argued, for example, that religion ordered and unified human lives, offered a "sense of security" for those in dire conditions, projected an ideal of a universal human family, and provided a basis for the social worker's sense of vocation.[6] In general, he said, religion expanded the natural inclination of people to perform acts of charity. When one looked back at the communal sharing of the early Christian church, one could see the "heights of social responsibility [to which] men can rise when driven by religious passion."[7] Niebuhr meant by religious passion the zeal or energy one could muster for the difficult task of serving the social needs of people. He explained the way religion generated this energy as follows:

> Religion, with its sense of dependence upon a Supreme Being, with its emotional commitment to the will of that person, [and] with its belief in the benevolent aid of that person for the achievement of our highest aims, is able to create a white heat of sublime emotion which devours all lesser passions and interests, leaving the soul purged of its distracting and confusing preoccupations and redirected toward the highest goal that it is able to conceive.[8]

The self that is unified by religious emotions is more centered and directed toward one goal than a self confused and caught in a web of competing claims and interests. Niebuhr felt that religion inspired an optimistic attitude toward the improvement of life and this process of "stereotyping optimism" enabled both the social worker and his or her clients to reach beyond the limits of their ordinary strivings to obtain results they would not be able to produce by their own uninspired efforts.

---

[4]In "The Sentiment of Rationality" James called it "the subjective method, the method of belief based on desire" (157). He also referred to this willingness to act energetically to advance a cause without any prior verification of its worthiness as the "serious" or "strenuous mood" (ibid., 86). Or, in another place, he dubbed it a "faith-ladder" by which one moves from holding a thing as "fit to be true" to holding for oneself that "it shall be true" and that "I will treat it as if it were true" ("Reason and Faith," in *Essays in Religion and Morality*, 125).

[5]New York: Columbia University Press.

[6]*The Contribution of Religion*, 39-44 and 63-75.

[7]Ibid., 3.

[8]Ibid., 39.

Religion was described by Niebuhr as the basis for optimism about life despite life's difficulties and tragedies: "Religion is the hope that grows out of despair," he said. "It is the ultimate optimism which follows in the wake of a thorough pessimism."[9]

Here we glimpse one of Niebuhr's earliest uses of the Jamesian eschatological principle. Niebuhr found in James the assertion that one of the fruits of the religious life is its unification and intensification of "personal energy."[10] Like James, Niebuhr asserted that religion is beneficial primarily in its effects upon human emotions and motivations. Religion is, Niebuhr said, "an affair of the emotions" which "animates the religious devotee" by making him or her capable of "a nobility which the rationalist can never compass."[11] "Religion is madness," he said, and "it may be noble madness," but one did not find it among those cool and calm thinkers who are unmoved by religious sentiments.

In anticipation of his later criticism of social thinkers such as John Dewey and John Childs, Niebuhr here contrasted the energizing capacity of a dynamic religious faith with the enervating capacity of abstract thought. Religious faith provided a motive power in believers which he felt was lacking in the activities of those whom Schleiermacher once called religion's "cultured despisers." For Niebuhr, as for James, faith motivates, but reason stagnates. His distinction between the pragmatic value of faith and reason, of the priority of heart over head, became one of the enduring features of his thought.[12]

For Niebuhr, both ancient Judaism and early Christianity were examples of the capacity of religion to generate energy for social change. Middle class religion in America was too complacent and too focused on individual sins to be of much help in the social sphere. The one modern example of religion's motive power he found to be adequate was the religion of the proletarian. This was the proletarian's belief that the ultimate goal of Communism, the creation of a classless society, was attainable. Niebuhr viewed this as a kind of eschatological faith:

[Communism, he said,] is fanatic. It has one goal, an equalitarian ideal for society, and everything else is sacrificed for that goal. It, like all religion, is constantly saying, "This one thing I do." That is what ought to be said if we have found the one thing worth doing. But alas! it is so difficult to know if, and when, we have.[13]

[9]Ibid., 72.

[10]*Varieties of Religious Experience,* 162.

[11]*The Contribution of Religion to Social Work,* 57. In his essay, "The Unhappy Intellectuals," *Atlantic Monthly* 143 (June 1929): 794, Niebuhr said: "The function of religion is to preserve life's highest irrationality, the urge toward the ideal."

[12]I argued this point in an unpublished paper, "Reinhold Niebuhr's Realism and Three of Its Critics," presented at a round table discussion, annual meeting of the American Academy of Religion, Chicago, Illinois, 21 December 1982.

[13]*The Contribution of Religion,* 60. Niebuhr's religious interpretation of Communism is discussed in Dennis P. McCann, *Christian Realism and Liberation Theology: Practical Theologies in Creative Conflict* (Maryknoll NY: Orbis Books, 1981) 28-37.

Here Niebuhr seemed to view Communism with both admiration and scepticism. He admired its expression of the passionate drive that a religious eschatology gave to individuals. Yet he also seemed to question whether Communism was the best expression of such a religious zeal in the interest of social justice. He implied that one could not be certain that the right set of eschatological concepts was to be found there. He viewed the religion of the proletarians positively because of the "apocalyptic" element in its vision of the just or "redeemed" society,[14] but he did not portray Communism then nor later as an unqualified good. What impressed him was "the tremendous moral energy which that vision inspires" for it is proof, he said, of the fact that "men do not move toward high goals without religious passion."[15] Thus, for Niebuhr, Communism, or "proletarian religion," as he sometimes called it, was, like "all vital religion" in that "it does create an energy which is beyond the capacities of rationalists."[16]

What I have shown thus far is that in his interpretation of religion's role in social work, Niebuhr used James's view that religion generates moral energy. For Niebuhr at this time religion alone had "the power to destroy the old and to build the new."[17] That Niebuhr used the eschatological principle of William James in *The Contribution of Religion to Social Work* is clear. But this was not his only use of it. In the other book that he published in 1932, *Moral Man and Immoral Society,* Niebuhr also made use of the theme. I turn now to an examination of that use of it in the latter work.

Niebuhr opened *Moral Man and Immoral Society* with an introduction in which he attacked the social strategies of educators, such as John Dewey, and social scientists, such as John Childs.[18] He suggested that "moralists, religious and secular" trusted too much in the social efficacy of reason combined with "a religiously inspired goodwill."[19] He viewed them as naive in their reliance on the objective analysis of a social problem and in their assessment of the degree of religious sentimentality within the general population which might contribute to social change. Such moralists did not realize the depth and pervasiveness of human self-interest, especially in its collective or group manifestations of nations, classes, and races. This failure of the social theorists led Niebuhr to offer a corrective vision which distinguished between "the morals of groups and those of individuals."[20] Niebuhr proposed to show

---

[14]*The Contribution,* 91.

[15]Ibid., 92-93.

[16]Ibid., 93.

[17]Ibid.

[18]Niebuhr knew each of the figures he had criticized. John Childs taught at Columbia Teachers College and was a member, along with Niebuhr, of the Union for Democratic Action, a political coalition dedicated to social change. John Dewey taught at Columbia University across the street from Niebuhr at Union Theological Seminary. He also chaired the League for Independent Political Action, a third-party organization on whose executive committee Niebuhr served. See Richard Fox, *Reinhold Niebuhr: A Biography* (New York: Pantheon Books, 1985) 197.

[19]*Moral Man and Immoral Society,* xii.

[20]Ibid., xxii.

that "moral and rational factors" alone did not lead to social change. The self-interest of human groups was so strong, he said, that "covert types of coercion and force" must be injected into social conflicts if change is to occur. Social conflict is "inevitable," he argued, and in such conflicts the force and power of the privileged must be met by the use of force and the quest for power by oppressed groups.[21]

In his discussion of the relative merits of reason, religion, power and force, Niebuhr once again used the eschatological principle of William James. Groups, such as the industrial workers and Afro-Americans, needed something more than mere rational analysis of their situation or the goodwill of the public. What they needed, Niebuhr said, was sufficient "morale" to pursue change in spite of the overwhelming odds against them. Such a morale was the result, he said, of "the right dogmas, symbols and emotionally potent oversimplifications."[22] The industrial workers would need to believe "more firmly in the justice and in the probable triumph of their cause, than any impartial science would give them the right to believe, *if they are to have the energy* to contest the power of the strong."[23] Such "motive force" was not, in Niebuhr's view, a product of "the cool objectivity of science."

Niebuhr's mention here of the energy oppressed groups would need to strive for justice was another use of James's view. He again rejected reason as an effective means for achieving social change and advocated instead the energizing power of morale based on faith in the ultimate triumph of one's cause. This faith needed to be grounded in appropriate "dogmas, symbols and . . . oversimplifications" if it were to inspire the "morale," "motive force," or "energy" oppressed groups needed.

Niebuhr argued, however, that the workers should not place their ultimate trust in the "victory of revolutionary socialism" envisioned by Marxists. As a pacifist, he rejected violent revolution as a means of social amelioration. Instead, he recommended an "evolutionary," nonviolent form of parliamentary socialism, based in part on a model of socialism he had encountered during his trips to England and through his friendship with the British socialist, Sir Stafford Cripps. Niebuhr envisioned the creation of a coalition of workers, farmers, and their sympathizers from society at large, working together to improve society.[24]

In a more critical analysis of socialism than he made in *The Contribution of Religion to Social Work*, Niebuhr stated that some socialists may not recognize that faith was needed in the efforts to achieve their goals. He noted that many socialists had become "too completely rationalistic to understand the roots of human fervor," namely, a vital religious apocalypticism. Such socialists had unwittingly fallen into "liberalism," which by now Niebuhr viewed as a bankrupt political philosophy. In the process of this ideological degeneration socialists had relinquished the "eschatological element" in their position. To give up hope in the realization of their "ultimate goal," namely, an equitable and just society, meant the "sacrifice of

---

[21]Ibid., xv.

[22]Ibid.

[23]Ibid., xv; emphasis added.

[24]Ibid., 218.

[socialism's] religious fervor and the consequent loss of [its] motive power."[25] By compromising socialism's "moral potency," socialists suffered a real loss in energizing power. Every increase in "rationality," brought a decrease in morale. Niebuhr explained:

> The naive faith of the proletarian is the faith of the man of action. Rationality belongs to the cool observers. There is of course an element of illusion in the faith of the proletarian, as there is in all faith. *But it is a necessary illusion, without which some truth is obscured.*[26]

By "illusion" Niebuhr here meant what James had called "over-beliefs."[27] Such a belief affirmed hypotheses which may have little immediate empirical support, but which were validated when faith produced the desired result. For James, "the most interesting and valuable thing about a [person] was his[/her] over-beliefs."[28] Niebuhr, following James, believed the most interesting thing about a social philosophy was its necessary "illusions." Niebuhr had translated James's personal energy into a more political view of the energizing capacity of religion. In *Moral Man* he incorporated James's conception into his own politics of social conflict. He concluded this book by reaffirming the need for these illusions, but added that members of society should not expect to build "individual ladders to heaven and leave the total human enterprise unredeemed of its excesses and corruptions."[29] "The most important of these illusions," he said, "is that the collective life of mankind can achieve perfect justice." In a passage which has all the prophetic power of the very zeal he was advocating, Niebuhr elaborated:

> Justice cannot be approximated if the hope of its perfect realization does not generate a *sublime madness* in the soul. Nothing but such madness will do battle with malignant power and "spiritual wickedness in high places."[30]

This "spiritual wickedness" was the enemy against which both James and Niebuhr fought. They both knew that the dream of its defeat was not realized without great effort. I have shown that it was from James that Niebuhr derived his view that religion expanded the range of human energies.

While both James and Niebuhr in their own ways made significant contributions to this activist view of religion, Niebuhr's contribution contained a rather vexing problem which makes his legacy less valuable today than that of James. I turn now to this problem, namely, Niebuhr's application of this view to the social struggles of industrial workers and Afro-Americans.

---

[25]Ibid., 220-21.
[26]Ibid., 221; emphasis added.
[27]*Varieties of Religious Experience*, 387-98.
[28]Ibid., 398.
[29]*Moral Man*, 277.
[30]Ibid.; emphasis added.

III

Any number of of critical assessments could be offered about Niebuhr's use of James. For example, Niebuhr did not have in 1932 as thoroughgoing a sense of the presence of evil in the world as had James, a sense which one can find in James's *Varieties of Religious Experience.*[31] One could also note that Niebuhr could have been more explicit about his use of James. But Niebuhr was often lax in his citation of thinkers to whom he was indebted. However, later in life, looking back over his career as a social and religious thinker, Niebuhr acknowledged to some degree that he owed much to William James. "I stand in the William James tradition," he wrote to one of his biographers. "He was both an empiricist and a religious man, and his faith was both the consequence and the presupposition of his pragmatism."[32] This remark stood in contrast to earlier versions of his intellectual biography wherein he cited primarily European thinkers, such as Ernst Troeltsch, as significant contributors to the development of his thought.[33] Niebuhr's later view of his connection with the empirical/pragmatic tradition in American philosophy was founded, at least in part, on specific features of his early work, as this essay has shown.

I note with sadness that Niebuhr abandoned the Jamesian view soon after 1932 and that this was a real loss in terms of the relevance of his position for contemporary social and political philosophy. Niebuhr's legacy would be more relevant had he not abandoned the insights he had gleaned from William James. Among other things, his view would be more compatible with liberation themes in many contemporary Latin American, Black and women's theologies. Instead, his view has become a source of comfort for conservative thinkers such as Michael Novak.

Even if he had not abandoned his use of James, I would find objectionable his less-than-consistent use of James in his analysis of the role of religion in the struggles of Afro-Americans in contrast to his more thorough treatment of the situation of industrial workers. He saw so clearly that the workers would need to make use of religion's millenial vision in their quest for justice, but he failed to show in an equally clear and persuasive way that Afro-Americans also could advance toward justice through the energizing capacities of their religious faith. He came quite close to making this point clear when in *Moral Man* he said that Afro-Americans (child of his age, Niebuhr used the term "Negroes") possessed "peculiar spiritual gifts" which could enable them to conduct nonviolent boycotts against their oppressors.[34] He unfortunately never spelled out clearly what these gifts entailed nor what millenial hopes Afro-Americans should have. Were they the same as those of the workers? Were the problems of economic and racial justice so similar that the same tactics would work

---

[31]I am indebted to Romney Moseley of Emory University for this insight into one difference between James and Niebuhr.

[32]Letter to the author quoted in June Bingham, *Courage to Change: An Introduction to the Life and Thought of Reinhold Niebuhr* (New York: Charles Scribner's Sons, 1972) 224.

[33]Richard Fox, *Reinhold Niebuhr: A Biography,* 146.

[34]Ibid., 254. For Niebuhr's later views on race, segregation, and the nonviolent tactics of Martin Luther King, Jr., see Ronald Stone, *Reinhold Niebuhr: Prophet to Politicians* (Nashville: Abingdon Press, 1972) 144-45; and Richard Fox, *Reinhold Niebuhr,* 281-83.

for both? It is this inconsistency in his treatment of the proletarian and the Afro-American that I find appalling in a writer as sensitive and insightful as Niebuhr. It is not surprising that feminist theologians have also found Niebuhr's theology to be similarly limited in its omission of any adequate analysis of the situation of women.[35]

I have shown in this paper that Reinhold Niebuhr for a time borrowed a very useful idea from William James, the idea that religion energizes individuals and groups for the difficult task of striving for social change. Though his use of this idea did not continue into the mature period of his political and religious thought, an awareness of his use of James reveals his early affinity for at least one American thinker and suggests the legacy he might have left if he had learned even more from the American empirical tradition.

---

[35]Judith Plaskow, *Sex, Sin and Grace: Women's Experience and the Theologies of Reinhold Niebuhr and Paul Tillich* (Washington DC: University Press of America, 1980).

Bernhardt's Philosophy
and the Study of World Religions

James A. Kirk

William H. Bernhardt was not a historian of religions and did not claim a specialized knowledge of any religious tradition outside of the western Christian heritage. He was a philosopher of religion—which both identified his mode of approach and the subject of his primary concern—generic religion. This should not imply that he was ill-informed or uninterested in the specifics of non-Christian religions. In fact, a claim could be made for his highly specialized and detailed knowledge of Roman religion in the Augustan age, of Trobriand Island religion, and concerning cults in Colorado, as well as a general knowledge of world religions characteristic of liberal scholars of the early twentieth century. He earned graduate degrees from Garrett, Northwestern, and The University of Chicago in the years from 1922-1927, and the inclusiveness of his interpretation of religion reflects the breadth of critical inquiry which would be taken for granted from those comprehensive institutions. His library was wide ranging and up to date on world religions, and he had read critically, in both English and German, the major studies then available. Nevertheless he was not primarily a student of world religions. He used no Asian research language and never published an article that would have been classified as "world religions." His first full time teaching position was as an Assistant Professor of Philosophy (Central College, Fayette, Missouri) and "philosopher" was his primary vocation throughout a long academic career. His contribution to the study of world religions, therefore, is primarily in the area of philosophical clarity and rigor.

I remember vividly a somewhat Lincolnesque episode in which he was showing me around his home study and library—occupying almost the entire basement level of his house—when he spied an old envelope sticking out from between two dusty books. He pulled it out, smoothed out the wrinkles, and reviewed the notes he had jotted down while on the train from Chicago to Denver, in 1928, en route to a job interview at The Iliff School of Theology, where he served for 35 years from January 1929. (I have no idea how many of his student assistants over the years may have enjoyed the same amazing experience.) His notes offered the hypothesis that religion is primarily concerned to aid human beings in those areas in which their technological self-confidence is insufficient. He held that hypothesis tenaciously through the next fifty years, refining it, testing it, verifying it, using it in the education of clergy and teachers as to what they are primarily about in the study and practice of religion. Recollections of William H. Bernhardt by his students almost always include reference to his remarkable clarity, his directness, and a kind of disturbing simplicity. He sometimes left one with the feeling of possible misunderstanding, because his interpretation seemed to be too straightforward to be philosophy.

What then, as a philosopher of religion, did he contribute that would be particularly relevant to the student of world religions? In my view, the fundamentals of his work have turned out to be most important. He offered critically important preliminary definitions and procedures. He started with the observation that "religion" taken as a whole is too untidy a term for critical use. Some philosophers and anthropologists (e.g., Frazer and his descendants) have seen religion primarily in terms of what people *do* that is religious—acts of worship, prayer, cultic gestures and the like. Others have been concerned primarily with religions as *bodies of belief,* systems of thought and interpretation. Still others have approached the subject primarily in terms of the values sought and achieved, the purposes served. Sociology and anthropology in the first quarter of this century had delivered an awareness of the usefulness of dividing institutional behavior into three aspects or elements. These three operate together in the complex we call religion. His terminology is also a clue to his fundamental contribution. He called these three aspects: function, reinterpretation, and techniques. Recent interpreters have suggested that religions are myth/ritual complexes serving psychological and social needs. It is a variation on Bernhardt's theme—just as his analysis (as he acknowledged) was a variation on conventional sociological interpretation of many human institutions in terms of their functions, ideological structures and modes of operation. "Function," Bernhardt defined as, "the ends, aims, goals, purposes or values realized or believed to be realized religiously."[1] He firmly believed that it was only in this area that there was serious likelihood of being able to identify the commonality in all the forms of religion. For the ideological component of religions he used the term "reinterpretation," and for the whole area of ritual and practice he used "techniques." This terminology obviously has an emotional and ideological neutrality which was important to Bernhardt's analytical style, and relevant to the student of world religions. Such frameworks avoid the intellectual gymnastics such as may be involved in considering nontheistic "theologies" and do not offer advantages to one religious formulation over others. He used the term, "reinterpretation," because he held that a culture offers, as a presupposition, a commonsense, traditional, or scientific interpretation of oneself and one's world which is reworked under the impulse of religious needs or interests. Of this he says,

> In this reinterpretation, many concepts emerge, from the "churinga"
> of the Australians studied by Durkheim to the "mana" of the Melanesians
> to the Gods of the higher religions; from the "interior being" of the primitive Australian to the soul of modern man; from the protective and saving

---

[1]William H. Bernhardt, "Philosophy in the Study of Religion," *The Iliff Review* 9/2 (Spring 1952): 9.

qualities of the primitive's "churinga" to the saviors of high religions. The reinterpretative phase of religions contains a large number of concepts believed to denote or designate available realities.[2]

One can see how from the outset it was intended that this form of analysis should be applicable to any particular religion which one might wish to study. However, it also had special relevance to the academic study of religion as conducted in the west. He pointed out that the curricular divisions characteristic of modern theological education have developed from these phases of religion—the philosophical analysis of functions (lamentably, now often neglected in theological education), the theological disciplines elaborating the reinterpretive content (both Biblical and systematic), and the practical disciplines dealing with the techniques and concerns of religious leadership.

This elementary analysis may seem too simple to be very useful, but in fact it addresses problems which continue to be of major academic concern. The opening assertion that "religion" per se is too loose a term for critical use, precedes Wilfred Cantwell Smith's careful analysis in *The Meaning and End of Religion*[3] by a couple of decades, but seems more fruitful for religious inquiry. Smith has documented abundantly and with precision the view that the term "religion" as we find it in use is not either as ancient as it sometimes appears to be or as clear as scholars are wont to assume. Bernhardt had no argument with that. He would, however, say that if we are to develop a critically useful definition (or theory) we must become aware of the different aspects already included within the term and of the various kinds of critical scholarship which may be involved in clarifying them. Smith finally abandons the term "religion" as deceptive and turns to the term "faith" instead. This relocates the deceptiveness. As Donald Crosby has explained in his *Interpretive Theories of Religion*,[4] the enterprise in which Bernhardt was engaged was more than a search for a terse definition. The Bernhardtian endeavor to clarify the issues was a comprehensive and theoretical approach. Secondly, the particular phases into which he divided religion form a framework for analysis which is very broadly useful. It is a structure which can be employed in the writing of texts or teaching of courses on world religions, dealing with each tradition in turn in terms of (1) both the common and the unique functions which that tradition serves, (2) the conceptual interpretations offered by that religion (and how these ideas relate to the functions), and(3) the ritual and dramatic activities characteristic of each form of religion. No general text on world religions has come to my attention which has a framework so clear. Bernhardt's framework can be maintained from one religion to the next because it is abstract, analytical and conceptually neutral. Some approaches have procrustean beds of questions which all religions are supposed to answer (almost invariably derived exclusively

[2]Ibid.

[3]Wilfred Cantwell Smith, *The Meaning and End of Religion* (New York: The Macmillan Co., 1962).

[4]Donald A. Crosby, *Interpretive Theories of Religion* (The Hague: Mouton Publishers, 1981).

from those questions which the author's preferred religion does in fact offer to answer), but most recent world religions texts have abandoned any serious hope of comparative analysis and try to analyze each tradition entirely in its own terms. Analysis by means of function, reinterpretation, and technique permits the religions under study to be described in their own terms, but allows also cross cultural comparison of similarities and differences in functions, in conceptual structures, and in the active religious life. Thirdly, the intensive effort to develop and use an analytical vocabulary which is evenhanded, as precise as possible, and which describes each tradition in ways which are not alien to that tradition, is really important for the student of world religions. A meta-language which will distort as little as possible and allow for the unfettered statement of the case as each tradition sees it performs an immense intellectual service to the interpreter of religions.

The central problem in the analysis of religion, according to Bernhardt, is the definition of religion. It seems quite clear that, although he addressed many significant philosophical problems in a long and productive teaching career, more time and effort was devoted to the complex of issues connected with the definition of religion than to any other problem. Of course, this was not accidental. There were two fundamental reasons for it. One was the importance of knowing where to begin. The education of clergy, to which he was devoted, was designed to serve the leadership needs of religious institutions. In the late 1920s and early 30s American Protestant churches were doing many things. The architecture and furnishing of their buildings tell the story. They were building gymnasiums and theatrical stages to provide for recreational interests and dramatic presentations. The Social Gospel was in full swing, making education, legislation, social criticism prominent in ecclesiastical circles. Bernhardt told a story about a train wreck, at which the Catholic clergy moved among the victims giving prayers, last rites, supportive liturgical service for the dead and the injured, while Protestant clergy organized a coffee service from the remains of the dining car. He asked simply, ''Is a theological education essential to an effective refreshments detail?'' He had of course no quarrel with social improvement and was much engaged in it himself, nor did he regard the provision of coffee at the scene of a public disaster as unworthy in itself. He was extremely concerned that the fundamental and historically central function of religion should not be forgotten or neglected amid the many ''good things'' which churches and their leaders might do. The problem of definition was important to him because it was vital to the effective leadership of the young men and women he was helping to equip. Secondly, the problem of definition was important because, despite a plethora of definitions in the field, it appeared that none of them had ever been tested under rigorous standards of analytical inquiry. Most definitions of religion by philosophers or theologians were simply postulated for the purposes of the issue at hand. Such postulated definitions might be very clever, might in fact even be fully correct, but ''postulation'' is not a very adequate basis for verification. Among the more systematic philosophers and social scientists who had occasion to need a working definition of religion, the method of ''simple enumeration'' was (and is!) most common. A proposed definition is stated carefully and several instances or examples of its truth are shown. Such definitions can hardly be entirely wrong, since the cases examined, at least, demonstrate them. However, in the critical analysis of methods of verification, simple enumeration does not appear to be very adequate. The search for positive examples of the truth of one's hypotheses tends to blind one to possible inadequacies in the formulation and to render negative instances quite invisible. If all that one has to do to show that he speaks the truth is to give an example, almost anything one can imagine can be shown to be true—there is one example of almost anything somewhere. Scientific inquiry is not guided by such simplistic methods, but uses a more comprehensive form of verification called "functional analysis." This method of inquiry requires a particular kind of hypothesis which will explicitly predict the relationships of at least two functional variables. This hypothesis invites falsification. It can be maintained as valid only when the predicated relationship is valid in every case. A single contrary instance invalidates the hypothesis as stated. Bernhardt applied this far more rigorous method to the definition of religion. It is necessary to describe his procedure briefly. We are after a *critical, working definition* which has been shown, by a complex and rigorous method of empirical examination, to be correct.

The first step is a kind of commonsense postulation. Several "commonly acknowledged" examples of "religion" must be accepted. This is necessary in order to have a body of experiential data which may be examined in the refinement of the definition of what is "religious" about these conventionally accepted religions. Very controversial cases may be set aside for later examination, but on the whole the "common language" sense of the term must be accepted as a point for the initiation of inquiry. This is different from the "common language" philosophers who emerged to prominence a couple of decades later. Bernhardt does not suggest that "common use" is the end of the argument, but that it is the beginning of more systematic inquiry.

The second step is the formulation of an hypothesis based on functional variables. In this case he refined the notion of an inverse variation between religion and human confidence in technology. In the most comprehensive written version he stated it in this way.

> The area in which religious behavior may be employed is determined by men's confidence or lack of confidence in the adequacy of their knowledge and skills to meet specific needs. The areas of human experience in which knowledge and skills are believed to be adequate are called secular; those in which adequate knowledge and skills are not available are religious. Religious behavior, in terms of this hypothesis, is a form of value-achieving activity whose functional areas are determined by the limits of men's confidence in their ability to achieve desired ends.[5]

The variation which he needed to trace to verify his hypothesis was the relationship between technological confidence and religious behavior. For this purpose he selected three cultural situations with a very wide range of difference in technological development and confidence. He utilized Malinowski's studies of the people of the Trobriand Islands, compared and contrasted with Roman religion and culture of the

---

[5]William H. Bernhardt, *The Analysis of Religion* (Denver: The Wesley Press, 1954) 28.

Augustan Age, and twentieth century North American Methodist churches. He also
coined the term "meta-technology" to "designate all attempts to introduce extran-
atural or supernatural force or forces into natural technological processes. One may
define it more simply, perhaps, as the attempt to utilize supernatural means to achieve
technological results."[6] This enabled him on the one hand to take full account of those
cultures in which religion and magic were thoroughly intertwined and yet later to distinguish between religion (as adjustment to the nonmanipulable) from metatechnology (as purported supernatural adjustment *of* the nonmanipulable). For this purpose
he examined Malinowski's distinctions between religion and magic. He quotes from
Malinowski's *Magic, Science and Religion, Myth in Primitive Psychology,* and his
article on "Anthropology" in *Encyclopedia Britannica.* He agrees that the principal
difference is between change in the objective circumstance [the goal of magic] and
change in the subjective response [the goal of religion]. Unlike Malinowski, Bernhardt did not suppose that a clear differentiation, recognizable to the persons involved, can always be made between these orientations in some primitive cultures.
He also quotes social anthropologist, Clark Wissler, who suggests that various methods, including some which would be classified as magic and some religious, are
available to the *shaman,* or religio-magical leader. Where such experts differ, Bernhardt held, it would be inappropriate for the philosopher to require greater clarity.
The term "meta-technology" allowed him to refer to a magico/religious complex in
such an undifferentiated situation. One important result is that religion is seen as continuing to perform its fundamental function even in a society which has abandoned
magic as a suitable way of changing things. Once again we see his effort in the philosophy of religion to avoid terminology weighted on behalf of any one religious tradition or any particular type or level of culture.[7]

To make his examination as precise and comparable as possible he selected two
area of human concern where the technological and the metatechnological/religious
interact, namely food production and health. Food production and health are vital
concerns of all human societies, but confidence and technology for determining favorable results have changed greatly since ancient times. If his hypothesis were correct we should find extensive metatechnological and religious interest in food
production and in health related activities in those societies which had relatively little
technological development and correspondingly less in those where conventional
technology has come further in assuring an adequate food supply and understanding
of the conditions which support and promote good health. I need not recite many of
his findings. He relied heavily on the work of Malinowski, especially *The Argonauts
of the Western Pacific,* but also H. Ian Hogbin, W. H. R. Rivers, and C. G. Selig-
mann. He noted that the processions, dances and incantations of the Trobriand Islanders in protecting their yam fields from spirit theft and their deep sea fishermen
from the hazards of shark and storm stood in considerable contrast with their primi-

[6]Ibid., 31.

[7]William H. Bernhardt, "The Analysis of Religion," bound mimeograph edition (Denver, 1939) ch. 7, "The Trobriand Islanders: Garden Technology and Metatechnology," pp.
59-67.

tive plowing, and lagoon fishing which required little or no supernatural aid. He reports in considerable detail how, at the outset of the gardening season the village gardeners assemble at the residence of the priest/magician to begin the metatechnogical (magico-religious) activities which will control the luck factor, and how these ritualized activities are sharply differentiated from the routine and well known technological procedures of stirring the soil, planting, irrigating, and driving off wild animals. The things which they do not understand such as plant disease, the mysteries of growth itself, are colored with ritualized activity designed to assure their food supply. Metatechnology, Bernhardt reports, is utterly pervasive in Trobriand Society.

The Romans were considerably more sophisticated in their agricultural knowledge, and correspondingly less likely to engage in metatechnological activity in this area, but their knowledge of medicine still called for supernatural appeals to appropriate gods or goddesses to make up for the lack of knowledge and skill. In the modern world the Festival of Rural Life, and occasional prayers for rain (sometimes supplemented by native American rain dances) in times of severe drought are about all that remain of the elaborate religious interest in food production, and farming problems are seen to be economic, institutional, technical, distributive rather than theological. The medical situation remains more complex. Despite enormous gains in knowledge and skill (public and preventative health, medicine, surgery, pharmacology, etc.) people still suffer complex and technically inexplicable or irremediable threats to their life. Average life has been lengthened, but death (from something) remains the lot of all. For people who have access and familiarity with high-tech medical services, that is where they turn first for help and relief. [The existence of certain groups which as a matter of policy make the refusal of medical service important does not invalidate the hypothesis, since it is not the available service which is determinative, but their lack of confidence in it.] Since, however, even the finest technology may leave needs or interests unsatisfied, religion may still function fairly extensively in the areas of health concerns, especially in matters of life and death. For a long time both Bernhardt and many of his students engaged in testing this hypothesis in wider and wider situations. The quality of the examination of this hypothesis with respect to other religions varied considerably, depending particularly on the clarity of the student's understanding of what was to be sought. Bernhardt believed that even Henry Nelson Weiman appeared to have some trouble along this line, in an essay he wrote in application of Bernhardt's identification of the nonmanipulable as the central problem of religion.[8] However, the accumulation of data was overwhelming. Hinduism, Buddhism, Shinto, Islam, Taoism, Zoroastrianism were shown convincingly to serve to enable and facilitate human adjustment to the unsatisfactory and nonmanipulable aspects of experience. Confucianism and Judaism proved as recalcitrant to neat classification by this method as they are to others, but it was at least possible to identify both religious and secular aspects of these traditions more explicitly. We should not be surprised that a careful and methodologically sophisticated analysis should finally generally agree with the conventional wisdom about the names

---

[8]Henry Nelson Wieman, "Bernhardt's Analysis of Religion: Its Implications and Development," *The Iliff Review* 11/1 (Winter 1954): 48-57.

of the great religions.

There were other reasons, or at least concomitants, for this approach to the study of religion. By establishing at least one central function served by religions, Bernhardt believed that he had identified a significant criterion to be employed in the analysis of the ideological and ritual sides of religion. In what ways do these ideas and/or techniques serve human adjustment to the nonmanipulable?

Comparative studies which try to classify religions as "good, better, best" have little attraction for serious scholars. The analysis of the reinterpretations or structures of ideas and techniques or methods of practice in which different traditions address the general issue of adjustment to the nonmanipulable, makes possible a larger *comparative* understanding of their ideologies and practices. In addition to this base of comparability, Bernhardt also believed that he had initiated a line of inquiry which could penetrate many of the philosophical issues of religious thinking. It is obvious that he was using the assumptions of the social-scientific approach to religion, grounded fundamentally in the philosophical style of John Dewey and George Herbert Mead as mediated to him especially through Shailer Mathews and Gerald Birney Smith, as well, of course, as through other writers of the time, William James, Charles S. Pierce, C. Lloyd Alexander, Henri Bergson, Jan Smutts, and to a lesser extent A. N. Whitehead. He was comfortable in the "Chicago School"—and never abandoned its intellectual enterprise, the development of our *working knowledge of religion* and its many ramifications by means of empirically verified research. He knew clearly, what later philosophers have pronounced to be the post-modern disintegration of philosophy, that is, that all our thinking is based on assumptions. He did not regard this as disintegrating, but as challenging to the philosopher who should reduce assumptions to essentials (another application of Occam's razor). He called his own most basic assumption, "The Presupposition of Increasing Cognitional Efficiency"—an epistemological assumption leading to the employment of nonabsolutist metaphysical, theological and ethical assumptions and to the examination of the evidence of experience. He had a positive architectural task before himself moving from the essential assumptions which make critical thought possible, to the actual analysis of ideas and experiences by the employment of these assumptions and the methods they imply, to the development of a position he called "Absolute Immanence" and "Naturalistic Theism." Much of that is not of great interest to the study of world religions. It is an interesting example of a recent Christian philosopher/theologian engaged with the material of his tradition. It does make clear that monolithic claims about *the* Christian idea of God, etc. would be ill-informed concerning this kind of Christian thinking. The underlying implication of this architecture of thinking, however, is toward more widely applicable categories of interpretation, more religiously neutral criteria of analysis, more effectively comparable modes of interpretation. This is of interest in the study of world religions.

What are the specific weaknesses of Bernhardt's philosophical approach to religion with respect to the study of world religions? One of them arises from the very intensity of his effort to identify precisely *the* function of religion. He wanted to identify that, which, if omitted, would represent the end of religion. It was admitted at the outset that many other functions might be served by religious institutions, and it was entirely plausible to him that at least some of those other functions, which his hypothesis did not identify, might in fact be equally fundamental with adjustment to the nonmanipulable, and therefore, part of any truly comprehensive definition of religion. But in practical terms this possibility was generally neglected. Experience in the concrete study of other religious traditions has generally suggested that awareness of the particular and characteristic functions which each of them undertakes to fulfill helps very much in understanding them. Whether these functions are universally characteristic of religion as such is not the only important issue. Cultures are somewhat different in what they regard as problems needing solutions. To look only for those problems which they share may be to overlook the fascinating distinctiveness and some of the particularities of each of the religious traditions. Bernhardt helps us by showing that we should attend to the functions which a religion serves, but I think that we may want to look both for widely shared and for very particular functions.

Secondly, the rather considerable generality contained in the idea of "adjustment to the nonmanipulable" is both attractive and disturbing. The attractiveness is that it enables us to look at a religious tradition very broadly and to give attention to psychic values, social practices, traditional forms which we would not notice, if all that we were doing were looking for the idea of God or an equivalent idea. It lets the religion speak not only in its own terms, but in terms which may not previously have appeared as prominent in comparative or interreligious studies. The worry arises from the nonspecificity which this adjustment implies. It may be necessary to detail a list of specific and identifiable circumstances in which cultures do explicitly turn to religion, especially to specify particular psychological, social, intellectual, and existential needs or concerns to keep an analysis within limits. It has also become clear that one must find some way to incorporate the positive and inspirational power which religions communicate. They are not exclusively a "very present help in trouble" but also a source of awe, fellowship, and gratitude. Bernhardt was not unaware of this, but put the emphasis upon the "adjustment" factor because that was the one which had survived the rigorous analysis he had conducted. These other functions are mostly supported by instantiation, the method of simple enumeration, and while they may well deserve our consideration, did not, in his time at least, deserve our confidence.

Analysis by function is not fashionable everywhere! I have heard arguments dismissed with no justification other than that this is a "functional approach." The confidence which Bernhardt felt in the progress of knowledge by means of careful, verifiable examination of experience has waned greatly. Clarity by means of working definitions supported by appeal to evidence such as anthropological fieldwork and historical analysis is not so often sought. In the case of William H. Bernhardt, the search for operational definitions and integrated analyses led to the search for the function of religion. He never supposed, nor do any of his definitions permit one to imagine, that function was all that religion was about. He was fully prepared to analyze the reinterpretive-ideological structures in their own terms, and to consider the role of ritual, liturgy, and prayer in relation both to the ideas which they support and which give rise to them and to the purposes which these techniques are called upon to serve. Bernhardt once invited Julius Seely Bixler, author of *Notebook of an Unrepentant Liberal*, to Iliff. That self-confident, unassuming commitment was Bernhardt's as well as Bixler's—the unrepentant liberal, determined to get nearer to the truth of things in practical and clear minded ways. He provided tools useful not only for thinking in the tradition of which he was a part but also for the global scale, for the serious effort to understand the religious persuasions and commitments of others. He was not an historian of religions, but his contributions to clear thinking could be of considerable use to those who are.

Problems with Transcendence

Konstantin Kolenda

A big question facing the philosophy of religion today is whether to defend the traditional *dichotomy* between the natural and the supernatural or to shift toward vocabularies which endorse the *continuity* of religiousness with the rest of experience. In this paper I would like to argue that for many important reasons the first alternative has outlived its usefulness and that the second is more defensible. It is high time for religion to abandon its preoccupation with transcendence; it is doing more harm than good.

I

If there ever was a concept that asked for trouble by merely existing, that concept is transcendence. To regard something or some being as transcendent is to declare it to be inexplicable, that is, unilluminable by any *further* concept. Thus defined, God becomes the Wholly Other, beyond comprehension. Equally problematic become other synonyms for God's transcendence, including the idea of divine perfection. Having declared existence to be a perfection, thus inventing the ontological argument, St. Anselm nevertheless admitted that the idea of that than which nothing greater can be conceived tells him nothing about God's nature. A recent defender of the ontological argument, Norman Malcolm, agrees with St. Anselm and sees the value of the argument in merely preventing philosophy from blocking the road to faith.[1] Like Kant before him, Malcolm denies that theoretical reason has anything to do with religion; it cannot harm it nor help it. Religion has to take care of itself. In doing so, it cannot expect any positive contribution to the idea of God from the philosophical ideas of transcendent perfection.

Ever since William James's use of it in the title of his famous book, the expression "religious experience" has been favored by theologians and philosophers as providing a conceptual vehicle to bridge the apparent gap between the natural and the transcendent, secular and sacred. But one should not be misled by the empiricist sound of that expression; it is less innocent than it appears. If the dimension of transcen-

---

[1]Norman Malcolm, "Anselm's Ontological Arguments," *Philosophical Review* 69 (1960).

dence is taken seriously, then it is self-contradictory to say that something can be both transcendent and experienceable at the same time. By being experienced it *ceases* to be wholly transcendent. In this application, "experience" become problematic; as John Dewey warned, it becomes a "weasel word."[2]

Those who are lulled into uncritically accepting the notion of religious experience suppress the legitimate suspicion that in any attempt to *characterize* it, we renege on the initial claim that God is Wholly Other Transcendent Being, opaque to any conceptual characterization. One forgets that such a characterization is attempted when one refers to God as a He, that is, when one thinks of God in terms of a human grammatical category, a predicament hardly avoided by those who would limit themselves to the seemingly neutral "It" or "the One."[3] To represent God in terms of *some* human concepts is to suppose that to that extent God is not Wholly Other. God is certainly not wholly other when He is made conceptually accessible via the very rich and promising concept of a person. *Personalizing* the transcendent is a welltrodden path of attempted escape from transcendentalism. Its popularity is evident in the almost infinite variants of belief in a personal God, represented by a messiah, messenger, or avatar, and countless deities poetically proliferating in religious imagination.[4]

The route to God via personalization is attractive,[5] because it allows the believer to have it both ways—to affirm God's absolute otherness and yet present him as conceptually accessible.[6] That this move presents a problem for the understanding many astute religious thinkers did not fail to note. There is bound to be something *magical* about "religious experience." "I believe in order to understand," declared Tertullian. Such an "understanding" can only be a miraculous happening—the result of divine grace. Kierkegaard cheerfully admitted that from the point of view of reason, this is a scandal. But this only reinforced his faith. In his view, the mark of divinity is that it *strikes down* any and all pretenses of the human intellect. God *must* transcend all our concepts, and that is why the sign of true faith is a willingness to em-

---

[2]Some contemporary philosophers of religion warn against allowing the word "experience" to be taken in a conceptually "naked" or empty sense. "The authority of religious experience rests upon certain judgments about how that experience is to be explained." Wayne Proudfoot, *Religious Experience* (Berkeley: University of California Press, 1985) 236.

[3]The early Hebrews' prohibition against fully writing out God's name reflects uneasiness about representing God by human linguistic means.

[4]The qualification "almost" is appropriate, since some religions (e.g., Buddhism) do not insist on personalizing divine reality.

[5]In my *Cosmic Religion: An Autobiography of the Universe* (Prospect Heights IL: Waveland Press, 1987) I argue that central features of the idea of God are derived from the concept of person.

[6]A good example of trying to have it both ways is found in Paul Tillich's account of absolute faith: "Absolute faith, or the state of being grasped by God beyond God, is not a state which appears beside other states of the mind. . . . It is not a place where one can live, it is without the safety of words and concepts, it is without a name, a church, a cult, a theology. But it is moving in the depth of all of them." *The Courage to Be* (New Haven and London: Yale University Press, 1952) 188-89.

brace the paradox of Christianity—in Christ the infinite becomes finite. For Kierkegaard, and all other fideists, the radical distance between God and man *must* be preserved. But the obvious consequence of accepting this distance is that in "religious experience" the dichotomy between the human and the transcendent becomes absolute.

II

It is important to note that the other, classical Greek, strand in the Western tradition perceives a continuity among human values and does not follow the dichotomous path. In Plato's *Symposium* Socrates shows how an encounter with a beautiful object arouses a desire for *other* beautiful objects, thus initiating an endless quest for more and better examples of beauty, ending up in the Form of Beauty itself. To be sure, struck by the power of this urge to seek ever more perfect embodiments of Forms, Plato, unlike Socrates, attributed to them a sort of transcendent reality. But even he did not really *separate* the human from the divine. For him, human souls, divine from the outset, remain so throughout life, and the task of philosophy is to keep this divine nature from becoming submerged. The distinctly spiritual endeavor of philosophy consists in trying to recollect and to keep active one's aspirational capacities. Although at times the effort to keep this project going may involve a direct mystical vision of the World of Forms, good life on earth consists not in the separation from but in the *participation* in the Forms, which are always immanent in the natural world.

For Plato, and for his pupil Aristotle, human life is a pursuit of ideals. But pursuit of ideals is inherently creative, prompting human beings to pay attention to a hierarchy of realizable good. Although some values are perceived to be higher than others, there is a continuity among them; a lower good points to the higher one, and a higher one shows up a deficiency in the lower one. In the course of moving in either direction—rising or backsliding—a person learns that the movement toward or away from a greater perfection need not be arrested at any point and that the criteria of what is valuable are indefinitely stretchable. Although each kind of being has its corresponding telos, that telos operates not as a transcendent goal but as an immanent force.

One crucial difference between the classical Greek and the transcendental strain of the Judeo-Christian conception of the relationship of the finite to the infinite is that in the former the principle of continuity is preserved throughout. No leap of faith is required. To be sure, the task of self-perfection is arduous and requires hard work of mind and heart. But there is no difference *in kind* between the early and the later stages of the journey. One learns something about one's divinity by obeying even the faintest impulse to improve one's understanding and behavior. At the moment when Socrates was cheerfully drinking hemlock he was closer to the total range of his soul's potentiality than those around him, but his friends who understood and honored what he was doing had a glimpse of what was happening to him. And, as Plato reports, they were deeply touched by what they witnessed. They realized that they were on the lower rungs of the same ladder, but nevertheless they were ascending in the same direction of open-ended perfection.

To subscribe to Arisotelianized, naturalized Platonism is to see no problem with saying that in human life nature is constantly trying to become *super*natural, when this gloss is taken in the same innocent sense as the claim that any ideal transcends actuality. To say that human beings are naturally creative is to ascribe to them the capacity to strain toward actions and practices which would raise them above the level at which they actually find themselves at any given moment. Whenever they project ideals, they envisage an improved or refined state of themselves. The effort to make the ideal actual, at least potentially or in some idiosyncratic version, presupposes a desire and a capacity to change the world for the better.

III

The insistence on a radical discontinuity between the religious and all other possible states open to us exacts a heavy price. In order to show in what that price consists, we need to take into account some special features of being human. There are events in human life that call for a wholehearted acknowledgement and appreciation. We are sometimes witnessing actions, activities, and events that cry out for an autonomous response. Some call for rejoicing and celebration, others for condemnation and mourning. Not to give a deserved acknowledgement to an heroic or self-sacrificial deed, for instance, or not to notice transparently horrid evils, is a kind of fault or deficiency, perhaps a sign of dullness, apathy, or moral insensitivity. When a good action or an event is not taken note of, when the one who performs or witnesses it does not recognize its significance, that action or event is a victim of a betrayal; it is not seen in the way it deserves to be seen, as something special, worthy of note. Correspondingly, when an action is undeniably evil or an occurrence tragic, not to judge it as such, not to recognize its negative significance, is an injustice.

In sum, it is a special prerogative and a privilege of human beings that they have the capacity to offer confident judgments about things that matter to them. And it is precisely with regard to this capacity that the dichotomous conception of the religious dimension does its damage. A believer who sees an unbridgeable gap between himself and a transcendent God and who insists on an absolute discontinuity between human and divine judgment is prevented from allowing himself to make confident affirmations about anything—positive or negative. He is always looking over his shoulder, anxious to be confirmed and upheld in his judgment by the transcendent entity. Until this confirmation takes place, he deems all of his opinions and judgments ultimately untrustworthy. He makes them alright, but timidly, tentatively, with reservations. In doing so, he abdicates his own capacity to evaluate the meaning of his life. If the final authority on the meaning of what one is doing or experiencing is God as the Wholly Other, if only Transcendence can do real justice to what is happening, then one's own evaluation must remain provisional and tentative. The implication of this delegation of authority is that human acts of naming, registering, acknowledging, and affirming significant events cannot really come off. They must remain in abbeyance, because their eventual confirmation or sanction is deferred to a being regarded as transcendent, beyond human ken. In effect, one's own judgment about good and evil is not trusted and remains suppressed.

The result of such a deferring or delegation is that the world and human experience are devalued; lacking a transcendent imprimatur, nothing ever is given its due. Moreover, the possibility is allowed that from the point of view of the Wholly Other what looks like a tragedy or travesty, for instance, could turn out to be radically different. Simply in virtue of being finite, human judgment counts for nothing, or at least cannot be fully autonomous and sincere, even if it comes from the depths of one's being. Thus, deference to a wholly transcendent divine judgment keeps us in doubt and uncertainty about the meaning of all our perceptions and experiences, no matter how glorious or how horrible they may appear to us.

The knight of faith who adopts radical transcendentalism may regard it as an expression of humility. But as Nietzsche cautioned, we have reasons to suspect that motive; it may be a front for a kind of one-upmanship, a quest for power. To declare oneself incompetent but nevertheless protected by God's absolute if totally incomprehensible competence is a not-so-subtle hint that one's faith is superior to anyone else's faith. By claiming to be empowered by a God who is beyond the reach of any possible human judgment, one is also giving to understand that faiths which have a different understanding of God are false. Thus, the believer in radical transcendentalism is a candidate for an ultimate fanatic. There seems to be resemblance between such a fanatic and a fundamentalist. By treating the Scriptures as supernaturally revealed and as literally true, the fundamentalist rejects any and all candidates for alternative interpretations. Thus his vaunted humility toward the Divine Being is in fact a disguised condescension and even arrogance toward those who hold different opinions. Since the God he believes in is invulnerable to any representation that others may prefer, he is tempted to claim exclusive status for his allegiance to such an untouchable God. Such unconditional allegiance is often frightening, providing a ready excuse for the practice of dividing people into "us" and "them."

IV

If the motives for postulating a transcendent God are frustrating and suspect, what is the alternative? The suggestion I wish to make is that in order to be religious, we must play God. Lest this suggestion be seen as shocking, let me hasten to describe the sense in which I believe it to be plausible. The expression "to play God" can be explicated in a way that is not only defensible but also deeply religious. Let me explain.

What ultimate motives do believers ascribe to God? He is celebrated as a being who has the power to make things glorious. Most religious scriptures devoted much space to poetically rapturous accounts of how in exercising this power God experiences glory and bliss. But if God's supreme enjoyment is a concomitant of His awareness that what he creates is good, then human aspiration to inject goodness into the world can be seen as rightly accompanied by corresponding joy. If fulfillment of divine purposes for the world lifts it out of its neutral, humdrum, monotonous, chaotic, indifferent, meaningless and valueless state, then any analogous activity by human beings is in that sense godlike. Thus, "to play God" is not to be taken in the pejorative sense of arrogantly exerting power over things or people but in the sense of being a coworker in the effort to make oneself and the world better.[7] To be religious is to exert oneself on behalf of goals which would make aspects of the world over which one has some control into something worthwhile. As God's project is to induce the world to exhibit admirable qualities, so does every single instance of helping such qualities to arise. This is the positive sense in which finite beings can be said to play at being God.

There are good reasons why we, all human beings, should take up this function which theologians misguidedly assign to a transcendent being. If the world acquires its value-status from manifesting features judged to be good in themselves, then not to recognize and not to celebrate the worth of such features as they come to realization is a loss to reality as such. Conversely, to see oneself as helping such worthy features to emerge in the world is to see one's actions and reactions as important. To make the reality of these creative contributions conditional on confirmatory acts of an alleged transcendent being is to make their value status contingent on the existence of such a being. The acknowledgement of the intrinsic value of human acts is kept on hold and is made only conditionally, thereby implying that should God not exist, the value ascription could not be confidently made. But this is a no-win position. Whether the question of God's existence is answered negatively or positively, the actual evacuation of intrinsic value from occurring human actions cannot be reversed. By cancelling the consciousness of being really responsible for helping some goodness to come into the world, we diminish and sell short the world and our role in it.

The loss is greater than we might be inclined to suppose. Being conditioned to question, to minimize, or even to disclaim a personal responsibility for the way the world goes and by surrendering our judgment to the transcendent being, we are prevented from experiencing something which the scriptures describe as glorious. What that something is can be approximated by shifting attention to still another possible connotation of the expression "to play God." A religious imagination rightly sees God's playing his value-creating role as accompanied by sublime blissful experiences. These sorts of experiences flow directly from creative activity. That's why the Genesis story has it that when God beheld the world after making it, He proclaimed it to be very good, that is, He literally pronounced a *bene-diction*. Similarly, one may presume that when God rested on the seventh day, He must have been pleased with Himself and His handiwork.

The ubiquitous references to God's sublime bliss, to his perfect repose in paradise, may have an obvious explanation: there is no greater bliss than the consciousness of spreading goodness, mercy, and justice through the exertion of one's loving and creative powers. This is why one of the most popular synonyms for God is *Love*. Plato captured this motif perfectly when in his creation story he attributed the world's

---

[7]This conclusion is strongly defended by C. S. Peirce in his view of religion. According to him, the essence of religion is "the aspiration toward the perfect." *Collected Papers*, 8 vols. (Cambridge MA: Harvard University Press, [1-6]1931–1935, [7-8]1958) 6.426. As he puts it, "the ideal of conduct will be to execute our little function in the operation of the creation by giving a hand toward rendering the world more reasonable whenever, as the slang is, it is 'up to us' to do so." 1.615.

existence to God's desire to share His goodness with whatever was capable of reson-
ating with it. God's goodness overflowed; not being jealous, as Plato put it, He wanted
to share His goodness with the world created for that very purpose.

The sense of happiness arising from the consciousness of being responsible for
the emergence of something good or beautiful will elude us as long as we think of
ourselves as ultimately unworthy, always correctable by a transcendent power re-
lentlessly looking over our shoulder. But if we manage to shake off this Nagging
Qualifier, a sudden exhilaration may come over us, permitting us to recognize and
accept ourselves as undisputable originators of something good. R.M. Rilke captured this sense of exuberant joy and pride in what we have created.

> So, after all, we have *not* failed to make use of the spaces, these gen-
> erous spaces, these our spaces. (How terribly big they must be, when with
> thousands of years of our feeling, the're not overcrowded.) But a tower was
> great, was it not? O, Angel, it was though, even compared with you? Char-
> tress was great—and music towered still and passed beyond us.[8]

In these lines Rilke tells us what it means to transform the world for the better.
It means to "play God" to it, and to allow the exuberance of creative play to fill one's
being, taking pride in the realization that but for human efforts the world would be
deprived of its concretely experienceable value. When the Hindu thinks of the world
as divine lila, as God's self-absorbed enjoyment in the play and drama He is creating,
he does not exile this enjoyment to an imagined heaven.

It would be a great boon for religion if it took seriously the view that God is within
us, taking the claim in the modest sense that impulses we characterize as divine find
expression in our attempts to make sense of our lives, to pursue worthwhile objectives, and to work at introducing goodness into human experiences, ours and those
of others. Creative acts that bring about this result are not limited to people with larger
or special talents—artists, thinkers, heroic doers. Granted that they experience greater
than average joys, everyone, as Rilke noted, can at least sometimes exclaim: Life
here is glorious! Satisfactions derived from being a child, growing into a mature person, trying to enlist one's energies in projects of one's choosing, setting oneself against
evils and adversities, entering into relationships with others for various mutually beneficial purposes, witnessing the drama of the world around us—at home and abroad,
in a family circle or on the global, historical scale—all of them can enlist our attention and furnish materials for creative, productive responses, thus providing opportunities for injecting some goodness into the world.

It is the sum total of that goodness, as experienced not only by all human beings
but also by all sentient creatures, that constitutes the natural substance of the world
which deserves to be called divine. This is the vast dimension to which spiritual leaders of humanity— sages, religious thinkers, artists, and writers—have always tried
to call attention, detecting the spark of divinity even in the lowly ones. *This* is the
concrete locus of all meaning and value—not in some bad metaphysical fantasy of a

---

[8]Rainer Maria Rilke, *Duino Elegies,* trans. Leishman and Spender (New York: W. W.
Norton, 1939) seventh elegy.

world-transcending being. The value of the world lies not in that imaginary being but in the actual occurrence of all genuine satisfactions. To get an inkling of that vast sum, think of good things that happen to you (no matter how many or how few) and multiply them by the billions inhabiting the earth. No wonder Rilke felt that the cosmic spaces must indeed be huge to contain the feelings experienced by sentient, value-creating beings. Compared to the substance of *this* reality, the dream of transcendence is but a shadow.

Rethinking Empiricism in Theology

Randolph Crump Miller

In 1919, Douglas Clyde Macintosh published *Theology as an Empirical Science*. This was a step forward in the development of empiricism as a method. Grounded in a carefully worked out epistemology, developed in his 1915 volume, Macintosh could speak of experience and its object, whether secular or religious, with some degree of certainty. He identified his theory of knowledge as critical monistic realism, meaning that there is an overlapping of experience and what is experienced but that there are large areas that remain outside this overlapping.

Macintosh was critical of any idealistic epistemology and he was trying to avoid a realism that was either naive or dualistic. The key for him was the word "critical" which enabled him to make the careful distinction between what is really present and the overlapping that eliminated some aspects of experience and of the object.

Awareness depends on sense perception, but there are instances of a wider basis, which he called "perception in a complex" by which he meant

> that in the midst of a complex of colors, sounds, and other sense qualities, subjectively produced but objectively located, we are able to intuit or perceive the presence of a physical reality with qualities such as direction, distance, extent, shape, duration, motion, energy, and the like, none of which are sense-qualities, but none of which can be discerned except in and through sense-qualities, to which the stimulations they originate give rise.[1]

To some of his more rigid empiricist critics, this seemed to endanger his claim to be strictly empirical, for it allowed for the intuitive and imaginal as well as sense perception, but he stressed the fact that further empirical testing was necessary in such

---

[1] *The Pilgrimage of Faith* (Calcutta: University of Calcutta Press, 1931) 214-15. See the volume on Macintosh's epistemology and religious insights by Preston Warren, *Out of the Wilderness: Douglas Clyde Macintosh's Journeys through the Grounds and Claims of Modern Thought* (New York: Peter Lang, 1989).

cases. The final test was always immediate experience.

The center of Macintosh's empirical appeal is what he called "the right religious adjustment." This is recognition that

> on condition of the right religious adjustment, i.e., spiritual aspiration, concentration of attention upon the religious Object, self-surrender to that divine being, an appropriating faith, willed responsiveness, and persistance in the same, . . . a divinely functioning reality . . . tends to produce a desirable change in that direction of the will and character of the individual concerned, and this may be regarded as the basic, dependable "answer to prayer." [2]

He then proceeded to list a number of "laws" that describe how the process may develop in terms of ethics, health of the ethico-religious life, development of character, feelings of repentance, peace, joy, love, assurance, guidance, health and healing, and of social action in social groups and in society at large. [3]

This procedure provides "an empirical verification of the existence of God, defined as a dependable Factor, favorable to spiritual values, and responding to the right religious adjustment." [4] But this does not provide verification for any specific definition of the religious Object, Christian or otherwise. That takes one beyond the strictly empirical.

By relying on his critical monistic realism, Macintosh asserted that there is reality beyond what is experienced, which can only be an object of religious intuition and faith. If we can discover values as criteria for the divine as known, we can make them applicable also to what is not available to direct perception, to what is transcendent but only believed in. This becomes the basis for what Macintosh called "reasonable faith." We can safely assume a consistency between the divine as known and the divine as imaginally intuited, although we do not therefore have an adequate basis for claiming that God is *known*, for example, as a person. But we can apply a morally valuational norm to our developing concept of God. A morally perfect God would not do some things often ascribed to diety, for such a God would be dependable and consistent.

This was not enough. Macintosh wanted a deity good enough for our absolute worship and trust. This forced him to insist on religious intuition that provides a feeling of certainty about the God we need. This is subjective certitude, not knowledge, but is at least a theoretical possibility. He incorporated here the claim of "moral optimism," that "we may morally will to believe and to keep on believing as we must in order to be at our spiritual best." [5] Has the camel of tradition got its nose into the empirical tent?

Macintosh's insistence on the "right religious adjustment" was centered on knowledge of the religious Object, and this was an important point. H. Richard Nie-

---

[2] *The Problem of Religious Knowledge* (New York: Harper & Bros., 1940) 202-203.
[3] Ibid., 203-10.
[4] Ibid., 197.
[5] Ibid., 368.

buhr wrote that "the enduring contribution of empirical theology, from Schleiermacher to Macintosh, lies in its insistence on the fact that knowledge of God is
available only in religious relation to [God]."[6]

In 1927, Henry Nelson Wieman published *Religious Experience and Scientific
Method,* in which he developed an empirical approach not fundamentally different
from that of Macintosh. He stressed God as an object of immediate experience. If we
accept this, without further attempts to describe God's character, it becomes obvious
that God exists, for "all experience is the experience of something."[7] So an examination of religious experience becomes necessary. It is

> a merging of many experiences, and just that form which gives us the datum
> signifying God is not clearly distinguished from that which gives us our
> knowledge of earth and sky, and fellow [human beings] and social group.[8]

Because our tools for interpretation are insufficiently developed, we have all kinds
of superstitions, vague fancies, and even blindness to fact,[9] which accounts for many
of the absurdities in the history of theology. What Wieman wanted was a clarification
of experience which can be considered religious, an analysis of the data, and proper
inferences concerning the object.

Wieman gave a brilliant description of religious experience. He pointed to a variety of highly significant experiences, such as the sinking of the Titanic and the San
Francisco earthquake and the stock market crash and reactions to them.

> At such times one's attention ceases to be focused on certain definite objects
> and becomes diffusive. The ordinary objects of response being taken away,
> and at the same time the whole organism pervasively stimulated, brings into
> play innumerable impulses without any determining adjustment or estab-
> lished pattern. It is a state where one must necessarily be aware of concrete,
> unanalyzed masses of experience that surge in upon one. We do not mean
> that there is any conceptualized cognition of these masses of experience. That
> is exactly what we do not mean, for we have all along insisted on the dis-
> tinction between awareness of immediate experience and clear knowledge
> of an object.[10]

This may not be a momentous experience, but may come in the quiet of one's room,
coming upon us without warning. It is what Whitehead called a many-termed relationship, an experience of what F.S.C. Northrop called "the undifferentiated (im-

---

[6]See Bixler, Niebuhr, and Calhoun, *The Nature of Religious Experience* (New York: Harper & Bros., 1937) 112.

[7]*Religious Experience and Scientific Method* (New York: Macmillan, 1927) 29.

[8]Ibid., 30.

[9]Ibid., 31.

[10]Ibid., 37-38.

pressionalistically) aesthetic continuum."[11]

Wieman claimed that this experience is direct acquaintance with God, but that it does not tell us what God is. Like any scientific knowledge, we need to interpret the data. Following a brilliant analysis of many views of the purpose of religion and the nature of God, Wieman concluded:

For God is precisely that object, whatever its nature may be, which will yield maximum security and abundance to all human living, when right adjustment is made.[12] . . . Worship [of God] will arouse and organize [one's] impulses for the farthest swing of constructive achievement of which [one] is capable.[13]

At this point in their thinking, Macintosh and Wieman were in close agreement in their strictly empirical evidence for the existence of God, and were aware that this was indeed a minimum statement. Wieman worked within the boundaries of a naturalistic theism and began to move toward a distrust of all of experience. Macintosh persisted in starting with the right religious adjustment and moved by means of reasonable faith toward a supernatural interpretation of deity. He accused Wieman of being like "a tight-rope walker at a circus. At one time it almost seemed as if he were going to come down on the side of theism."[14] Over the years, Wieman kept refining his concepts (and there were many) of God, starting with "the growth of meaning and value" and ending with "creative interchange."

There is much to be said for Wieman's method and conclusions. Daniel Day Williams argued

that while Wieman's position stands apart from obvious trends, he has actually stated what has become the practice of people in wide areas of our culture, including much of the practice in the established religious institutions. When we ask what [people] actually put their trust in as revealed by their actions, we see that we may require something like "creative interchange" to describe the operative process to which we give our attention and even our devotion.[15]

Bernard Meland developed an interpretation of empiricism based more on Bergson and James, a view that emphasized what he called the "appreciative consciousness." He thought that clarity was often achieved at the expense of deeper and less specific meanings. Like James and Whitehead, he was suspicious of too much clar-

[11]F. S. C. Northrop, in *Religion and the Moral Predicament of Modern Man*, ed. Benjamin F. Lewis (Brooklyn: Pageant-Poseidon, 1972) 108.

[12]*Religious Experience and Scientific Method*, 381.

[13]Ibid., 383.

[14]*Is There A God?* by Henry Nelson Wieman, Douglas Clyde Macintosh, and Max C. Otto (Chicago: Willett, Clark & Co., 1932) 24.

[15]*Charles Hartshorne and Henry Nelson Wieman*, ed. William S. Minor (Carbondale IL: Foundation for Creative Philosophy, 1969) 56.

ity. He sought a "richer, thicker form of experience" of the "individual-in-community,"[16] which is where religion emerges. One moves from open awareness to appreciative awareness to creative awareness, which is "wonder becoming a creative force."[17]

Human experience reflects this kind of experience in various cultures through the myths and poetry that we have inherited and in the modern myths emerging in current metaphysical and religious insights. Some cultures resist the newer myths and others reject the older ones, so that we need to work on ways of communication that will bring about genuine community. Meland does not think that Western culture will eliminate the Jewish-Christian *mythos,* and we need to discover the resources within this culture to provide a sense of reality to a modern expression of religious faith.[18]

Meland's position was not far from Whitehead's in the emphasis on a richer and deeper experience. Whitehead spoke of what happens to people in their solitariness and in "the return from solitariness to society. There is no such thing as absolute solitariness. Each entity requires its own environment." Furthermore, "what is known in secret must be enjoyed in common, and must be verified in common."[19] Like the other empiricists, Whitehead claimed very little verified knowledge about God on the basis of experience, but he pointed to a "permanent rightness" both as efficient and final cause. Any concept of deity is within a metaphysical system and beyond the views of any particular religion.

> God is the ultimate limitation, and His existence is the ultimate irrationality. For no reason can be given for just that limitation which it stands in His nature to impose. God is not concrete, but He is the ground for concrete actuality. . . . The general principle of empiricism depends upon the doctrine that there is a principle of concretion which is not discoverable by abstract reason. What further can be known about God must be sought in the region of particular experiences, and therefore rests on an empirical basis.[20]

Whitehead begins with what he called the "sense of 'worth,' . . . the sense of existence for its own sake."[21] In its primitive stage it is "the vague grasp of reality, dissecting it into a threefold scheme, namely, 'The Whole,' 'That Other,' and 'This-My-Self.' "[22] It is a value experience. This dim and vague reaction to the environment leads to the sensory activities arising from the human body. "Clear, conscious

---

[16]Bernard E. Meland, *Higher Education and the Human Spirit* (Chicago: University of Chicago Press, 1953) 48-78.

[17]Bernard E. Meland, *Faith and Culture* (New York: Oxford University Press, 1953) 162-63.

[18]See Meland, *Seeds of Redemption* (New York: Macmillan, 1947) 41; "How Is Culture a Source for Theology?" *Criterion* 3 (Summer 1964): 19.

[19]*Religion in the Making* (New York: Macmillan, 1926) 137; see 16, 47, 58.

[20]*Science and the Modern World* (New York: Macmillan, 1925) 257.

[21]*Modes of Thought* (New York: Macmillan, 1938) 109.

[22]Ibid., 110.

discrimination is an accident of human existence. It makes us human."[23]

When "our sense of the value of the details for the totality dawns upon our consciousness," we have "the intuition of holiness, the intuition of the sacred, which is the foundation of all religion."[24]

> We owe to the sense of deity the obviousness of the many actualities of the world, and the obviousness of the unity of the world for the preservation of the values realized and for the transiton to ideals beyond realized fact.[25]

Nancy Frankenberry, in her *Religion and Radical Empiricism,* traces the story from William James to Alfred North Whitehead, with a treatment of logical empiricism as a prelude to her penetrating analysis of James, Dewey, Wieman, Meland, and Loomer. We find here a critical rethinking of radical empiricism. She writes:

> The never fully resolved difficulty of Meland's empirical realism, as it is also of James' psychology and Wieman's contextualism, is to reconcile the prereflective flow of dynamic felt qualities in lived experience with the structures of reflective and linguistic expression. . . . I would argue that radical empiricism should recognize a reciprocal and even codeterminate relation between experience and language. . . . [This] will . . . entail a certain inescapable relativity in matters of faith, and especially in connection with any empirical discernment of what is called "god." To attempt to report such a discernment is to acknowledge that the experience is conditioned and limited by language which is at once both an instrument of expression and largely also the conditioning medium of experience itself. . . . To whatever extent language and experience are reciprocal influences. One way of speaking about God, rather than another, will have profound importance in encouraging attention to central aspects of experience rather than others, and even in eliciting certain experiences rather than others.[26]

Frankenberry concludes with a chapter comparing Buddhist thought with Whitehead. The emphasis here is on what Whitehead called "subjective form" and Frankenberry calls "felt qualities," which in process thought make up and emerge from "the processive-relational matrix of all experience."[27] Frankenberry's conclusion is that what Buddhists and radical empiricists "are talking about is that to which the concepts 'God' and 'Emptiness' are applied, and by which they are justified."[28]

Radical empiricism is based on a realistic epistemology, with the presupposition that we have direct experience of reality, including God. But all empirical conclu-

---

[23]Ibid., 116.

[24]Ibid., 120.

[25]Ibid., 102.

[26]Nancy Frankenberry, *Religion and Radical Empiricism* (Albany: State University of New York Press, 1988) 141-44.

[27]Ibid., 177.

[28]Ibid., 188.

sions are technically tentative. There is no ultimate guarantee that the sun will rise
on schedule tomorrow morning. If God is both necessary and contingent, we need to
start with other than empirical evidence for God's necessity. According to Charles
Hartshorne, there is need for abstract a priori reasoning to establish God's existence
and for empirical evidence to believe in God's accidental or generating qualities.[29]

> What we can clearly infer as to God is only [God's] abstract essence, and
> the wholly abstract is no actual value. The concrete actuality of God is in us
> only in so far as we, with radical ineffectiveness and faintness, intuit it.[30]

The distinction made by Hartshorne is asserted in different ways by others. Macintosh started at the empirical pole, and he believed that the right religious adjustment established the existence of God but provided no details as to God's nature,
similar to James' distinction between his basic concept of a divine "More" and his
overbeliefs. Wieman remained more strictly empirical, but his interpretations seemed
to some to go beyond the empirical evidence. Meland saw the necessity of using myths
and models to form theological concepts and made much more use of the meanings
to be found in various cultures. Whitehead granted that the concept of the primordial
nature of God arose from his general system which provided a basis for empiricism,
and used empirical evidence for the consequent nature of God.

If we grant, with the major empiricists, that we have evidence for believing in
the existence of God, but not any theoretical certainty about the characteristics of God,
we are forced to move into the area of James' "overbeliefs" or Macintosh's "reasonable faith." "Being sure in religion," wrote Ian Ramsey, "does not entail being
certain in theology."[31] "We can be sure about God; but we must be tentative in theology."[32] For Ramsey, the certainty lay in commitment, as it did for Wieman, but
the expression of it was always in terms of models which need to be revised and reconstructed with each passing age.

Ramsey knew that the use of models for God took one beyond the possibility of
verifiable deductions. But they stand or fall on the basis of what Ramsey called "empirical fit." Both scientific and theological models "arise out of, and in this way become currency for, a universe that discloses itself to us in a moment of insight."[33]
Science needs verifiable deductions and religion empirical fit.

Ramsey spoke of "disclosures," by which he meant an activity which imposes
itself on our experience. It is closely related to insight or intuition, and it leads in the
case of religion to a vision. Here he recorded Whitehead's statement:

> That religion is strong which in its ritual and its modes of thought evokes an
> apprehension of the commanding vision.[34]

---

[29]*A Natural Theology for Our Time* (LaSalle IL: Open Court, 1967) 51-52.

[30]*The Divine Relativity* (New Haven: Yale University Press, 1948) 92.

[31]*On Being Sure in Religion* (London: Athlone Press, 1963) 47.

[32]*Christian Discourse* (London: Oxford University Press, 1965) 89.

[33]*Models and Mystery* (London: Oxford University Press, 1965) 19.

[34]*Christian Discourse*, 66.

Ramsey paraphrases Whitehead as follows:

> What is disclosed as the topic of a religious vision is 'something real, the greatest present facts, what gives meaning to all that passes, whose possession is the final good, the ultimate ideal.' Yet when we come to speak of it, no interpretation will be complete, all our discourse will be inadequate, partial, and approximate. Hence, with respect to an adequate interpretation we can say, again with Whitehead, that it waits to be realized, is a remote possibility, eludes apprehension, is beyond reach, that it is, if not a hopeless, certainly an endless quest.[35]

When Whitehead said that this is "a vision of something which stands beyond, behind, and within, the passing flux of immediate things," he provided modifiers for the primary model of God which alerts the listener to an imperative force which is more than mere description.

Ronald Hepburn, from a different point of view, provided support for this approach. He wrote:

> It is the little words—'outside,' 'inside,' 'behind'—that cause the logical trouble, when they are applied to the world as a whole. . . . But do these words *altogether* fail us? Do they not express a range of haunting and memorable human experience at least better than other words at our disposal? Perhaps we can be empirical even here. For many people there are times when the world loses its ordinariness and takes on a disturbing, derivative, transfigured look; when awe deepens to numinous awe.[36]

Ramsey's point was that all religious language needs such qualifiers in order to communicate effectively. If we are going to lead or help others to understand what we say about God, we need models which can disclose a personal relationship that is logically odd but which is open to empirical fit, for only then can there be an objective reference. And this we may call "God," but even this use is not descriptive; it is metaphorical.

Metaphor is the primary means of religious expression. Image thinking, story telling, poetic expressions and forceful models are found throughout religious literature. "No animal ever understood a metaphor: that belongs to intelligence," wrote Horace Bushnell.[37] The prophets loaded the Hebrew mind with rich images and metaphors that carried over into the New Testament and traditional Christian symbols and creeds. The early Christians, trying to understand Jesus' death, found in their own Jewish tradition the metaphors of lamb, fire, and blood. The parables may be

---

[35]*Models and Mystery,* 71.

[36]Ronald Hepburn, "The Gospel and the Claims of Logic," *Religion and Humanism* (BBC Publications, 1964) 14. See Ramsey, *Models for Divine Activity* (London: SCM Press, 1973) 63.

[37]Horace Bushnell, "Our Gospel a Gift to the Imagination," *Building Eras* (New York: Scribner's, 1881) 252.

thought of as drawn-out metaphors. The disciples are called living epistles. We can think of Jesus as parable (McFague). Many metaphorical phrases are rich in imagery, as in "For *of* him and *through* him, and *to* him," or "One God and Father of all, who is *above* all, and *through* all, and *in* you all.[38] Such concepts have a richness that analytic procedures cannot match, yet they are open to interpretation in terms of process thinking and to tests of empirical fit.

Whitehead moved from philosophical language to poetic images and symbolism in speaking of God as love, who is "a little oblivious to morals," as "tenderly saving the turmoil of the intermediate world by the completion of his own nature." "He is the lure for feeling, the eternal urge of desire." "He does not create the world, he saves it; or, more accurately, he is the poet of the world, with tender patience leading it by his vision of truth, beauty, and goodness." "He is the binding element of the world. The consciousness which is individual in us, is universal in him; the love which is partial in us is all-embracing in him." "He is not the world, but the valuation of the world." "God is the great companion—the fellow-sufferer who understands." "The power of God is the worship he inspires." We never get rid of wonder and mystery.[39]

Whitehead rejected some traditional models for deity. He wrote:

> The brief Galilean vision of humility flickered throughout the ages, uncertainly. . . . When the Western world accepted Christianity, Caesar conquered. . . . The Church gave unto God the attributtes which belonged exclusively to Caesar. . . . the Galilean origin of Christianity . . . does not emphasize the ruling Caesar, or the ruthless moralist, or the unmoved mover. It dwells upon the tender elements in the world, which slowly and in quietness operate by love; and it finds purpose in the present immediacy of a kingdom not of this world. Love neither rules, nor is it unmoved; also it is a little oblivious to morals. It does not look to the future; for it finds its own reward in the immediate present.[40]

Charles Hartshorne, in his delightfully titled *Omnipotence and Other Theological Mistakes,* points to a number of models that no longer have meaning for those who discern the changing theological climate. To think of God as absolutely perfect and unchangeable places two qualifiers in conflict, for to be perfect must mean being capable of change. God will respond to different situations and creatures according to the needs and cares that emerge.

Most hymnals have eliminated the hymn, "God the Omnipotent" who is "King who ordainest thunder thy clarion, the lightning the sword." This, says Hartshorne, is "the *tyrant* ideal of power."[41] God decides everything that happens, and wills that

---

[38]Ibid., 265.

[39]See my *The American Spirit in Theology* (Philadelphia: Pilgrim Press, 1974) 156.

[40]*Process and Reality,* corrected edition, ed. David Ray Griffin and Donald W. Sherburne (New York: The Free Press, 1978) 342-43 [520-21 in earlier edition].

[41]*Omnipotence and Other Theological Mistakes* (Albany: State University of New York Press, 1984) 11.

we will freely make the identical decision. In contrast, the biblical model is the parental role. Wise mothers and fathers do not try to determine what their children will do, but they do use persuasive love to guide them into right decisions. In this sense, we can use father and mother as models for speaking about God. Furthermore, "there is an aspect of real chance in what happens." Freedom implies chance. There is chance or randomness in nature. We need not only to qualify our view of God's power but we also need to develop a theology of chance.

Furthermore, says Hartshorne, although God knows or prehends the past and the present, even God does not know what has not yet occurred. If God knows the future which is not yet, then he knows falsely. And if God does not yet know the future, God can grow in knowledge, and the doctrine of omniscience needs to be qualified to have currency in today's world.

God's love is not an intellectual love but consists of "feeling of feeling." It is compassion or sympathy or empathy in a literal sense. The RSV translates it as "steadfast love." So Hartshorne concludes on this topic, "Much more appropriate is the idea of a mother, influencing, but sympathetic to and hence influenced by, her child and delighting in its growing creativity and freedom."[42]

When we think of persons-in-relation as an organic view of ourselves in the world, we begin to seek models for God that make sense of an "I-Thou" relationship. Virginia Mollenkott writes that "This *Thou*, this Absolute relatedness, may be referred to as He, She, or It because this *Thou* relates to everyone and everything. . . . This *Thou* is a jealous God . . . jealous . . . that He/She/It be recognized everywhere in everyone and everything."[43]

We need, then, to find personal models for God. Sallie McFague claims that "this is not to say that God is a person or that personal language describes or defines God. It is to say, rather, that to speak of God with the aid of or through the screen of such language is better than some other way of thinking."[44] This allows one "to reflect a view of God's activity in the world as radically relational, immanental, interdependent, and noninterventionist."[45]

McFague suggests that we experiment with three models not often used: God as mother, as lover, and as friend. She has worked out a careful and insightful defense of these models, but she says there are more of them, especially when we are addressing God in prayer. She writes that

> when we address God as mother, father, lover, friend, or as judge, healer, liberator, companion, or yet again as sun, ocean, fortress, shield, or even as creator, redeemer, and sustainer, we know that these terms are not descriptions of God.[46]

---

[42]Ibid., 58.

[43]*The Divine Feminine: The Biblical Imagery of God as Female* (New York: Crossroad, 1983) 113-14; quoted by McFague in *Models of God* (Philadelphia: Fortress, 1987) 203.

[44]*Models of God*, 82-83.

[45]Ibid., 83.

[46]Ibid., 181. See Sallie McFague, "The World as God's Body," *The Christian Century* (20-27 July 1988): 671-73.

Such models of these have an empirical base, although the base may be something like Macintosh's value producing factor or Wieman's growth of meaning and value. Only on this basis can we attempt to find models that speak to us today. But models are the product of culture and can outlive their usefulness. They are the product of human imagination, drawing on the human capacity to reflect on the data of experience. We can expand our concepts of God through metaphysical and logical thought, and we find that most of our language is poetic and metaphorical. But ultimately we face the question of a model's basic truth and this turns us to Ramsey's test of empirical fit. As Whitehead reminds us, the models we took from Caesar have served to alienate us from a God who cares, and Hartshorne has shown such theological mistakes as omnipotence, omniscience, and love without emotion. But we are being presented with new models or with refurbished old ones with the proper and logically odd qualifiers, and perhaps we can continue to look for additional models that reflect both empirical methods and process thought.

William Bernhardt's Theory of Religious Values

Charles S. Milligan

The purpose of this essay is to provide an exposition and analysis of Bernhardt's* theory of religious values.[1] Bernhardt held that there are certain values that accrue as a result of religious practices and interpretations. These values, so remarkably diverse in various cultures and periods of history, are more or less universal in essence when understood in relation to those aspects of life that are beyond human control. Religion functions, he argued, in relation to what he called "the nonmanipulable"—those aspects of life that are destructive of human values and for which there are no techniques and knowledge available and adequate to control the destructive situation. My focus in this essay will be on those religious values that emerge as an adjustment to the nonmanipulable aspects of life.

After having examined Bernhardt's theory of religious values, I will propose two additional hypotheses as extensions of his theory. The first is that there are different *levels of religious values*. The second is that religion inevitably operates by means of *a principle of indirection*.

A third hypothesis will be proposed, which represents something of a disagreement with Bernhardt's views, namely, that there has been a categorical change in the

---

*Writings of William H. Bernhardt cited in the notes are abbreviated as follows.

AR *The Analysis of Religion.* Denver: The Iliff School of Theology, 1939.

CQG *The Cognitive Quest for God.* Denver, 1971. Published by a corporation no longer incorporated but whose name is now used by an entirely different firm (Criterion); therefore inquiries should be sent to the Iliff School of Theology rather than to the original publisher.

FPR *A Functional Philosophy of Religion.* Denver, 1958, 1969.

OT *Operational Theism.* Denver, 1971. (Bound together with CQG.)

TR "Truth in Religion," *The Iliff Review* 22/3 (Fall 1965): 5-50.

[1] William H. Bernhardt (1893–1979; Ph.D., University of Chicago, 1928) was Professor of Philosophy of Religion at The Iliff School of Theology in Denver, Colorado from 1929 to 1964, and over the years taught courses as well in theology, ethics, social philosophy, history of religions, sects and cults.

form which the nonmanipulable takes in modern life. As a consequence there are substantial changes in the values that are operative in religion. If correct, this has further consequences in how religion is regarded by those who understand this change in the human situation and in the beliefs and interpretations pertaining to their religion.

1. Worldview and Methodology

Bernhardt's basic intellectual orientation was rigorously naturalistic, understanding that to mean an integrated natural world open to investigation and operating in accordance with principles of order and causality. The abbreviated way of saying this would be that "all reality is law-abiding," but since that type of language is often associated with a mechanistic (Newtonian) cosmology, a more qualified statement is necessary. Put negatively, this form of naturalism rejects mechanistic materialism on the one side and idealism (that is, that reality is fundamentally mental) on the other. Reality consists of something like "neutral stuff," rather than being a machine or a mind, yet having a vast range of potentialities. It also rejects supernaturalism, any radical bifurcation of the universe, all esoteric claims for a special pathway to truth (or of epistemological privilege), and every form of authoritative or divinized revelation. In this regard he was in conformity with many of the leading figures of "the Chicago School."[2]

Along similar lines, his methodology was that of empiricism. Human experience is the ultimate court of appeal. It simply happens to be the only one available to us. We must be quick to add that it is experience examined by means of refined, systematic, and critical reason, providing provisional conclusions without any pretentions of infallibility or finality. This approach has much in common with pragmatism, but emphasizes far more the role of system and theory. Thus Bernhardt preferred the terms "functionalism" and "operationalism" to pragmatism. He often spoke of "checkable consequences," and stressed that "it is better to live in terms of verified probabilities than of unverified certainties."[3] He was enthralled with problems and theories of methodology and wrote a number of papers devoted to aspects of it, such as, "The Presupposition of Absolute Demand," "Approximation: The Presupposition of Proximate Realization," "The Presupposition of Increasing Cognitional Efficiency," and "History and the Logic of All or None." It was characteristic of him that in virtually every subject to which he turned his attention, he began with an analysis of diverse methodologies used there—generally in more detail than some students thought necessary. At the same time, such was his fascination with methodologies and how it is that they and their presuppositions shape conclusions, that he awakened a serious interest in others in this austere subject.

Having emphasized his naturalism and empiricism, I think I should add that his spirit and attitude were thoroughly irenic, rather than dogmatic or authoritarian. His patience with students who were struggling to think things through, including many

---

[2]The period referred to here is the 1920s and 1930s, although Professor Bernhardt was in touch with H. N. Wieman, S. J. Case, B. Loomer, and others for some years beyond that.

[3]OT 192; TR 47. On basic assumptions, listed later, see FPR, 34-35.

who simply refused even to entertain an understanding of an empirical approach to religious studies, was legendary. What I wish to make clear is that his tolerance as he listened and discussed was never such that it obscured where he stood, what he thought and why he thought that.

It is in order now to list his basic assumptions as prefatory to consideration of his metaphysics. Here, again, I will be listing things with a minimum of comment, reminding you that he gave detailed exposition to these items. Basic assumptions cannot be proved, of course, but can be subjected to reexamination and evaluation in terms of their utility, necessity, and apparent congruence with what appear to be reasonable conclusions. As Bernhardt enumerated them, these were his basic assumptions (or necessary metaphysical presuppositions): 1. Belief in an order of nature; 2. Knowledge of nature depends on observation of brute facts; 3. Belief that entities are related functionally, which is to say that "in a more or less orderly world, changes which occur concomitantly may be presumed to be related causally or determinately, that is, functionally."

We turn now to Bernhardt's metaphysics in which these assumptions operate. He regarded metaphysics as "essentially a matter of organizing knowledge as adequately as possible." Or, as he defined it formally, it is

> the organization of the all-pervasive characteristics, qualities, trends, or tendencies of the Existential Medium [all reality whatever] in order to provide a framework for the understanding of man and that in which he exists.[4]

He termed that all-pervasive interpretive structure of his metaphysics *Episodic Durationality*. This provides a more particular designation for the general position which I called naturalistic empiricism. As Bernhardt unpacks his meaning of episode and duration, it turns out (as I see it) to be very close to Whitehead's meaning of the "organismic" view and the phenomenon of "concrescence" (emerging in definite particularity), or what Dewey meant by the quality of specifiability.

Episodic Durationality is explicated through fifteen categories.[5]

A. Categories of Existence	B. Categories of Relation	C. Categories of Modality
Episodicity	Compresence	Spatiality
Directional Momentum	Emergence	Temporality
Modifiability	Multiplicity	Limitation
Stability	Nonneutrality	Determinateness
Quality	Transeunce	Culmination

The presumption is that no one of these terms can be adequately subsumed under one of the other categories, and also that anything which is can be adequately dealt with under some combination of these categories. The three groupings "constitute the framework for the organization of knowledge which constitutes metaphysics as we

[4]OT 152.

[5]"A Metaphysical Basis for Value Theory and Religion," *The Iliff Review* 15/2 (Spring 1958): 14; ch. 2 of OT, pp. 156ff.

understand it.[6]

In the light of this bare outline of Bernhardt's metaphysics, our question is, where are values to be found within this categorical scheme, with its claim to present a minimum but adequate universally comprehensive vocabulary? The question is singularly challenging to this type of naturalism since all but one of the categories appear to be akin more to physics than to biology, let alone psychology or the humanities. On the surface there is no apparent connection with attributes which would be associated with worth and significance as meant in ordinary discourse. The one exception is the category of quality, but quality is not synonymous with value. In philosophical understanding quality has a much broader meaning than value. Any attribute of an object or event—such as weight or color, velocity or frequency, extension or opacity—is a *quality* of an object to which it belongs. Yet it is altogether clear that Bernhardt did not subscribe to an epiphenomenalistic interpretation of value. He regarded values as real, designatable, definite, and subject to human evaluative judgment with some degree of warrantability. How, then, do values fit into his categorical scheme?

2. The Nature of Value

After having examined several philosophies of value (Aristotle, Bernard Bosanquet, Nicolai Hartmann, and Dewey), Bernhardt notes that they tend to be either concerned with the realization of ends or the appreciative aspect. On most subjects Bernhardt was given to analysis and drawing lines of distinction, however, here he calls attention to the need to assimilate divergent views into one broader view. An adequate theory of the nature of value must include both dimensions: the ends-realization and the appreciative.[7]

> These two categories may not in actual fact be separable. It is possible that they are divergent emphases of an inclusive experience or episode.
> Tentatively, then, we may say that this analysis of four quite different value systems indicates that value "facts" consist in experienced events, occurrences or activities characterized by culminations, consummations or realization accompanied by satisfactions, appreciations and enjoyments, or at least with feelings that the culminations are proper or fitting, that is, satisfying.[8]

As for the question of cultural diversity and thus whether any defensible universal assertions can be made, he asserts that

> There are profound differences in the way in which these satisfactory culminations are interpreted. These are variants. . . . The invariants for which

---

[6]OT 157.

[7]"Value Theory and Religion," *The Iliff Review* 15/1 (Winter 1958): 11; ch. 1 of OT, p. 141.

[8]"Value Theory and Religion," 13; OT 143.

we are seeking are found in the category presented in the preceding paragraph. [Characterized by culminations, consummations, or realized satisfactions.]⁹

This portrayal of the underlying commonality of value attributes which are pervasive through "profound" cultural diversities, leads to an exposition of five factors which, he claims, are present in value situations. As nearly as I can determine, Bernhardt's view was that there is no such isolatable reality which can be designated as values. For values are adjectival in nature. That is, they inhere in other things or events and are attributes which characterize certain specifiable events, thus qualities of events; they are not independent essences, subsistents, or substances. This does not make them less real or significant than stones or bread, persons or galaxies. Here are the characteristics of the adjectival qualities which we recognize as values.¹⁰

1. *The Emergence of Novelty.* This simply refers to the observable fact that things change and sometimes the changes are such that they are regarded as productive of value or an increase in value. Novelty, he observed, is not limited to the human realm, but is found repeatedly in nature.

2. *Tension, Momentum, or Directionality.* Tension refers to the types of situation in which a value realization process began with some sense of need. He acknowledged that this is often the case, but pointed out that there are instances of spontaneous value appropriation. Also, he had come to the conclusion that "there is a factor of directional momentum operative at all levels of existence." By directional he meant a persistent tendency or trend.

> The universe is dynamic, and it is directional. And what is true of the whole appears to be true of the lesser wholes. With the emergence of some novelty, the new contains its own directional momentum with its own tendency toward some culminative activity.¹¹

The similarity here with the creative evolutionists, such as Henri Bergson, Samuel Alexander, C. Lloyd Morgan, and Jan Christian Smuts, is quite apparent.

3. *Culminative or Consummatory Results.* This is directly related to his designation "episodic." For an episode is a "set of events that stand out or apart from others as of a particular moment."¹² A value event stands apart from other similar events which are not of singular importance. A commonplace illustration will show how this can be. Imagine that you are walking down the street in an unfamiliar city and that you pass another pedestrian. You walk on later and pass yet another pedestrian. The first encounter was of value; the second was not. Anyone could fill in a senario to explain the difference. If the first person met was an old friend and unexpected in that place, the encounter could have led to animated conversation cul-

---

⁹Ibid.
¹⁰OT 143-47, 170-74.
¹¹OT 145.
¹²OT 146.

minating in memorable and gratifying news, plans, and shared memories. By way of contrast, the second pedestrian was a stranger and in fact was encountered, but the event led to no culminative consequence.

Episodes which are valuable do occur and pass away, but they are not thereby ephemeral will-o'-the-wisps. They have definite outcome and leave some type of durable significance.

> These culminative results are never absolutely or finally satisfactory. . . .
> Yet culminative results are never wholly lost. They appear to be cumulative
> in nature . . . [with] a cumulative factor at work which carries something
> of each earlier value experience into those which emerge later.[13]

4. *Changes in Quality-Potential.* Bernhardt accepted the view often expressed that qualities are characteristics of objects which produce effects in other objects. This is, plainly, a view which presupposes not only that qualities have this potentiality for effects beyond themselves, but also that objects or events or processes have a capacity for receiving and being modified by qualities in other objects/events/processes. This is "universal modifiability."

> Each experience, *something lived through,* leaves its imprint upon us phys-
> ically and psychically. Each day leaves us older, each experience may leave
> us more mature. The first is called the aging process, the second the matur-
> ing process. Both refer to modifications produced or evoked by factors op-
> erating within us or without, or both. The culminative events or experiences
> defined as valuable have this capacity also.[14]

5. *Satisfactoriness.* The danger with regard to this attribute of value is that it will be understood to mean simply having pleasant sensations in connection with an event or activity, or simply a judgment that one's chosen course of action will be or has proven to be congruent with hopes and expectations. Bernhardt assigns a deeper and more complex meaning to satisfactoriness. There is, he claimed, a "feeling tone which accompanies all activity." It is deepened and enriched when the culmination of the event is not merely gratifying because of having met our expectations, but in addition "satisfies the structure of our feelings."[15] Perhaps we can use the metaphor of resonance and say that when an event fully meets the criterion of satisfactoriness, it resonates with a larger pattern of our purposes as well as meeting the particular need at hand. The value event is then continuous with and harmonious with the total experience.

> The relational is essentially cognitive, the event is intuitive, an immediate
> participation in the event itself with the feelings normal to such a relation-

---

[13]Ibid.
[14]Ibid. He acknowledges a particular debt to Wieman regarding this concept.
[15]OT 147, 172-73.

ship.[16]

Furthermore, satisfactoriness in this larger sense may well include elements of dissatisfaction, not merely in the stages leading to a culmination, but in the culmination itself. Hence this is quite different from Augustine's aesthetic theodicy where evil is viewed as temporary discord, enriching the larger pattern and absorbed into a perfect culmination. In actual life experiences there are many highly valuable and fulfilling events which nevertheless contain aspects of regret or loss. Just as Bernhardt would reject the presupposition of absolute demand, so he would reject the demand that our fulfilling experiences must be perfect. The demand for certainty or claims for perfection are not attributes of refined insight, but characteristics of immaturity.[17]

In summary, Bernhardt's theory is that values are relational, culminative, and satisfying in nature. They are not substances or essences, but modifying attributes of episodic events. They are *combinations* of qualities which in their interrelated pattern have the five characteristics that have been ennumerated. In Bosanquet's terminology (but not his metaphysics), they are *wholes* and are generally experienced as successive realizations of wholeness.[18] They are marked by both the realization of ends and the response of appreciation.

> The term value refers to, denotes or designates those culminative episodes which satisfy some need, interest, or directional momentum of living beings. Disvalue or evil consists in that which thwarts or prevents these satisfying culminations.[19]

3. Religious Values

The simplest and most direct way to come at Bernhardt's view of religious values is to say that religious values are those— whatever they are—which come into being as a result of religious activity and thought. The appropriate question then becomes: Are there certain values which emerge from religious practices which are more persistent and universal? Bernhardt calls these invariant, in contrast with values which vary substantially from one religion to another, even one person to another.

It should be emphasized that in speaking of religious values, he is not making the claim that there are certain goods or states of being which are unique to religion and which exist only in connection with religion. The term refers rather to those *life values* which religion engenders, strengthens, and enriches.[20] As we observed in the

---

[16]OT 147.

[17]Cf. AR 296-97; FPR 120; TR 33-34 and passim.

[18]OT 135. Cf. H. H. Potthoff, *God and the Celebration of Life* (New York: Rand McNally, 1969) 188-89.

[19]OT 147.

[20]Cf. John Hick, "Faith as Interpretation," *Classical and Contemporary Readings in the Philosophy of Religion,* 2nd ed. (Englewood Cliffs NJ: Prentice-Hall, 1970).

previous section, actual values are found in particular instances. In this regard Bernhardt belongs with the Nominalists in the medieval debate with the Realists. The reality of values is not located in any abstraction or generalization, but in the experiences
of individual persons in communities. From such particular experiences we can make
reasonable generalizations about types of values, such as moral, cognitive and aesthetic.[21] Religious values combine cognitive and aesthetic (that is, emotional and appreciative qualities). Thus in his frequent definitions of religion he often used the term
"aesthetic-noetic behavior."

In Bernhardt's analysis of the function of religion he found that the factor which
consistently calls forth religious practices—in a wide variety of cultures and periods
of history— to be the "nonmanipulable," that is, an undesirable circumstance which
is beyond control by means of the knowledge and skills available.

> Religious behavior is a complex form of individual and group behavior
> whereby persons are prepared intellectually and emotionally to meet the
> nonmanipulable aspects of existence positively by means of a reinterpreta-
> tion of the total situation and with the use of various techniques.[22]

It might appear from this that as knowledge and technology increase, religion will
necessarily diminish. And of course there are some life problems where religion used
to be used, but is no longer because there are now effective means of control. However, Bernhardt argued that the increase of technology merely shifts the location and
form of the nonmanipulable. Ignorance,or awareness of the limits of our knowledge,
provides one example. Increased knowledge does not diminish the boundary where
ignorance impinges upon the known. The more one knows, the more areas there are
where one is aware of being ignorant.[23] Furthermore, in ancient times one could master a significant part of the realm of knowledge. Thanks to the knowledge explosion,
we can master only small areas of limited fields of knowledge.

The nonmanipulable can be denoted in terms of its consequence: frustration. If
frustration is the thing which calls forth religious responses, it is all too clear that
although the items which cause frustration have changed, frustration is as intense a
human problem as ever. It is with reference to that that we find emerging religious
values. The value which persistently is found emerging from religious practice of
whatever sort is *morale*. Morale is the maintenance of *courage, confidence,* and *hope*
in the face of frustration and demoralizing circumstances.

> Religious techniques are thus morale-building and morale-maintaining ac-
> tivities. They enable individuals, in greater or lesser degrees, to maintain
> courage, confidence, and hope in normal life as well as in the crises of life.
> In normal life there are factors, unsatisfactory yet inescapable, which tend
> to deprive life of its zest and meaning. Active participation in religious tech-

---

[21]OT 147.

[22]FPR 157.

[23]Cf. W. C. Tremmel, *Religion—What Is It?*, 2nd ed. (New York: Holt, Rinehart, and
Winston, 1984) 22.

niques should counteract this devitalizing effect of normal living. In the crises of life, when one's dearest possessions are jeopardized, religious techniques, familiar through long practice, may prevent the disorganization of behavior, or aid in its reorganization if it has become disorganized. Furthermore, these techniques may enable individuals to reestablish the beliefs or regulative principles by which they have been living, but which were shaken by the crisis.[24]

There may well be other values produced by religious participation. Bernhardt has no objection to that unless a religious leader or institution pursues a tangential value to the utter neglect of religion's central and invariant value: morale, which consists in courage, confidence, and hope.[25]

Bernhardt was concerned to combat two serious misconceptions about religion and to do so by means of empirical data. On the one hand there were those who equated religion with magic and thus dismissed it. They did not notice that religion is compensatory and adjustive or that religions have had a remarkably tenacious place in people's lives despite a dismal record of repeated failures in producing bumper crops, continuous health, and victory in war. Something else was going on, namely an inner source of strength and spirit in the face of such defeats, the gift of their religion.

On the other hand, the more prevalent threat from within academe came from those who some years ago saw religion as essentially ethics in disguise. Bernhardt had no axe to grind against ethics—after all, he taught it by choice for several years— but he did have such an objection to confusion and what he viewed as muddle-headedness. The ethical record of religion is not any more studded with stars than is the magical record. I do not recall that Bernhardt mentions this, but I have noticed that frequently well meaning people engage in social action and religio-ethical language with demonstrable ineffectiveness, under the illusion that they have "done something about the problem." What they have accomplished is generation of reassurance and self-satisfaction within themselves—in a word, morale for facing life in an unsatisfactory world.[26] I must add that I report this observation with sadness, because

---

[24]FPR 132-33. Cf. AR, 270, and W. H. Bernhardt, "More Things Are Wrought by Prayer," *The Iliff Review* 1/2 (Spring 1944): 64; Tremmel, *Religion—What Is It?*, 60-64; Potthoff, *God and the Celebration of Life*, 57-58; C. S. Milligan, "An Examination of Bernhardt's Definition of Religion," *The Iliff Review* 11/1 (Winter 1954): 7ff. In addition, attention should be called to Professor Tremmel's paper in this present series, which adds later reflections on the function of religion as conceived by Bernhardt.

[25]FPR 161-62.

[26]ARP 297. Bernhardt devoted detailed attention to analysis of the position which claims that religion is a subcategory under ethics and that religion is really ethics in disguise. The first of these positions is represented by Kant and largely derives from either his thought or the British notion, frequently expressed and just as frequently dismissed, that religion is primarily for the purpose of controlling the young and keeping them in line, as e.g. "Religion is morality tinged with emotion." The second position is represented by R. B. Braithwaite, *An Empiricist's View of the Nature of Religious Belief* (Cambridge: Cambridge University Press, 1955), where he argues that religious statements or assertions are actually expressions of one's inten-

I have been an activist all my professional life. It is for that reason that I deplore action on behalf of good causes, which does not promote the cause but rather the gratification of the promoters and participants. One's religious faith may indeed motivate one toward work on behalf of social justice. But there is something to be said for being clear about what the purpose of such involvement is and also clear about what one's religion has to contribute, which is not special wisdom as to what is true or guarantees of infallibility as to strategy and tactics. What religion has to contribute is inner strength and durable persistence, which may be for good or ill, and as far as I can see is the one as often as the other.

There is no better statement of the function of religion in Bernhardt's view than in these familiar verses:

> We are afflicted in every way, but not crushed; perplexed, but not driven to
> despair; persecuted, but not forsaken; struck down, but not destroyed. . . .
> . . . to be strengthened with might through the spirit in the inner self. . . .
> So we do not lose heart. Though our outer nature is wasting away, our inner
> nature is being renewed every day.
> This is the victory that overcomes the world, our faith.[27]

However, it was not scripture, but Epictetus who set Bernhardt on this line of thought. "We must make the best of those things that are in our power, and take the rest as nature gives it. What do you mean by 'nature'? I mean, God's will."[28]

Bernhardt's theory of what constitutes central values of religion was not original, nor did he think it was. His contribution was in providing a disciplined empirical basis for the claim and in a strong argument to the effect that the need for these values— courage, confidence, and hope—has not diminished with the advance of science and technology. The line between these and other variant values may not be as clean cut as he thought, but I believe he was quite correct in his claim that when religious institutions and teachings lose sight of their special contribution in terms of inner strength and spirit, the results are unfortunate.[29]

---

tion to follow a specified policy of behaviour. Santayana came close to this view in *Reason in Religion* (New York: Charles Scribner's, 1905), suggesting that religion gives "its symbolic rendering of that moral experience which it springs out of and which it seeks to elucidate." (14) This is odd in view of the major thrust of his book, viewing religious "truth" as poetry and presenting a view very close to Bernhardt's: "Prayer . . . will not bring rain, but until rain comes it may cultivate hope and resignation and may prepare the heart for any issue, opening up a vista in which human prosperity will appear in its conditioned existence and conditional value." (36).

[27]2 Cor. 4:8-9; Eph. 3:16; 2 Cor. 4:16; 1 John 5:4, respectively.

[28]*The Discourses of Epictetus* 1.1, which Bernhardt quotes in AR, 213, and refers to again in FPR, 157 n.1. He gives credit to Professor William L. Bailey of Northwestern University for introducing him to Epictetus and the concept of religion as basically an adjustment. I have been able to track down only a limited amount of information about Bailey, but enough to judge that he was a colorful, active, and stimulating teacher with many lively interests.

[29]TR 13.

4. Three Additional Hypotheses

1. *Levels of Religious Values.* My proposal is that religious values operate at three levels of awareness.[30] These are not ones of higher and lower significance, but of psychological differences. First, there are those which are directly stated and emphasized, the "official" values. These may be for rain, righteousness, health, justice, upright morality, etc. Secondly, there are the implicit values, acknowledged but stated only incidently and not emphasized. They may be for status, fellowship, economic benefit, ego gratification and the like. Thirdly, there are the unconsciously sought values, which may be suppressed or simply of such nature that they cannot be achieved if made self-consciously explicit. These may be exhibitionistic, vengeful, sacrificial, redemptive, narcissistic, salvific, etc. Morale may be involved in any or all of these levels, it is such a collective term.

Among the frustrations of modern life is the stress of having to be continuously goal-oriented. I suspect that religion needs to provide renewal and relief from that, heightening self-awareness rather than more self-consciousness, more need for performance and less for a justifying rationale.

2. *The Principle of Indirection.* This principle asserts that religion is most effective in the long run when it operates by means of cultivation rather than manipulation, by indirection rather than by direct mechanical means. Its language is more like that of love and poetry than science and commerce, often implicative and metaphorical. There are some rituals in *all* religions which have little direct resemblance to their functioning purpose, recognizing of course there are others which are direct dramatizations of their purpose. It is not merely in Judaism and Christianity that many teachings are clothed in the imagery of nature. For in growing crops we tend soil and water, nutrition and weeding, far more in enhancing the plants' environment than by direct action upon the plants. That is indirection.

This is not to deny the necessity for instruction at the appropriate time, but merely to note that many of the most sustaining values of religious participation emerge as by-products of activities and as side effects of the mythos, theology and cognitive reflection. It is at the more sophisticated religious level that there is the danger of being overly self-conscious with neglect of the more patient, more trusting, processes of cultivation which permit fruition and culminations to occur in their own way in due season.

3. *The Principle of Categorical Change.* One of Bernhardt's methodological presuppositions is that "Religion must be defined in terms consistent with its historic function rather than as any given individual may wish to define it."[31] It is reasonable enough that there be historical continuity, but I have slowly come to recognize categorical change within sequential continuity. I believe this has happened with regard

---

[30]I have developed this view in more detail in "Navajo Religion— Values Sought and Values Received," *The Iliff Review* 3/3 (Fall 1946) and 4/1 (Winter 1947). I have a copy of Bernhardt's lectures on the history of religions (unpublished ms) and although I want to be forthright in saying that this theory of levels of religous values is mine, in reviewing his lectures on world religions I have no reason to believe my theory to be at odds with his views.

[31]FPR 46.

to the nonmanipulable *in modern, privileged, technological societies,* with consequent changes in religious values and techniques, as well as doctrine.

For ages on end humans struggled with insufficiencies. These were of power, energy, knowledge, weapons, conveniences, speed. All that has changed for us. Our frustrations are ones of disposal, selection, finesse, over-choice, boundaries. Consider power. It becomes a parable of many circumstances to picture an automobile that will go over a hundred miles an hour caught in the five o'clock gridlock. The excess of unusable power mocks its owner. We worry more about a prolonged dying process than about death. So many of the causes of modern frustration are *impalpable,* being due to arrangements, far away developments, bureaucratic management. The more we have, the more we are mocked by our powers and possessions when they are unusable or when our world crumbles. Poets and dramatists have depicted this from every angle. The nonmanipulable confronts us in new guises— impalpable and mockingly. It is not primarily lack of knowledge and skill.

As a result, new values, mostly not yet clear, are needed in response to the new frustrations. Bernhardt said repeatedly that the God concept is essential to religion and that God becomes our "highest good."[32] That appears to me to be less true than formerly. Picture a house filled with art and conveniences whose occupant's once lovely marriage has ended in divorce, or a farmer who has survived crop losses but not increased interest rates as the auctioneer's gavel comes down, or a laborer of skill and integrity replaced by automation or the decline of the domestic steel market, and you begin to comprehend the modern form of demoralization. God talk turns out to be strangely unhelpful for many such, and yet morale and inner resiliency are needed more than ever.

Morale is still a good term for what is needed, but we must expand the list of "courage, confidence, and hope" to include a sense that life is meaningful and of worth. Spiritual strength, rejuvenation, focus, perspective—all that and more—are needed, but even for the very devout the forms which engender those qualities have changed.

These thoughts are admittedly impressionistic and inadequately developed here.[33] My purpose has been to suggest a line of questions and thoughts which may be of worth for further reflection and which emerge. as a result of having once again worked through the writings of a deeply revered teacher and friend, William Bernhardt.

---

[32]FPR 116, 164. Cf. Bernhardt, "God as Dynamic Determinant," *The Journal of Religion* 23/4 (October 1943): 276-85; "The Present and Future of Religious Liberalism," *The Journal of Bible and Religion* 11/4 (November 1943): 195-201; "Reason in Religion," ibid. 15/3 (July 1947): 133-38.

[33]On uncertainty of present trends, see TR, 13, and CQG, 126-28, an interesting topic illustrating our groping in religious studies is ecology. A recent study issued by the Association of Theological Schools barely mentions the ecological crisis in one sentence, although secular scientists and scholars rank this on a par with nuclear threats to human survival.

Charles F. Potter
On Evolution and Religious Humanism

Mason Olds

Speaking both generally and historically, in the West people of religious faith have believed in the existence of God, that right actions were predicated on the will of God, and that the believer was immortal and would be rewarded for faithfulness. Most often these beliefs were explained in terms of a metaphysical dualism, involving a natural realm and a supernatural realm. Furthermore, those doctrines which could not be proved by reason were thought to be justified by divine revelation. To be religious was to believe such doctrines and to be nonreligious was to refuse to believe them.

However, beginning about 1915 in the United States, a number of liberal religious thinkers began to repudiate, if not refute, these tenets. They maintained that one could in the best sense of the word be religious without believing any one of these doctrines. The term employed to designate this position was Religious Humanism.

Though Charles Francis Potter did not arrive fully at the Religious Humanist position until about 1925, he did adopt it, and became a popular spokesman, continuing to promote it until his death in 1962.[1] Potter advocated a religion without God, believing that intellectual honesty led him to "agnostic atheism"; he thought that it was the will of humans which determined what right actions were rather than the will of God; and he maintained that the evidence pointed to the fact that humans were mortal and that doctrines about personal immortality were pure fantasy. Moreover, he argued there was insufficient evidence supporting the claim about a supernatural realm, so he accepted a monism which focused on the natural realm. Rather than revelation being self-authenticating, he felt such claims spurious; so he thought the way to separate truth from falsehood was the scientific method. Hence Potter, like others of his

---

[1]The basic facts about Potter's life are contained in his autobiography, *The Preacher and I* (New York: Crown Publishing, Inc., 1951). His obituary appeared in the *New York Times,* 5 October 1962. For a more complete study of Potter's thought, see my *Religious Humanism in America: Dietrich, Reese, and Potter* (Washington DC: University Press of America, 1977) esp. 159-200.

theological tribe, repudiated the foundational doctrines of Western religious thought; and, yet, at the same time he advocated a religion without God.

Potter and Evolution

Following the publication of Charles Darwin's *On the Origin of Species by Means of Natural Selection* (1859), a heated debate ensued among scientists and among religious thinkers, and between scientists and religious thinkers. And of course with the appearance of *The Descent of Man and Selection in Relation to Sex* (1871), which confirmed the fears of the antievolutionists, that the Darwinians thought humans were a part of the evolutionary process by means of natural selection, the debate spread. In the United States evangelical religion began to split on this and other related issues. In one camp were the Modernists who thought religious beliefs should be reconciled with the development of science. Therefore they were willing to accomodate religious thought to such movements as evolution and historical criticism. However, there were in the other camp, the Fundamentalists who denied the validity of such modern developments. They felt the Modernists were selling out some important ingredients of the historic faith to the secular world.

With respect to evolution, there were several important issues. The first had to do with the age of the world. According to the Fundamentalists, the world was created ex nihilo less than six thousand years ago; whereas, the Modernists were willing to entertain the possibility that the world was billions of years old, and creation was continuous. The second issue dealt with the creation of humans. The Fundamentalists followed literally a Genesis account which had man "specially created" by God in an instant and with woman "specially created" by God from man's rib also in an instant. The Modernists accepted the theory that life had evolved on our planet, that more complex forms of life had developed from less complex forms by means of natural selection, and that humans were the latest to evolve in this long process. These two issues had implications for a third issue, namely, the authority of the Bible. The Fundamentalists saw clearly that if the Modernists were correct, then Scripture was not an infallible source for religious faith and practice. Of course, the Modernists accepted the view that the Bible was not infallible, but they thought that rather than being literally the word of God, it *contained* the word of God. According to the Modernists, the Bible tells that God is the creator, but it does not explain how creation came about. Evolution offers an explanation as to how God creates. So shortly before the First World War, these issues were hotly debated in the mainline Protestant churches.

By 1914, Potter had relinquished his fundamentalistic interpretation of religious faith and had become a Modernist. His shift in faith was represented by his transfer of ministerial fellowship from the Baptist Church to the Unitarian Church. Having served three Unitarian Churches in rapid succession, he became the minister of the West Side Unitarian Church in New York City (1919–1925). While at West Side, the conflict between the Fundamentalists and Modernists was hotly debated with the focus often on evolution. The Fundamentalists made a well-organized, concerted effort to pass laws in the various states to prohibit the teaching of evolution in the public schools, and even amend the federal Constitution to that end. In some states, such as

Tennessee, they were successful; whereas, in other states like Minnesota they were defeated. Of course, this attempt to outlaw the teaching of evolution raised important issues about academic freedom, which also had implications for free speech. Along with evolution, these issues had high priority with the Modernists.

Potter was the modernist minister at West Side, but at Calvary Baptist Church, just a few blocks away, was John Roach Straton, the pastor, who was the unchallenged leader of Fundamentalism in New York. In early December 1923, Straton brought together such well-known Fundamentalists as Thomas T. Shields of Toronto, J. Frank Norris of Forth Worth, and William Jennings Bryan to launch a campaign against the Modernists. As the newspapers carried stories of the meetings and reported personal attacks on Modernists, especially liberal Baptists and Unitarians who were personal acquaintances of Potter, Potter retaliated with the eventual outcome being the Straton-Potter debates. Originally five debates were scheduled, but only four were actually held. The first was in Calvary Baptist Church before an audience of over twenty-five hundred, and the other three were in Carnegie Hall before a packed house. For our purposes, the second debate was most important, for it dealt with the question "Resolved, That the earth and man came from evolution."[2]

Potter of course took the affirmative, and Straton the negative. Potter's basic thesis was that "at no time has a transcendent God interfered with the universe, but that God has been immanent in the evolutionary processes from the very beginning; that every upthrust of this life-force has been a manifestation of God; that you and I are manifestations of God, rather imperfect, to be sure, but progressing toward better things."[3] The kind of creation Potter believed in was "absolutely continuous, and if so, it becomes evolution."[4]

Straton argued that unless the biblical story of creation was true it is impossible to account for humans appearing on earth. His argument was, "The gap between dead matter and sentient life has never been bridged except by guesses."[5] He went on to maintain that acceptance of Darwinism had led to "animalism" and that this had a corrupting influence on morals. In fact, he argued that it had led to "a degrading of womanhood" and degeneracy in our literature, sensuality in dramatic art, and divorce; and that "Germany took Darwinism, applied it literally to develop the philosophy that 'might makes right' and then bore down upon an unsuspecting world in 1914."[6]

Though two of the judges were "eminent justices of the New York Supreme Court" and a third "a lawyer of prominence," they awarded the debate to Straton.

---

[2]For the text of the debate see John Roach Straton and Charles F. Potter, *Evolution versus Creation* (New York: George H. Doran Co., 1924). For a liberal interpretation of the debate, see Jenkin R. Hockert, "Sidelights of the Second Debate," *The Christian Register* 103 (7 February 1924): 149-50. A more recent defense of evolution is contained in [No author cited], *Science and Creationism: A View of the National Academy of Sciences* (Washington DC: National Academy Press. 1984) 5-26.

[3]Straton and Potter, *Evolution versus Creation,* 28.

[4]Ibid., 29.

[5]Ibid., 50.

[6]Ibid., 106.

In 1925, the Scopes Trial was held in Dayton, Tennessee, and Potter attended as "librarian and Bible expert for the defense," and covered the debates for *The Christian Register,* a Unitarian publication in Boston. In many respects the Scopes Trial was a recapitulation of the second Straton-Potter debate on evolution. Only this time the central characters were Clarence Darrow and William Jennings Bryan and the stakes were higher. As Bryan had collaborated with Straton in the debates, most of Bryan's arguments were very similar to those of Straton, even many of the phrases: for example, "I'm not so much interested in the age of the rocks as I am in the Rock of Ages." Likewise Darrow had Potter work up a list of inaccurate historical statements in the Bible based on higher criticism, but apparently Darrow was able to use only a few of them. Incidentally, Potter was convinced that those people in Dayton who instigated the Scopes Trial received the idea from reading about the Potter-Straton debates in the newspapers.[7]

Two months before the Scopes Trial, Potter resigned as minister of the West Side Unitarian Church, and at that time was moving theologically from his Modernist position—containing in a rather confused way elements of both deism and pantheism—to that of nontheistic humanism. Once Potter took this final step the evolutionary model had a central place in his religious thought, for he employed it to explain both how humans arose in the world and their place in it. He used the term "saltations" to refer to the great "jumps ahead in evolution." In other words, there are periods in the evolutionary process in which very little appears to be taking place and then there is a significant development which can be definitely discerned. He also refers to these saltations as "crises."

In Potter's scheme there are four major saltations or crises. The first was the move from nonliving matter to matter which has life. He says:

> Long, long millions of years ago, then there came a point in the process of evolution when gradually changing combinations of chemical elements on the surface of this planet began to live and move and have being.[8]

Although it is not clear as to how this change occurred, the development of inert matter into living matter was called by Potter the first great crisis or pivotal point in the evolutionary process.

The second crisis came millions of years later after life had developed through many forms and took on consciousness. According to Potter, primitive forms of consciousness are found in lower forms of animals, though the level of thinking in them is not nearly as highly developed as it is in humans. Just as nonliving matter contains the same chemical elements as living matter, so the earliest forms of life had in them the elements of consciousness.[9]

The third crisis of the evolutionary process arrived when consciousness became self-consciousness, that is, when the thinking animal realized that it was thinking. In

[7]Charles F. Potter. "The Real Origin of the Dayton Trial," *The Christian Register* 104 (6 August 1925): 765-66.

[8]Charles F. Potter, *Creative Personality* (New York: Funk & Wagnalls Co., 1950) 10.

[9]Ibid., 34.

other words, the evolutionary process has now produced a self-conscious being who can recognize itself. It is this capacity for self-recognition which differentiates humans from other animals, so that this third crisis deals with the advent of humans.

The fourth crisis is much more speculative than the first three, for it is predicated upon the belief that a new crisis is imminent, that human evolution is on the verge of taking a jump ahead.[10] Potter realized there are all varieties of humans, some who are hardly self-conscious and others who are well-developed personality types. It was in this group of the higher personality type that he expected a new crisis. He referred to the next stage as being "cosmic conscious." He explained that cosmic consciousness is

> that state of mind into which an individual may enter during which he is conscious of the cosmos. In this state of mind, he becomes intellectually and emotionally aware of the universe as definitely and closely related to himself. He recognizes himself as an integral part of the universe, and even in spirit identifies himself with it. He partakes of its creative nature. He becomes cosmically and creatively conscious.[11]

Before the appearance of humans on the stage of history, the evolutionary process had been largely blind, dependent upon chance, and trial-and-error-or-success. With the coming of humans the process became self-conscious and for the first time the possibility of consciously directing the evolutionary process became a real option. As humans evolve, chance and experiment can be taken over by conscious creative control.

Although it is impossible to know what humans will become, it is obvious they have not reached their highest potential. On this point, Potter's view is rather similar to that of Jean-Paul Sartre. namely, with certain exceptions, humans make themselves into the kind of human beings they wish to be. Potter explains: "Draw a picture, an outline, of the man you would like to be, the man you ought to be. Or the woman. Then set about painting it with the best materials and skill you have or can get."[12] The great men of the earth pose challenges to those not so great. The world would be improved if the virtues of the few great men were possessed by the many. Hence one of the ways to formulate the picture of the man you would like to become is by studying the lives of great men. This is possible because "there is a projective power in many whereby he can extend his personality beyond the limits of his former self and thus obtain a larger selfhood."[13] And a part of this larger selfhood is cosmic consciousness.

In summary, Potter developed an evolutionary scheme that contains four crises. With the first crisis came "life," with the second came "consciousness," with the

---

[10]Ibid., 11.

[11]Ibid., 12.

[12]Charles F. Potter, *Humanizing Religion* (New York: Harper & Bros. Publishers, 1933) 201.

[13]Charles F. Potter, *Technique of Happiness* (New York: Macaulay, 1935) 172.

third came "self-consciousness," and with the fourth will come "cosmic consciousness." An example of the latter was Jesus. Potter evaluated him highly because of
his creative personality and his cosmic consciousness. However, it is important to
emphasize that Potter did not interpret Jesus' greatness in terms of theism and supernaturalism, but rather from a naturalisitic and humanistic perspective.[14]

Potter and Religious Humanism

As Potter did not create the theory of evolution but employed it in his "theology," he also did not create the perspective referred to as Religious Humanism. John
H. Dietrich was certainly one of the earliest proponents of this radical interpretation
of religion, for he carefully chose the term to describe his position as early as 1915.
Dietrich's hour-long addresses presented at the First Unitarian Society of Minneapolis were attempts to explicate "a systematic theology" of Religious Humanism. Also,
Curtis W. Reese, the minister of the Unitarian Church in Des Moines, Iowa, was
advocating a similar point of view under the title "Religion of Democracy." When
Dietrich and Reese met at the annual meeting of the Western Unitarian Conference
in Des Moines, in 1917, they discovered they were theological brothers under the
skin. In fact, the Religious Humanist movement has its beginning with their meeting,
for shortly thereafter Reese adopted Dietrich's terminology. About the same time,
Professor Roy Wood Sellars, philosopher and Unitarian, at the University of Mich-
igan, promoted Religious Humanism in his book *The Next Step in Religion* (1918).

The point is that Potter, though he was aware of the Religious Humanist movement shortly after its inception, did not become identified with it until about a decade
later. Yet, when he did "convert" to it, he became one of its most dynamic and en-
thusiastic promoters. For instance, with a great deal of publicity, Potter became
founder and leader of the First Humanist Society of New York (September 1929).[15]
Potter's enterprise was not without controversy even within the Religious Humanist
movement itself. Dietrich and Reese thought the best strategy for promoting humanism was to work within the established liberal denominations, whereas Potter sought
to establish Religious Humanism as an independent denomination.

In 1933, the humanists issued "A Humanist Manifesto" to the American people
which caused much debate.[16] It contained fifteen articles. Perhaps, the first two will
provide a sense of its perspective. The first article affirms that "Religious humanists
regard the universe as self-existing and not created." And the second states "Humanism believes that man is a part of nature and that he has emerged as the result of
a continuous process."[17] Obviously, the first is a repudiation of the traditional doctrine of creation ex nihilo and the second a denial of the "special creation" of humans. Sellars wrote the first draft of the document, and it was only slightly altered

[14]Potter, *Humanizing Religion*, 223.

[15][No author cited], "Now a Creedless Cult," *The Literary Digest* (16 November 1929): 23.

[16]"A Humanist Manifesto," *The New Humanist* 6 (1933): 1-5.

[17][No author cited], "First Humanist Assembly," *The Christian Register* 113 (1 November 1934): 665.

by members of a committee. Potter, as well as Dietrich and Reese, signed the Manifesto.

From the time Potter founded the First Humanist Society of New York until his death, he lived rather precariously on lecturing and writing. He wrote on many non-religious subjects and published in many of the popular magazines, such as *Reader's Digest, Saturday Evening Post,* and *Esquire.* At the same time he remained a strong advocate of what were considered liberal causes. In 1938, for example, he was a founder and director of the Euthanasia Society of America. He was also active in the birth control movement, the abolition of capital punishment movement, an advocate of "civilized divorce laws," and a staunch supporter of women's rights. In addition he worked on behalf of book promotion believing that the reading of good books would raise the cultural level of America and thus strengthen democracy. In fact, he appeared before both Senate and House committees urging a lower postal rate on books.

Though Potter was in demand as a lecturer and magazine writer, he did publish a number of books. However, for our purposes, I mention only three which contributed to the promotion of Religious Humanism. The first was *Humanism: A New Religion* (1930) which provided a kind of theological manual for humanism. Then came *Humanizing Religion* (1933) which contained fourteen of Potter's addresses to the Humanist Society. *The Creative Personality* was published in 1950; and in this work Potter picked up on one of the themes of *Humanism: A New Religion,* namely, that in humans the evolutionary process takes on consciousness which leads to personality and the concomitant need for humans to develop their personalities to the fullest. The concept of personality played an important part in Potter's thought since the early days when he became a Unitarian. Originally he interpreted it within a theistic context, but later it was interpreted within a purely naturalistic one.

As we have seen, Potter was a man of many talents, and certainly made his contributions to the humanist movement, several of them we have noted. Being in New York and having a talent for gaining headlines, he without doubt gained more publicity for the movement than any other single individual. Also, as we have seen, Potter attempted to move beyond Unitarianism and to establish humanism as an independent movement. Wallace P. Rusterholtz in his evaluation of Potter says, "To Potter, credit is chiefly due for divorcing Humanism from Unitarianism."[18] Furthermore, as noted, Potter was a social activist and a living example that humanist principles could be put into practice. Harry Elmer Barnes evaluated Potter this way:

> Dr. Potter's unique contribution was to write the best popular statement of the Humanist position and to take Humanism beyond enlightened doctrine into diversified and effective social action in behalf of human betterment. . . . Dr. Potter has been primarily the dynamic man of action in propagating and practicing Humanism.[19]

---

[18]Wallace P. Rusterholtz, *American Heretics and Saints* (Boston: Manthorne and Burack. Inc., 1938) 302.

[19]Harry Elmer Barnes, "Dr. Potter and American Humanism." *The Humanist* 12/1 (1952): 40.

But to return to Potter's theology, he believed that religion and gods were created by humans, and he understood religion in a functional sense, that is, religion was
created by humans in order to help them obtain some goal. Specifically, Potter said,
"But religion itself is but a means to an end, the improvement of man. It fails if it
does not further that purpose."[20] For him, the basic end of religion was the improvement of human personality. It is the improvement of personality both individually
and socially rather than the worship of God that is the end of religion.

Appealing to both Confucius and Buddha, Potter argued that religion is not necessarily connected with God. He observed, "To the average Westerner, a Christian
of Europe or America, for instance, religion without God is almost inconceivable.
But in the East, religion without God is no novelty."[21] As he could find no evidence
that personality exists as a separate entity apart from humans, his Religious Humanism was then a religion without God.

Potter and Philosophical Theology

I have attempted to place Potter within the context of his time and place. Both
the issues of evolution and Religious Humanism were components of that context.
Though his thought was similar to that of other Modernists and Humanists, he thought
through the issues for himself and staunchly defended his conclusions. Hence, he not
only reflected the thought of his time, but also contributed to it.

It is interesting to recall that the context out of which Religious Humanism arose
was the same as that which provided the development of modern process thought.
Whitehead's *Religion in the Making* (1926), contained lectures presented at King's
Chapel, a historic Unitarian Church in Boston. In 1937, Charles Hartshorne published *Beyond Humanism* and a journal article, "The Philosophical Limitations of
Humanism." Both these process philosophers were developing positions which repudiated supernaturalism in Neoorthodoxy and Thomism on the one hand and naturalistic humanism on the other. Though Potter was not the specific target of the
criticisms against Humanism, being an active participant in the humanist movement,
the criticisms certainly apply to his thought.

Potter, along with other humanists, however, thought that through the centuries
the attempt to reconcile traditional religious doctrines with new thought had so glossed
over the original meanings that the time had come to discard the traditional doctrines
such as God and personal immortality. For instance, article six of the Manifesto states:
"We are convinced that the time has passed for theism, deism, modernism, and the
several varieties of 'new thought'." The Religious Humanists were certainly aware
of Whitehead's thought and would have included it under "new thought." There is
no reason to doubt that Potter thought that Religious Humanism was a legitimate and
viable alternative to the various religious perspective promoted at that time, including process thought.

---

[20]Potter, *Creative Personality*. 113-14.

[21]Charles F. Potter, *Humanism: A New Religion* (New York: Simon and Schuster, 1930)
62.

If philosophical theology be distinguished from kerygmatic theology by critical reflection without appeal to revelation, and if it be differentiated from the philosophy of religion by acknowledging a religious commitment, then Religious Humanism has a legitimate claim for serious consideration in discussions about philosophical theology. Paul Tillich spoke of religion as ultimate concern, and theology as reflecting on that ultimate concern.[22] The ultimate concern of Religious Humanism is humanity in both its individual and social dimensions. Of course, Tillich would view such concerns as penultimate and therefore idolatrous, whereas Religious Humanists would contend that Tillich's ultimate is pure fantasy based on the need for wish fulfillment. Obviously the question of ultimacy is an appropriate one for philosophical theology, and it certainly is raised by Religious Humanists in a way that is rarely raised by other religious perspectives.

Fred Streng refers to religion as a system that has a theory about significant transformation,[23] and of course philosophical theology arises out of reflection on that transformation. Potter spoke of the uncreative and the creative personality. He thought there was an impersonal force in the universe which came to consciousness in humans. By choosing and aspiring to reach one's particular expression of the creative personality, one could employ that force by channeling it in the direction of one's ego ideal. Through this process the individual is transformed from an uncreative to a creative personality. Part of article eight of the Manifesto states, "Religious humanism considers the complete realization of human personality to be the end of man's life, and seeks its development and fulfillment in the here and now." If Streng's criterion for religion and theological reflection is correct, then once again Religious Humanism qualifies as an apropriate subject for philosophical theology.

In conclusion, I have presented briefly Potter's thought on the subjects of evolution and Religious Humanism. I have not argued for the truth or falsity of either. In fact, I have not even presented Potter's own arguments for supporting these doctrines. I have merely tried to convey a perspective on religion which often is ignored. It certainly has a place in a discussion of philosophical theology. Whether one accepts it or not is another matter, but it does offer an alternative to supernaturalism, Thomism, theistic existentialism, and even process thought.

---

[22]Paul Tillich, *The Dynamics of Faith* (New York: Harper & Bros. Publishers, 1957) 1-4 and passim.

[23]Frederick J. Streng et al., eds., *Ways of Being Religious* (Englewood Cliffs NJ: Prentice-Hall, Inc., 1973) 6-12.

Herbert of Cherbury
A Much-Neglected and Misunderstood Thinker

David A. Pailin

Herbert of Cherbury (1583?–1648), adventurer, diplomat, poet, historian, philosopher, and theologian, is a fascinating figure who combines the medieval with the modern and the sensible with the quixotic. Although not as widely remembered as his younger brother George Herbert, the poet, pastor, and divine, he deserves to be considered seriously. He was one of the first English writers on metaphysics and on comparative religion. He is also commonly—though questionably—alleged to be the "father" of that radical line in English theological understanding called "deism."

In his basic attitudes Herbert of Cherbury shares many of the characteristics of enlightened modernity. He regards reason as the common and unifying factor in humanity, as the ultimate ground of sound judgments, and as the proper way to decide about religious belief. He tries to discover the nature of true understanding and to secure toleration on the basis of universally accepted principles. At the same time he is influenced by Hermetic notions of the harmony of the One and the All, and considers that "judicial astrology" (*Autobiography*, 50) can provide some knowledge of the future. He was a probing philosopher who also wrote a pompous autobiography, a rational theologian who refrained from publishing until he had received a sign from heaven. Although respected in his own century as a person of "great learning and strength and wit" (Baxter, 556), his writings are marred by obscurities and inconsistencies. It is perhaps not surprising that his pioneering works have neither been widely studied nor greatly appreciated.

Basic Thought

Herbert justifiably sees himself as an original thinker who philosophizes "freely" (cf. DV 73) and who recognizes only the authority of reason. Although he may have valued his links with contemporary thinkers and although his works reveal extensive reading in classical, scholastic, and Renaissance literature as well as in the *corpus hermeticum,* it is a mistake to regard him as an uncritically eclectic writer who presents a number of incompatible elements which happen to have appealed to him. He is, rather, to be seen as making use of a range of ideas culled from a variety of sources in order to develop his own doctrines on the nature of truth, of understanding, and of religion. So far as his position suffers from internal tensions and unresolved conflicts, these are due to his failure to think through his pioneering ideas thoroughly enough rather than to his borrowing from others.

The underlying aim of his philosophical and theological works was to find a way of avoiding or, at least, of minimizing the significance of religious disputes by establishing basic points of agreement which no one in their right mind would reject. His attempt has two aspects. On the one hand there is a metaphysical investigation into the nature of truth and into our way of perceiving what is true. Here Herbert is engaged on the formal tasks of discovering what is meant by speaking of something as "true" and of determining the proper procedures for finding the truth. On the other hand Herbert also undertakes the substantive task of identifying some of the truths that all people recognize to be such—or would do so if they understood things correctly! Here his thought is particularly concerned with religious belief—and it is also here that the fiercest criticisms of his views arise.

Underlying Herbert's investigations into the nature and content of truth is his commitment to rational reflection. To a large extent the religious disputes of his day were the result of disagreements about the location and interpretation of supposed authorities. Herbert rejects the appeal to sacred texts or to divinely authorized institutions or persons as the final arbiter of what is true. In their place he asserts the authority of reason. Although he holds that the overall providence of God ensures that only what is true receives universal assent, he regards reason as our unquestionable judge of what is true. He is accordingly one of the first to set out the modern view that religious faith and religious authorities are only acceptable if they are rationally justified.

Unfortunately Herbert is no more able than others to show how the canon of reason can operate decisively in many matters where people disagree. In particular he fails to provide any incontrovertible tests for distinguishing between the right and the wrong uses of reason. Sometimes he says that individuals must use their own judgement—but this leaves us with the problem of how to choose where the truth lies when people disagree about it. On other occasions he suggests that individuals must let their reason be judged by the standard of universal consent. This, however, is no satisfactory solution since fundamental disagreements arise just because there is no universal consent about what is true.

On the basis of his commitment to the canon of reason Herbert presents in *De Veritate* an attempt to determine the nature and conditions of true understanding. It involves epistemology, psychology, and methodology. Among the conclusions is a most interesting treatment of the relationship between thought and its objects. Here he anticipates and seeks to avoid basic problems with the Lockean and the Kantian views of this relationship.

Locke argues that our ideas of objects are the result of the impressions that they make upon us. One difficulty with this view is that it does not recognize any initial activity by the experiencing mind in shaping what it apprehends as the objects of its experiences. A century later Kant reversed this approach, maintaining that what we know as objects depends on our modes of cognition. A difficulty with this view is that it implies that we cannot justifiably claim to know what things are like in themselves. We can know only how they appear to us when grasped and filtered through our sensational and mental processes. Herbert essays a third position. He maintains both that our minds are actively involved in the process of coming to knowledge and that we can know reality as it really is. His doctrine is that our minds contain a myriad of what he called "faculties." Each of these "faculties" corresponds to a particular possible object in reality. True knowledge occurs when the mind actively interacts with an experienced object to select the exactly corresponding "faculty" for perceiving that object as it actually is.

A basic problem with Herbert's doctrine is that of justifying the claim that our minds contain as many faculties as there are potentially knowable objects in reality. Not only is it difficult to envisage how the human mind could have this capacity; it seems impossible to find any way of substantiating the claim that it is so equipped.

Herbert also asserts that we have a special form of perception that directly senses when we have grasped an object in terms of its corresponding faculty. This gives rise to another problem. It would be a great relief to be able to hold that when we have a certain intellectual feeling accompanying a perception, we have an incontrovertible indication that we have perceived something as it is and therefore our knowledge of it must be correct. Unfortunately it does not seem possible to justify such a claim.

Nevertheless, in spite of fundamental problems with his epistemological doctrine, Herbert should be given credit for recognizing that a satisfying theory of knowledge must take account of two things—the activity of the mind and our ability to perceive things as they are. What he seeks to develop is an epistemology that endorses the commonsense view of truth.

Another fundamental doctrine in Herbert's theory of knowledge is that of the "common notions." It is a mistake to consider that Locke conclusively demolished Herbert's position in his attack on innate principles. For Herbert the common notions are not principles of which every person is consciously aware. They are rather principles that are initially latent in everyone. They only emerge to conscious recognition in those individuals whose minds are provoked by appropriate experiences. What is common to everyone is a basic structure of understanding through which any individual, when suitably stimulated, may become aware of these common notions. When they are explicitly grasped, though, the common notions are universally recognized by normal and honest people to be undoubtedly true. Herbert also describes them as being the result of God's providential concern that we should be able to perceive the truth.

On the basis of his doctrine of the common notions, Herbert holds that conflicts may be solved and agreement achieved. All that stands in the way is bad faith and mental abnormalities. The former is culpable, recognizable, and removable. The latter, he apparently assumes, are not so prevalent as to halt the establishment of practically universal consent to these fundamental truths. While, however, since his time doubts have justifiably arisen about Herbert's doctrine, to reject its position is no light matter. If there are no universally recognized "common notions" by reference to which we can in principle sort out our differences in understanding, we seem committed to an ultimate relativism that threatens the significance of any final appeal to rational reflection.

Herbert's Understanding of the Common Notions of Religion

At the end of *De Veritate* Herbert lists what he considers to be the five common notions of religion. These are

1. There is a Supreme God.
2. This Sovereign Deity ought to be Worshipped.
3. The connection of Virtue with Piety . . . is and always has been held to be, the most important part of religious practice.
4. The minds of men have always been filled with horror for their wickedness. Their vices and crimes have been obvious to them. They must be expiated by repentance.
5. There is Reward or Punishment after this life.   (cf. DV 291-300)

If these are common notions, it follows that the religious beliefs and practices of humanity must provide evidence that they have been recognized by people throughout the world. In his comparative study of different religions, *De Religione Gentilium*, Herbert argues that this is the case.

There is, of course, much evidence that suggests otherwise. Herbert deals with some of it by holding that it shows how priests have distorted and perverted the beliefs contained in the common notions in order to use religion for their selfish advantage. As for the remaining evidence that challenges his position, he argues that either it is misunderstood because of ambiguity in the use of words or it needs to be interpreted as making symbolic references to the basic truths of religion. Herbert thereby manages to attack priestcraft and to condemn superstition while maintaining that many of the apparent ascriptions of divinity to sun, moon, stars, and heroes are in fact indirect references to the reality and attributes of the one true God.

Herbert's knowledge of other religions was limited. His interpretation of what he did know was often forced in order to fit his theories. What is significant, though, is the appreciative sympathy which characterizes his attitude to other religions. On the grounds that God's providence is universal, he seeks in them recognition of the truth. He thus belongs to that band of theists who perceive that God cannot credibly be regarded as concerned with and known by only a segment of humanity.

The Charge of Deism

Theologically Herbert has persistently suffered from a bad press. This focuses on the charge that he is the father of deism in England. One of the first to press this charge is Thomas Halyburton in *Natural Religion Insufficient and Revealed Necessary* which first appeared in 1714. Philip Skelton repeats it in *Deism Revealed* in 1749. Five years later John Leland's classical *View of the Principal Deistical Writers* states that Herbert is not only "the most eminent of the deistical writers" but also "the first remarkable Deist in order of time" (Leland, 1:3).

Is the description justified? Was Herbert himself a deist and was he the intellectual father of deism in England? These are distinct questions. An author may unwittingly generate a movement that is significantly at odds with his or her own self-understanding.

First, let us briefly consider the paternity issue. Did deism in England develop from the work of Herbert, whether as legitimate offspring or unintentionally so far as Herbert is concerned? The paucity of references to Herbert in what are generally regarded as deistic works produced at the end of the seventeenth century and during the first half of the eighteenth century together with their different philosophical approach to questions of religious truth suggest that he was not significantly responsible for the views expressed in them.

Apart from Charles Blount the so-called deists hardly mention Herbert. Their neglect is probably to be understood as the result of a number of factors. In the first place Herbert's writings reflect an earlier period of thought. His eclectic use of scholastic ideas, the works of Renaissance humanism, and the *corpus hermeticum,* as well as his occasional but sympathetic remarks about "judicial astrology," could well have led to his being regarded as old-fashioned at a time when radical thought was self-consciously "modern." Secondly, the significance of his insights are obscured by lack of clarity in their expression. Thirdly, John Locke's *Essay Concerning Human Understanding* not only was widely, though incorrectly, considered to have decisively refuted Herbert's basic doctrine of the common notions; it also led to Herbert's favored appeal to the intrinsic teachings of reason and to some supposed *consensus gentium* being largely replaced by arguments based upon empirical and historical considerations. These showed that matters were much less uniform than Herbert's discussions had recognized. Fourthly, in post-revolutionary (that is, post-1688) England the battle for toleration and comprehensiveness, which had been central to Herbert's concerns, was no longer of such interest. The major issue now was the significance of claims about revelation. Although Herbert had some pertinent views on this matter, they were not extensive and in any case were probably unknown to most of the protagonists in the radical debates about the reasonableness of belief in the post-Lockean period. Fifthly and finally, it is likely that Herbert's work was not given as much attention as his reputation might suggest because it was not radical enough to please the leading "deistic" critics of traditional belief while it was considered too radical to please those who wanted to defend such belief.

So far, then, as a paternity suit lies against Herbert with respect to deism, the evidence strongly indicates that he should be found not guilty.

But even if Herbert was not the *father* of English deism, is it nevertheless correct to deem him to be a "deist"? This is a complicated question, not only because of the need to tease out the evidence about Herbert's own position but also because of the primary need to define what is meant by the description "deist."

In both contemporary and later discussions the term "deist" is imprecise though widespread. Then, as now, the term was generally used pejoratively, but what exactly was being criticized thereby has to be determined from the context. The intrinsic connotation of the term itself is unclear. As Harold Hutcheson puts it in reference to those classically regarded as "deists,"

> If Blount, Gildon, Toland, Collins, Woolston, Tindal, Morgan, Annet, Chubb, and Dodwell, to name the most prominent, all shared a common creed, if even a majority of these consciously took "a common philosophical position," no one to my knowledge has yet succeeded in stating that creed or position.   (Hutcheson, 220)

To ask, then, if Herbert of Cherbury was a "deist" is not a precise and may not be a fruitful question. Instead, therefore, let us end by outlining an answer to a more interesting question, namely, What does Herbert believe about God, humanity, and their relationship?

The Religious Beliefs of Herbert of Cherbury

Herbert's views on religion emerged in response to three concerns. In the first place he was disturbed by two attitudes in contemporary thought, especially noticeable in discussions of religious belief. On the one hand there was the bigotry of those who held fanatically to the truth of certain beliefs; on the other there was the skepticism of those who reacted to such assertions by doubting whether anything significant could be established in such matters. Herbert wants to find a way of determining the truth that avoids these two evils. Secondly, Herbert was deeply suspicious of claims to divinely sanctioned authority in religious matters. He therefore seeks to establish some way by which ordinary people—the laity—may distinguish the relatively simple contents of authentic religion from the inauthentic complexities and self-seeking corruptions introduced by priestly ambition. Thirdly, there was a universalism in his sympathies that makes him deeply unhappy with suggestions that God's providence and salvation are not fully available to a large proportion of humanity through no fault of their own.

What, then, do Herbert's writings indicate about the nature and content of his religious beliefs? They show, in brief, that he has a firm and living conviction of the reality and gracious activity of God as the lord and parent of all humanity and of humanity's duty to respond to God by living a virtuous life.

The Reality of God

Herbert has no doubts about the existence of God. He considers that the universality of this conviction is only obscured by the use of different names to identify God. Among the attributes he ascribes to God are those of blessedness, eternity, goodness, justice, and wisdom. Indeed, whatever quality "exists in us in a limited degree is found absolutely in God" (DV 211). God is both the origin and end of all things, and the providential means by which they subsist. God hears and answers prayer, giving "divine assistance in times of distress." "Experience and history," furthermore, show that God rules the world "with absolute justice" (DV 292).

Herbert not only regards the reality of God as established by its being a common notion. He also holds that the reality of God is indicated by the character of the world. For instance, he suggests that no one who studies anatomy could ever be an atheist since the human body is so "strange and paradox[ic]al" (*Autobiography*, 59). Against the Epicurean view that the world is a product of chance, he offers versions of the argument from design. These use the analogies of a watch and of a musical instrument to reach the conclusion that the diverse and opposed constituents of nature are superintended by "some one Supreme God" (RG 160; cf. 257ff.).

His remarks about God make it clear that Herbert does not understand the divine to be a remote, uninvolved First Cause. God for him is a continually and intimately involved Providence.

Immortality

Herbert holds that human beings do not perish with death. They have a postmortem existence in which they find the fulfillment that is unobtainable in this world. He thus presents arguments for immortality that bear some resemblance to Kant's view of it as a postulate of the practical reason. Each "inner faculty" is directed towards the attainment of the supreme good. This, however, is not to be found "in this life, where everything changes and decays." Since, therefore, we cannot be content with what this life affords, we "must press on, until we reach a principle that is eternal." Immortality is hence essential if we are to attain the "object of the inner faculties" (DV 198; cf. *Autobiography*, 31ff., 300).

Furthermore, while Herbert accepts that "we have at present no more knowledge about the future than the knowledge we had of it in the womb" (DV 124; but cf. 125), he maintains that in the postmortem state God rewards righteousness and "avenges crimes" that went unpunished in this life (DV 301). Here again we find that Herbert's God is no uninterested and uninvolved Ultimate. The divine is a morally concerned agent from whom nothing is hidden.

Revelation

It is important to appreciate that Herbert's religious beliefs include the recognition of divine acts of revelation. Although he carefully limits any appeal to such events, he does not doubt that they occur and that they have authority for those to whom they occur. He is concerned, however, to distinguish between "the deliveries of divine faith" (that is, events in which revelations occur) and "the traditions of historical faith" which transmit reports about such revelations (DV 81). Since the latter are matters of report, they are subject to the possibility of corruption during their transmission to the present.

Furthermore, while Herbert holds that "revealed truth exists," the nature of its truth is quite different from that discerned by our faculties. It "depends upon the authority of him who reveals it." Because of the danger of mistaken identification in alleged cases of revelation, Herbert puts forward four conditions which ought to be fulfilled before a supposedly revealed truth is accepted to be such. First, it should be given in response to proper invocations of the divine. Secondly, it should be given directly to an individual. What is "received from others as revelation" is "not revelation but tradition or history." Thirdly, it should recommend what is good. Fourthly, it should be accompanied by a sense of the divine spirit. If these conditions are fulfilled, we must "recognize with reverence the good will of God" in making known to us what "surpasses human understanding" (DV 308ff.).

Revelation, though, is not only a matter of the divine manifestation of truths that lie beyond our grasp in the general providence of God. It covers "every original impulse of pity and joy which springs in our hearts"—all those "movements of conscience and prayerful impulses" that mark the activity of particular divine grace in human lives (DV 310). It further includes, as seems to be the case with the Decalogue, truths that are in principle discernible by rational reflection as common notions but that God mercifully communicates to us directly to ensure that we grasp them without error (cf. DV 312).

Although Herbert distinguishes between revelations directly received and historical reports about them, he does not deny in principle that revelations binding on the present may have been given in the past. If, however, past revelations are to be regarded as still authoritative, they must not merely meet the four criteria for revelation which he has laid down: those who cite revelations given in former times must also provide convincing proof, first, that these revelations were actually given by God; secondly, that they were accurately recorded when they were given; thirdly, that they have been correctly transmitted down to the present; and, fourthly, that they are still necessary as articles of faith (DV 309-310; cf. RG 365-66).

Nevertheless, while Herbert thus recognizes in principle that revelations may exist that have general significance, he regards our faculties and the universal providence of God as normally sufficient to provide the knowledge which we need. Where revelations are given, they should be regarded as of only private significance unless they contain clear instructions to the contrary (cf. DV 303-304, 311-12).

That Herbert's references to private revelation are not purely theoretical is shown by his report that after writing *De Veritate* he was uncertain whether to publish it. He therefore prayed to God as the "Giver of all inward illuminations" for "a sign from heaven" to indicate what he should do. He received one—"a loud though yet gentle noise" that "came from the heavens" and that he took to be a sign to publish (*Autobiography*, 248-49). His comments on this incident are further evidence that Herbert believes that God acts in particular ways as well as through a general Providence.

Prayer and Worship

Another characteristic of Herbert's religious position is that he considers prayer to be important and efficacious. Toward the beginning of *De Veritate* he reports that in the face of religious controversies, he "sought no other hold but that of God." He consequently describes what finally was published as "the product both of Nature" (through the use of his reason) "and of Grace" (DV 77-78).

The second of the common notions is that God is to be worshipped. Accordingly people act correctly in offering to God "supplications, prayers, sacrifices, acts of thanksgiving." In developing this notion Herbert asserts that "God does not suffer us to beseech Him in vain, as the universal experience of divine assistance proves." God acts by special providence as well as by general in answer to people's expressed needs (DV 294). Herbert's own faith is no notional entertainment of a set of ideas about a remote Absolute. It involves a living relationship with God expressed in prayer to God and expectations of divine response.

Salvation

Herbert's understanding of repentance and moral goodness as the sole requirements for salvation is a major implication of his appreciation of the universality of God. Soteriologies that exclude particular groups of people for no fault of their own are incompatible with the basic nature of God as the "Creator, Redeemer, and Preserver" of all (*Autobiography*, 60). Salvation, therefore, cannot be a matter of a response to persons, teachings, or events that are not knowable by everyone (cf. DV 137).

In Herbert's judgement the condition of salvation is virtue: "none . . . can justly hope of an union with the supreme God, that doth not come as near to him in this life in virtue and goodness as he can." Those who lack virtue must seek "by a serious repentance, to expiate and emasculate those faults, and for the rest, trust to the mercy of God" (*Autobiography*, 60-61).

Herbert may be optimistic in holding that people often sin only because they mistake "a true good for that which was only apparent" but he is not an unqualified universalist. Those who deliberately choose to offend God may receive "infinite punishment" (*Autobiography*, 61). In spite of these warnings, though, his major concern is to understand salvation in a way that is compatible with the majesty and mercy of God and with the state of humanity worldwide.

The Bible

Herbert's attitude to the Bible is in line with the rest of his theological understanding. Aware that different religions appeal to different sacred books he holds that their teachings must be tested against the judgement of "right reason" (RL 99). In particular what in the Bible is to be regarded as "the very word of God" and as "necessary to salvation" is what expresses the "catholic truths" of the common notions since these are "the undoubted pronouncements of God." As for the biblical records of miracles, prophecies, rites, sacraments, and ceremonies, these are to be understood as there to clarify and sanctify "our catholic truths" (RL 101). The common notions thus provide a hermeneutical tool for identifying what is authoritative within the Bible.

Herbert does not uphold the view that everything in the Bible is equally "the pure and undisputed word of God" (RL 99). Although he says that he has "profound respect" for the Bible, finding it a "source of consolation and support," he allows that its text may sometimes be corrupt and its interpreters mistaken (DV 316). Indeed, his treatment of the story of Adam shows considerable freedom. He asks, for instance, how "the Soul of *Adam* can be said to be made after the Image of *God*; if he were altogether *ignorant* of *Good* and *Evil* before his Fall." As he points out, "if before he had eaten" the fruit "he was entirely ignorant of *Good* and *Evil*," he could not have understood "the Prohibition of it." He asks "the learned *Divines*" to explain the matter in a way that "may be clearly understood, and evidently prov'd to the Capacities of the Laity" (RG 265-66)!

Faith and History

Herbert's treatment of historical judgments in *De Veritate* anticipates problems of the relationship between historical judgements and religious faith that Lessing classically posed. On the one hand Herbert emphasizes that historical judgments can never be other than probable. Lessing's "accidental truths of history can never become the proof of necessary truths of reason" (Lessing, 53) is foreshadowed by Herbert's "How precarious, therefore, are the foundations of any important belief which rests only on the evidence of historians" (DV 322; cf. 316, 320). As for Lessing's other, crucial, and neglected insight that there is a categorical distinction between judgements of history and religious faith (cf. Lessing, 54), this is presaged in Herbert's statement that "the traditions of historical faith are distinct from the deliveries of divine faith, not merely by the method by which they are perceived, but by the whole breadth of the sky" (DV 81). Nevertheless, while Herbert distinguishes between historical and religious judgements, he makes no attempt to bridge what Lessing describes as the "ugly great ditch" that separates them. He felt no need to engage in such an exercise. His belief in God was, as he put it, "not derived from history, but from the teaching of the Common Notions" (DV 315).

The Theological Significance of Herbert of Cherbury

While Herbert's writings express a living theistic faith, they show him to be an independent thinker who anticipates a number of later concerns. Even though his works indicate a lack of interest in the significance of Jesus Christ and of the sacraments, he was not a self-conscious radical who deliberately set out to overturn traditional Christian faith. He was, rather, an inquiring believer who, by thought, faith, and prayer, sought to identify the authentic belief of the truly "Catholick and Orthodox Church" (RG 368; cf. RL 133), belief which he considered must be reasonable, simple, and universal.

As *reasonable*, this belief should overcome the doubts of skeptics while avoiding the extravagances of fanatics, whether Roman Catholic or Protestant. By identifying, through his metaphysical investigations, the common notions of religion, Herbert considered that he had both discovered the essential contents of this reasonable belief and shown the rational necessity of assenting to it.

As *simple*, this belief exposes the erroneousness of the complications introduced into the pure religion of the common notions. In this respect Herbert shares that "liberal" approach, be it Renaissance, Enlightenment, or modern, that looks for a reasonable faith that is also a simple faith, free from the burdens of priestly pretensions, traditional embellishments, and expensive rituals.

As *universal*, this belief highlights the theistic unsatisfactoriness of views that implicitly, if not explicitly, restrict the extent of divine providence. Herbert is not merely concerned to identify a faith that should bring an end to the conflicts within Christianity. His grasp of the attributes of God convinces him that all humanity is dependent upon God and the recipient of divine care. Any limitation of divine providence contradicts the justice, oneness, and boundlessness of God. The basic principle of Herbert's theistic understanding is that God is "the common Father" of all people (RL 105).

How is Edward Herbert, first Baron Herbert of Cherbury, to be summed up? In the end it may be fairest just to say that he was himself. Perhaps, however, one final comment on him may be allowed in order to redress the balance of his theological reputation. It is a comment by Richard Baxter. In spite of criticizing the views of Herbert of Cherbury, Baxter writes,

> I would they would learn of him, that the being and perfections of God, the duty of worshipping him, and of holy conformity and obedience to him, and particularly all the Ten Commandments, the necessity of true repentance, and the rewards and punishments of the life to come, with the soul's immortality, are all *notitiae communes,* and such natural certainties, as that the denial of them doth unman them. To know this, and to live accordingly, would make a great alteration in our times; and Christianity could not be disrelished by such that so know and do.
>
> (Baxter, 522)

Works Cited

Edward, Lord Herbert of Cherbury. *The Autobiography*. Ed. S. L. Lee. London: John C. Nimmo, 1886. (*The Life of Edward Lord Herbert of Cherbury, Written by Himself*, to 1624, published in 1764.) [Cited as *Autobiography*.]

_____. *Lord Herbert of Cherbury's De Religione Laici*. Ed. and trans. Harold R. Hutcheson. New Haven CT: Yale University Press, 1944. (Originally published with "Appendix ad Sacerdotes" as *De Causis Errorum*, 1645.) [Cited as RL.]

_____. *The Antient Religion of the Gentiles, and Causes of Their Errors Consider'd*. Trans. W. Lewis. London: 1705. (*De Religione Gentilium Errorumque apud Eos Causis*, 1663.) [Cited as RG.]

_____. *De Veritate*. Trans. M. H. Carré. Bristol: J. W. Arrowsmith for the University of Bristol, 1937. (*De Veritate, Prout distinguitar a Revelatione, a Verisimili, a Possibili, et a Falso*. 1624, enlarged 1645.) [Cited as DV.]

Baxter, Richard. *More Reasons for the Christian Religion and No Reason against It*. Printed in *The Practical Works of the Rev. Richard Baxter*, ed. W. Orme, vol 21. London: James Duncan, 1830.

Halyburton, Thomas. *Natural Religion Insufficient; and Revealed Necessary to Man's Happiness*. Edinburgh, 1714.

Hutcheson, Harold R. "Lord Herbert and the Deists." In *Journal of Philosophy* 43 (1946): 219-21.

Leland, John. *A View of the Principal Deistical Writers*. London, 1754.

Lessing, Gotthold E. *Theological Writings*. Trans. H. Chadwick. London: Adam and Charles Black, 1956.

Locke, John. *An Essay concerning Human Understanding*. London, 1690.

Skelton, Philip. *Deism Revealed, or, The Attack on Christianity Candidly Reviewed*. London, 1749.

F. E. Abbot
Science, Nature, and God

Creighton Peden

American Philosophical Theology in the latter part of the nineteenth century was dominated by the intellectual revolution generated by the publication of Darwin's *Origin of the Species*. A significant philosophical theologian in this intellectual revolution, although relatively unknown today, was Francis Ellingwood Abbot (7 November 1836–23 October 1903). In 1861, while still a theological student, Abbot wrote a key document in the Darwinian debate entitled "The Phenomena of Time and Space," which was published in 1864 as two articles in the *North American Review*. These articles established Abbot at home and abroad as a very promising young thinker.

An important result of the Darwinian revolution for American philosophical theology was the emergence of the "Free Religious Movement." Abbot was a key figure in this movement. First, the intellectual foundation of the Free Religious Movement was expressed by Abbot in a review article entitled, "Positivism in Theology," published in 1866 in the *Christian Examiner* (80:234-67). Second, he wrote the constitution and was a moving force in establishing the Free Religious Association, a central element in the Movement. Third, he founded and served as Editor from 1870 to 1880 of *The Index*, which became the official publication of the Free Religious Asosociation. Fourth, he contributed significantly to the development of American philosophy and theology through his four major books and hundreds of articles. The purpose of our remarks will be to explore Abbot's views on science, nature, and God.

Having postulated as the foundation for philosophy the affirmation "human knowledge exists," Abbot turns to the scientific method for the discovery of the facts of nature. These facts are an understanding of the relations of things in nature, which is a system of the universe itself. Rejecting the Spencerian philosophy of the "unknowable," Abbot contends that science must refuse to admit the existence of any "insoluble mystery." All science has as its starting point *faith in the Universe*. "By this I mean an assumption, deeper than an argument can reach, that the universe is a whole or unit, that all its parts stand to each other in the relation of perfect mutual adaptation, and that all its laws are harmonious elements of one underlying, all-penetrating, all-comprehensive Law. In other words, I mean that the assumption of a *perfect unity in limitless variety* is the absolute condition of all scientific study of existence."[1] Abbot readily agrees that this fundamental postulate about science cannot be proved; but he does contend that if it is denied, all science is impossible. The proper way to view science is as the democracy of the intellect. The principle of authority upon which revealed religions rely, is rejected and in its place science proclaims the principle of freedom—meaning observation and experiment, analysis and synthesis, criticism, intuition, and thought itself:

> . . . : either an external world independent of human consciousness is known to exist, or else all human science is false. By no logical subterfuge can this issue be escaped. If the discoveries made by science are real or true discoveries, if the relations they reveal in the nonhuman universe are real or true relations, then scientific realism is no assumption, no begging of the question, no taking for granted of the point at issue, but the most absolutely *proved truth* which the intellect of man has ever wrested from the mystery in which he dwells. The claim of science to be real knowledge of a real and intelligible universe is the voice of the collective experience and reason of mankind; it is a claim so solidly grounded that the hardest sceptic durst not call in question the particular truths of which that knowledge is the sum.[2]

Without there being a relationship between thought and being, thought is valueless. The "veracity of the human faculties" rests on the "veracity of the universe." The verification of any hypothesis must exist in its ability to account for all the facts; and the hypothesis for an independent, external world is the only one into which all the facts of human experience will exactly fit. Therefore, modern science in its practice has planted itself immovably on the objectivity of the cosmos, as a "working hypothesis" long since verified and now transformed into a demonstrated theory. Science moves us from the mere world of thought to the realm of real existence, forbidding us to believe anything disproved by facts or to accept as true anything not supported by facts. However, the key issue is this:

> The spirit of freedom is the spirit of reliance on universal Nature, the spirit of confidence that universal harmony is best secured by giving the freest possible play to the native faculties of humanity, the spirit of fearless expectation that all immediate discords thus ensuing will be caught up speedily into the general movement of the great overture of history. It is this spirit which most ennobles man, because it tends most directly to bring him into unison with the world in which he lives no less than with the laws of his own individual development.[3]

---

[1]F. E. Abbot, "A Radical's Theology," *Radical* 2 (1867): 591-92.

[2]F. E. Abbot, *Scientific Theism* (Boston; London: Macmillan and Co., 1885) 68-69.

[3]F. E. Abbot, "The World-Orchestra," Harvard Archives, "Free Religion," vol. 4, pp. 1-19.

Reason alone is the authority of science, but it is the authority of universal reason. This is neither the reason of one or a few, often repudiating the obligation of conformity to the law and facts. Rather, it is "the reason which is universal, impersonal, grounded on absolute and irreversible laws of intelligence, discoverable only by the submission of all individual thought to the test of verification and direct appeal to the facts of nature."[4] However, science does not pretend that this authority of universal reason is infallible; nothing is infallible that is human. Science only provides the nearest approximation to the absolute truth itself. Universal reason is the highest appeal, respecting all individuals' rights but furnishing a common appeal when they differ. "In short, it is the authority of Nature and Truth in their universality, and can be denied by no one who understands what it means."[5]

According to Abbot, science has not adequately addressed the problem of the existence or nonexistence of the purely moral element in Nature or in humans, who are but a part of Nature. Science is in a preparatory and merely physical stage, but it is moving in the direction of a spiritual philosophy of the universe. So far science has brought about the destruction of the old distinction between "natural" and "supernatural," leaving humanity as an integral part of Nature. What is required is for science to include within its study the moral and spiritual consciousness of humans. "Despite all his littleness and deformities, Man is the highest of all studies; and the highest thing in him, the glory of his humanity and the recondite route of his connection with the boundless universe which has evolved him, is a presence of a moral nature which shines out fitfully through all his feebleness or wickedness, and now and then bursts forth with a splendor incomparable and unapproachable by aught besides."[6] By applying the scientific method to the subject matter of religious ideas, Abbot believes that science will relate one's moral and spiritual being to the universe as a whole. This extension of the scientific method to include the spiritual in humans will make it possible to bring all verified phenomena into relation with each other as part of one coherent system, laying the foundation of a new philosophy in which moral consciousness will hold a central focus—"not as an unrelated fact of merely human significance, but rather as a fact related to every other in the universe, and presenting the only position-point whence the universe can be apprehended as a unit."[7] Having rejected the supernatural and revelation, science appears to be destroying traditional religion. However, by carefully applying the scientific method to moral and spiritual consciousness, the truth contained within the supernatural religions should be more clearly demonstrated by disengaging it from the superstitions in which it is wrapped.

Abbot's theory of truth divides truth into three kinds. First is the Real Truth or truth of Being or of Things, meaning the realities of the universe wholly independent of all thoughts concerning them. The only criterion of truth of Being is experience. The human brain uses the senses as instruments of research in acquiring all that it

---

[4]F. E. Abbot, "Four Authorities," *The Index,* arch. 4, 1875.

[5]Ibid.

[6]F. E. Abbot, "The Glory of the Human," Harvard Archives, "Free Religion," vol. 4, p. 29.

[7]Ibid.

means to learn of the truth of Being. Second is the truth of Thought or Formal Truth, with everything's being true that does not violate the laws of logic. The former is altogether independent of thoughts, while the latter is altogether independent of things. However, both of these kinds of truth are practically worthless unless joined with the third type—the harmony of Science or Real Knowledge. Since the truth of Science or Knowledge is simply the correspondence of thought with things—the harmony between our thinking and the realities of the universe—the criterion of scientific truth is simply the combination of experience and logic. However, there is no absolute criterion of truth, for we cannot escape the possibility of error. The third kind of truth is a reflection of the universe, its facts and laws in our minds, and is the type of truth needed above all by every person. Abbot explains:

> Here lies the difference between the sane and the insane man. The sane man brings his thought into harmony with Nature, perceives things as they are, and acts accordingly. But the insane man mistakes his own feverish fancies and wild hallucinations for actual facts; and he, too, acts accordingly. Knowledge is sanity; ignorance is a species of insanity. We are all insane when we presume to act on insufficient knowledge. Truth, therefore, is the great need of every soul, inasmuch as our action is at all haphazard, as likely to end in disaster and misery as in happiness, until we have brought our thinking into harmony with the actual conditions of life and the real facts of Nature.[8]

Truth lies in establishing an equation between the interior thinking and the outward reality. What is required is individual discovery and universal recognition. This process can be accomplished by bringing before mind after mind the relations that exist objectively in nature, resulting in a universal recognition of Nature's system. This process could not occur if either Nature had no intelligible system or the individual had no power to discover that system— if, all in all, individuals had no common intellectual capacities subject to universal laws. Thus, the law of nature is obedience to Nature.

Belief is mainly an intellectual act and should have an intellectual, not emotional, basis. It is futile to build belief on anything except evidence. However, the intellect cannot deny its own perceptions of truth, for it must see what it does see. Yet, the intellect requires discipline. It must be taught to recognize the whole universe as its proper field of activity, emancipated from all allegiance except to the fundamental laws of the scientific method. The disciplined intellect requires freedom to build perception upon perception, fact on fact, experience on experience, until dreams have been vanished and the foundations of belief are solidly established on reality.

The undisciplined mind of prescientific religions has attempted to solve the enigma of Nature's creation by postulating a supernatural god external to and superior to nature. This god is supposed to be responsible for every event in Nature through the fiat of divine will. The disciplined scientific mind, in light of the theory of evo-

---

[8]F. E. Abbot, "What Is Truth?" *The Index*, 18 January 1870.

lution, provides a different perspective of Nature. It finds Nature infinite in space; its duration infinite in time; Nature's Cause infinite, imminent, and omnipresent.

"Outside of Nature," "above Nature," or "superior to Nature," are nonsense phrases—phrases which are mere empty sounds signifying nothing. Nature is all there is; there is no supernature beyond nature. All events in Nature occur in accordance with purely natural laws:

> Nature is all-sufficient, all-comprehensive, all-sustaining, and self-sustaining. All events in the past and the present and the future are bound together indissolubly by the uniformity of changeless laws. Throughout their entire course, they have been, so far as human reason can discover, the steps of an endless process, which is an endless evolution of the universe. The unity of Nature working by natural laws and natural causes in the direction of gradual development—that is the history of the universe as written by human Reason in the name of science.[9]

According to Abbot, the laws which govern nature are simply diverse manifestations and modes of a single, infinite, omnipresent force. The same Power that is the law of human destiny guides the stars, speeds light through the abyss of space, governs the invisible play of chemical affinities, and holds atoms and constellations alike true to their function in the sublime economy of the universe. Science is now able to demonstrate that all the physical phenomena of the universe manifest a single, all-pervading cause. This capital force, which prescientific religions vaguely conceive as being somewhere up in the skies, really manifests itself throughout the boundless universe and is round about us and all other things. Nature is alive and its life is the life of God. The activity of God humans behold is the changeless uniformities of Nature.

Nature is but another name for the orderly manifestation of infinite thought. There is an ever-active Intelligence directing the steady ongoings of nature. Abbot explains:

> Prior to the existence of every organic being, its ideal or type exists in Nature, molds plastic matter in strict accordance with its own law, and presides like an invisible architect over the construction of the new edifice of life... I claim it is an indisputable truth of science, as well as of common experience, that organic forces build up each new living structure in the strictest accordance with the typical form of its own species...for my own part, the simple fact alone proves to me, almost with the force of absolute demonstration, that intelligence is the root of outward Nature and pervades the universe as omnipresent and ever-active cause.[10]

Another way to conceive of this intelligence is as the "One Creative Spirit" directing the everlasting becoming of Nature. All the disorder which seems to reign in Nature is actually unperceived order. To the One Creative Spirit chaos is itself cosmos. Har-

---

[9]F. E. Abbot, "The Ascent of Man," *The Index,* 12 September 1872.

[10]F. E. Abbot, "Human Ideals," *The Index,* 2 April 1870.

mony, order, cosmos "consist in the perpetual unfolding embodiment of an infinite thought in infinite time, a never-ending progression or march of creation which is at every step conformed to the perfect life of God."[11] Thus, Nature is the visible manifestation of the Divine Life.

Abbot addresses the problem of evil and contends that evil, as seen by humans, is really Evil. However, he raises the question whether Evil must be as we see it? Since he supports the position that Nature is governed by natural laws, Abbot, from one perspective, postulates that the seeming chaos of human life is actually the cosmos of a perfect "providence of law." Yet, the principle that a person's chaos is God's cosmos is severely tested when applied directly to the world of moral life. While we are free in all moral choices, it is at this point our freedom ends for, having made our choices, consequences follow by inexorable laws. The consequences are the laws of moral reaction and include both retribution for evil and benediction for good. Abbot attempts to resolve this problem of evil by postulating that eventually a divine cosmos will evolve in which spiritual evil either positively belongs or is overcome. "Over the ocean of human life moves ever the Creative Spirit; through the inner tempest it moves, stilling the storms and educing order out of the very riot of disorder."[12] Every person is a creation—a spiritual cosmos—of the indwelling God. We each become the creator of our own character through the limited power of self-creation, occurring under the fixed laws which determine organization and circumstances. To a certain extent we can foster or famish our good intentions and, thus, contribute toward advancing or retarding the development of cosmos. In essence, Abbot attempts to resolve the problem of evil by viewing evolution as a great symphony of nature. The process of evolution is a passage from the imperfect toward the perfect:

> The only way to explain the admission of even partial discords into a great musical work is to concede the impossibility of obtaining general harmony of the highest order without them; and so the only way to explain the existence of evils in the vast overture of Nature is to concede the same absolute impossibility. Ultimate necessity, dependent upon no will, but conditioning the exercise of all will, stands as the only explanation of evil, no matter what hypothesis of causation be adopted.[13]

According to Abbot, the theory of evolution provides a new way of contemplating the universe, which is heliocentric and not geocentric. Instead of viewing the universe from the standpoint of the individual ego, the proper approach is from the universal consciousness of the human race as a part of human nature. Abbot is rejecting the old conception of the Ego plus cosmos, with the Ego posited on one side and cosmos on the other as if they were some sort of coordinates and equal facts. The more adequate approach is to conceive the Cosmos as the one, integral, all-embracing reality in which the Ego has its proper limited place. Humans are an integral part

---

[11]F. E. Abbot, "Chaos and Cosmos," *The Index,* 3 September 1870.

[12]Ibid.

[13]F. E. Abbot, "The World-Orchestra."

of Nature— or the inclusion of Mind in Nature. Nature speaks through each person, calling on each to unhinge his or her own intellectual and moral nature in order "to bring the human mind into the highest possible harmony with nature."[14]

There is a Moral Harmony of the Universe and humans must dedicate themselves to participate in this Harmony. This participation occurs when one attempts to obey the laws of truth, justice, and benevolence in all of one's active dealings with humankind. Through this process of voluntary obedience one serves one's own highest welfare by serving the highest welfare of all. However, this does not mean that such obedience will always result in an increase in individual happiness. Rather, it may be necessary in order to promote the general happiness of all to sacrifice one's own happiness. Still, the highest object of an individual's life is to promote this Moral Harmony personally by obeying the moral law. One should seek to become possessed by this ideal myth of the Moral Harmony of the Universe so that it constitutes one's dominant life purpose. Abbot writes of the individual's responsibility:

> Of the universe, he himself is a part; and, so far as he is part of it, the harmony of the universe depends upon the degree of conformity which he freely establishes between his own action and the universal laws of moral being. What to others will be a mere vague abstraction—because of truth, of justice, of purity, of benevolence, of freedom, of order—will be to him that Moral Harmony of the Universe to which he owes allegiance through the mere fact and recognition of himself as a moral being.[15]

In addition to contending that humans should strive to be in harmony with the universe, Abbot argues that the only conceivable or possible explanation of an ethically constituted humanity must be the ethically constituted universe as a whole. Agnostics countered this view by denying all knowledge of the constitution of the universe as it is making it impossible to admit its ethical character. Abbot returns to his argument that modern science eventually will move beyond a study of only physical events and will develop an ethical science which will focus upon the cosmic conditions of moral life. Modern ethical science will present "the conception of ethical relations which are as universal and necessary as mathematical relations, superior to all force or power, and dependent upon no will, human or divine."[16] The ethical constitution of humanity will then be seen as the strongest possible truth of the ethical constitution of the universe. The Cosmos is to be viewed as one mathematically and ethically—proclaiming the Moral Harmony of the Universe.

For Abbot, Nature and God are the same. It is no longer necessary to seek God outside or above Nature, for modern science has laid the foundation for a natural idea of God in the discovery of the principle of the simple unity of force throughout the

---

[14]F. E. Abbot, "Centennial Oration on Alexander von Humboldt, *The Index*, 10 September 1870.

[15]F. E. Abbot, "Disinterestedness in Morals," Harvard Archives, "Free Religion," vol. 4.

[16]F. E. Abbot, "Wagons and Stars," *Practical Ideals* 1 (June 1901): 2.

universe. The principle of unity derives from the principle of the conservation or persistence of force, coupled with the metamorphosis of the "properties of matter" into "modes of action." This combination results in the more consistent view that matter does not exist distinct from force, and that all forces are resolved into one Force. Abbot is not saying that this principle of unity constitutes the idea of God; rather, he postulates "that the discovery of this unity has first made possible the development of a monotheism based exclusively on scientific grounds."[17] Instead of searching the Scriptures of prescientific religions, one now studies Nature for an understanding of God. The theory of evolution also provides an important insight that the history of the universe is a connected whole. There is one Force which has followed the pathway of evolution in the becoming of the universe, leaving legible traces to human intelligence employing the scientific method. Based on the scientific study of Nature, the only cause that can explain evolution is the ever-present activity of Mind.

> If what I have been saying is of real value, it will appear that the two great discoveries of modern science, the conservation of force and the law of evolution, must eventually give to it a vast impulse in the direction of religious inquiry. The one establishes a unity of the universe in respect to Force; the other establishes the unity of the universe in respect to Law. One Force rules throughout Space; one Law rules throughout Time; and the Force and the Law are themselves explicable as *one* only as *Mind*. To this conclusion I believe that modern science is cautiously but surely approaching.[18]

Abbot rejects a notion that there is a Divine center of intelligence in Nature, contending that the intelligence of Nature cannot be centralized or localized because it is boundless. He especially notes that intelligence in Nature is not concentrated in humans, for humans are only tiny sparks of this universal Intelligence. As a part of Nature, humans are aware of the All-Intelligence, just as the All is conscious of the All. Between humans and universal Intelligence exists the most real of all relations. However, Abbot rejects as inadequte speaking of God as a person or personality. "The utmost that we know of personal being is so trivial when we speak of Being itself, that I can find no statement so satisfying as this— *God is not less, but infinitely more than Person.*"[19] The scientific study of Nature affirms the idea of God, the grandest product of the human mind. For Abbot, "the God of Science is an infinitely nobler object of worship than the gods of the world's historical religions."[20]

---

[17]F. E. Abbot, "The God of Science," *The Index Tracts,* no. 11, p. 16.

[18]Ibid., p. 19.

[19]Ibid., p. 21.

[20]F. E. Abbot, "The Ascent of Man," *The Index,* 12 September 1872.

Philosophical Theology and Provincialism:
Reflections on the Thought of Josiah Royce

John K. Roth

I speak of course as a native Californian, but I do not venture to limit even for a moment my characterization by reference to my own private experience.
—Josiah Royce, 1898

The statement above first appeared in an address that the American philosopher Josiah Royce (1855–1916) gave to the National Geographic Society. It serves well not only as a departure point for this essay but also as a motto for Royce's career. Royce valued his California upbringing. Those formative experiences in the American West remained fundamental as he developed the far-reaching theories that brought him fame in the cosmopolitan academic centers of the American East and in their transatlantic counterparts as well.

Ever the keen observer of life in the West, this California youth transmuted into Harvard philosopher never experienced a "Golden State" replete with urban sprawl, freeways, smog, Hollywood, and Disneyland. He would find much to deplore in contemporary California, just as he did when he lived there or looked back on his native state. But Royce always appreciated that California was different. He believed, for example, that its climate and geography encouraged distinctive types of individuality. They enriched the One and the Many that Royce took reality to be.

Shortly before his death, Royce located the origin of his philosophical interests in a sense of wonder at once provincial and universal. Royce's early home was a California mining town named Grass Valley, a place only five or six years older than himself. He heard his elders describe it as a new community. The boy, however, noticed abandoned mines, rotting structures, and graves. They all looked old. The land's majesty, moreover, was anything but recent. Ages were in it. What, the young Royce wondered, was really new in this particular California dwelling together where his life began? Such puzzlement led him to many destinations, few of them reached by routes that a gold-country lad could guess in advance.

As a philosopher, Royce was intensely interested in what religions share. That broad concern, however, never led him to lose sight of religion's particularity. On the contrary, when Royce wrote about the social consequences of belief in God, his philosophy included a place for *provincialism*. This paper concentrates on that latter aspect of his thought. Its inferences are Roycean, which is to say that they are not new insights. But like many of the points that Royce drove home, they may be overlooked because they are so basic as to be obscured. Specifically, then, this paper explores the following propositions: (1) Contrary to conventional wisdom, provincialism has much in its favor. (2) Lacking "a wise provincialism," as Royce called it, religion in particular is impoverished. (3) A critical human need—the upbuilding of loyalty to loyalty— depends largely on religion's ability to nurture the right provincial touch. The preceding verb "explores" is used advisedly. This essay's style is not to argue directly for the truth of those ideas, but instead to let Royce's thought encourage wonder about their validity.

Provincial California

Royce published his National Geographic address—"The Pacific Coast: A Psychological Study of the Relations of Climate and Civilization"—in his 1908 book, *Race Questions, Provincialism, and Other American Problems*. He regarded this collection of essays as "an effort to apply, to some of our American problems, that general doctrine about life which I have recently summed up in my book entitled *The Philosophy of Loyalty*."[1] Royce's paper on "The Pacific Coast" noted how California's regional identity developed. The changes, Royce believed, were important for understanding loyalty and provincialism's place within it.

Beginning with the '49ers, Royce discerned three stages in the more than half-century of California life he knew. Early on, he recalled, "nearly everything was imported."[2] Large-scale agriculture seemed unfeasible, and, in turn, people's roots remained in eastern soil. Exemplified by what Royce called "the lynching habit," social instability abounded. Within a decade, however, a marked change occurred.

Although many prospectors rushed to California without intending to stay, significant numbers soon realized that they would in fact remain. Isolated from the East, these men and women decided "to create a community of which it was worthwhile to be a member."[3] Between 1860 and 1870, provincial California emerged—a place "self-conscious, independent, indisposed to take advice from without, very confident of the future of the state and of the boundless prosperity soon to be expected."[4] If that description continues to hold more than a grain of truth, it is far from the whole story, as Royce's third stage makes clear.

Isolation, which made provincialism unavoidable, gradually diminished. Spanned symbolically as well as physically by transcontinental railroads, West was linked with East. The uniqueness of California, concluded Royce, consisted of the attempt to blend "provincial independence . . . with the complex social influences derived from the

[1]Josiah Royce, *Race Questions, Provincialism and Other American Problems* (New York: The Macmillan Company, 1908) v.

[2]Ibid., 211.

[3]Ibid., 212.

[4]Ibid.

East and from the world at large.'' [5] Nearly a century later, Royce's observation—
"the California of today is still the theater of the struggle of these opposing forces"—
commends itself. [6] This ferment creates waves of the future.

Memories and Hopes

As Royce well knew, waves of the future—especially those from Pacific shores—
can storm away essential ties that bind families and friends, causes and commitments. Thus, Royce summed up his prolific career in saying that ''my deepest motives and problems have centered about the Idea of the Community.'' [7] The value of
community first impressed him as he experienced the West's rugged ways. His appreciation for it grew with observation that progress increases when people faithfully
pursue their best convictions and yet remain true to each other in exchanging, de-
bating, and evaluating different points of view. A trust that God is ultimately faithful
to creation in a healing and loving manner also played a role. Whatever the factors,
Royce's thought did center on community, and thus it focused on loyalty and provincialism, too.

Royce believed that a community exists just to the degree that persons share
memories and hopes, which include ethical commitments and collective responsibilities. Those memories and hopes typically contain elements that are broadly philosophical and even universalizing in their religious dimensions. Royce believed such
elements were crucial, but he insisted that ethical commitment and collective responsibility are never abstract. Without commitment to a particular cause, which entails practical work in definite times and places, loyalty exists in word alone. The
unavoidably particular nature of communal relationships, of course, may create as
many problems as it solves. For many commitments set up conflicts—internal and
external—that cancel out the good. Hence, if human meaning depends on commitment, and if shared commitment is the basis of communal ties without which our existence is severely impoverished and perhaps ultimately incapable of survival, then
those views of Royce's all suggest why provincialism rightly fascinated him.

Unsophisticated, narrow, countrified—those are just a few synomyms conjured
up by the term "provincial." Usually we do not want the word applied to ourselves,
although it serves well enough to disparage views or persons not to our liking. Royce,
however, reconsidered whether "provincial" deserves to be an uncomplimentary
description or an anachronism for which only cosmopolitanism is the antidote. Provincialism, he believed, is certainly not an end in itself. In that guise it is dangerous.
But provincialism can be virtuous, especially when it encompasses wisdom that recognizes how the particular and the universal should nurture each other. No oxymo-
ron, wise provincialism was precisely, Royce believed, what the United States would
need as the twentieth century unfolded. Any quick dismissal of that claim is unwar-
ranted.

---

[5]Ibid., 214.

[6]Ibid.

[7]Josiah Royce, *The Hope of the Great Community* (New York: The Macmillan Company,
1916) 129.

190   God, Values, and Empiricism

To illustrate, consider the French statesman and philosopher, Alexis de Tocqueville, whose tour of the country resulted in his classic, *Democracy in America*. The sesquicentennial of the publication of its first volume was observed in 1985. Volume II did not appear until 1840, but following up on his early impression that nothing characterized Americans so much as their emphasis on equality, Tocqueville began his book's second half with a chapter "Concerning the Philosophical Approach of the Americans." "Less attention," he there observed, "is paid to philosophy in the United States than in any other country of the civilized world."[8] Nevertheless, continued Tocqueville, "of all the countries in the world, America is the one in which the precepts of Descartes are . . . best followed."[9] Prizing individualism so much, he explained, Americans are Cartesians in their propensity to display "a general distaste for accepting any man's word as proof of anything."[10] Instead they rely on "individual effort and judgment" to determine what they believe."[11]

As with most of the American qualities he discussed, Tocqueville found "the philosophical approach of the Americans" possessing both assets and liabilities. Skepticism might nurture a praiseworthy critical attitude; self-reliance could produce desirable innovation. But a cunning consequence was the undermining of authority, tradition, and communal loyalty. That result, in turn, could lead to other mischief. For where reliance on authority and tradition are severely undermined, people still seek confirmation in the judgments of others. The despotism of unthinking conformity, which is a long way from the public spirit that ensures real freedom and community, is not far behind.

Tocqueville's uneasiness about American individualism was justified, and the consequences for our national well-being are enormous. In sum, while American individualism honed ingenuity and industry that led to positions of economic and political world leadership, the same spirit drew Americans further apart even as they lived closer together in conformity. Now giving self-fulfillment precedence over civic virtue and a publicly responsible loyalty, Americans care more for individual wealth than for their commonwealth. To those remarks Royce might have added that a wise provincialism could provide much that the United States needs.

A Wise Provincialism

In *The Philosophy of Loyalty*, Royce developed his thesis that the meaningfulness of human life depends on loyalty, which he initially defined as "*the willing and practical and throughgoing devotion of a person to a cause.*"[12] Although the details of it cannot be elaborated here, Royce's analysis led him to conclude that the most fundamental principle of the moral life can best be articulated in terms of the general

---

[8]Alexis de Tocqueville, *Democracy in America*, ed. J. P. Mayer, trans. George Lawrence (Garden City NY: Doubleday Anchor, 1969) 429.

[9]Ibid., 429.

[10]Ibid., 430.

[11]Ibid., 429.

[12]Josiah Royce, *The Philosophy of Loyalty* (New York: The Macmillan Company, 1908) 16-17; Royce's italics.

cause of *loyalty to loyalty*.[13] But if one's fundamental moral responsibility ought to be that of being loyal to loyalty, is that idea anything more than a formal principle devoid of concrete content? Absolutely, said Royce, and the reasoning drew upon his wise provincialism.

The Philosophy of Loyalty devoted only a few pages explicitly to provincialism.[14] In 1902, however, Royce had prepared a substantial essay on the subject, which he read as the Phi Beta Kappa Address at Iowa State University. Recognizing that his theory of loyalty could become persuasive just to the extent that he illustrated its applicability to contemporary life, Royce included a version of the 1902 article in *Race Questions, Provincialism, and Other American Problems.*

Delineating his topic, Royce called a province "any one part of a national domain, which is, geographically and socially, sufficiently unified to have a true consciousness of its own unity, to feel a pride in its own ideals and customs, and to possess a sense of its distinction from other parts of the country."[15] Provincialism, then, meant "first, the tendency of such a province to possess its own customs and ideals; secondly, the totality of these customs and ideals themselves; and thirdly, the love and pride which leads the inhabitants of a province to cherish as their own these traditions, beliefs, and aspirations."[16] Given these definitions, what most interested Royce was the question of provincialism's worth. He defended the thesis that "in the present state of the world's civilization, and of the life of our own country, the time has come to emphasize, with a new meaning and intensity, the positive value, the absolute necessity for our welfare, of a wholesome provincialism, as a saving power to which the world in the near future will need more and more to appeal."[17]

That thesis did need defending. Throughout history, not least in the United States, the violence of sovereigns, sects, and sections has produced a deplorable record that argues for movement beyond the provincialism that spawned it. Precisely because of that record, however, Royce believed that the world had been changed in ways that defined "a new social mission which the province alone, but not the nation, is able to fulfill."[18] Rightly practiced, enlightened provincialism would itself be a way beyond "narrowness of spirit" and "jealousies between various communities."[19] It would, in fact, foster loyalty to loyalty.

Again, Royce stressed, one cannot be loyal to "a mere abstraction called humanity in general."[20] Loyalty to loyalty means commitment in a particular time and

[13]For further discussion of these themes, see my introduction to *The Philosophy of Josiah Royce,* ed. John K. Roth (Indianapolis: Hackett Publishing Company, 1982).

[14]See §7 of ch. 5, "Some American Problems in Their Relation to Loyalty," in *The Philosophy of Loyalty,* 244-48.

[15]Josiah Royce, "Provincialism," in *Race Questions, Provincialism, and Other American Problems,* 61.

[16]Ibid., 61.

[17]Ibid., 62.

[18]Ibid., 64.

[19]Ibid., 64-65.

[20]Ibid., 67.

place and to specific causes. True, such loyalty does enjoin attitudes that encompass a breadth of humanitarian concern, but Royce's point was that without a provincial base this concern will have little substance. If a wise provincialism is desirable, however, Royce denied that it could be taken for granted. Modernity tends to erode it.

First, mobility makes us strangers much of the time, and where provincial ties do exist, such communities do not easily expand to make newcomers truly welcome. A second factor that both threatens provincialism and intensifies its importance is what Royce identified as "the levelling tendency of recent civilization."[21] Life becomes imitative to the point of homogenization. Not far behind is "a dead level of harassed mediocrity."[22] There are, of course, gains to be found in mobility, standardization, and uniformity. Likewise, provincialism requires its own conformities. As it confronts the levelling tendencies of modern civilization, provincial character nevertheless can be a countervailing force that nurtures both individual initiative and loyalty to loyalty. Third, at least where popular government is concerned, the levelling tendencies that worried Royce could develop into the spirit of a mob. That spirit is characterized by a lack of self-criticism and self-restraint. Those desirable qualities Royce found more likely to predominate when relatively small groups of persons interact with each other. As he saw prophetically, "a nation composed of many millions of people may fall rapidly under the hypnotic influence of a few leaders, of a few fatal phrases . . . which tends to make the social order, under certain conditions, not only monotonous and unideal, but actively dangerous."[23] Just because a wise provincialism accentuates local pride, loyalty to one's immediate community, and willingness to remember the best in particular traditions, the resulting contrasts with the larger levelling tendencies in society provide a fertile field for critical consciousness to sustain freedom against its enemies.

Apart from the benign influence of provincialism, contended Royce, "the nation by itself is in danger of becoming an incomprehensible monster, in whose presence the individual loses his right, his self-consciousness, and his dignity. The province must save the individual."[24] To combat the danger, Royce drew attention to four elements that a wise provincialism incorporated. First, a wise provincialism is not so much boastful about local accomplishments but instead is genuinely idealistic—it longs continuously for the community's improvement. Second, a wise provincialism is not closed to the values that other communities contain but instead seeks to learn from them, interpreting and incorporating those insights in its own way to strengthen the provincial community.[25] Third, as a new generation is educated, the goal of a wise provincialism will be to arouse curiosity about other communities but at the same time to foster a sense of responsibility for the welfare of the home community and

---

[21]Ibid., 74.

[22]Ibid.

[23]Ibid., 95.

[24]Ibid., 98.

[25]In passages that retain a contemporary ring, Royce describes the Japanese as a people who are adept at learning from others and at adapting this learning to their distinctive ways. See ibid., 103-107.

then to ensure that opportunities for exercising responsibilty are made available. Finally, urged Royce, a wise provincialism will not overlook the significance of sacrifice that aims "to put in the form of great institutions, of noble architecture, and of beautiful surroundings an expression of the worth that the community attaches to its own ideals."[26] Where such sacrifice accompanies the other traits he outlined, Royce believed there was little likelihood that provincialism would become too confined. On the contrary, by thus idealizing itself, provincialism would remind people that its major contribution is to be a vital part that enriches the whole.

Provincial Religion

Taking seriously the derivation of "provincialism" from "province," Royce underscored how the traditions associated with a state, city, or town would be at the heart of a provincial spirit. Thus, his account of a wise provincialism says little explicitly about religion. But there is nothing in his definitions to make impossible that provincialism could include loyalty to the local in diverse senses. For instance, much religious life involves identification with a congregation that gathers in a specific place. Such a congregation will share concerns and activities that reach well beyond the local. Yet it will also express local ways and aspirations. Indeed those particular elements will influence how it enacts more universal concerns. If we cultivate the loyalty that Royce urged, religion that is wisely provincial contributes a significant source of strength.

Not always wisely, religion and provincialism commonly go together. That relationship exists because religion tends to retain elements of exclusivity that harbor narrowness. But religion's advantage, even where exclusivity and narrowness are found, is that this provincialism does include elements of the universal. Usually, for example, there is a vision of the good that is all-encompassing, and the particularity of a tradition is oriented toward its view of the whole. Granted, religion may be dogmatic about its claims to truth, and when that happens even its vision of the good becomes dangerously narrow. But here the point to make is as follows: If religion's provincialism can be made wise in the Roycean sense, then religion is a powerful base for fostering the ideals that Royce desired to encourage. For quite natural to religion are the qualities and the motivations toward the provincialism he prescribed as an antidote for social ills such as rootlessness, levelling to "a dead level of harassed mediocrity," and the conformity of mass politics that invites totalitarian control.

To illustrate, consider some of religion's best forms, ones that in principle could characterize its practice in countless local situations. First, accompanying religious life that exists in communal form and in a particular location, there will be found a drive to keep improving and not to be satisfied, let alone merely boastful, about what has been accomplished in that place. Awareness that a tradition's memories and hopes must be enlivened in concrete settings will blend with conviction that loyalty to them requires a special giving, one recognizing that the right ideals are never totally fulfilled on earth and yet that effort toward them intensifies life's significance. Second, the effectiveness of such religious practices, it is recognized, does depend on open-

---

[26]Ibid., 108.

ness to what others are doing and to what they have to teach. But the eye watching in those directions is also turned to perceive how the appropriate lessons can be interpreted locally to serve the ideal causes that religion extols. Third, religion at its best constantly seeks to educate the young to carry forward the memories and hopes that give it vitality. Again, the recognition is that this learning must extend far and wide, even to the point of risking that the young will abandon the religious community. But that recognition also includes the insight that unless there is a match between the breadth of training and opportunities for service within the tradition, the life of a religious community will be impoverished as one generation succeeds another. Finally, in its particular ways, religion does take seriously the notion that beauty belongs in the service of the ideal. The styles, structures, and sounds may vary, but for those who care about a shared religious life, there is usually a concern to create places and moments of beauty. Not only local spatially, they will also reflect particular traditions and even a specific locale as they praise and honor what is good and thereby idealize it further.

These qualities, which are natural to religion at its best, can help keep people armed against the social ills that Royce wanted a wise provincialism to combat. Indeed, unless we look to the religious life to provide this provincialism, we probably overlook its most promising source. For a wisely provincial religion understands that the orders of historical flux, human society, and political might are not all that exist. They are relativized by power that transcends them for good, and in whose service it is the proper task of the finite beings of the world to labor. At the same time, by putting those beliefs to work in its particular times and places, religion can provide a home for those on the move. It can forestall the levelling Royce feared by supporting the conviction that individual persons and communities count and that they do so precisely because they can do good things that no one else can accomplish. Finally, through loyalty to its unique perspectives, religion can help to prevent the loss of freedom to tyrannical political authority.

Overarching all these traits of a wisely provincial religion is the fundamental Roycean theme that full personhood is achieved neither atomistically nor in isolation but through committed relationships. Royce offered one of his best insights when, speaking "as a native Californian," he went beyond his own personal experience to urge that those relationships can and should be nourished by a wise provincialism, one that should and can be found especially in religious life.

Immortality
Objective, Subjective, or Neither?

D. W. D. Shaw

Two entirely different circumstances have prompted entry upon well-worn but dangerous paths with a return to the question of immortality. The first was an occasion some years ago in Edinburgh in the course of Marxist-Christian dialogue when the subject was "What may we hope for?" It was perhaps to be expected that the Marxists would have an easier time of it than the Christians, and so it turned out as they spoke with confidence about "the classless society," the transformation that would be wrought, the new history that would begin with its inauguration. When the Christians' turn came to articulate the "Christian hope," they soon had to admit that there were almost as many different versions on the hope as there were Christians: certainly varying from a literal heaven as a continuation of this life but with all restrictions on happiness removed, to a literal hell—as total separation from God— through a host of other versions between these two extremes, including transformation of this life without any reference to the future at all. What was clear was that there was no one agreed manner of expressing a Christian perspective on death, and what, if anything, may reasonably be hoped for thereafter.

The other circumstance is what I am beginning to see as the critical situation of funeral rites and the language used there. To take but one example—a local one to me—the words of committal in the 1940 *Book of Common Order* were as follows: "Forasmuch as it hath pleased almighty God to take unto himself the soul of our brother/sister here departed, we therefore commit his/her body to the ground, earth to earth, dust to dust, and ashes to ashes, in sure and certain hope of resurrection to eternal life through our Lord Jesus Christ."[1] Note the unambiguous reference to "soul" and "body" and "resurrection to eternal life." In the latest edition of the *Book of Common Order* (1978) the recommended words of committal are much more cautious: "We have entrusted our brother/sister . . . into the hands of God, and we

---

[1](London: Oxford University Press, 1940) 177, approved for use in the Church of Scotland.

now commit his/her body to the ground, earth to earth, ashes to ashes, and dust to dust; having our whole trust and confidence in the mercy of our heavenly Father, and in the victory of his Son, Jesus Christ our Lord, who died, was buried, and rose again, and is alive and reigns for ever and ever."[2] This is much more of a Christological confession: no mention of the soul, no mention of resurrection to eternal life. Doubtless this change of emphasis was thought to be theologically sound. What it does do is draw attention once again to differences, not to say confusions, that exist in what Christians think, or, perhaps more to the point, what they think they are supposed to think about death. Has the idea of a soul been ditched altogether? Is the language of resurrection to be studiously avoided? Is "eternal life" merely a euphemism for living well now with no future reference? This is obviously an area of the greatest possible pastoral importance, and this, combined with the confused apologetic situation the Marxist dialogue threw up, certainly seemed amply to justify a return to and reexamination of this theme.

All that is proposed here is to sketch in rough outline a number of possible perspectives currently being offered, and then, greatly daring or perhaps with crude naivete, to suggest a way forward.

First to be considered are theories of *objective immortality*. As guide here I follow Charles Hartshorne, whose approach is similar to but much more systematic than Whitehead's. It is true that Whitehead said that his system was "entirely neutral" on the question of survival after death[3]; it is also true that Hartshorne concedes that "personal survival after death with memory of life before death is hardly an absolute absurdity."[4] Nevertheless, neither thinker believes in "personal survival." For Hartshorne, an individual lives and dies—and as far as that individual is concerned as a thinking, acting, relating subject, that is the end of the matter. But in a sense it is not an end of the individual. For everything the individual is or has been has its place everlastingly in a totality—God—from which the individual can never pass. Death is not the destruction of the individual: it is rather "the last page of the last chapter of the book of one's life, as birth is the first page of the first chapter. Without a first page, there is no book. But given the first page, there is, insofar, a book." Books can be truncated, brought to an end too soon before the theme has had a chance to develop. "And such truncations can be tragic. But they do not affect the reality of the book, which is there, written forever."[5]

But we have to distinguish between what Hartshorne calls "retained actuality" and "reality in the form of further actualization." In the case of the death of a loved one, the realized actuality of the loved one lay in his or her thoughts, feelings, de-

---

[2](Edinburgh: Saint Andrews Press, 1978) 94.

[3]Alfred North Whitehead, *Religion in the Making* (London and New York: Macmillan, 1926) 107, quoted in John B. Cobb, Jr., and D. R. Griffin, *Process Theology. An Introductory Exposition* (Belfast: Christian Journals, 1977) 124.

[4]Charles Hartshorne, "Time, Death, and Everlasting Life" in *The Logic of Perfection and Other Essays in Neo-Classical Metaphysics* (La Salle IL: Open Court Publishing Co., 1962) 253.

[5]Ibid., 250.

cisions, perceptions. "These are evermore as real as when they occurred. But it does not follow that new thoughts, feelings, decisions, are occurring 'in heaven,' having the stamp of the same individuality; or that friends who died earlier are now being conversed with in new dialogues, and so on. This would be new reality, not the indestructibility of the old."[6] Continuing his analogy of the human life as a book, Hartshorne asks concerning the potential readers of this book, after the final chapters have been written, who are they? They could be future human beings—posterity, in other words, but Hartshorne rejects this as inadequate. Even our contemporaries cannot know the exact quality of our feelings, the exact intentions of our acts: how could our successors possibly achieve this? In fact, as far as preserving the book is concerned, there must be a reader who is not subject to the incurable ignorances of human perception, understanding, and memory—and that reader is God! So Hartshorne concludes that "our adequate immortality can only be God's omniscience of us." "He to whom all hearts are open remains evermore open to any heart that ever has been apparent to him. What we once were to him, less than that we can never be, for otherwise He himself would lose something of his own reality."[7] So "death cannot mean the destruction, or even fading, of the book of one's life; it can only mean the fixing of the concluding page."[8]

This notion of "objective immortality" has been transposed into a specifically Christian key by, among others, Norman Pittenger.[9] For Pittenger, the "Last Things" are not dismissed as illusory, but refer specifically to the here and now. The sting is not to be taken out of death. "We all die, and all of us die."[10] Judgment is to be interpreted as God's appraisal of a whole human life, not simply at the end of that life but at all points within it, coupled with the actual consequences of our sin, being in a state of gracelessness in which we find ourselves unable to become the people we are meant to become. "The appraisal that God makes is worked out in what he does—or, in words that describe the creative advance as we know it, the appraisal is worked out in terms of what is taken into, and what is rejected from, the 'consequent nature' of God, God as he is affected by what occurs in the world; and then in what use is made of what has been last taken or received in the furthering of the project or purpose of God, the information of good 'in widest commonalty shared'."[11]

"The only *reward* that love can offer is more opportunity to love; its only punishment can be failure on the part of the lover to continue in loving. The only reward promised to those who love God or do his will is really the presence of God and the joy of 'seeing him'; while the punishment is the alienation from his presence and that joy, the result of not loving which the victim has imposed upon himself."[12] Indeed,

[6]Ibid., 251.

[7]Ibid., 252.

[8]Ibid, 253.

[9]Particularly in *"The Last Things"* in a Process Perspective (London: Epworth Press, 1970); also After Death Life in God (London: SCM Press, 1980).

[10]Pittenger, The Last Things, 35.

[11]Ibid., 58.

[12]Ibid., 49.

Pittenger makes a telling if unkind point when he reminds us that to want God and something else (including continued existence after death) is not genuinely Christian. "It is not a matter of God and a lollypop!"[13] "He who seeks God in order to have something more does not know what he is seeking" (St. Francis de Sales).[14]

" 'Resurrection of the body' is not ignored but is to be rather innocuously translated into such a proposition as this: the love which God manifested in the life and death and victory of Jesus is indefeasible: the totality of the material world and of human history as well as of everyman in that history who with his brethren has achieved good in his existence in the world is usable by God."[15] "Thus the resurrection is not something that will take place in the distant future when the scroll is opened and a Grand Assize is held. It is a present reality in the faith of the Christian. The 'Christian hope,' grounded in Christian faith, is a present experience; indeed, that hope, like the love which is participant in Christ is in that faith. The living in Christ—by which I mean living 'in love' as a human possibility which has been 'represented' for us in the Man Jesus—as Christ lives in those who respond and hence know what love is: this is, at this very moment, our hope of glory."[16]

I have to admit that after I have got over the shock of the sheer negativity of such a view—"objective immortality"—its appeal increases. There is a certain logic about it; it is not brain-splitting, and has a commonsense quality about it that makes it comprehensible and if not "scientifically grounded" (perish the phrase) at least not scientifically unacceptable. These days, that must be considerable bonus. More than that, it is consistent with a lot at least of the Old Testament data, which is surely not to be written off by theologians as primitive and irrelevant, and from a specifically Christian point of view, most importantly of all, it is thoroughly theocentric. The concentration is on *God* and his future, rather than the future that an individual might desire or require. So much thought of an afterlife is so thoroughly unimaginative and self-centered—my friend's picture of "sitting on a comfortable cloud with an inexhaustible supply of gins and tonic" is, after all, only a mild caricature: "the cigars are wonderful" type of heaven is by no means yet dead. To require a theocentric approach is surely no bad thing—and "objective immortality," while it is certainly not too exciting from the individual's point of view, does at least end up by giving God the glory. (See 1 Cor. 15:28: "and thus God will be all in all.") I should perhaps add that it is not, in the end of the day, a million miles removed from the kind of approaches advocated by theologians of a certain neoorthodox or even existentialist bent![17] I think, therefore, that it has to be taken very seriously by anyone who wants to speak about everlasting life or immortality, and that there is a lot more mileage left in it yet.

[13]Ibid.
[14]Ibid., 49-50.
[15]Ibid., 76.
[16]Ibid., 77.
[17]Cf. Eberhard Jüngel, *Death. The Riddle and the Mystery* (Edinburgh: Saint Andrew Press, 1976).

Nevertheless, even though I think I am appreciating "objective immortality" more and more, how "religiously satisfying" it is is another matter. If all that is meant by belief in "the life everlasting" and the "resurrection of the body" is that "love is the greatest thing" and that God cannot forget what we have been and done, how does this differ from belief in the finality of death and, with death, the frustration of all potentialities and possibilities? Furthermore, without a great deal of straining, it is certainly not reconcilable with much of the New Testament, or the faith and hope of the martyrs, or the simple belief of generation upon generation of Christians. It is in effect a rather complacent, middle-aged or old man's creed: "I've had my chance; if, after sixty or seventy years, I still don't know right from wrong or still haven't learned to love, what chance have I in any future life of doing any better? God knows who I am and what I have been, and he can use the great or little I have done in the opportunities he gives my successors." That may be all right for an old man. But, as Dostoyevski's Ivan would say, "What about the children?" What about lives cut short in infancy or in a gas chamber, whole futures cut off by drought or starvation? What is there for even God to remember, let alone anyone else? What price "objective immortality" now?[18] It is not surprising that different answers have been sought, which do allow for something that might be called "subjective immortality," and to these I now turn.

This is a theme with many variations mainly to do with the survival of the body. At one extreme, there are those who maintain that we shall live again after death with our own bodies in some way reconstituted, or at least in some sort of continuity with our present bodies. This surely requires a lot of swallowing. The slightest acquaintance with natural processes of decay, to put it no higher than that, would seem to rule it out, and it is interesting to note that it is precisely because this is ruled out and no alternative is to them conceivable that some commentators[19] insist that immortality of any kind goes by the board.

At the other extreme of subjective immortality are those defenders of the concept of "soul" or "self" or "person" or "the I" who insist that a postmortem physical or quasi-physical body is neither possible nor necessary. For them, a complete account of human life cannot be given without reference to the nonphysical or nonmaterial ("mind," "soul," and so forth) and this essential part of the individual is, they claim, because nonphysical, "survivable," if I can coin an admittedly ugly word, on the disintegration of the body. Defenders of the "soul" like H. D. Lewis[20] can put up a strong case and Ryle's "ghost in a machine" has proved extremely lively.[21]

In between these extremes are, firstly, those who concede that for life of any kind some kind of body is necessary. For them life after death requires a body of

[18]See Fyodor Dostoyevski, *The Brothers Karamazov* (London: Penguin Books, 1958) esp. bk. 5, ch. 4, "Rebellion," 276ff.

[19]E.g., Bernard Williams and Antony Flew, in H. D. Lewis, *Persons and Life After Death* (London: Macmillan, 1978) esp. 49ff. and 94ff.

[20]E.g., H. D. Lewis, *The Elusive Mind* (London: Allen Unwin, 1969); also *The Self and Immortality* (London: Macmillan, 1973) and R. Swinburne, *The Evolution of the Soul* (London: Oxford University Press, 1988).

[21]G. Ryle, *The Concept of Mind* (London: Penguin Books, 1966).

some kind, for example, an "image body" (H. H. Price)²² or a "replica body" (John Hick)²³. It should be noted that for both the proponents of "surviving soul without body" and the proponents of "surviving soul with some kind of body," great stress is laid on examples of telepathy, "veridical hallucinations" (Paul Badham)²⁴ and of mystical experience as enabling some kind of communication and so of life. Some people may feel, as I do, that while neither telepathy nor mystical experience is to be written off as illusory, the evidence is not such as to justify the heavy demands these survival theorists seem to make on it.

Also to be included in the "subjective" camp are those who take an existentialist or metaphorical line. For them, "immortality," "life everlasting," and so forth are not to be taken literally as referring to some future existence after death. Rather they are to be used to refer to a quality of life than can be experienced now, life with a capital 'L', if you like, experiences that go beyond what can be seen, touched, heard (that is, observed), commitments to which one gives one's personal backing now, and so transcends the spatiotemporal world. I am thinking here of thinkers as different in other respects from one another as Rudolf Bultmann and his followers, D. Z. Phillips²⁵ (following Wittgenstein) and I. T. Ramsey, late bishop of Durham, who made such an ingenious, if sadly brief, contribution to the debate.²⁶ I am perhaps also thinking of St. John.²⁷ Although Ramsey equates "immortal" with the nonspatiotemporal (without which a full account of human existence cannot be given), I call this type of approach metaphorical, because of its refusal to discuss the possibility of future, postmortem existence.

Of particular interest was the attempt by John Cobb to expound something like "subjective immortality" in "process terms."²⁸ Cobb tries to develop Whitehead's concept of the "Kingdom of Heaven" as an image of hope, to be set in relation to other images of hope, such as the "City of God" (for example, Augustine) and "the resurrection of the dead" (for example, Wolfhart Pannenberg).²⁹

In his critical development of Whitehead's "Kingdom of Heaven," Cobb acknowledges that the doctrine of "objective immortality" is a legitimate interpretation of Whitehead, but not the only possible one. If I understand him aright, Cobb wanted to claim that what is preserved in God's consequent nature or the "Kingdom of Heaven" is not merely the objectivity of everything that has happened in the world, but an element of subjectivity as well. He bases this on an elaboration of Whitehead's doctrine of perishing and objectification. In the succession of occasions or events that constitute our cosmos there is a flow of feeling from object to subject. Something of

---

²²"Survival and the Idea of Another World," in J. R. Smythies, ed., *Brain and Mind* (London: Routledge & Kegan Paul, 1968).

²³*Death and Eternal Life* (London: Collins, 1976).

²⁴*Christian Beliefs about Life after Death* (London: Macmillan, 1976).

²⁵*Death and Immortality* (London: Macmillan, 1970).

²⁶*Freedom and Immortality* (London: SCM Press, 1960).

²⁷John 17:3.

²⁸*Christ in a Pluralistic Age* (Philadelphia: Westminster Press, 1975).

²⁹*Jesus—God and Man* (London: SCM Press, 1968; Philadelphia: Westminster, 1973).

the subjectivity of each occasion is thus preserved by a successor, if only partially and momentarily. But God knows the events of this world both in their objectivity and their subjectivity. In the Kingdom, the subject is preserved as subject with its immediacy. This means that for Cobb, persons as persons inhabit the Kingdom, both in their objectivity and in their subjectivity. These persons (in the Kingdom) are not to be conceived as closed within themselves. Cobb quotes Lewis Ford and Margery Suchocki in their development of Whitehead's vision. "There can be no clearly defined border of the personality. What obtains is more likely a center of personality which then extends and flows to others in the giving and receiving which is the harmony of God. This is fitting, for the temporal purpose of personality was primarily suited to the greater intensity of feeling made possible by the complex structure of personality. This intensity now having been achieved it may now be put at the disposal of its ultimate purpose—the enrichment of the whole. In the process, the narrow confines of the self have been lost, but not its subjective reaction to the universe as a way of experiencing that whole."[30]

Cobb continues: "To the extent that the narrow confines of self are lost, those who can conceive no fulfillment that is not of the personally identical individual will find Whitehead's vision of hope unsatisfactory. *But it is doubtful that an eternal self-identity can be truly envisioned as fulfillment.* What is reasonably required is a participation and redemption of the human actuality, not that this be conceived in the categories of individualism. This reasonable requirement is met by Whitehead's vision in harmony with that of the perfection of love. There is a dynamism in the Kingdom of God. This suggestion is made that in God the occasion experiences an enlarged and enlarging world which contains new occasions as they come into being and each occasion would experience the consequences of its own actions."[31]

Cobb of course contends that Christian reflection on what Whitehead means by the Kingdom can indeed bring into closer relation with Christ as the resurrected Jesus. He claims that the structure of existence in the Kingdom is in the direction of the structure of Jesus' existence. In the Kingdom, events and persons are open to each other and to God. They become what God can make of them. They exist for him. Most important of all, Jesus himself exists in the Kingdom. Cobb describes the experience of the Kingdom in this life as the love of God providentially flowing into the world and when he does so, the experience to which he points is the one that has been effective in human history because of Jesus. He concludes that if it is Jesus' message that makes the Kingdom real for us in anticipation, and if it is the structure of Jesus' existence that foreshadows what existence in the Kingdom is to be, then the notion that unity with the resurrected Jesus is of peculiar importance for the blessedness of the Kingdom[32] is not as farfetched as it may initially seem.

There, then, is an extensive, though certainly not exhaustive, sample of perspectives on immortality, ranging from total denial to a lively postmortem existence. Clearly there is no consensus, even among Christian theologians. I have classified

---

[30]Cobb, *Christ in a Pluralistic Age,* 247-48.
[31]Ibid., 248.
[32]Ibid., 250ff.

them in terms of "objective" and "subjective" immortality, including in the latter the more existential "life-with-a-capital-L" type and Cobb's imaginative extension of Whitehead. Another way of classifying them would have been to distinguish those where the emphasis is largely anthropological, and those where the emphasis is mainly theological. Among the former would be those which concentrate on a description and affirmation of "the soul" or something like it and posit its nondestruction at death. They also conceive of life after death as analogous to life and its interpersonal communication before death. Also included would be those who conceive of two different kinds of human life, one with a small 'l' and one with a capital 'L'. Among the latter—the ones with the mainly theological emphasis—would be those which look to God to supply a postmortem body of some kind, to make the "person" identifiable, with not too many questions asked as to the how, why, and wherefore. The danger of the former is that they tend not to meet the religious requirements of a theory of immortality, while the danger of the latter is that they fail to meet the requirements of rationality.

Perhaps we could determine to avoid a one-sided emphasis on either theology or anthropology and insist all the way through on recognizing the relation of the human being to God, in other words combining a theological with an anthropological starting-point. If, as theologians, it is impossible to give a complete account of the human being without recognizing the relation to God, then it would also be impossible to speak of the end or the future of human being without taking into account the relation to God. Given at least Christian assumptions, this is indeed the case. If, with the New Testament, we speak of God as love,[33] the one aspect of the love of God is his *concern,* which in fact imparts a value to human life as a whole and to individual human lives which it and they would not otherwise have. God's concern gives value not only to the individual during his or her life but at the point of death, and if what St. Paul speaks of as the "inseparability of God's love"[34] with which nothing, not even death, can interfere, then this must have some significance for "life everlasting." On this account, what suggests that physical death is not necessarily the end of the story is not the alleged existence of indestructible soul but the confessed existence of the indestructible love of God.

If we pursue the theme of God's love even further, the Christian perspective acknowledges, with the doctrine of incarnation, however understood, as the most profound aspect of God's love, God's *identification* with the human condition.[35] This being so, we are surely entitled to rely on this identification in death as in life. If God does not die, then God's identifying with the dying does not die. God will not allow what we are or what we have been to be lost (compare objective immortality). Is it not possible to think of human life as being, not absorbed, but united with God, finding fulfillment in him? Even if, on this view, we could not claim literally to see our lost loved ones again, yet the conviction could be advanced as realistic that they could, with us, be united with God, fulfilled—jointly, together, not in isolation.

---

[33] 1 John 4:16.

[34] Romans 8:39.

[35] See J. McIntyre, *On the Love of God* (London: Collins, 1962) 150ff.

Perhaps this would help to put new confidence and integrity into the words we use at Christian funerals. It would not, of course, answer all the questions. There would, for example, still remain the one really awkward question, Ivan's question, "What about the children?" It might just be that further reflection on the concept of imagination[36] might help us here. If, let us say, the child dying, whose life appears to be utterly wasted or frustrated, is really related to God, if such a child is really the object of God's concern and the subject of his identifying love, we would have to allow that God not only knows the child, but can imagine all that the child might be. As it is God we are talking about, this would not be wishful thinking, or fantasy, but experienced and imagined reality that would not perish with the child's death. There would be a sense in which the child not only lived on in God but through God's imagination is capable of fulfillment in God. I appreciate that this is a wide, even wild claim, but is it necessarily utterly ridiculous?

I have strayed along the path of speculation far enough. I gave as a title to this essay before I wrote it "Immortality. Objective, Subjective, or Neither?" I think now I should have called it "Objective, Subjective, or Both"! Further, since I have concluded with "imagination," perhaps a poet ought to have the last word.

From "Now that May has gone"

I have never been able to believe
In an after-life, yet now that May has gone
I find myself hoping for her continuation.
I like to think of her in some safe place
Meeting her mother and father whom she never knew. . . .
When my own time comes
If there are to be unimaginable revelations
I would want her to tell me about them.
It would be her voice I would want to listen to,
The glories of eternity would be incidental.
I have to confess, though, that I do not think
We shall ever see each other again.
But I look up at the stars above the house
With wonder and longing. . . . [37]

---

[36]See J. P. Mackey, ed., *Religious Imagination* (Edinburgh: Edinburgh University Press, 1986) and J. McIntyre, *Faith, Theology, and Imagination* (Edinburgh: Handsel Press, 1987).

[37]From Robin Jenkins, "Now that May has gone," *The Scotsman*, 8 June 1988 (copyright © The Scotsman Publications Ltd., Edinburgh.).

The Birth of God

Frederick Sontag

1. The Modern Experience

Although atheism (disbelief) has been an undercurrent in every religious tradition, Nietzsche is credited with popularizing the theme of "the death of God." Zarathustra came down from the mountain and proclaimed to a startled group: Have you not heard that God is dead? For many reasons the theme of the death of God has been prominent, if not dominant, in religious thought ever since. Marx and Engels proclaimed the material determination of all thought, which eliminated the Hegelian stress on Spirit as the driving force in life. The advance of modern science has for many, if not for a majority, eliminated the need to refer to God as the explanation for the created order.

The forces unleashed by the proclamation of the death of God are undeniable; they have shaped the intellectual, and even religious, climate of the past century. But one major premise has attached itself to this idea that now needs examination. Along with his stress upon the determining force of a divine Spirit, Hegel had a trust in a dialectical development of history, and he assumed a notion of "Progress," that events moved forward in an upward spiral never to return to their origin. However, our recent disillusionment with the notion of "Progress" is almost comparable to the effect of Nietzsche's announcement of the death of God. Contemporary science, which underwrote the idea of Progress with legitimacy, is now nearly devoid of the notion that modern science has brought irreversable progress to the world of human affairs.

If the idea of progress is either in question or has largely been abandoned, if all peoples stand in the same place where all others before them began, if scientific knowledge lets us fly but does not necessarily solve human problems, then the death of God that was experienced in one time may not be an irreversable phenomenon. Let us grant Nietzsche his prophetic role and admit that many long-powerful notions of God have lost their hold over us, but let us also admit that nothing prevents God from being born again. No intellectual happening in human affairs should be considered irreversible. If God can and did die, God can also be born again. Are we now, then, living in the age of the Birth of God?

If so, certain facts become clear: In spite of human efforts to fix one immutable idea of God for all believers, 'God' has always been a flexible, multiple notion. Thus, Nietzsche forgot to ask if all Gods died at the same time or if it was only one idea of God whose time had passed. Yet if we accept this possibility, we know that God cannot be immutable, as has so often been proclaimed, since ideas about the divine not only vary but are subject to the phenomenon of dying and rising. That God should die—and be born again—need not be a notion alien to the nature of God. Rather, it can be a description of the essence of divinity. If so, is God then robbed of the traditional notions of omnipotent power and stability which always have stood so much in contrast to our human impermanence and weakness?

The concept of 'immutability' has been one way of asserting God's power and permanence. Yet, perhaps our experience of the death of God can reveal to us that this is not the only way to establish divine power. Rather than abolishing God permanently, as Marx and Freud hoped to do, the death of God can give rise to a new insight into the divine nature, if we use the death of our cherished God for that purpose. All Gods need not be viewed as deposed from omnipotence in the death of one God. Instead, we may find that we face a divinity powerful enough, as we are not, to undergo a formal death, or to become absent for a time, and yet to be born again. Christians have long used this concept, which they derived from Jesus' words, about being "born again." But they have failed to extend this notion to see that their human experience of rebirth may be simply a reflection of a central feature of the divine life, that is, controlled absence and calculated rebirth.

Of course, one problem with this discovery about God, which arises from an experience of divine death, is that we now realize that no one concept of God can ever be fixed and made free from change. If God undergoes death in our eyes and then escapes fatality only to be born again, this means that new insights into God's nature emerge with each rebirth such that no description of the divine nature can be fixed as final. Just as God eludes death, so God eludes our final conceptual grasp. Divinity appears and disappears and reappears in our lives, but the nature of a God who has this capacity will retain an element of final mystery. The full power of divinity can be preserved, but it will of necessity exceeed any final intellectual grasp and fixed formulation.

Perhaps, then, one reason for the occurence of the death of God was the determination of the Age of Rationalism to do away with all mystery and to put all concepts, including God, on a clear, rational basis. Surely this was Descartes' aim and also Spinoza's. When we attempt to confine God to our grasp, we sadly learn, God dies. The divine escapes us, eludes our conceptual hold, in its death and in its birth. But as a result we come to realize that divinity's power and self-control are such that it will be born again, if only to prove that what is divine lies beyond our control. The human religious spirit has always expressed ecstasy when experiencing the birth of God in its own spiritual life. Such is the report of the mystics too. What may not have been evident to traditionalists of the religious life is that, in experiencing the birth of God interior to their spiritual life, they were at the same time experiencing the essence of God's own nature.

God, as well as man, can be born again. The experience of renewal and transformation in our religious life is but a reflection of the divine life in ours. The experience of the death of God in the modern age was a truth but only a half-truth. God can, God will, be born again, a fact we know now to be integral to the divine life. For Christians, viewing God in such a light greatly relaxes the incomprehensibility of Jesus' death and resurrection. In our experience of God, absence and death are crucial, but so is rebirth, we discover. God's presence in human affairs, as in the divine life itself, is never without alternation, never without disappearance and return. To accept this fact about God's nature makes the universal instability of all religious life and all theologies understandable in terms of God's own nature.

Do we have any control over either God's death or eventual rebirth? Our religious sensitivity is never permanent but is easily dulled or lost. When this occurs, in individuals or in religious communities, God dies; the once prominent divine presence disappears. Honest purveyors of religions have always recognized this phenomenon, even when reluctant to admit it publicly for fear of disappointing the faithful. But not all have seen that the source of this religious experience stems from, and is revelatory of, God's own nature and inner experience. To be religious, to be faithful, essentially comes to mean to be willing to suffer the "dark nights" of God's death, as well as our own, and to be willing to wait for God's chosen, and for us unpredictable, moments of rebirth.

Such is, of course, neither a popular nor an easy view of God. It does not offer a tranquil religious life. Augustine long ago said our present experience of God is not enough; we want to possess God permanently, and we seek our security by wanting to possess a fixed truth. Certainly to be human means to desire this, as Plato recognized about human love even before Augustine. But this demand stems from our insecurity and our vulnerability and the human feeling of our ultimate lack of power. This fact tells us much about human nature, this desire for absolute stability and unchangeableness, but perhaps it says little about God, although theologians have projected these qualities upon God as they seek a stable source of satisfaction. We learn most about God, then, when we experience his death and when we see if we are able to wait through to an experience of the birth of God. In God's birth and death divinity is most fully disclosed to us in its inner life.

As we seek to study God (or really, all Gods) we should have discovered a primary clue from the death and birth of God. That is, we must constantly search out new insights into God, since our experience tells us that the current visions we have of divinity, which may seem vital and even overpowering, have every liklihood of being embraced by death as their time comes. If this is true, we know there cannot be one concept of God. We have had many notions of divinity, and the modern hope to finalize our notion of God (such as Descartes) seems only to have percipitated another death of God, perhaps more wide spread in its resulting atheism than any previous rejection of God. No fixed concept can hold divinity. Thus, we know we live in an age of the rebirth of Gods. Theism must once more be pluralistic or fail. Therefore, we need a multiplicity of notions of God, some hopefully novel in their suggestion of how Gods might be conceived.

This approach via the innovative and plural notions of God reflects the Birth of God, the alternative which Nietzsche overlooked in the excitement of his discovery that one God had died. Strange as it may seem, the plurality of our notions of God does not deny monotheism versus polytheism. Many have thought of monotheism as a signal of enlightenment and progress. But our discovery of the possibility for the birth of God does indicate that arguing for monotheism will never result in a single, once and for all dominate, concept of God that will never change. But if monotheism remains possible even with many notions of God, all fixity in our concept of God is ruled out. Change may or may not be compatable with all ideas of God, but change in our conceptualization, plus experiencing the death and the birth of God in our inner life, has become a fact in the post-modern religious world. Eventually, as our inner experience works its way into our outer public life, God will either be again declared dead or else reborn.

2. The Contempory Experience

Many have experienced the death of God, Nietzsche in his intellectual revolution and theologians in the 20th century "after Auschwitz." But if after the notion of the death of God has taken hold, a thought as alien to classical theologians as to metaphysicians, we now discover that God can also be born again, how does this transform other notions we might have of, or approaches we might make to, God?

We argue that God is found "only in certain contexts." That the awareness of God's existence is contextual, that in one situation one person might be aware of divinity and in another time and place not. This lack of universality is not so strange if we accept God's ability to die and to be reborn.

It follows that it is crucial to find the right time and place for God; otherwise, no awareness may be experienced. Actually, this is not the such a radical notion if one examines Hebrew or Christian scriptures. God appeared as a presence or disappeared according to the divine will and the apostacy or faithfulness of the people. It is insulting to the majesty of divinity to think that God would be available at any time or place on command and without consideration of the worthiness and receptivity of those who might experience the divine presence. Surely in Jesus' case some experienced God through him while others in a different frame of mind or disposition were alternately enraged in their opposition or became indifferent.

If this phenomenon seems obvious from religious history, although many fail to realize it, we must ask, "What might be the divine context in our day?"; otherwise we will find God absent. Of course, if what we say is true of God's relationship to us, we are persuing a somewhat elusive object. If in relation to us God is elusive by nature, our problem is how to make an elusive presence real for us, how to make concrete what appears unstable. In considering the human problem, we should not overlook the past and present function of religious symbols. Rituals seem able to relate a group of people to the divine presence. Perhaps in their attention to the divine power which religious symbols display, we can find assistance in our project of approaching God.

On the other hand, we must remember that religious symbols have also had the function of shielding us from God, a naked confrontation whose presence might destroy us. Symbols, then, have a contradictory role, to reveal divinity and to shield us from its overbearing power. Perhaps this corresponds to the death and birth of God. God can become obscure, distant, alien; God can appear or be brought into our presence on the divine initiative. How, then, do we discover these crucial symbols and learn their effective use? Of course, it is also true that absence and silence might be one appropriate context, as well as one full of rich and antique symbols. This is a more austere, a more demanding context, but perhaps it fits the qualities of divinity which transcends our context and all contexts, who dies and rises at will.

Since we have talked of God's birth, silence could mean the experience of God's death. This is sometimes how the divine absence appears to one who waits. Yet, somewhat ironically, silence can also be a context which, after quiet waiting, God appears or is reborn in the instant. In this regard, we must note that sustained solitude is often necessary. In the midst of things and people and the rush of activities, it may be easy for us to lose God or for God to die. Solitude, on the other hand, is a hard context for busy people to learn to tolerate and to use. Once acclimated, however, it may provide the space needed for any significant divine disclosure or reappearance. If solitude becomes a matter of our inner disposition, it should teach us that God's life or death depends a great deal on our inner state.

Evil and wanton destruction, when they come, also seem to have the effect of causing God to disappear, particularly if our view of God has been one of a being who is "the source of all good." Again, in an interesting contrast, if we do not follow the advice given to Job after experiencing evil to "curse God and die," but if we gear ourselves up to do battle against all the evil and destruction known to us, the God lost in the dispiriting experience of facing unmitigated evil may be reborn as our energy is rekindled to resist. We break out of the world of silence into supportive action for those facing loss or destruction. Words and actions (and God) can be born out of silence. Finally, we act; we speak out again.

We face a God of contrasts. Silence can be the place to discover God born again, but the rush of violent forces also may be revealing. God spoke to Job "from the heart of the tempest." Oddly enough, as the desert fathers discovered, being left alone can bring an increase of self-centeredness, a dwelling on minor myseries, not a sense of a divine presence in solitude. The rush of powerful forces, on the other hand, can destroy or numb us, but it can also strip us of unnecessary concerns and open us to other presences. St. John of the Cross found God in the dark night of the soul, or rather after passing through it. From all this we learn that no single context, situation, or formula can be thought of as a sure avenue to God. The divine nature is less fixed than verbal statement.

We are not without clues of the ways to God. They come from the experience of others and from our own, but none lead to certainty. In this case, what can a "proof" of God's existence mean, since "proof" should mean universally acceptable. But a God who can be born again, we are learning, cannot be a divinity who conforms to prescriptions. The fact that "proof" becomes impossible for the God who can die and be reborn does not mean we learn nothing. Rather, the inapplicability of standard forms of proof tells us something about a God who defies proof. If divinity in its nature can be elusive, the fact that proofs fail to capture and hold such a nature gives us a clue as to the dynamism, and the independence, of a being who is fully divine.

What Religious Naturalism Can Learn from Langdon Gilkey
Uncovering the Dimension of Ultimacy

Jerome Arthur Stone

This study is part of a larger project of developing a religious naturalism. This project includes an attempt to enrich religious naturalism by exploring the theocentric tradition of viewing human life from an ultimate viewpoint. In the West this tradition includes Augustine, Luther, Calvin and the neoorthodox and goes back to Jesus, Paul, and the prophets.[1] Specifically, I have been exploring Tillich, the Niebuhr brothers, and now Langdon Gilkey to see what religious naturalism, which is my developing position, can retrieve from this tradition.[2] I seek to incorporate some of the insights of theocentric theology into a naturalistic framework.

I assume that the general contours of religious naturalism are familiar to the reader. I do not intend to articulate them here.

I

Gilkey's project is to uncover an ultimate dimension in contemporary secular life. He does this not by analyzing explicit statements of secular self-understanding, since they reject or ignore ultimacy. Rather, he explores feelings and behavior in order to uncover a forgotten and unsymbolized horizon of ultimacy. He is guided in this project by the theocentric tradition. Since he conceives this search as only a prolegemenon to theology, he seeks merely to show the secular meaningfulness of God-language, not to claim its validity. This ultimate may be experienced either positively or negatively, as God or as a threatening emptiness, the Void.

---

[1]This list sounds provincially Protestant. Mea culpa!

[2]For a sketch of the writer's own religious naturalism, see his "A Minimal Model of Transcendence" in the *American Journal of Theology and Philosophy* 8/3 (September 1987): 121-35.

I shall focus on two books by Gilkey, *Naming the Whirlwind* and *Religion and the Scientific Future.*[3] I concentrate on four types of experience in which Gilkey finds this awareness of an ultimate horizon. These are the awareness of contingency, of relativity of meaning, of the ambiguity of freedom, and also certain elements in cognitive inquiry.

1. He suggests that we first become aware of ultimacy as a problem when we experience our contingency, when we cannot find an ultimate source to our life. Then an infinite Void at the depths threatens all we are and do. We feel emptiness and anxiety, perhaps despair. These feelings elicit strange behavior. We frantically look for something to fill up the emptiness and have a fanatical attachment to our answers. Hence an accurate picture of the human condition must use the categories of despair, meaninglessness, idolatry, the demonic and fanaticism. Like animals we act in order to survive, but unlike animals there is a drive toward ultimacy in this action.[4] A rival, the boss, the stock market, the latest news can become symbols of Fate, of an ultimate insecurity. The ultimacy of this threat gives the quest for survival and power its panicky and endless character with demonic possibilities. The search for job and financial security, status, office politics, career maneuverings, and professional jealousy all partake of this infinite dynamic.

Normally our security is socially supported. Our anxiety is compounded when we sense the finitude of our community and social fanaticism arises. The panic which comes from this sense of foreboding is one of the driving forces of historical life.

However, there are also signs of a positive creative power. There is a joy of life, a sense of vitality, of fulfillment at the use of our powers, a joy in community and personal intercourse. These common experiences buoy us up, make us glad to be alive and refuel our existence. These are religious, not just physiological experiences. They are experiences of being, of reality. There is ultimacy in these experiences since: (a) being is not one of our values but is the basis of them all, (b) this sense of reality is given to us, not created and controlled by us, and (c) it appears within us as the ground of what we are, unlike finite things which appear over against us.

2. Ultimate meaninglessness is as deep a threat as the loss of existence. People need meaning in life, not just physical security. Meaning is the sense that our life and activities have or will someday have some sort of value, the sense that what we are and do is worthwhile. We need not be conscious of this feeling, but it is manifest in

[3]Langdon Gilkey, *Naming the Whirlwind: The Renewal of God-language* (Indianapolis: The Bobbs-Merrill Company, 1969) pt. 2; *Religion and the Scientific Future. Reflections on Myth, Science, and Theology* (New York: Harper & Row, Publishers, 1970) chs. 2-4. For brevity I am omitting Gilkey's brief discussion of temporality; also his very rich treatment of historicity in *Reaping the Whirlwind: A Christian Interpretation of History* (New York: The Seabury Press, 1976) esp. ch. 2. We do not have the space to elaborate Gilkey's use of Augustine, Heidegger, Kuhn, Lonergan, Polanyi, Rahner, Toulmin, and, above all, Tillich. See esp. Gilkey's *Gilkey on Tillich* (Los Angeles: Crossroads Press, 1989). For a segment of my own naturalistic critical interpretation of Tillich's notion of agape as a moral norm, see my "A Tillichian Contribution to Contemporary Moral Philosophy," in *Being and Doing: Paul Tillich as Ethicist,* ed. John J. Carey (Macon GA: Mercer University Press, 1987).

[4]See Gilkey's reference to R. Niebuhr in *Naming the Whirlwind,* 321n.

the energy which we pour into meaningful activities and in the loss of the sense of reality when we can find nothing constructive to do. We find that our purposes are as vulnerable as our being. There is a relativity to all our projects. The farm one generation builds, the families we nurture, the institutions and communities we help fashion, the books we write are all forgotten ere long. Who can even recall where a grandparent is buried?

The meanings which elicit our enthusiasm and powers are relative, so they must participate in a total system of meaning to overcome the threat of relativity.[5] Secularity understands this in practice, for it finds such total systems in the glory of one's career, nation or race, the myth of Progress, or the eschatologies of the revolutionaries. Each myth tends toward idolatry, and if made ultimate will result in destruction or despair.

When the ultimate context of meaning of a culture starts to crumble, the proximate meanings vanish. How silly to get excited over something relative and transient. Hence the demonic efforts of the privileged to protect at all costs the meaning which stems from their status.

The sense of the significance of what we do is an unearned gift. Like the affirmation of existence, the sense of the meaning of life is given to us. You cannot say, "I shall enjoy my work" or "I shall have a new set of hopes." The love of something as worthful cannot be willed. As in the quest for ultimate security, there is common grace wherever we experience the meaning and creativity of our particularity.

3. The third area in which ultimacy may be uncovered is that of freedom and autonomy. Every decision we make, every answer to the question, "Should I?," affirms a standard to evaluate the alternatives. This norm has an ultimate or sacred character, for it is the foundation of the value of our existence and functions as an ultimate to which we give our lives and from which we expect to receive blessings. The sacred is now felt as an unconditional moral will which obligates and judges us.

Again we have possibly idolatry and the demonic. Another ultimate appears, the tendency to give an unconditioned commitment to the well-being of one's self and one's group. We have a spiritual center such that if anything happens to it we fall to pieces, life means nothing. The center of such ultimate concern can vary: one's own power, career, family, group, but each sets up an idolatrous absolute. Such a center of concern is ultimate in that unconditioned loyalty, transcending other loyalties, is given to it. A person will do anything, sacrifice anything for it. Hence it functions as a god. Frequently this leads to the infinite expansion of the needs and desires of self, which uses its rational and moral powers to justify this striving after its interests and security. The self is in bondage to its own well-being.

Often our idolatrous concerns lead us to act inhumanely. Thus greed, dishonesty, bias, ruthlessness and aggression stem from idolatry and the demonic. An analysis of freedom, this time as guilty freedom, leads to a judgment on our tendency to be unloving and to support injustice. The sacred is now opposed to us.

The sense of unworthiness and isolation which this experience of guilty freedom brings can be destructive, resulting in a feeling of unreality, loss of emotion, or bit-

---

[5]See Martin Heidegger, *Being and Time* (New York: Harper & Brothers, 1962) 182-95.

terness. This sense leads to a search for self-acceptance and renewed community. We can seek relief in an unrealistic self-image or a finite community of acceptance, such as a friend, analyst, or group. But our efforts to prove our innocence are futile because others don't accept our doctored accounts of what happened. A finite community of acceptance is not the answer, for it shares in our conflicts and, if we receive acceptance from it, we are in danger of losing our integrity and freedom.

Ultimacy appears in this third area because: (1) the need for acceptance is unconditional, (2) this acceptance recreates the self from beyond itself, and (3) the acceptance is unconditional in the knowledge of ourselves (for only an acceptance that knows us thoroughly is worth anything) and unconditional in its acceptance. What we need is not acceptance based on the assurance of our innocence but forgiveness of the guilt we know full well is there. Only the grace of the ground of life can heal without destroying our autonomy. Neither nature nor history contains such a power.[6]

4. A fourth area in which Gilkey finds ultimacy is in cognitive inquiry, epitomized by science. Here there are three points of ultimate intent: (a) the passion to know, (b) the global visions and theoretical structures presupposed by scientific inquiry, and (c) the affirmation of what is judged to be true and the self-affirmation of the knower, in short, motive, presupposition, and affirmation.

> a. Scientific inquiry demands a determination to know . . . patience, rigor, self-discipline, and hope—and all of these presuppose a deep passion to know. . . . All scientific repugnance at prejudice, the closed mind, unexamined answers, and lack of rigor in facing uncomfortable truths, depends on this underlying eros to know.[7]

This eros has an element of ultimacy. The passion on which science depends must be an ultimate passion to find and adhere to the truth. It is an affirmation of the good of knowing for its own sake, an affirmation of the value of a set of cognitive standards. It is this affirmation that sustains the search for an intelligibility not yet found. Such an affirmation is unconditioned. It involves an affirmation of a rationality which is there to be found even if I cannot demonstrate its existence, and a commitment to the ultimate value of that search and that achievement. Thus the first element of ultimacy in scientific inquiry involves the affirmation that knowing is possible and the commitment to scientific integrity, the disdain for anything but the beauty, order and simplicity of scientific explanation, and the refusal to affirm anything but what is veridically based on the evidence.

b. The second element of ultimacy in cognitive inquiry is that it requires a conditioned absolute, a fundamental theoretical structure which is believed to be true. For experience is intelligible only in relation to a method of inquiry, and data are determined as relevant only in relation to a theory about the data. For it is in terms of such a theoretical structure that the welter of facts is so ordered as to be manipulable, investigable, and intelligible. A conditioned ultimate, a vision of things which

---

[6]*Naming the Whirlwind*, 409.
[7]*Religion and the Scientific Future*, 48-49.

is held to be nonrelative, is presupposed in all knowing. Here again an aspect of ultimacy is present in scientific inquiry.

c. The third element of ultimacy in inquiry involves the virtually unconditioned grasp of what is judged to be true plus the self-affirmation of the knower as a knower. To begin with the virtually unconditioned grasp of what is judged to be true, a theory has conditions. If the conditions turn out to be the case, we say that our theory seems correct or probable. A rational judgment about a theory is thus made when, as far as can be determined, no important questions are left outstanding which would render the judgment vulnerable, when the judgment is virtually unconditioned and its content must be affirmed to be so. Here an "element of ultimacy in judgment enters: when the satisfaction of the conditions is seen and so the proposition is seen to be virtually unconditioned."[8]

A second element of ultimacy in judgment is

> that once having seen the unconditioned character of our judgment—that our theory "checks out" and that we can say "it is so"—*then* we cannot refuse to judge, nor can we remain in suspension. . . . In seeing, therefore, the unconditioned character of the judgment, we are compelled to affirm it. We do not then act as we *want*; we act as we *must,* that is, as rational beings.[9]

Furthermore, there is the still deeper certainty that in this situation I know myself as a knower.

> All cannot be relative and tentative in inquiry: else we would never judge this to be the case, nor could we discriminate among hypotheses. . . . The process of inquiry cannot move forward unless it steps somewhere on firm ground, . . . the virtually unconditioned character of contingent judgments and our unconditioned affirmation therein of ourselves as knowers.[10]

These then are the four areas in which Gilkey claims to have uncovered the forgotten dimension of ultimacy in our contemporary life. Although we cannot give here a full account of Gilkey's theory of language, we should sketch his idea of the value of religious discourse for common experience. For Gilkey, words clarify and so give meaning to the felt character of a shared situation. By thus thematizing our experience words help give more precision and shareable form to our dim and inchoate experience. Secularism has no language for the dimension of ultimacy, resulting in an improverishment of the human spirit. Its myths and false ultimates are unchallenged and "its joys are left uncelebrated and so unexperienced, its terrors uncomprehended and so unconquered."[11]

---

[8]*Religion and the Scientific Future,* 57.
[9]*Religion and the Scientific Future,* 58.
[10]*Religion and the Scientific Future,* 60-62.
[11]*Naming the Whirlwind,* 306.

II

Before proceeding to a critique of Gilkey, perhaps the writer should sketch his own underlying approach. The variety of religious naturalism which I propose might be called "minimalism." It is an alternative to the dichotomy between theism and secular humanism. Between these two viewpoints there is room, generally overlooked, for a "tentative affirmation of a minimal degree of transcendence." The motive is that "if a strong assertion is hard to defend, a more cautious and more restrained model" of divinity "will be better able to answer the doubts of our age while providing some of the support and prophetic criticism which the traditions have offered."[12]

This minimalism rests upon an ontological reticence. After all, the major arguments for the reality of God make a leap over a breach in the argument at the important point. Appeals to revelation or authority are also questionable. To accept any putative revelation or authority as genuine is already to affirm the reality of God. Why should we accept the claim of one revelation over another? The Qu'ran seems as valid an authority as does the Bible and *vice versa*. The fertility of our imaginations and our tendency to wish-fulfillment suggests continuing caution against the uncritical affirmation of our ideas, a restraint upon our metaphysical urges. Our judgment about these things must be made on "partial but persuasive reasons, a weighted ontological wager." Since caution is in order and since there are no cogent reasons for affirming the reality of God (or whatever full Transcendent), I advocate an ontological restraint resulting in a minimalist approach to transcendence.

Drawing upon Edward Scribner Ames and Shailer Mathews, I propose the following as a model for "God" or, as I prefer, "the divine."[13] *"The divine" is a human symbol for a plurality of challenging norms and creative powers which transcend the present situation as perceived.* In other words, God is a collection of situationally transcendent powers and norms.

This symbol is neither subjective nor objective. It involves an interplay between real objective factors in experience and a unifying, abstractive human response to these factors.

"The divine" refers to both powers and norms. The temptation of some forms of naturalism is to ignore the real powers and treat God as a symbol for ideals or norms only.

In the interaction of a person with the natural and human environment there are processes at work which are resources for that person. When one of these resources transcends the limited resources of the situation as perceived by the person, I call this a situationally transcendent power. By this I mean that the process, natural or human as it is, is comparatively superior in power and worth to the processes within the situation as previously perceived.

---

[12]Jerome A. Stone, "A Minimal Model of Transcendence," *The American Journal of Theology and Philosophy* 8/3 (September 1987): 121.

[13]Edward Scribner Ames, *Religion* (New York: Henry Holt and Company, 1929) 151, 178; Shailer Mathews, *Is God Emeritus?* (New York: The Macmillan Company, 1940) 29-35.

A paradigm for the situationally transcendent power is the occurrence of unexpected healing. The doctor, drug, healing power of the body or some interaction of these factors can be called divine, provided that they are transcendent to the situation as perceived. Situational transcendence is relative to a personal or temporal point of view. What is unexpected or uncontrollable for the patient may not be so for the doctor, and what is unexpected before the healing may become expected in a similar situation. Or, when interpersonal relationships are trapped in guilt or alienation, sometimes unexpected forgiveness or reconciliation can come as an unexpected and unmanipulable resource of healing and challenge to be healed.

These resources are also ambiguous in worth. "The divine" is a substantive term with the force of an adjective, referring only to the worthwhile and valuable aspects of these resources.

By "situationally transcendent norm" I refer to any norm that continuously transcends any attempt to attain it. It is an aspect of "the divine" if it continues to be a challenge no matter what is achieved in pursuit of it. Let us take the search for truth as an example. "The truth is an ideal, never fully attained, which functions as a continual demand that we push toward that goal." Likewise, "the pursuit of beauty, moral goodness, or justice" or other meaningful but unattainable pursuit can be taken as the pursuit of a situationally transcendent norm or demand.[14]

III

We come now to the question of what naturalism, minimalist or otherwise, can make of all of this. It must first be recognized that a yearning for the ultimate is a key part of human experience and behavior. Gilkey is correct in this. His hermeneutic of our secular life rings true. His sketches of terror at the Void and of rejoicing in "common grace" are on target. His uncovering of ultimacy in our secular life brings into focus the presence of this hunger for absolutes in people who reject or ignore formal religion. Critics of religion often miss this point by claiming that this yearning for the infinite is a vestige of the primitive past or is created by organized religion. Institutional religion no more creates this yearning than do soap operas create a nostalgia for love.

Naturalism asserts that there is no ontological reality which satisfies this hunger for the unconditioned. There is no Ground or God which satisfies our yearning for the absolute any more than there is, as far as I can tell, a heaven which satisfies our longing for immortality or a perfect love which satisfies our romantic yearnings. I cannot support this contention here. I will merely say that given a survey of the available evidence, insights and arguments, I have made a wager (a weighted wager, since I believe there is a preponderance of reasons to do so) that there is no such ontologically supreme reality.

Gilkey seeks to provide a justification for a theistic, particularly a Christian, outlook on life. I find four types of rationale which he provides. Space permits only the briefest sketch of these and my replies. (1) Gilkey asserts a dichotomy between faith and despair or idolatry. But there is another possibility: resignation of all absolutes

[14]Stone, "A Minimal Model of Transcedence," 130.

with openness to innerwordly transcendence and vulnerable commitment to penultimate values. (2) He asserts the need for religious language to thematize the experiences of ultimacy, as we just saw, and also freedom and destiny and Fate and bondage of the will. My reply is that an enriched naturalism can also symbolize these experiences. (3) He recognizes that the justification of theological affirmations involves a revelatory illumination and personal validation. I have moved away from such a validation and reject the authenticity of such an experience in my own life. (4) Gilkey argues for God as the ground of a temporal process.[15] As I see it, such an argument is a *non sequitur*.

The problem for a naturalist's reflection on religion is to develop a way of thinking about ultimacy lest life be impoverished and undisciplined at its depths. We need a theory of ultimacy which will: (1) challenge false absolutes and our fanaticisms and frantic searches for the infinite, (2) give rational support for our personal efforts at renunciation of the ultimate, and (3) help us to comprehend the unease, even terror, at the loss of the positive Ultimate, and yet to celebrate the temporary joys and partial victories which are real and concrete.

The vision I suggest leads to a philosophy of critical openness. It makes three challenges: (1) to be critically open to the gifts of life, (2) to be critically committed to proximate ideals, and (3) to renounce the ultimate.

1. Gilkey is correct. There are experiences of what the tradition calls "common grace" and we need to be open to them, although we also need to be critical, lest we accept any foolish or dangerous gift. Within the naturalistic framework such an experience may be conceived of as an awareness of a resource which is transcendent to the situation as perceived. A cup of water, a reconciling word, a healing medicine may be situationally transcendent resources, unexpected and uncontrolled gifts to heal and renew. The challenge is to be critically receptive to these gifts.

2. We are called to responsibility to proximate ideals, causes, institutions and persons. We must respond to such calls, although we must be critical in such commitment lest we succumb to phony or corrupt challenges or waste our efforts on trivial or overweening demands. In short, we need to be ready to revise our values and ideals and to make our commitments with critical loyalty. Within the naturalist framework such commitment is a revisionary process directed towards values transcendent as regulative ideas.

3. Gilkey is also correct that we constantly go after false absolutes. There can be terror and despair at glimpsing the Void and this underlies much of the ennui and boredom, frantic activity and escapism of our life. The approach of naturalism is to work through the grief which comes from losing our ultimates, to work towards a hard-won personal maturity. The loss of the absolutes, like the loss of parents, of loved ones, the betrayal of our first loves and hopes can end in cynicism or in grasping after false hopes. Or it can result in a maturity, sometimes painfully won, which gives up the hope of winning the ultimate, only to receive the small, but concretely real joys which belong to the finite. We must learn to appreciate the short-lived cherry blossoms. These are the three challenges which stem from a philosophy of openness

[15]*Reaping the Whirlwing*, ch. 12.

as I conceive it: (1) critical openness to the gifts of life, (2) critical commitment to proximate ideals, and (3) a mature renunciation of the ultimate.

Let us recapitulate the four areas of experience where Gilkey claims to uncover ultimacy and see what they look like from the viewpoint of a naturalism which also looks in the direction of ultimacy but finds no positive ultimate.

1. First there is the two-sided experience of contingency. On the one hand, Gilkey claims that when we really experience our finitude we either find an ultimate source of our existence or else we plunge into despair or into an endless panicky striving for ultimate security. On the other hand, when we experience the joys of life we are in touch with the unconditioned source of our existence. Such experiences point to the ultimate, Gilkey claims, because existence is the basis of all of our values, not one among them, and also because they are given to us, we do not create or control them.

Naturalism, as I understand it, can recognize, on the one hand, our despair and our endless striving for security. However, since there is no ultimate source of our being, we must face the Void honestly and summon, with appropriate help from our friends, what courage we can. We must give up the quest for ultimate security and engage in reasonable prudence, being ready to risk or even abandon security where it seems appropriate. In the middle of Gilkey's triad of despair, frantic striving and a glimpse of the positive Ultimate, we must situate ourselves with courage and prudence.[16] This is a difficult, never finished task.

On the other hand, naturalism can join with Gilkey in openness to the gifts of joy in existence. However, neither as "given" nor as the "basis" of our other values are these positive experiences of existence signs of ultimacy. True, these gifts are largely not the result of our creation or control, but their givenness means they come from beyond us. It does not mean they come from beyond everything. In the technical language of our minimal model, these gifts bringing joy are situationally, not ultimately, transcendent. Also, Gilkey claims that such joy in existence is of a different order than our other values since without existence these others values could not be. But this foundational quality of existence merely means it is the necessary condition of the realization of other values. It does not mean it derives from an ultimate source.

2. Gilkey's analysis of the second area of experience, meaningfulness and its threatened loss is similar to his analysis of contingency. We search for a sense of worthwhileness to what we do, but this calls for an ultimate context of meaningfulness. On the one hand, relativity and transcience threaten our meanings. Without such an ultimate context the proximate meanings vanish. On the other hand the gift of a sense of worth of what we do is unearned and thus points to an ultimate source.

Again naturalism can applaud Gilkey's analysis of human striving after ultimate meaningfulness. Once again, however, we must renounce an ultimate context of meaningfulness. We must face the issue of just how silly it is to be excited over prox-

---

[16]A commentator has suggested that I ponder the relationship of my thoughts on courage and prudence to Epicurus and Hume. I have given some thought to the relationship of my minimalism to Hume and have long recognized but not explored my affinities to Stoicism. These are both inviting avenues to explore.

imate meanings. The answer is that we may be appropriately excited, ready even to sacrifice our life, but with a saving touch of irony, a realization that our passion is for proximate concerns. Again we must situate ourselves in the middle between despair, fanaticism, and an acceptance of a positive ultimate. Gilkey, along with many others, sees either all or nothing, either an ultimate context of significance or no significance at all. And modern man often feels and acts out of a similar dichotomy. But the truth probably lies in avoiding the extremes, in an acceptance of the fragmentary but authentic worth of finite causes. The farms and schools we build will vanish, but our work for them has genuine albeit partial and temporary worth. With Gilkey I find much of our sense of worth unearned and unbidden. But this is a sign of our finiteness, not a sign of the ground of all finite meaning.

3. Next is the area of freedom. For Gilkey every choice affirms a norm of selfhood which has a sacred character since it is the foundation of the value of our existence. It is that to which we give our lives and from which we expect to receive blessings. The sacred here obligates and judges. Furthermore, to summarize Gilkey, freedom leads to an unconditioned concern for the well-being of one's self and one's group, leading to the infinite expansion of desires, bondage of the self, cruelty, in short, to idolatry and demonic behavior. In turn, guilty freedom results in a search for self-acceptance and renewed community. But another self or finite community is no answer. Others don't accept our efforts at self-justification, are guilty themselves, and our dependence on their acceptance threatens us. Only the ultimate ground of life can accept us unconditionally, with a thorough knowledge of ourselves, without destroying our autonomy. Naturalism can agree that obligation and judgment are transcendent in the sense of pulling the self beyond its narrow confines. However, obligation and judgment are not transcendent in the sense of being rooted in ontological ultimacy.

In addition we can appreciate Gilkey's analysis of guilty freedom which is far more profound than that of ordinary secular self-understanding. However, there is no ultimate acceptance. There may be partial forgiveness and fragmentary reconciliation. Such reconciliation is situationally transcendent, for it is not in our power to predict or to control and it might be strong enough to bring us back from the abyss of despondency or worse. We must learn to accept the absence of unconditional reconciliation. This requires real grief work and some of us may not achieve it or may hide from the depth of their own evil. We must also learn to accept fragmentary offers of forgiveness, which also is difficult. Indeed, the offers may not appear. We can hope, but not presume. In turn we must make our own offers of restoration, negotiating the line between self-abnegation and false pride, knowing that we all have fallen short. Who is sufficient for these things? None of us knows for sure.

4. Finally Gilkey claims to uncover three points of ultimate intent in cognitive inquiry, namely, motive, presupposition, and affirmation. These are: (a) the eros to know, (b) global visions and theoretical structures presupposed by inquiry, and (c) the grasp of what is judged to be true and the self-affirmation of the knower. (a) The eros to know is a passion involving the belief that knowing is possible and the commitment to the discipline of inquiry. This eros is unconditioned because the affirmations of the possibility and the intrinsic worth of knowing, even when this possibility and goodness cannot be shown, are unconditioned affirmations. (b) The theoretical

structure required to use any method or data is a conditioned ultimate, a particular vision held to be nonrelative. (c) When the conditions for a rational judgment about a theory turn out to be fulfilled, the judgment is virtually unconditioned, we are compelled as rational beings to affirm it and further we have an unconditional affirmation of ourselves as knowers which is the basis of all rational judgment.

Gilkey's analysis of science is valuable, challenging an extreme objectivism. These three elements of inquiry give an experiential root to God-language within the cultural enterprise of science and thus partially establish its meaningfulness. This does not show the validity of God-language, as Gilkey is quite aware. From a naturalistic outlook these elements of motive, presupposition, and affirmation are best described as having ultimate intent, but as not being grounded in an ontological ultimate. They point to certainty in the midst of relativity, particularity and tentativeness. They are finite footprints on the path of inquiry, not traces of an ontological ultimate.

In short, what naturalism can learn from Gilkey is that our yearning for the ultimate is present in both our feelings and our behavior. We must learn to face, with a seriousness often lacking in naturalism, this striving after the ultimate, our anxiety of not finding it, and our demonic and idolatrous attempts to secure it. While some of us may not accept his vision of a positive ultimate, he has shown that this striving is a powerful component of normal human existence and that we must come to terms with it.

A God of Power
or a God of Value, Another Look
The Debates between William H. Bernhardt
and Henry Nelson Wieman, 1942–1943

J. Alton Templin

It was in the early 1950s, while I was a student at The Iliff School of Theology that I first met Henry Nelson Wieman. He came for a lecture and on that morning most classes were cancelled so we could hear the presentation of this scholar about whom we had heard very much. His book *The Source of Human Good* had been available a few years, and most of us had read it in philosophy of religion or in theology classes. We were all aware of certain differences between Wieman and our own professor, William H. Bernhardt, and were eager to see how Wieman would elaborate his ideas since we had already discussed all the shortcomings. As the discussion period began, several students began centering down on certain questions to bring out the differences we anticipated. Wieman was well aware of what was going on, and midway in the discussion period he leaned over the pulpit in our chapel and said "Gentlemen, this is the only school where when I speak, they call me a conservative." This was all it took to clear the air and to bring us into a very fruitful discussion that morning.

Actually there was very much appreciation for what Wieman was writing, and the differences between the theology of our faculty and our guest when seen in the larger theological world were only slight. I say this remembering that the early 1950s was a time when neoorthodoxy was still very influential in some circles; Paul Tillich was highly regarded in other areas; Existential theology such as that espoused by Nels Ferre was talked about widely; while for Methodists there was the continuing influence of personal idealism stemming from Boston. Indeed, Bernhardt and Wieman were very close together in world view; two advocates of what then was known as "religious naturalism" but which later would come to be known as "process theology." It seems to me, however, that the point at which they differed still merits consideration, even though process theology has come of age, and itself is expanding in several different directions.

This discussion is helped by the fact that Bernhardt and Wieman had engaged in an extended discussion in the early 1940s—almost a decade before I had heard of either of them. Bernhardt was finishing his Ph.D. at Chicago when Wieman first went there to teach in 1927. They began a relationship which continued throughout the lifetime of both of them. Their exchange was begun by an article by Bernhardt entitled, "An Analytic Approach to the God Concept," published in 1942. Thereafter the articles appeared in 1943 in the *Journal of Religion,* two articles each by Wieman and Bernhardt. Finally in the January 1944 *Journal of Religion* Wieman presented a short response, or conclusion to the discussion. Let us follow them through this discussion, noting their major points in five major articles and Wieman's conclusion.[1]

In the first article Bernhardt compares and contrasts two categories for discussion concerning God—or two general classes to which all entities we label "God" belong. The first category Bernhardt calls *Agathonic Realism,* based on the Greek word related to value. Data for this concept of God are related to the values which are of use or enjoyment for the human race. Later in the article he calls this approach the "moral-personal" understanding. He refers to several of Wieman's published works of the 1930s to show that this is a very good example of the *agathonic* approach to the God concept, or that concerned with human values.

The second general category for data concerning God Bernhardt calls "pure realism," indicating a more inclusive, scientific and even metaphysical orientation. Data for this category are appropriated from what is dominant or controlling in the Existential Medium whether valuable for the human race or not. Elsewhere Bernhardt refers to this as the absolute or the existential approach, and God is "the determiner of destiny" in the words of James Bissett Pratt. We might think of this as a cosmological orientation, and God is the "divine determinant." Bernhardt places himself in this second category.

After summarizing these two different approaches, Bernhardt not only points to criticisms of the agathonic approach, but recognizes criticism of his own position as well. He believes the agathonic category is overly selective, using only the data which relate directly to human value. He admits that the alternative approach, however, while including all data from whatever source, sometimes has difficulty in finding order or direction. Furthermore, the data may be true for cosmic concerns, but may seem far removed or be relatively unimportant for human values, because human appropriation or useability is not the main objective.

Bernhardt concludes his first article with the supposition that there is no empirical or pragmatic way to determine which of these categories is to be chosen. This choice depends on what one considers the function of religion. If, in the case of Wieman religion functions as a source of human value, the agathonic category is the log-

---

[1]The articles on which this paper is based are as follows. William H. Bernhardt, "An Analytical Approach to the God-Concept," *Religion in the Making,* 2 (March 1942): 252-63. Henry Nelson Wieman, "Can God be Perceived?" *Journal of Religion* 23 (January 1943): 23-32. Bernhardt, "The Cognitive Quest for God," *Journal of Religion* 23 (April 1943): 91-102. Wieman, "Power and Goodness of God," *Journal of Religion* 23 (October 1943): 266-75. Bernhardt, "God as Divine Determinant," *Journal of Religion* 23 (October 1943): 267-85. Wieman, "Reply to Dubs and Bernhardt," *Journal of Religion* 24 (January 1944): 56-58.

ical approach. If, on the other hand, religion is understood as a method whereby the believer can exist in hope and confidence in face of those elements of our experience which are not necessarily amenable to basic human values, one chooses the dynamic category, concerning the power of God. Bernhardt states his understanding of the function of religion to assist one to adjust one's understanding and one's life in face of the nonmanipulable elements of our reality, such as death or ignorance of ultimate purpose.

Wieman's first article is entitled "Can God be Perceived?" and grows out of the question in the discussion concerning whether God is a perceived reality, or is inferred. Wieman argues the first while Bernhardt opts for the second. The seeming difference turns on how the term "perception" is understood, and in this case Wieman's is much more inclusive than Bernhardt's. The usual meaning of perception refers to an awareness which one can have by using one's five senses—feeling roughness, or seeing red, for example. By using this definition only, Wieman agrees God is not perceived in this way.[2]

He expands the idea by introducing several qualifying additions to his definition. He argues that a perception is a psychophysical happening, and is neither true nor false. If we look afar we may "see" a man walking, but as we get closer we realize it is a bush instead. Our original perception was not in error, only the conclusion we drew was erroneous. The object, whether bush or man, caused shadows and contrasts in my vision which seemed at first to be a man, but later proved to be a bush.

Beyond the basic perception of shadows of bushes, rising smoke or flashing lightning we must bring our human understanding. When we place this perception in the total context of our experience we qualify, or inform, our perception that that is really a bush. From rising smoke we assume certain things such as that there is or was a fire. Therefore, we complete our perception by incorporating it into our larger frame of reference. Since our perception is neither true or false, but it is only our interpretation of the perception of what our senses brought to our awareness that is true or false, Wieman concludes that perception and inference must always be interrelated. He argues, therefore, that God is never an inferred reality only, but must be a perceived/ inferential reality, or must be based on a perceptual inference. With this definition I don't think Bernhardt would disagree, but he places his emphasis in another direction, as we will note shortly.

If God can thus be perceived and if these perceptions can be interpreted in a meaningful way into our total experience, why is it that a large percentage of the population, or even of religious believers cannot or at least do not perceive God? Why is it stated that God is hidden? Wieman denies that the hiddenness of God is based on some metaphysical reality beyond the reaches of human ability. Epistemologically he is very much in the process theology camp, but hiddenness is still a problem. God is hidden because our sociohistorical awareness has not progressed to an extent sufficient for our having a contextual awareness into which the reality of God can be integrated. For example, he uses the illustration of a chair as perceived by some primitive culture would not be perceived as "chair," but would seem to be a piece of a

---

[2]Wieman, "Can God be Perceived," 27-28.

tree, maybe a magic symbol, a work of creative art, or even fuel for fire. The perceivability of the chair was there as much for that culture as for ours, but something would be lacking. He suggested that if Aristotle should suddenly be confronted by a vehicle like one parked outside this building, with four wheels, he would not perceive ''automobile'' because at first he would not have the sociohistorical background to make an interpretation of the object ''automobile'' in any meaningful way.

Similarly Wieman argues that ''God cannot be perceived until those meanings are developed in some strand of history and in some community which are necessary to the occurrence of those perceptual events which enter into the structure of that creativity which generates the appreciative mind and the appreciableness of the world.'' Here Wieman introduces the idea of an ''appreciative awareness'' on our part which is necessary to complete the process which began as simple perception. This simple perception has been augmented when we qualify it by adding context and interpretation.

An accurate perception leads us to go behind the perception to a larger context. It bids us look behind the created good, or behind the end result of a process to the creativity which makes the created good possible. Correctly perceived, this creativity is what he calls ''God,'' and he summarizes it in these words. ''The value of God is the value not of the gifts but of the giver. Not the goal but the source, not the golden eggs but the goose that lays them, not the grains and fruits but the creative earth, not the products of love but the loving, not beauty but the generator of beauty, not truth but the source of truth, not moral righteousness but the creator and transformer of righteousness, not the profits of industry but the ultimate producer, not the goods but the creativity, must be given priority over all else if we would escape destruction, have salvation, and know the true and living God.''[3]

Hence, God as the source of human good depends on our entering into the process of perception, inference, integration and appreciative awareness. God is thus hidden from many because they have not been socioculturally-psychologically nurtured or conditioned to perceive the nuances of this understanding of God, and have not developed the necessary appreciative awareness to be part of the developing process. Thus Wieman can write that ''the greatest gift of God to man is appreciation. When this appreciation is turned away from its creative source, we have original sin. It is the chief cause of man's blindness to the presence of God.''[4]

The following article by Bernhardt is entitled ''The Cognitive Quest for God.'' *Cognitive,* that is, in contrast to Wieman's emphasis on *perception.* Wieman had indicated that a discussion of the transcendence-immanence question might be more primary than that of categories such as value (agathonic) or power (dynamic). As part of his cognitive quest Bernhardt proposes three approaches to the immanence-transcendence question, or he asks ''What is the relation of God to nature?'' First, there is the possibility that God and nature are mutually exclusive, and that God completely transcends nature. Bernhardt calls this the concept of *absolute transcendence,* when no method of reasoning such as epistemology or logic is able to gain any un-

---

[3]Wieman, ''Can God be Perceived,'' 25.
[4]Wieman, ''Can God be Perceived,'' 29.

derstanding of God. Second he suggests the concept of partial inclusion or *partial transcendence,* in that God is partly related to our natural world and partially transcendent to it. Finally, the third concept he calls *absolute immanence,* in which God is totally within the natural realm, and knowable by means of methodologies we would use with any other discussion—reason, logic, analysis, perception and so on.

It is evident that both Wieman and Bernhardt accept the presuppositions of the third of these concepts, so their difference cannot be analyzed in these terms. The question of whether the category of value or of power is chosen, and the reasons for choosing the one or the other, remains.

Bernhardt then analyzes Wieman's use of the term perceptual/inferential reality with relation to God. Bernhardt agrees with Wieman in this expanded usage, but argues that Wieman is needlessly broad in this definition and that because too much is included, precision is lacking. He proposes a further clarifying terminology. In the usual understanding of perception we expect one of two types of objects, the microcosmic or the macroscopic. The first is not observable with the naked eye without the aid of a microscope, but given the necessary equipment, microscopic objects are observable and thus perceived. Likewise, with the proper equipment the macroscopic are also perceivable. Bernhardt suggests, in addition to these two terms a third term. Since some realities on which we depend are not observable by the normal perception processes, Bernhardt suggests the term "Heteroscopic." Such realities are gravity, evolution, historical events, or God. None of these is observable with either a microscope or a telescope, and certainly not with the naked eye. Bernhardt calls these heteroscopic or inferred realities, but reality nevertheless. Wieman continues to think of perceptual/inferential realities.

Arguing that the above distinctions are still subsidiary to his main concern of determination of categories of value or power, Bernhardt introduced a conceptual analysis of the relation between nature and what is conceived to be the supernatural. He argued that the more limited one's views or understanding of nature, the more a supernatural realm is presupposed to fill in the gaps or complement the understanding of an individual. As one's understanding of and confidence in nature—the existential medium—increases, the need for a God of the gaps lessens. He concludes "finally, if one's primary view of nature is rich and inclusive enough to serve as objective referent for all that he experiences, the meaning one ascribes to God-as-supernatural will diminish to the vanishing point."[5]

From this understanding Bernhardt would develop the idea that there is a functional relation between our concept of reality or nature on the one hand, and the religious understanding, and the techniques we will develop in response. The Trobriand islanders, as studied by Bronislaw Malinowski, feared the power of ocean waves or currents, so had elaborate rites to appease the gods before every fishing expedition. Most of us have enough knowledge of tornadoes, hurricanes, or earthquakes that we do not have elaborate religious rituals in face of these natural phenomena, although I hear now and then of some groups praying for rain, or of those who pray for medical cures rather than trust medical science. We may be afraid of these situations, and

---

[5]Bernhardt, "Cognitive Quest for God," 99.

justifiably so, but this is not really a part of our religious reaction.

Bernhardt introduced this type of argument to begin to prove the priority of the category of power as we develop religious responses to that which we consider non-manipulable in our experiences. The responses that are developed are as diverse as are the many groups' understandings of nature and the natural happenings. Bernhardt thus argued that God, conceived of as power—even with many interpretations—was the common element in the development of primitive and also present-day religious practices, liturgies and techniques to bring hope and meaning in face of what are conceived as nonmanipulable happenings. I suggest in this, however, that he has moved at least one step toward Wieman's views in that how we adapt, or what understandings we conceive are related to what is meaningful, and seems to bring value to human understanding. God may be power, but our reaction is related to our human values as we understand them.

The fourth article in the series Wieman entitles "The Power and the Goodness of God." He begins by insisting that since categories are the structure the thinking mind gives to experiences, hence experiences are more basic than categories. He proceeds to justify his category for God as value by constructing a fourfold outline of creativity on which all human advancement depends if it is to be meaningful and fulfilling. He lists several Christian virtues such as lack of fear, love, appreciation, keeping one's vision in face of hardship and persecution. Then he asks the question, "What sort of reality can produce this quality of life if we give ourselves over to it?" His answer is not belief, for belief is an intellectual formulation drawn from actual realities within one's life.

His answer to this question is *Creativity*. He makes slight modifications from what Whitehead or Bergson meant by their use of the same word, but he admits his meaning is sufficiently like theirs to use this word in preference to all others. The fourfold outline is summarized thus. First, when I communicate with another I get a new perspective, so emergence of new perspectives is the first step. Second, one integrates the new perspectives into the diverse perceptions which already make up one's unique personality. One becomes gradually a different person through integrating new perspectives. Third, one expands his vision of the appreciable world with each new insight. This appreciable world is thus a product of this same creativity. Fourth, when our mind has been changed by the emergence of new ideas, and the appreciable world has expanded we can understand our neighbors better and at a deeper level. "Creativity generates mutual understanding, brotherhood, fellowship—all that makes us humanly akin to one another."[6] It is interesting to note that this is the concept of creativity elaborated in his later book *The Source of Human Good*.

Wieman insists, however, that this creativity works outside each of us. Its benefits come gratuitously, and we can do nothing to promote them, save being open to these possibilities. The increase of understanding that comes to us through a certain experience could never be anticipated by us, for it is beyond our power to effect. One sure way to thwart this creativity, however, is to be content with created goods, or transitory accomplishments.

---

[6]Wieman, "Power and Goodness of God," 270.

In some concepts of religion the more proficient one becomes in manipulating the world or the humanity surrounding one, the less is God needed. Wieman insists just the opposite. "The more power man has, the more faithfully must he follow the divine requirement of creativity working by way of intercommunication of interests. Otherwise his augmented power of achievement only magnifies the evils of life."[7]

Finally, however, Wieman insists that power and goodness of God finally merge into one. Both are encompassed finally in symbols of the faith. Power is symbolized in a baby wrapped in swaddling clothes, and a criminal crucified between two thieves under the law symbolizes Goodness. I submit to you, however, that this moves well beyond perception and involves rather, an inferred, or interpreted meaning in addition.

In the fifth article Bernhardt elaborates his own ideas of a God understood in the dynamic category. He argues that we must first decide what the function of religion is, in the past as well as in the present, and construct a hypothesis which covers all examples we have. He states it in these words: "Religion is a complex form of individual and group behavior whereby persons are prepared intellectually and emotionally to meet the unsatisfactory or inescapable aspects of existence positively, that is, with confidence, courage and hope."[8]

Bernhardt believes it follows that when one's understanding of what is or is not understood in one's environment changes, one's religious understanding also changes. That is, when one's knowledge and skills develop, the part of our experience where religious activity seems relevant is relocated. This accounts for many reinterpretations or theologies which have been developed, but each of which fulfills the above function in its own way. According to Bernhardt's understanding, religion does not become obsolete or outmoded or even illusory as Freud argued, but it changes its locus to fulfill the same function in a different, or in a "higher" culture.

This definition according to function fits the dynamic category, a God of power. The reinterpretation, or conceptual framework, however, involves human values. On this level he states that "religion is a complex form of individual and group behavior designed to nourish, sustain, or cherish some human interests or values by means of (1) an interpretation or reinterpretation of persons and situations concerned and (2) the employment of certain techniques."[9]

Thus, while Bernhardt argues that God is the "divine determinant," the way we as a religious people relate to this reality involves our perceptions, our felt shortcomings against the context of our own sociocultural understandings. It also concerns our human values as we seek to interpret the inexorable situations of life in a way which has meaning and provides courage and hope to the believing and reacting community.

Bernhardt believes his category for deity as dynamic is substantiated through the method of functional analysis. According to this analysis different understandings of our "existential medium"—whether simple and primitive, or sophisticated and sci-

[7]Wieman, "Power and Goodness of God," 274.
[8]Bernhardt, "God as Divine Determinant," 281.
[9]Bernhardt, "God as Divine Determinant," 280.

entific—result in different means by which the same function of religion is exemplified. At one level food gathering is surrounded with many religious practices such as prayer or incantations, while at another level food gathering involves a trip to the supermarket which is not usually considered a religious ritual. The same can be true in our limited or more expanded understanding concerning medical practices—to pray or to innoculate, or to perform surgery, for example. Thus Bernhardt concludes that religious interests *always* center in what is considered by any people as critical, or precarious or nonmanipulable. It seems that the above holds true even though there are objective failures—that is, the storm was not averted, or the sick did not become well. There seem to be sufficient subjective successes to prove religion's right to continued existence, albeit in many different forms.

It is interesting here to note that Bernhardt has introduced the subjective as well as the objective aspects of religion. According to the objective, he states: "In religious behavior people submit to, commit themselves to, collaborate with, or identify themselves with God as dynamic determinant in the endeavor to maintain serenity and poise in the presence of the unsatisfactory and inexorable conditions of life."[10] At the same time the subjective values are spelled out. "Religion . . . has aided people when they faced conditions which were to them at their level of culture critical, precarious, uncontrollable. It has prepared them to meet these unsatisfactory and inescapable conditions in terms of intellectual revaluations and emotional controls when objective manipulation was impossible. . . . One becomes convinced that people have found . . . spiritual values in their religious life--[such as] the inner poise and strength with which to meet life's inexorable conditions."[11]

Bernhardt's final comparison between the categories being discussed is that whereas the dynamic category tries to encompass all reality as it is, or as it is understood, the agathonic category analyzes reality as one wishes it might be, or as it has a bearing only on the valuing individual. Bernhardt asserts that the first is related to scientific or philosophical objectivity, while the latter is more personal and subjective.

In his concluding comments Wieman merely reiterates points to which he has alluded in earlier articles. He insists that "religion must be approached with religious symbolism and not in terms of scientific analysis."[12] Bernhardt would undoubtedly agree although he would put a higher priority on scientific analysis at the beginning of the process. Wieman denies that he is subjective as Bernhardt asserted. Rather, the creative event does not necessarily provide what the believer assumes he or she wants, but may result in something more complex that could not have been imagined. For example, a combination of H_2 and O results in something that could not have been predicted or imagined based on either of the original elements. Wieman is partly correct when he states that Bernhardt "is really interpreting religion and God in terms of value although ostensibly he is repudiating that approach."[13]

---

[10]Bernhardt, "God as Divine Determinant," 284.

[11]Bernhardt, "God as Divine Determinant," 282-83.

[12]Wieman, "Reply to Dubs and Bernhardt," 56.

[13]Wieman, "Reply to Dubs and Bernhardt," 58.

Conclusion

While Bernhardt and Wieman remained friends throughout their careers, their differing methodologies and emphases made them sound quite different. Bernhardt could be categorized as a "philosophical" theologian, in which theology must be conceived in cognitive, analytic, scientific, intellectual terms. Precision of terminology was his uppermost concern, without which one could not be sure analysis could proceed in a logical or intelligent manner. Wieman, on the other hand, could be categorized as an "empirical" theologian in that theology related to the total experience of an individual or of a society before cognitive or intellectual analysis is developed. Bernhardt and Wieman seemed to disagree because they conceived of the theological task as different enterprises, based on different presuppositions, hence arriving at differing results.

Wieman emphasized "appreciative awareness" rather than careful cognitive precision. The total human experience was the basis of his theology, and the experience of "creative interchange" in a human life was more decisive than any analysis or speculative construction with reference to the experiential. The philosophical construction was not denied, but he argued that the experiential was prior and more basic. Therefore, he sought to analyze "what operates in human life with such character and power that it will transform an individual as one cannot transform himself or herself. . . ." as he stated in many ways in his writings. This was not analytically precise, nor philosophically definable, according to Bernhardt's criticism. Wieman did not think this precision was the most important aspect of his, or any, meaningful humanly motivating theology.

Bernhardt, on the other hand, was more concerned with cognitive definition, or as he called it "increasing cognitional efficiency," than he was the more broadly experiential data. He was comfortable in the scientific and abstract formulations of theories rather than the more existential aspects of human experiencing. For this reason Bernhardt was critical of Wieman's emphasis on perception of God at work in actual human experiences. Bernhardt was accurate when he accused Wieman of shifting in his career from a scientific and metaphysical basis for theology, to an analysis of social questions, and finally to transformation within individual persons. Bernhardt believed this was a movement away from theological precision; but Wieman argued he was moving more to the individual where the only transformation of human living could be determinative.

Given their different understandings it hardly seems possible that Wieman could conceive God in other than the agathonic category, the arena where human beings are influenced by the creative event, and become enriched in the process. This refers indeed to the value-producing experiences of the human life. Wieman could use symbolism, art and poetry to capture the depth of human experiences, and referred to "appreciative awareness" as one gave himself or herself to existential immersion in the deepest, even unconscious, aspects of life. On the other hand, Bernhardt emphasized the theoretical construction which he believed could help to explain the dynamic elements of a culture, the changes that take place in religion when another part of cultural interpretation changed. All aspects of culture are related, he thought, and developed or were modified in predictable "concomitant variations." Theology for him referred not to human perceptions or life-transforming experiences, but was based rather on careful analysis and critical, logical, intellectual constructions. Bernhardt was not comfortable using symbolism, poetry or art. He could not appreciate the beauty of a symphony orchestra, for example, but on one occasion when he dutifully attended a concert admitted he heard only "noise." Wieman thought of theology as a help in an understanding of real personal and transforming experiences. Bernhardt thought of theology as a construction of logical explanations of experiences after they happened or had been observed.

As we look at the debates forty years later we realize that neither emphasis is the whole story in theology, and many of us, I am sure, would be tempted to use certain aspects of each approach in contemporary theological analysis. At a risk of seeming too simplistic in summary, or of failing to understand their differences, I should like to hazard some suggestions as to how the values of the two seemingly diametrically opposed undertakings can be related to each other.

First of all, they both presupposed a process world view. Both insisted on what Bernhardt called God's divine immanence. No concept of God as "wholly other" or knowable in other than normal human epistemological categories was meaningful.

Second, while Bernhardt related his concept to the existential medium, or had a scientific or metaphysical orientation, Wieman did not deny this in his own work. As his career progressed Wieman seemed to be less interested in what he called "metaphysical speculation." He thought his religious understanding could be more profitable if he emphasized the personal-and social-based analysis. I submit that this is a difference of emphasis, not a difference of theology.

Third, while Bernhardt emphasized the nonmanipulable realities in an objective sense, he left room in religion for subjective understanding as an individual sought wholeness and meaning through theological reinterpretation. Wieman emphasized human value, but was not oblivious to how this was based on a larger reality on which we are dependent, and which we cannot ourselves control. Wieman merely refused to speculate beyond knowable or perceived human experiences.

Fourth, while Bernhardt insisted on being objective in his analysis, he had room for the subjective. Wieman, seemingly subjective, did not deny nor ignore the larger objective reality. They disagreed on which was more important in the theological enterprise.

Fifth, Bernhardt emphasized philosophical analysis and precision of definition, while Wieman seemed to be more concerned about what produced quality of life. In this I think we see, again, not a dichotomy but a different emphasis.

Sixth, and finally, it seems to me that when related to the universal function of religion Bernhardt emphasized power and scientific realism, which Wieman did not really deny. When it came to the existential level of relating religion or theology to individuals both emphasized the integrative or meaning-producing aspects of human value. Wieman called this the perception of the personality-enhancing experiences of life, while Bernhardt emphasized reinterpretation which adapted his theoretical construction to real human concerns.

Consequently, while Bernhardt and Wieman agreed at the outset of their debate that there was a necessity to distinguish between a God of power or of value, they came to their theological task from two different directions. We all must live both in the world of scientific realism at one level, and the world of human perception of and appropriation of meaning and value at another level. While these may be analyzed from different viewpoints, they are really two sides of the same coin of human life in today's world. We are subject to the forces which can be analyzed in all natural sciences, the reality of gravity, of sometimes unpredictable wind currents which produce tornadoes or floods, problems such as plagues, earthquakes or sudden infant death. At the same time the human personality seeks meaning and value through surrendering to the "grace" of the creative event. Religious values can also come through the hope-producing and life-affirming understandings arising from reinterpretation of the dynamic realities of our experiences so they can be appropriated in the human community.

Bernhardt's Functional
Philosophy of Religion

William Tremmel

In this essay my intention is to present some of the thought of William Henry Bernhardt in his examination of the nature of religion, and his work in developing a functional definition of religion.

Bernhardt had a passion to know what he was talking about, especially when he talked about religion. Those of us who knew him became quite aware that he was, in an irenic way, the nemesis of fuzzy thinking. Even so, in the preface to his *A Functional Philosophy of Religion,* he admits that at first, during his years of formal education, definitional vagueness and unverifiability in religious cognition did not bother him much at all. He wrote:

> Many theories concerning the nature and function of religion were presented to me during my years of graduate work at Garrett . . . Northwestern . . . Chicago. The task of validating one of such definitions did not arise until I began teaching Christian Theology [at] Iliff. . . . Then I found it necessary to arrive at some conclusions concerning the nature of the work upon which I was engaged. The question . . . was . . . : *On what grounds [was I] justified in accepting one definition of religion in preference to others?*

That was in 1929. Those of us who studied with him after 1929 (or at least during the 1940s) can testify that he, indeed, took the question of definition and verifiability quite seriously. Among other things, he became interested in dealing with the glut of definitions that give our discipline more the character of a fiction than a science.

To make sense in a study of religion it seems reasonable even if simplistic to say a good definition of religion would be helpful. And, of course, we have "good" definitions by the score. All sorts of persons, eminent and otherwise, come up with good definitions of religion. For example, that father of anthropology, Edwin Tylor, defined it quite simply as "belief in Spiritual Beings."[1] In more recent times Alfred

---

[1] Edwin Tylor, *Primitive Culture* (New York: Gordon Press, 1974) 1:383.

North Whitehead declared it to be "what an individual does with his own solitariness."[2] That giant of eighteenth-century philosophers, Immanuel Kant, declared it to be "the recognition of our duties as divine commands."[3] A generation after Kant, Friedrich Schleiermacher discerned "the common element of religion" to be "the recognition of ourselves as absolutely dependent."[4]

And, of course, we have the definition of that fellow who said, "Religion ain't doin' nobody no harm; leastwise not intentionally; and anyways not very often."

Bernhardt began to face the dilemma of too many definitions when he faced his first religion classes at Iliff in 1929. About this he later wrote:

> Students of religion . . . find it practically impossible to agree upon what it is they are to study. This state of affairs becomes evident as soon as one examines books purportedly written on religious subjects. [They] may find [themselves] reading ethics tinged with emotion; or [sociology] written with more than customary fervor; [or abnormal psychology] written by one who finds the field wholly absorbing and therefore concludes that it is religious; or [they] may find [themselves] reading the impassioned writings of some philosophical physicist whose chief emotional satisfaction is found in his struggle with fundamental concepts, and who is thus convinced that his physics is religion.[5]

For all this, Bernhardt concluded that probably most of the various views on religion—What is it?—can be classified in four groups.

First, there are supernaturalistic definitions, for example, James Frazier's definition that religion is "the propitiation or conciliation of powers superior to man which are believed to direct and control the course of nature and of human life."[6]

Second, we find those definitions that stress the ethico-social interests of humankind, for example, A. E. Haydon's "religion is the shared quest of the good life."[7]

Third, we find those definitions (which Bernhardt himself was more inclined to endorse) that might be called the adjustive definitions. Such definitions, he pointed out, go back at least as far as Epictetus (first century A.D.), who as a slave knew all about unsatisfactory/inescapable aspects of life. Epictetus addressed these aspects and stated a religious proposition for living life successfully *in spite of.* "We must," he said, "make the best of what is under our control, and take the rest as its nature is.

---

[2]Alfred North Whitehead, *Religion in the Making* (Cleveland: World, Meridian Books, 1969) 16.

[3]Immanuel Kant, *Religion within the Limits of Reason Alone,* trans, Theodore M. Greene and Hoyt H. Hudson, 2nd ed. (La Salle IL: Open Court Publishing, 1960) 142-51.

[4]Friedrich Schleiermacher, *The Christian Faith,* ed. H. R. Mackintosh and J. S. Stewart (Edinburgh: T. & T. Clark, 1948) 5-18.

[5]William Henry Bernhardt, *A Functional Philosophy of Religion* (Denver: Criterion Press, 1958) 1.

[6]James Frazier, *The Golden Bough,* one-vol. ed. (New York: Macmillan Co., 1922) 50.

[7]A. E. Haydon, *The Quest of the Ages* (New York: Macmillan Co., 1929) ix.

How, then, is its nature? As God wills."[8]

More recently Paul Tillich made reference to the same sorts of unsatisfactory, inescapable, human anxieties. He classified them as fate and death, emptiness and meaninglessness, guilt and condemnation—anxieties we cannot escape, and to which we must address religion in our attempts to achieve *The Courage to Be*, in spite of.

Finally, Bernhardt identified those definitions of religion that are based in deep emotional experience. The essence of religion is feeling. Thrill. Which may at times become intense enough to be an ecstasy.

In these four types of definition, and in other conceptions, investigators assume they have discovered the essential nature of religion, and that their conclusions are based upon the careful use of admissible data. But, as we can see, religion so declared is almost anything and everything.

Intrigued by this, Bernhardt began to target his attention on the methodologies used in arriving at most definitions of religion, and he concluded that most often scholars utilize John Stuart Mill's old Method of Agreement (also called Simple Enumeration or Empirical Generalization). This method consists of two operations—clarification and verification. Clarification involves identifying a problem and formulating a hypothesis that seems to be relevant to that problem. Then comes verification. This consists of determining what empirical evidence is admissible in the validation or the invalidation of the proposed hypothesis; then one must search for and gather such evidence.

Trouble comes in the fact that different persons can get different conclusions depending on where they start their hypothesizing. Different definitions are verifiable depending on the hypothesis proposed. It is the presupposition that determines where one looks for evidence.

Bernhardt demonstrated this with two examples. First he pointed out how A. E. Haydon, looking at religion, hypothesized that religion is a "shared quest of the good life." Haydon then rather easily identified a volume of instances supporting this hypothesis—a volume of instances of people sharing in a quest for the good life.[9]

Next Bernhardt presented Rudolph Otto, and said of him, "[After] many years of patient study of the religious life of humanity [Otto] concluded that religion was essentially an experience of 'the Holy Other.' . . . He then gathered many instances of this form of experience, selected from the religious history of mankind. . . . Both men [Bernhardt continued] relied upon the Method of Agreement as their instrument of verification proper."[10] And both men invented persuasive definitions of religion that are miles apart—one based in ethico-sociality, the other in psycho-spiritual experience.

A truly defining-answer must be somewhere else, had to be arrived at by some other method. Bernhardt turned to a method common in modern science—the Method of Concomitant Variations, or Functional Analysis. This method proceeds on the

---

[8]*Arrian's Discourses of Epictetus*, trans. W. A. Oldfather (London: William Heinemann, 1926) 1.1.17.

[9]See Haydon, *The Quest of the Ages*, 14.

[10]Bernhardt, *Functional Philosophy*, 24.

premise that concurring variations may be indications of causal relations, that is, concomitant variations may be indications of functional connections. If two phenomena are observed to change with some regularity, it is likely (not guaranteed, but likely) they are somehow causally related. An example of this method can be seen quickly in the work of Louis Pasteur (1822–1895) in his (1865) scientific report regarding the origins of bacteria. As anybody can see by observing fertilization in grape juice, or the souring of milk, or putrification of meat, microbes (bacteria) occur magically— by the miracle of spontaneous generation. That is obviously the case. But Pasteur doubted this. He got the idea that such "generation" was the result (the function) of dust in the air—dust carrying the microscopic spore of the "miraculously" appearing bacteria. So he set up a concomitant variations experiment. He filled sixty glass bulbs with sterile mediums. Twenty of these he opened in dusty air; twenty in less dusty air; and twenty in the high Alps where there was very little dust in the air. The results: in dusty air, 8 of the 20 sterile mediums were contaminated, developed bacteria; in less dusty air, 5 of the 20 were contaminated; in Alpine air, only 1 was contaminated. Concomitant variations may be indications of causal/functional relations.

Observe that Pasteur did not do precise mathematical quantifications of dust-in-air. Quoting Bernhardt, "He was content to prove that a discernible difference in the dust content of the air resulted in a discernible difference in the number of bulbs affected."[11] That was enough for Pasteur, and enough to launch the science of microbiology.

Could such a method be employed in understanding the cause and nature of religion? Bernhardt thought it was worth a try.

Take, for example, the simple religious activity of praying for rain. Compare the probable number of times, during a drought, one can expect people to pray for rain in the dry-land wheat farming of far-eastern Colorado (where my wife comes from) with the probable number of times we can expect such praying in the deep-well irrigated wheat farming in middle-eastern Colorado (closer to where I come from). If you can reasonably expect fewer prayers in the irrigated area than in the nonirrigated area, would you not suspect (in a Pasteurian way) that you might be on to something? You might have a clue to religious behavior. Could there not perhaps be some functional connection between praying for rain and irrigation technology?

Bernhardt sought concomitant variations not simply in prayer activities, but in all attempts to introduce extranatural/supernatural control into natural processes. He called this metatechnology.

He established a hypothesis, and then set out to verify it through the method of functional analysis. The hypothesis was/is: "Religious behavior is a complex form of individual and group behavior whereby persons are prepared intellectually and emotionally to meet the nonmanipulable aspects of existence positively by means of a reinterpretation of the total situation and with the use of various techniques."[12]

To verify his hypothesis, Bernhardt examined technology and metatechnology in three widely different cultures—a primitive culture (that of the Trobriand Islanders

[11]Ibid., 36.
[12]Ibid., 157.

of the South Pacific), an ancient culture (that of the Romans of the Augustan age), and a contemporary, modern culture (the culture of the people who today call themselves United Methodists).

In his examination, Bernhardt demonstrated that, indeed, in those areas of critical concern in human life, which are precarious and often beyond human control, religious belief and practice were elaborately evident. He discerned also that with the advance of technological control (with the reduction of the nonmanipulable aspect of critical issues) metatechnological techniques became peripherally used, or not used at all. In each of the cultural situations examined, the people made extensive interpretations of the origin, meaning, and destiny of human life. They reinterpreted (the term Bernhardt preferred) life from their religious points of view. Then, in terms of their reinterpretations, they dramatized their beliefs (their theologies) in dramatic actions. They performed religious rituals.

We should observe that Bernhardt did not identify metatechnology—people attempting to introduce extranatural/supernatural force into natural processes—as religion. Rather he emphasized that with religious beliefs and behaviors (sometimes including metatechnology) people condition themselves ''intellectually and emotionally to meet the nonmanipulable aspects of existence positively. . . . '' Whether the world changed or not, the people changed. This was the important point. Concerning this, Bernhardt wrote:

> Historically . . . religious behavior was essentially metatechnological. Persons sought for supernatural or magical aid in their attempts to conserve their values. Present-day information leads one to believe that all such metatechnological activities were futile so far as objective results were concerned. . . . At the same time, religious behavior continued despite its metatechnological impotence because it served . . . in other ways. It had subjective success which more than compensated for its objective failures. . . . Religious behavior, in other words, aided individuals to make subjective adjustment to situations not subject to objective control at the time, and to do so without loss of morale.[13]

With the advance of technological control, it would seem reasonable to expect religion gradually to disappear. But no, it is not religion that begins to disappear so much as the metatechnological aspects of religion that begins to disappear. Religion does not disappear because we are still caught in Tillich's destiny and death. . . . We must seek not only for physical control (technology), but, also, for spiritual control—''to make subjective adjustments not subject of objective control . . . and to do so without loss of morale.'' We need the courage to be, not just physical survival.

Bernhardt did not identify religion with metatechnology. He simply used technology and metatechnology to discover the basic function and method of religion. In doing this he analyzed the nature of religion into three phases that can be diagrammed under three headings; namely, function, reinterpretation, and technique.

---

[13]Ibid.

First, the function of religion is to effect (quote) "subjective adjustment in situations believed to be nonmanipulable in terms of available knowledge and skill." The function is, of course, the "why" of religion—why it is done.

Having thus identified the function of religion as subjective adjustment, Bernhardt identified two interrelated dimensions involved in doing religion. First, reinterpretation— the intellectual aspect of doing religion. Here the subjective adjustment consists of making some kind of transcending, spiritual sense out of the world where a person finds himself. What's it all about? Why am I here? And especially, What is the meaning of this happening? "Emergent in this reinterpretation [dimension] are such concepts as *soul, God,* or *gods, heaven, hell,* etc."[14] This is the dimension of theology, mythology, doctrine. In the second dimension of the methodology (which Bernhardt calls technique), the "subjective adjustment consists . . . of overt behaviors" performed in an effort to control the disruptive emotions evoked by inescapable and unsatisfactory situations.[15] Here we do the things we are persuaded to do in the name of religion— pray, posture, perform, what-have-you.

All this amounts to recognizing that humans are the peculiar animals—the ones who don't just live in *the* world, but who also live in *their* world—worlds of technological sophistication (greater or lesser) and worlds of driving, creative imagination.

We're the ones who want to know not only that we are and where we are, but why we are. We're the self-conscious, self-centered animals who are absolutely loaded with imagination. What if we could fly like birds? Imagine! Only a few years ago, a fantastic idea. Yet here we are at this conference. Flew like a bunch of birds because somebody imagined it.

I often suspect that air-conditioning is the product of one of our ancestors, shivering in a cave somewhere in the Neanderthal Valley, who suddenly imagined how nice it would be to have some of that prairie-fire stuff right here in his cave.

We imagine and we make from our imaginings. We imagine and we make from our imaginings fantastic worlds. But that's not all of it, or even half of it, and especially not the religious dimensions of it. Because of self-centeredess and imagination large amounts of human thought and emotional response are on the negative side— the dark side: the side of threats and catastrophes, the side of how to deal with such things in some kind of subjective adjustment.

In this world it doesn't take long to discover that nobody ever gets out of life alive, or out of life even half of what one wants. Why not? What's it all about? Human imagination does not limit itself to technological inventions or aesthetic accomplishment. It operates even more fantastically in psychospiritual dimensions. Why am I here? Surely it's not meaningless.

We ask such questions and try for answers. But, of course, initially the questions and answers are already institutionally available to us, and we are already culturally conditioned. We do not invent our religions. We are born into them. After awhile we may do some additional reinterpreting— perhaps try to make the religious satisfac-

[14]Ibid., 158
[15]Ibid.

tion more personal and/or try to make better sense of the theologies and rituals we have inherited from a long-ago world.

Bernhardt was keenly aware of the new world that emerged in the last 400 years, and he wanted to define religion in a way that would let it make morale-sustaining sense in this contemporary world.

He was convinced that this contemporary world must learn to do religion in a nonmetatechnological fashion. He knew that historically religious behavior was essentially metatechnological. But present-day information, he said, indicates that such activity is "futile so far as objective results [are] concerned."[16]

There are, indeed, an increasing number of people in the world who are beyond belief in any form of metatechnology. Metatechnology is out, but not necessarily is religion out. The needs are still there, and out of such needs new religious reinterpretations and techniques are emerging and will continue to do so.

As an example of this, I shall present here excerpts from a letter from a father to his daughter, a young woman distraught by the approaching death of a friend's baby. Both the daughter and the child's mother needed some kind of better answer than the usual "God's will." They were hurting for an answer from their twentieth-century world. Both are very modern young persons (the daughter herself being a scientist). Neither could accept any metatechnological hocus-pocus.

The father tried for an answer. What he wrote speaks of life, value, the world, and God in ways that both exemplify Bernhardt's functional analysis, and, also, reinterprets life, value, the world, and God, in ways compatible with Bernhardt's theological position with reference to God.

Bernhardt held, with his old Chicago School colleagues, that there is no supernatural order. God, he said, is the Directional Momentum, or the Dynamic Determinant in this natural order: a momentum-dynamic to which humans can turn in search for spiritual support when confronted with situations that are both horrendous and uncontrollable.

Within this tradition, the father wrote:

A man your mother and I met when we were at the University of Chicago (Charles Hartshorne) wrote a book recently called *Omnipotence and Other Theological Mistakes*. This title suggests that maybe there are other ways of thinking about God and this world—where it came from where it's going, and our place in it. . . .

You're a scientist. As a scientist you know the scientists' fantastic story of how we got here—from Big Bang 15 billion years ago, to our geosphere 4.6 billion years ago, where in another billion years, things cooled down enough for the biosphere to form. Then sometime about 100 thousand years ago that part of the biosphere called homo sapiens began to show up. And for the first time in all those years of incredible happenings, questions began to be asked: What's it all about? Why am I here? Who made it? Why is it so flawed? Good, legitimate questions, but not so easy to answer, either 100

[16]Ibid., 157

thousand years ago, or now.

Seen with a scientist's eyes you can, perhaps, begin to see that the whole business from Big Bang to homo sapiens has something to tell us about the whole affair, and our place in it. First . . . it should be obvious to us that [this universe] is not a chaos. . . . It has come from somewhere. It is going somewhere. And one of the fantastic harmonies-in-complexity that has already arrived are the tears in the eyes of a person asking, "Why leukemia in this little one."

A wonderful thing has happened in this universe. It took 15 billion years for it to happen. But it is such a rare and beautiful thing that the time was worth it. At least on this little planet, in this second rate solar system, the miracle of all miracles has happened. We call it love.

To be born, and to live, and to love, and to give your own particular gifts to life, that's what it's all about. And the sadness? That's the price we pay for the gift of life that was given to us. You see, the universe was not created for us. We're simply . . . part of it. But a special part, for we are the ones (perhaps the only ones in all the universe) who ask, "What's it all about? Why is it flawed? Why did God let that happen?"

Why did God? I'll hazard a twentieth-century guess. It is . . . because God's place in the world is not that of an omnipotent creator . . . "up there" running it according to some mysterious, hidden Jobian plan. Rather, God is the creative passion that set it all going in the first place, and keeps it all going—the passion that dreams of ever-increasing complexity and harmony . . . the passion that is the allurement of what might yet be if we but choose it. . . .

There are viruses in this world and there are babies in this world. Both are products of the creative passion. Each has its place in the scheme of things. And when they cross in an unplanned encounter it is not only the earthly parents who weep, but the "divine parent" also weeps. The beauty has been distorted. . . .

Dr. Bernhardt closed his book on functional analysis by acknowledging that his functional approach to a definition of religion "is closely related to [the thought] of several members of the recent Chicago Divinity School faculty."[17] He also gave credit to an earlier teacher at Northwestern who first (without, I suspect, even knowing it) set Bernhardt off in his search for religion, what is it, and how and why we do it. Toward the end of his *A Functional Philosophy of Religion,* Bernhardt wrote, "My own interest in this approach was awakened when under the teaching of Professor William L. Bailey, in Northwestern University, in 1925, I became acquainted with the thought and sayings of Epictetus."[18] "We must make the best of what is under our control, and the rest as its nature is. 'How is its nature?' As God wills."

In saluting Dr. Bernhardt, I thought it appropriate to salute the teacher who aimed him in an adjustive/functional direction.

---

[17]Ibid., 179
[18]Ibid., 157 n.1.

William James on Victorian Agnosticism: A Strange Blindness

James Woelfel

The views of William James on agnostic attitudes and arguments regarding theistic belief were uncharacteristically harsh and wide of the mark. A "radical empiricist" who was profoundly open and sensitive to religious experience in all its variety and in its most exotic forms, James was strangely insensitive to the varied and often anguished experience of his contemporaries who broke with Christianity for conscience's sake and challenged its religious authority. A late-nineteenth-century American intellectual, living in the age of Dwight L. Moody and a pervasive religious anti-intellectualism, James warned gravely of the human danger of the agnostic spirit and a triumphant science, but was inexplicably reticent about the stultifying effect on human minds and lives of so much that called itself Christianity. A polymath who knew well a wide range of thinkers and ideas and could sympathetically characterize views with which he disagreed, James contented himself with truncating and caricaturing the outlook of notable agnostics such as T. H. Huxley.

I want first to describe James's monochromatic characterization of agnosticism and why he thought it was wrong-headed. Then I will contrast with his depiction a summary of the self-definitions and sensibilities of nineteenth-century British agnostics and the specific case of Huxley. I will be critical of James throughout my presentation, so in my conclusions I will focus briefly on his contention that agnosticism and atheism amount to the same thing.

The chief sources for James' presentation of and argument with agnosticism are certain of the essays in *The Will to Believe and Other Essays in Popular Philosophy* (Cambridge: Harvard University Press, 1979), notably "Is Life Worth Living?," "The Sentiment of Rationality," "Reflex Action and Theism," and of course the title essay "The Will to Believe" itself.

1. James on Agnosticism

In the essays to which I have just referred James argues for our intellectual right to believe theistically. Human thinking is always in the service of our practical, willing nature. Metaphysical beliefs that frustrate our deepest religious and moral desires and fail to provide cosmic support for our positive actions in the world are doomed to practical failure. Agnostic and atheistic outlooks, which doubt or deny realities transcending the phenomenal order, fall within this category. They demand that we subordinate our practical need for existential meaning to a strict evidentialism. At the other extreme, intellectual beliefs that outrun our passional demands in the direction of a mystical or philosophical absolutism fail us by saying much more than we know or need. James calls such views "gnosticism."

The truly rational middle way— understanding "rational" in its Jamesian sense as satisfying harmoniously our perceptual, conceptual, and practical needs—is a broad, "minimalist" theism. By this James means belief in a cosmic personality analogous to ourselves who interacts with us in purposive and caring ways. Such a belief enables us in both our thinking and our living to satisfy the demands of our "passional nature" and open us to whatever larger dimensions of reality there are, while realistically avoiding speculation and presumption about the details of those larger dimensions.

In developing these views James characterizes agnosticism in an almost wholly unsympathetic way. Both the substance and the tone of his remarks are negative. He portrays agnostics as arrogant and aggressive, enemies of the religious spirit and heralds of an intellectual Philistinism. At the practical level agnosticism is no different from atheism: not only do both outlooks fail to provide adequate foundations for human hope and positive action in the world, they actually undermine hope and morality. Let me document these generalizations with some specific examples.

James almost never refers simply to "agnosticism." He commonly links it with "materialism," speaking of "materialisms and agnosticisms" ("Reflex Action and Theism," 106) and "the materialistic or agnostic hypothesis" ("The Sentiment of Rationality," 75). He never straightforwardly identifies agnosticism with materialism, but by repeatedly linking the two he strongly suggests to his listeners and readers that they amount to the same thing. At minimum we have here a kind of guilt by association, and in the context of James's insistence on the indissolubility of belief and action he genuinely thinks that they amount to the same thing at the level of human living: a practical atheism.

By forging a close connection between agnosticism and materialism, James suggests that agnosticism, like materialism, is a full-blown worldview of a particular kind rather than a cautionary epistemological principle and a cluster of attitudes that express themselves in a variety of forms and practices. One would never suspect from James' characterization, for example, that the Victorian agnostics (Huxley is a prominent example) were typically agnostic about whether materialism is true or not!

The other familiar manner in which James refers to agnosticism reinforces the suggestion that it represents a kind of describable worldview. He often calls it "agnostic positivism" ("Is Life Worth Living?," 50). The term "positivism" was in wide currency among late-nineteenth-century intellectuals. In the narrower sense it referred to the "positive philosophy" of Auguste Comte. But Comte had famously argued that the progress of human knowledge necessarily passes through three stages— the theological, the metaphysical, and the scientific—and that the Western world had entered upon the last and highest stage, the scientific understanding of the world. Comte confidently described a confidently advancing scientific spirit and body of knowledge, and he worked it out into a detailed worldview which some who were influenced by the sciences emulated. Hence people came to use the term "positivism" in the broader sense to mean what James calls "scientificism"—what today we would probably call "scientism": the elevation of scientific knowledge into an all-sufficient and all-embracing metaphysics.

In the contexts in which James uses the terms "positivism" and "agnostic positivism" he almost invariably discusses the limitations of science and the presumptuousness of scientism. "Certain of our positivists," James writes, "keep chiming to us, that, amid the wreck of every other god and idol, one divinity still stands upright—that his name is Scientific Truth, and that he has but one commandment, *Thou shalt not be a theist,* for that would be to satisfy thy subjective propensities, and the satisfaction of those is intellectual damnation." This is "the religion of exclusive scientificism" ("Reflex Action and Theism," 104-105).

Indeed, just as he ties agnosticism inextricably to materialism, James always identifies agnosticism with scientists, science, and scientism. Since materialism is normally the metaphysics of scientism, we thus have the unholy trinity agnosticism-scientism-materialism. The fact that most of the eminent Victorian agnostics, although greatly influenced by scientific knowledge and the scientific spirit, were neither scientists nor materialists is not a discovery one can make in the pages of James' essays.

James perceives the agnostic and the scientific materialist as aggressive, undermining theistic faith and more generally narrowing human horizons and blunting human sensibilities. Identifying the agnostic-scientistic mentality with the erection of the principle of parsimony into an intellectual absolute, he writes of these "knights of the razor": " . . . when I see their fraternity increasing in numbers, and, what is worse, when I see their negations acquiring almost as much prestige and authority as their affirmations legitimately claim over the minds of the docile public, I feel as if the influences working in the direction of our mental barbarization were beginning to be rather strong, and needed some positive counteraction." ("Reflex Action and Theism," 105)

What, according to James, is the intellectual position of the agnostic? James correctly sees that agnosticism involves evidentialism, which holds that the reasonableness of one's beliefs is deteɪmined by the nature of the evidence one has in support of those beliefs. On a benign view of agnosticism, this means simply that the agnostic believes that we should reserve judgment or be skeptical about confident assertions of a number of religious and metaphysical claims, on the grounds that the evidence available to us is simply insufficient as a basis for reasonable belief.

But it should be clear by now that James' construal of agnosticism is anything but benign. He characterizes the agnostic reliance on evidentialism in this way: " . . . the agnostic 'thou shalt not believe without coercive sensible evidence' is simply an expression . . . of private personal appetite for evidence of a certain peculiar kind." ("Is Life Worth Living?," 51) Notice here how the evidentialist principle becomes a commandment and is stated in its most extreme form: "without coercive sensible evidence."

James insists that, contrary to the agnostics' view of themselves, agnosticism is not a neutral suspension of judgment but an actively negative position, at both the theoretical and the practical level. He lumps the agnostic together with the atheist and the materialist as an "anti-theist." The agnostic is a "faith-vetoer" who is "shut . . . up in snarling logicality." ("The Will to Believe," 30-31) As James familiarly argues in "The Will to Believe," "Scepticism . . . is not avoidance of option; it is option of a certain particular kind of risk. . . . [The sceptic] is backing the field against the religious hypothesis, just as the believer is backing the religious hypothesis against the field." ("The Will to Believe," 30)

Since "belief and doubt are living attitudes and involve conduct on our part," agnosticism is a practical atheism. James draws from this the following conclusion: "And so if I must not believe that the world is divine, I can only express that refusal by declining ever to act distinctively as if it were so, which can only mean acting on certain critical occasions as if it were *not* so, or in an irreligious way." ("Is Life Worth Living?," 50-51) James makes it clear elsewhere that what he has in mind here is an inextricable link between religion—or more specifically theistic faith—and morality. Agnostic doubt, like atheistic denial, undermines not only a positive, hopeful attitude toward our human place in the cosmos but also thereby the foundations of a positive morality! In a remarkable passage James writes that

> . . . it is often practically impossible to distinguish doubt from dogmatic negation. . . . He who commands himself not to be credulous of God, of duty, of freedom, of immortality, may again and again be indistinguishable from him who dogmatically denies them. Scepticism in moral matters is an active ally of immorality. Who is not for is against. ("The Sentiment of Rationality," 88-89)

Here James indiscriminately mixes religious questions (God, immortality) with moral issues (duty, freedom). In this passage and elsewhere he seems unmistakably to claim that skepticism about the former entails skepticism about the latter, both in thought and in practice. A number of the major moral philosophers of the Western world would want to insist, by contrast, that both a positive morality and its justification are possible independently of theistic belief. The nineteenth-century agnostics fully shared this view, and abundantly exemplified a positive morality in their actions. I shall briefly return to James's assumption—a central one in his treatment of agnosticism—that "Who is not for is against" in my conclusion.

2. Agnostics on Agnosticism

When we test William James's account of agnosticism by the actual self-definitions, thought, and lives of the great Victorian agnostics, it turns out to be a serious distortion. Agnosticism was never a definite worldview or metaphysical outlook, but rather an attitude toward the problem of knowledge and truth, particularly with regard to religious claims, that articulated itself in a range of ideas and styles. While some of the leading British agnostics were definitely influenced by Comte's positivism—one thinks particularly of John Stuart Mill, Harriet Martineau, and George Eliot—they adapted it to their own uses and were much less dogmatic about it than was Comte. They widely rejected, and even poked fun at, Comte's attempt to found a "religion of humanity" with its new church and priesthood. (Huxley called it "imitation ecclesiasticism.'') While the Victorian agnostics were deeply influenced by scientific methods, the results of scientific discovery and research, and positivism's strictures regarding the possibility of transempirical knowledge, most were not themselves scientists and varied in their applications of these principles and practices. Very importantly, they also—and the scientist Huxley just as surely as the rest—appealed broadly to common sense and general moral considerations as well as to scientific knowledge in making their case.

Many of the eminent Victorian agnostics were raised in deeply pious Christian homes; some were the daughters and sons of clergymen. A few, like Leslie Stephen, were for a time Anglican priests, while others continued to consider themselves incurably religious even after they left their childhood faith. For some in these categories breaking with Christianity and the church was a slow and extremely painful process. Most retained an affection and admiration for the person of Jesus, and respected the Christian tradition for the good they believed it continued to manifest amid the narrowness and superstition.

What James interpreted as negativity and aggression toward faith is more accurately to be seen as lively and conscience-informed criticism of highly dubious and often arrogantly proposed religious claims. The leading agnostics such as Huxley, George Eliot, and Harriet Martineau were also large-spirited and humane individuals who normally respected the humanity of their opponents even as they vigorously disagreed with them. When we read of the widespread vilification to which freethinkers were subjected in the nineteenth century and the opportunities that were closed to them because they had the courage of their convictions, it is clear who really had the power and who was often using it aggressively in the service of narrow and unworthy ends. As for James's fear that agnostics, together with scientistic materialists, would contribute to a general ''mental barbarization,'' what do we actually see when we look at the nineteenth-century British agnostics? To a remarkable degree we see persons of great intellectual breadth and aesthetic and moral sensitivity—humanists in the fullest sense of the term. There is no better example of this than Huxley, the distinguished biologist whose wide-ranging essays also gained him a reputation as one of the eminent men of letters in Victorian Britain.

The relationship of the British agnostics to nineteenth-century theological currents is illuminating. They skillfully argued that many defenders of Christian orthodoxy agreed with them on their main point—that human reason is incapable of knowing anything about the supernatural—but then irrationally went on to insist that we have certainty about the supernatural on the arbitrary basis of faith and revelation. The Victorian agnostics were on the whole sympathetic to the efforts of liberal theologians of the day—among them Anglicans such as the contributors to the highly controversial *Essays and Reviews* (1860), F. D. Maurice, and Charles Kingsley, and Unitarians such as James Martineau—precisely because they saw an agnostic humility about the affirmations of faith informing their reflections. James's attack on agnosticism is especially ironic at this point, since as I have indicated, he advocated a ''minimalist'' theism and insisted on being strictly agnostic when it came to *Aberglaube*—to filling in the details.

James's accusation that both agnosticism and atheism undermine moral commitment and activity, by depriving people of trust in a friendly universe, is—if I may pointedly invoke evidentialist considerations—unsupported by actual human evidence. It is specifically and eloquently refuted by the Victorian agnostics, who were notable for their moral passion and energy, their integrity and humanity.

Now I want to turn from my general characterization to a specific example of the spirit and practice of Victorian agnosticism. I must restrict myself to focussing on Thomas Henry Huxley, but he is an appropriate representative since he invented the term "agnosticism" and was one of its most influential embodiments. I could have chosen representatives from a long list and a wide range of distinguished nineteenth-century British agnostics: among them the mathematician W. K. Clifford (whom James called "that delicious *enfant terrible*"), the biologist Charles Darwin, the novelists George Eliot and Thomas Hardy, the political economist Harriet Martineau, the philosophers John Stuart Mill, Henry Sidgwick, and Herbert Spencer, the lawyer Fitzjames Stephen and his historian brother Leslie Stephen, and the poet Algernon Charles Swinburne. Perhaps even Matthew Arnold belongs here, since the author of *Literature and Dogma* interpreted God and the significance of Jesus entirely in terms of human experience. Simply to cite the names of such a variety of thinkers and writers suggests a range not only of intellectual articulation but also of sensibilities bound up with agnostic views regarding theism. In his famous essay entitled "Agnosticism," published in 1889, Huxley recounts how he came to coin the term by telling about his early intellectual development. "When I reached intellectual maturity," he relates,

> and began to ask myself whether I was an atheist, a theist, or a pantheist; a materialist or an idealist; a Christian or a freethinker; I found that the more I learned and reflected, the less ready was the answer; until, at last, I came to the conclusion that I had neither art nor part with any of these denominations, except the last. The one thing in which most of these good people were agreed was the one thing in which I differed from them. They were quite sure they had attained a certain "gnosis,"—had, more or less successfully, solved the problem of existence; while I was quite sure I had not, and had a pretty strong conviction that the problem was insoluble. (*Selections from the Essays* [Arlington Heights IL: AHM Publishing Corporation, 1948] 87)

When he later became a member of the celebrated Metaphysical Society, Huxley says, "most of my colleagues were *-ists* of one sort or another," while he seemed sadly lacking in a label. "So I took thought," he wryly reminisces, "and invented what I conceived to be the appropriate title of 'agnostic.' It came into my head as suggestively antithetic to the 'gnostic' of Church history, who professed to know so much about the very things of which I was ignorant. . . . "After Huxley introduced the term to the Metaphysical Society, showing that he too "had a tail, like the other foxes," it caught on quickly—appropriated by many freethinkers as an apt label for their similar views, and cursed by many theologians and ecclesiastics as atheism or infidelity under another name. (88)

Huxley offered an explicit definition of agnosticism in his essay "Agnosticism and Christianity" (1889):

. . . speaking for myself, and without impugning the right of any other person to use the term in another sense, I . . . say that Agnosticism is not properly described as a "negative" creed, nor indeed as a creed of any kind, except in so far as it expresses absolute faith in the validity of a principle, which is as much ethical as intellectual. This principle may be stated in various ways, but they all amount to this: that it is wrong for a man to say that he is certain of the objective truth of any proposition unless he can produce evidence which logically justifies that certainty. This is what Agnosticism asserts; and, in my opinion, it is all that is essential to Agnosticism. (92)

This formulation of agnosticism is one of the premises that formed the basis of the "ethics of belief" debate that so exercised the members of the Metaphysical Society and Victorian intellectuals generally, a debate in which James participated in the lectures and essays of the 1880's and 1890's to which I have referred. It was John Locke who influentially propounded the notion that the moral duty of truthfulness involved "the not entertaining any proposition with greater assurance than the proofs it is built on will warrant." David Hume reaffirmed the principle, familiarly in his statement that "the wise man proportions his belief to the evidence," and through John Stuart Mill it became the thesis that pitted leading Victorian Christians and skeptics against each other in debate.

What strikes me in reading Huxley is the careful, open-minded, and undogmatic way in which he applies the evidentialist principle to a range of issues. Like most of the Victorian agnostics, he was influenced by the critical theories of knowledge of Hume and Kant and believed that reason is limited to the realm of spatiotemporal phenomena. Huxley freely granted that all sorts of things are possible or conceivable as candidates for reality, but the lack of evidence for them demands in some cases suspension of judgment and in others outright skepticism.

Something of the wideness of Huxley's use of the agnostic principle can be seen in the following remarks from his essay "Agnosticism and Christianity":

The extent of the region of the uncertain, the number of the problems the investigation of which ends in a verdict of not proven, will vary according to the knowledge and the intellectual habits of the individual Agnostic. . . . What I am sure about is that there are many topics about which I know nothing; and which, so far as I can see, are out of reach of my faculties. But whether these things are knowable by any one else is exactly one of those matters which is beyond my knowledge, though I may have a tolerably strong opinion as to the probabilities of the case. (93)

On this basis Huxley himself did not believe that he could confidently pronounce on such issues as theism vs. atheism, idealism vs. materialism, and the immortality of the soul. There was simply insufficient evidence to decide one way or the other on these matters.

Invoking Bishop Butler's maxim that "probability is the guide of life," Huxley certainly had his opinions on at least some metaphysical questions as to where the preponderance of the evidence pointed. For example, on the use of the terms "natural" and "supernatural" he wrote: "For myself, I am bound to say that the term 'Nature' covers the totality of that which is. The world of psychical phenomena appears to me to be as much part of 'Nature' as the world of physical phenomena; and I am unable to perceive any justification for cutting the Universe in two halves, one natural and one supernatural." (100) Interestingly, I do not think James disagreed in principle with this view. As an empiricist he would talk only about the world of experience, although as a "radical" empiricist he defined experience very "thickly" and holistically. James understood God as one reality among many comprising a pluralistically understood universe, not a "ground of being" existing "outside" the universe.

Huxley's care in distinguishing between doubt and denial is evident in his discussions of biblical interpretation, in which this natural scientist showed himself to be well-read in the biblical criticism of the day. One of his favorite texts for exposing the intellectual dilemmas of Christian orthodoxy was the gospel story of Jesus and the Gadarene demoniac. In the course of a critique of theological interpretation of the story, Huxley grants that, strictly speaking, there is no a priori refutation of the possibility that demons exist and can transfer from humans to pigs:

> For anything I can absolutely prove to the contrary, there may be spiritual things capable of the same transmigration, with like effects. Moreover I am bound to add that perfectly truthful persons, for whom I have the greatest respect, believe in stories about spirits of the present day, quite as improbable as that we are considering. (80)

Nevertheless, he goes on to say, the church's "evidence on this particular matter" is "ridiculously insufficient to warrant their conclusion." (81)

It is worth remarking that Huxley the agnostic, who by James's lights represented the narrowly scientistic forces making for our "mental barbarization," argued for many years that the Bible should be used as an instrument of popular education. In his 1870 essay "The School Boards: What they Can do and what they May do," he praised the biblical literature in lofty humanistic terms:

> . . . for three centuries, this book has been woven into the life of all that is best and noblest in English history; . . . it has become the national Epic of Britain . . . ; . . . it is written in the noblest and purest English and abounds in exquisite beauties of mere literary form; and, finally, . . . it forbids the veriest hind, who never left his village, to be ignorant of the existence of other countries and other civilizations and of a great past, stretching back to the furthest limits of the oldest nations in the world. By the study of what other book could children be so much humanized and made to feel that each figure in that vast historical procession fills, like themselves, but a momentary space in the interval between the Eternities; and earns the blessings or the curses of all time, according to its efforts to do good and hate evil . . . ? (Quoted in *Selections from the Essays,* 103-104)

In achieving these ends, Huxley went on to say, instruction in the Bible must be taken out of the hands of clerics and approached in terms of history, literature, and ethics rather than of theology.

Huxley maintained that the agnostic quarrel was not with what he called "scientific theology," but with ecclesiasticism, which he called "the championship of a foregone conclusion." (93-94) While he is not altogether clear about what he means by "scientific theology," he refers to scientific theologians with respect as Christian thinkers who are trying freely and boldly to rethink Christianity in modern and intellectually respectable terms:

> . . . the Agnostic, knowing too well the influence of prejudice and idiosyncrasy, . . . can wish for nothing more urgently than that the scientific theologian should not only be at perfect liberty to thresh out the matter in his own fashion; but that he should, if he can, find flaws in the Agnostic position; and, even if demonstration is not to be had, that he should put, in their full force, the grounds of the conclusions he thinks probable. The scientific theologian admits the Agnostic principle, however widely his results may differ from those reached by the majority of Agnostics. (94)

Huxley had in mind liberal theologians such as those I have mentioned, and also Henry Mansel of Magdalen College, Oxford, who spent his last years as Dean of St. Paul's. Huxley referred to him as an "eminently agnostic thinker." (86) In his 1858 Bampton Lectures, especially in their published form as *The Limits of Religious Thought Examined,* Mansel stirred up a good deal of controversy by arguing, on the basis of Sir William Hamilton's "philosophy of the unconditioned," that the transcendent is by definition "incognizable and inconceivable," so that there can be no speculative knowledge of God attainable by reason and independently of revelation. Huxley's remarks on "scientific theology" can in a larger sense be taken as a characterization of the liberal theologies that became increasingly prominent in the late nineteenth and early twentieth centuries.

Raised in what he called "the strictest school of evangelical orthodoxy," Huxley, like almost all the eminent Victorian agnostics, was keenly sensitive to the fact that "the process of breaking away from old beliefs is extremely unpleasant; and I am much disposed to think that the encouragement, the consolation, and the peace afforded to earnest believers in even the worst forms of Christianity are of great practical advantage to them." (89) He went on to say, however, that "If agnostics lose heavily on the one side, they gain a good deal on the other. People who talk about the comforts of belief appear to forget its discomforts; they ignore the fact that the Christianity of the Churches is something more than faith in the ideal personality of Jesus. . . . " (90)

Like Hume and Mill, Huxley thought that the contribution of Christianity as foundation and improver of morals was a decidedly mixed one, and like them he saw no intrinsic connection between theistic faith and a positive morality. "The causes which have led to the development of morality in mankind," he wrote, " . . . will not cease to operate because a number of ecclesiastical hypotheses turn out to be baseless. . . . " (98)

In a longer study I could add to the testimony of Huxley those of other leading Victorian agnostics: Leslie Stephen, the historian-biographer whose essay "An Agnostic's Apology'' was a widely read articulation of the agnostic attitude in religion; Harriet Martineau, the political economist and translator of Comte's *Positive Philosophy*, whose intense religious piety as a girl translated itself into an adult passion for social reform; George Eliot, whose novels portray the religion of her childhood with sympathy while evaluating it in terms of its capacity for expressing community, love, and justice. They are joined by many others—scientists, writers, philosophers—who embodied the agnostic spirit in a great variety of ways and were on the whole admirable human beings.

3. Conclusions

I have offered criticisms of William James's evaluation of agnosticism throughout this study, and I trust that the testimony of Huxley's thought confirms those criticisms. In my concluding remarks I want briefly to mention Morton White's critique of James on agnosticism in his book *Science and Sentiment in America*. White focusses on James's argument that at the practical level agnosticism is a form of ''antitheism.'' James, says White, ''cannot find an action-counterpart of doubting which is different from the action-counterpart of disbelieving. . . . From a practical point of view, . . . they are both *against* the proposition that God exists because neither of them is for it.'' (New York: Oxford University Press, 1972, 197) For James, not to be for theism was to be against it, both intellectually and practically, and with White I would say that that is simply a mistake—an oversimplification and falsification of the actual views and behavior of the agnostics among his contemporaries. I would go on to observe that, in keeping with his prejudices on this score, it seems hardly ever to have occurred to James that the lives of many Christian believers very typically involve a large measure of ''practical atheism''—of living in the world *etsi deus non daretur*. The issue White raises is yet another facet—and an important one—of a systematic distortion of agnosticism that reveals a strangely blind side of one of our more expansive and open-minded philosophers.

About the Authors

Larry E. Axel is Professor of Philosophy at Purdue University. He is a graduate of the University of Indianapolis (A.B.), Yale University Divinity School (M.A.R.), and Temple University (M.A., Ph.D.). In addition to editing two books, he is the author of twenty articles. Axel serves as coeditor of the *American Journal of Theology & Philosophy* and as coeditor of the Highlands Institute for American Religious Thought series.

J. Edward Barrett is Professor of Religion at Muskingum College. He is a graduate of Susquehanna University (B.A.), Princeton Theological Seminary (B.D., Th.M.), and the University of St. Andrews (Ph.D.). In addition to twenty articles, he is the author of *How Are You Programmed?* and *Faith in Focus*. He is associate editor of the *American Journal of Theology & Philosophy*.

Francis W. Brush was Professor of Philosophy at the University of Denver until his retirement in 1977. He is a graduate of Wichita State University (B.A.) and Iliff School of Theology (Th.M., Th.D). In addition to holding a variety of administrative positions, his numerous publications include a series of articles on "Patterns of Thinking" in *The Iliff Review*, 1960–1966.

J. Harley Chapman is Professor of Philosophy and Humanities at William Rainey Harper College where he currently chairs the Humanities Department. He is a graduate of Emory University (B.A.), Columbia Theological Seminary (M.Div.), and the University of Chicago (M.A., M.A., Ph.D.). In addition to numerous articles, he is the author of *Jung's Three Theories of Religious Experience*.

Donald A. Crosby is Professor of Philosophy at Colorado State University. He is a graduate of Davidson College (B.A.), Princeton Theological Seminary (B.D., Th.M.), and Columbia University (Ph.D.). In addition to numerous articles and critical studies, he is the author of *Horace Bushnell's Theory of Language, in the Context of Other Nineteenth-Century Philosophies*; *Interpretative Theories of Religion*; and *The Specter of the Absurd: Sources and Criticisms of Modern Nihilism*.

William Dean is Professor of Religion at Gustavus Adolphus College. He is a graduate of Carleton College (B.A.) and the University of Chicago (M.A., Ph.D.). He has long been interested in defining a distinctively American strand of religious thought. Dean has worked toward this end in his two recent books: *American Religious Empiricism* and *History-Making History: The New Historicism in American Religious Thought*. Currently he is working on a study of an American religious crisis and resources for its correction in the American tradition of philosophy and theology.

Douglas Allan Fox is the David and Lucille Packard Professor of Religious Studies at Colorado College. He is a graduate of the University of Sydney (B.A.), the University of Chicago (M.A.), and the Pacific School of Religion (S.T.M., Th.D.). In addition to eleven articles, Fox is the author of five books, including *The Heart of Buddhist Wisdom* and *Meditation and Reality: A Critical View*.

Nancy K. Frankenberry is Associate Professor of Religion at Dartmouth College where she has also been cochair of the Women's Studies Program and taught feminist theory. She is a graduate of Marquette University (B.A.) and the Graduate Theological Union (M.A., Ph.D.). Frankenberry is the author of *Religion and Radical Empiricism* and numerous articles in scholarly journals.

Charley D. Hardwick is Professor of Religious Studies at the American University in Washington, D.C. In addition to degrees from Southern Methodist University and Drew University, he received his doctorate in philosophical theology from Yale University. As a student he received Danforth and Rockefeller theological fellowships. He has also been the recipient of Guggenheim, American Council of Learned Societies, and the American University Sabbatical Support fellowships. Hardwick is author of *Faith and Objectivity: Fritz Buri and the Hermeneutical Foundations of a Radical Theology* and *Religious Truth in the Absence of God*, as well as numerous articles. He served as editor of the "Aids to the Study of Religion" and "Studies in Religion" monograph series sponsored by the American Academy of Religion.

Charles Hartshorne is Ashbel Smith Professor Emeritus in Philosophy at the University of Texas at Austin. He has also taught philosophy at Harvard University, the University of Chicago, and Emory University, and has been a visiting professor in Japan, India, and Belgium. He is a graduate of Harvard University (B.A., M.A., Ph.D.) and has received honorary degrees from Haverford College and the University of Leuven, Belgium. Hartshorne is the author of seventeen books and several hundred articles and reviews.

Yeager Hudson is Professor of Philosophy and Department Chairperson at Colby College. He is a graduate of Millsaps College (B.A.), Boston University School of Theology (S.T.B.), Colby College (M.A.), and Boston University (Ph.D.). He is coeditor of the "Problems in Social Philosophy Today" book series. The author of numerous articles and four books, his most recent book is *Emerson and Tagore: The Poet as Philosopher*.

Tyron L. Inbody is Professor of Theology at the United Theological Seminary in Dayton, Ohio. He is a graduate of the University of Indianapolis (B.A.), United Theological Seminary (M.Div.), and the University of Chicago (M.A., Ph.D.). He serves on the editorial board of the *American Journal of Theology & Philosophy* and has contributed numerous articles to a variety of scholarly journals.

J. Dell Johnson is on the faculty of Stonehill College. He is a graduate of DePaul University (B.A.) and Harvard University (M.T.S., Ph.D.). His academic interests include theology and literature, especially the theological interpretation of myth and folklore, and the legacy of William James in American religious history.

James A. Kirk is Professor of Religious Studies at the University of Denver. He is a graduate of Hillsdale College (B.A.) and the Iliff School of Theology (Th.M., Th.D.). After early teaching and writing in the philosophy of religion, his recent publications have been primarily in Asian religions: *Stories of the Hindus: An Introduction* and coauthor of *Religion and the Human Image*.

Konstantin Kolenda is Carolyn and Fred McManis Professor of Philosophy at Rice University where he has taught since 1953 and served as department chairman from 1968 to 1975. He was a visiting professor at the University of Heidelberg, University of Texas at Austin, and the United States Military Academy. Among his published books are *Philosophy's Journey: A Historical Introduction; Philosophy in Literature: Metaphysical Darkness and Ethical Light; Religion Without God*, and *Cosmic Religion: An Autobiography of the Universe*.

Randolph Crump Miller is the Horace Bushnell Emeritus Professor of Christian Nurture at Yale University and the emeritus editor of *Religious Education*. He is a graduate of Pomona College (B.A.) and Yale University (Ph.D.). He has served as a visiting professor at fourteen universities and theological schools and has presented special lectureships throughout the world. Miller is the author of numerous articles and fourteen books.

Charles Milligan, Professor Emeritus of Philosophy of Religion, the Iliff School of Theology, is currently (1989) serving in sequence as visiting professor of religious studies at Mesa College, Grand Junction, Colorado; theologian-in-residence at the Windward Coalition of Churches, Oahu, Hawaii; visiting professor of religion, Colorado College, Colorado Springs, Colorado. He is a graduate of the University of Denver (B.A.), Iliff School of Theology (S.T.M.), and Harvard University (Ph.D.). In addition to numerous articles, he is the author of *Guide to Contemporary Philosophy of Religion*.

Mason Olds is Professor and Chair of the Department of Religion and Philosophy at Springfield College. He has also taught at Mount Holyoke College, Smith College, and Richmond College (London, England). He is the author of *Story: The Language of Faith; Religious Humanism in America*, and numerous articles.

David A. Pailin is Reader in Philosophy of Religion at the University of Manchester. He is a graduate of Cambridge University (M.A.) and Manchester University (M.A., Ph.D.). In addition to numerous articles, his publications include *The Way to Faith: An Examination of Newman's Grammar of Assent as a Response to the Search for Certainty in Faith; Attitudes to Other Religions: Comparative Religion in Seventeenth- and Eighteenth-Century Britain; Groundwork of Philosophy of Religion*, and *God and the Processes of Reality*.

W. Creighton Peden is Fuller E. Callaway Professor of Philosophy at Augusta College. He is a graduate of Davidson College (B.A.), the University of Chicago (B.D., M.A.), and St. Andrews University (Ph.D.). In addition to over eighty articles and ten books, Peden is coeditor of the *American Journal of Theology & Philosophy*, executive director of the Highlands Institute for American Religious Thought, president of the North American Society for Social Philosophy, and executive director of the Twentieth World Congress of Philosophy.

John K. Roth is the Pitzer Professor of Philosophy at Claremont McKenna College. In addition to his sixteen books, he received the 1988 Professor of the Year award from the Council for Advancement and Support of Education (CASE) and the Carnegie Foundation for the Advancement of Teaching.

William Shaw is Professor of Divinity and principal of St. Mary's College, St. Andrews University, Scotland. He is a graduate of Cambridge University (B.A.) and Edinburgh University, he studied theology at Edinburgh University, and was ordained as a Church of Scotland minister. Shaw is a leader in the World Alliance of Reformed Churches and has lectured widely in Europe and North America. He is the author of *Who Is God?* and *The Dissuaders*.

Frederick Sontag is the Robert C. Denison Professor of Philosophy at Pomona College. He is a graduate of Stanford University (B.A.) and Yale University (Ph.D.). He has published seventeen books and some two hundred articles in the fields of metaphysics and philosophy of religion.

Jerome A. Stone is on the faculty of William Rainey Harper College. He holds the Ph.D. from the University of Chicago. His articles include two studies of Paul Tillich and two studies of Samuel Alexander. A United Church of Christ pastor for eighteen years, he was the founder of the Danville (Illinois) Council on Human Relations and helped develop a Hispanic parish in Chicago.

J. Alton Templin is Professor of Church History and Historical Theology at the Iliff School of Theology. He is a graduate of the University of Denver (B.A.), the Iliff School of Theology (Th.M., Th.D.), and Harvard University (Ph.D.). Templin has done major research on theological developments in early sixteenth-century Netherlands, as well as studies on Luther, Calvin, and Zwingli. He is the author of *Ideology on a Frontier: The Theological Foundation of Afrikaner Nationalism, 1652–1910*.

William C. Tremmel is Professor and chair of the Department of Religious Studies at the University of South Florida. He is a graduate of the University of Denver (B.A.) and the Iliff School of Theology (Th.M., Th.D.). Tremmel has combined an active ministry in the Methodist Church with teaching and scholarly activity. In addition to numerous articles in scholarly journals, he is the author of nine books and monographs, the most recent of which is *The Jesus Story—in the Twenty-Seven Books*.

James Woelfel is Professor of Philosophy and director of the Western Civilization Program at the University of Kansas. He is a graduate of the University of Oklahoma (B.A.), the Episcopal Divinity School (M.Div.), Yale University (M.A.), and St. Andrews University (Ph.D.). Woelfel is associate editor of the *American Journal of Theology & Philosophy*. In addition to numerous articles, he is the author of *Bonhoeffer's Theology: Classical and Revolutionary*; *Borderland Christianity: Critical Reason and the Christian Vision of Love*; *Camus: A Theological Perspective*; and *Augustinian Humanism: Studies in Human Bondage and Earthly Grace*.

DATE DUE

HIGHSMITH   # 45220